THE EFFECTIVENESS OF ENVIRONMENTAL LAW

European Environmental Law Forum Series, Volume 3

THE EFFECTIVENESS OF ENVIRONMENTAL LAW

Edited by
Sandrine MALJEAN-DUBOIS

intersentia
Cambridge – Antwerp – Portland

Intersentia Ltd
Sheraton House | Castle Park
Cambridge | CB3 0AX | United Kingdom
Tel.: +44 1223 370 170 | Fax: +44 1223 370 169
Email: mail@intersentia.co.uk
www.intersentia.com | www.intersentia.co.uk

Distribution for the UK and Ireland:
NBN International
Airport Business Centre, 10 Thornbury Road
Plymouth, PL6 7 PP
United Kingdom
Tel.: +44 1752 202 301 | Fax: +44 1752 202 331
Email: orders@nbninternational.com

Distribution for Europe and all other countries:
Intersentia Publishing nv
Groenstraat 31
2640 Mortsel
Belgium
Tel.: +32 3 680 15 50 | Fax: +32 3 658 71 21
Email: mail@intersentia.be

Distribution for the USA and Canada:
International Specialized Book Services
920 NE 58th Ave. Suite 300
Portland, OR 97213
USA
Tel.: +1 800 944 6190 (toll free) | Fax: +1 503 280 8832
Email: info@isbs.com

The Effectiveness of Environmental Law

ISBN 978-1-78068-467-3
D/2017/7849/71
NUR 823

British Library Cataloguing in Publication Data. A catalogue record for this book is available from the British Library.

PREFACE

The present book is most welcome. This is in part because sufficient attention has not been paid to effectiveness in the past. The book shines a spotlight on the efforts of negotiators and lawyers to frame legal instruments with environmental objectives, together with strategies and mechanisms to ensure their effective fulfilment.

Recently, there has been an increased focus on the assessment of the effectiveness of legal and policy instruments in achieving their intended goals. In this context, the Paris Agreement on Climate Change provides one example of the need, expressed by states, to plan periodic meetings to collectively assess the overall efforts of mitigation, adaptation and other implementation measures.

That being said, we should remember that measuring the effects of the intended objectives is a rather difficult task. The question we might ask is: what exactly should be assessed? Should the results of a collective framework be evaluated or, rather, the various measures taken to ensure the effective implementation of an instrument? The latter might provide good indicators of the best road to follow in achieving a given objective. In addition, there is a need to define the methodology for assessing the effectiveness of an instrument clearly; the law has to partner with other disciplines in this respect.

Synergies among multilateral environmental agreements may contribute to greater effectiveness. Environmental issues are interdependent and there is an acute need to adopt a holistic approach towards the protection of the global environment, now more than ever. Climate change, the protection of the ozone, biodiversity and desertification regimes, to name but a few, are all closely linked and these interconnections need to be taken into account when measuring effectiveness.

The essential relationship between effectiveness and sustainability must also be subject to scrutiny. Sustainability cannot exist without the sound protection of the environment. As such, there is a need to better grasp the notion of effectiveness in the environmental field, so as to ensure the promotion of sustainable development.

The present book, edited by Sandrine Maljean Dubois, represents a critical milestone in the endeavour to shed light on the importance of effectiveness in the environmental field and to reflect on the appropriate means and measures by which to ensure the effectiveness of environmental instruments.

Laurence Boisson de Chazournes
Professor at the Faculty of Law of the University of Geneva
June 2016

CONTENTS

INTRODUCTION

The Effectiveness of Environmental Law: A Key Topic

Sandrine Maljean-Dubois
*Aix Marseille Univ, Univ Toulon, CNRS, DICE, CERIC, Aix-en-Provence, France**

Over the last five decades, there has been a rapid expansion in the use of law in the service of the environment. We now have a collection of legal instruments aimed at protecting the environment, at the international, regional, national and subnational levels, ranging from treaties to national legislations, from constitutional provisions to municipal regulations, from hard to soft law. There is certainly a breath-taking number of instruments today, as well as a variety of protected domains.

However, this impressive development in environmental law has not always been matched by corresponding improvements in environmental quality. The threats to our environment and, by extension, to our health have never been so numerous or serious. Ecosystems and natural resources are declining at an alarming rate. Yet, climate change is a reality. Environmental degradation is an ever-growing challenge. These threats jeopardize our children's future, and subsequent generations' futures, because of their long-term consequences, not to mention their irreversibility. Without sounding overly melodramatic, we must recognize that this is now a question of our very survival.[1]

Indeed, if successive environmental reports are to be given any credence, there is a steady decline in environmental quality, bringing into sharp focus questions relating to implementation, as well as questions related to the true value of the existing instruments. In brief, it gives rise to some questions about legal effectiveness.

* The author would like to thank Lavanya Rajamani for having accepted the publication of this text partially based on their common introduction of the book *La mise en œuvre du droit international de l'environnement / Implementation of International Environmental Law*, S. Maljean-Dubois, L. Rajamani (ed.), The Hague Academy of International Law, 2011, Martinus Nijhoff, 812 p.

1 See for example F. Biermann, 'Planetary boundaries and earth system governance: exploring the links' (2012) 81 *Ecological Economics* 4.

For this brief and modest introduction to a very rich conference topic, I will first underline that effectiveness has been a long-neglected issue. Secondly, I will try to define what is a polysemic term. Thirdly, I will remind the reader of the difficulties involved in assessing effectiveness. Lastly, I will try to identify some avenues by which to improve the effectiveness of environmental law.

1. THE EFFECTIVENESS OF ENVIRONMENTAL LAW: A LONG-NEGLECTED ISSUE

In the early years of environmental law – from the 1970s to the 1990s – a time characterized by "normative frenzy," the stress was primarily put on constructing a body of regulations aimed at environmental protection. As this body of regulations attained critical mass, academics and practitioners turned the spotlight on the causes for the relative ineffectiveness of a lot of instruments that had been adopted and the means by which to remedy it. The academics followed the same trajectory: after a phase of interest in the conditions for creation and content of new regulations, they began asking difficult questions relating to implementation and enforcement.

Indeed, the problem of the implementation of international environmental law has gradually emerged as a field of research in economics, political sciences and law[2], generating varied analyses, some more empirical, some more theoretical, with authors looking to qualify and even quantify[3] the degree of these instruments' effectiveness and to explain the disparities that emerge. This wave of introspection extended beyond international law to European[4] and national law.[5] But, and "even though environmental lawyers are probably the species of lawyers most interested in empirical research on the effectiveness of legal and policy instruments"[6], relatively few published works evaluate the effectiveness of domestic environmental legal systems.[7]

---

2 D. F. Sprinz, *Research on the Effectiveness of International Environmental Regimes: A Review of the State of the Art*, 1, Paper prepared for the Final Conference of the EU Concerted Action on Regime Effectiveness, IDEC, 9-12 November 2000, Barcelona.

3 H. Carsten and D. F. Sprinz, Measuring the Effectiveness of International Environmental Regimes, 45 *Journal of Conflict Resolution*, 630-652 (2000); and, D. F. Sprinz, The Quantitative Analysis of International Environmental Policy, in D.F. Sprinz, Y.Wolinsky-Nahmias (eds.), *Cases, Numbers, Models: International Relations Research Methods* 424 (2004).

4 See Communication from the Commission to the European Parliament, the Council, the European Economic and Social Committee and the Committee of the Regions on implementing European Community Environmental Law, COM/2008/773 final, 18 November 2008.

5 In French Law, this is reflected in for example the adoption of the law called "Bamier," no. 95-101 of 2 February 1995 related to the reinforcement of environmental protection, JORF no.29 of 3 February 1995, p. 1840.

6 M. Faure, "The effectiveness of environmental law: what does the evidence tell us?", *Wm. & Mary Envtl. L. & Pol'y Rev.*, Vol. 36 (2012) 295.

7 Chris McGrath, *Does environmental law work?*, Lambert Academic Pub, 2010, p. 21.

However, as environmental threats worsen, strengthening the effectiveness of environmental law seems to be a major challenge for the future.[8] Assessing the actual and projected *effects* of environmental measures is necessary for developing models or scenarios in relation to future trends in the state of the environment.

As lawyers, we do not have all of the keys on hand. Nevertheless, we have a great responsibility in participating in this assessment, in identifying the difficulties, obstacles and limits of legal rules and instruments and in exploring or even proposing solutions to policy makers. Improving the effectiveness of environmental legal systems is certainly an ongoing task.

2. EFFECTIVENESS: WHAT IS IT?

According to the Cambridge Dictionary, "effectiveness" means "the ability to be successful and produce the intended results". This is the usual meaning. As a working definition, effective rules or instruments are those that create a result that meets their objectives. The main question, then, is: does a legal rule or an instrument contribute to improve the environment or to achieve the intended policy objective? In that sense, measuring the "effectiveness" of laws means measuring the extent to which laws solve the problem they were designed to address. This is, without any doubt, the ultimate concern of legal rules and instruments.

2.1. EFFECTIVENESS AND OTHER RELATED CONCEPTS

Again according to the Cambridge Dictionary, "efficacy" means the "ability, especially of a medicine or a method of achieving something, to produce the intended result". In that sense, it could be used as a synonym for effectiveness.

In common language, compliance, implementation and effectiveness or efficiency are sometimes perceived to be interchangeable, but they do have specific connotations. This is why we need to clarify some potential ambiguities that deeply inform the theoretical discussion about the concept of legal effectiveness. To that end, I propose some working definitions.

The term "compliance" refers to a state of conformity or identity between an actor's behaviour and a specified rule.[9] As mentioned previously, if an instrument

---

8 This is a need that has also been recognized in the Fourth Program of the United Nations Environment Program (UNEP) for the development and periodic evaluation of environment law. *See* the Report of the meeting of senior government officials expert in environmental law to prepare a fourth Programme for the Development and Periodic Review of Environmental Law (Montevideo Programme IV),UNEP/Env.Law/MTV4/IG/2/2, 22 October 2008.

9 K. Raustiala, "Compliance & Effectiveness In International Regulatory Cooperation", 32 *Case W. Res. J. Int'l L.*, 391.

is not well-designed, the environmental problem will not be solved, even if there is a very good compliance rate.

It is important to distinguish between compliance with commitments *per se* and the true impact that commitments have on the actor's behaviour.[10] The latter is what matters; compliance is incidental. Take the example of Russia in the Kyoto Protocol. It is in full compliance with its commitments, because its economy, and thus its emissions, collapsed in the early 1990s. But this compliance is not the result, or not mainly, of behavioural change. Now their emissions are on the rise as their economy picks up.

For its part, "implementation" refers more to the process than to the result. These processes involve applying rules or instruments, providing administrative infrastructure and resources necessary to apply them, instituting effective monitoring and enforcement mechanisms and so on.[11]

Whereas implementation is usually a critical step towards compliance, compliance can occur without implementation. For instance, for international legal rules at least, this will be the case when an international commitment mirrors national law and practice, or where factors external to the legal process induce compliance.[12]

"Enforcement", then, is "the act of compelling compliance with a law".[13] I will deal with this notion in greater detail below.

Moving on to "efficiency", the question that arises is: "Have these objectives been achieved at the lowest cost?" It is not a matter of effectiveness, except where we consider that more efficient legal rules will be more easily implemented and for this specific reason should be more effective.

2.2. THE MULTIPLE MEANINGS OF EFFECTIVENESS

Even effectiveness has multiple meanings. More specifically, there are three levels of effectiveness, that are often mentioned as such in the literature:

1) legal effectiveness, meaning that the law is respected;
2) behavioural effectiveness, which shows whether the situation is different from what it would have been without the treaty, obligation, rules. In other words, it refers to the ability of the legal provisions to change people's behaviour or

---

10 D. G. Victor, "The Use and Effectiveness of Nonbinding instruments in the management of complex international environmental problems", 91 *Am. Soc'y Int'l L. Proc.* (1997) 242.

11 T. Risse, "Rational Choice, Constructivism and the Study of International Institutions." *in* Katznelson (I.), Milner (H.) (eds.). *Political Science as Discipline? Reconsidering Power, Choice and the State at Century's End*, 2001.

12 K. Raustiala, "Compliance & Effectiveness In International Regulatory Cooperation", *op. cit.*, p. 391.

13 Black's Law Dictionary, 8th Ed. 2004, p. 569.

to result in changes in the behaviour of socio-economic actors. The recipients of the legal rule – those to whom the law is addressed – could be public or private actors. They are to be distinguished from those affected by the law. Among public actors are the administrative and judicial authorities in charge of the implementation, monitoring, sanction of non-compliance, including penalties. They are the secondary recipients of the legal rule. The primary ones are those individuals to whom the law or the legal rule is addressed;
3) and problem-solving effectiveness, focusing more on the goals, interested in the aim of the legal provisions (has it been set too low?) and to how action is spurred towards achieving these objectives.[14]

An instrument could lead actors to try to reach solutions through a variety of initiatives and actions, including some that do not involve the instrument directly.

An instrument could have unintended effects or consequences.

It could even be counterproductive. However, this matter is no longer a matter of effectiveness then. According to the definition we have adopted, we cannot include effects in contradiction with the purpose of the legal rule, this would include effects producing a result that is opposed to the intended result.

Effectiveness is a phenomenon that is difficult, if not impossible, to comprehend and to explain. Even if we are to simply try to explain the legal effectiveness, it is quite difficult. Is the legal effectiveness spontaneous or due to an efficacious monitoring, together with severe penalties? Is the rule respected because it is considered to be good, justified or legitimate? Or is it motivated by fear of possible sanctions? Effectiveness is not only a question of fact; it also has a symbolic dimension.

Regarding international law, there are numerous theories that try to identify the factors that influence state-behaviour. Rationalist theories explain compliance in relation to the nature of the problem, the structure of the solution chosen and the costs and benefits associated with different behaviours.[15] Norm-driven theories focus on the power of ideas to influence state behaviour.[16] For instance, T. Franck argues that the legitimacy of rules and processes generates a "compliance pull."[17] A. Chayes supports "managing compliance" through financial, technical or informational assistance, or through interpretative dialogue.[18] Liberal theories suggest that liberal societies, because of their domestic reverence for the rule of

---

14 A. Rieu Clarke, J. Gooch, "Implementing international water agreements", in *Implementing Environmental Law*, P. Martin, A. Kennedy ed., The IUCN Academy of Environmental Law, 2015.

15 K. Raustiala, "Compliance & Effectiveness In International Regulatory Cooperation", *op. cit.*, p. 405.

16 *Idem.*

17 T. M. Franck, "Legitimacy in the International System", 82 *Am. J. Int'l L. 705* (1988).

18 A. Chayes et al., "*Managing Compliance: A Comparative Perspective*", in *Engaging Countries: Strengthening Compliance with International Environmental Accords* (E. B. Weiss and H.K. Jacobsen eds, 1998).

law, are more likely to comply with the decisions of international tribunals than illiberal states, etc.[19]

Indeed, to reach the problem-solving effectiveness, which is the most important, instruments need to satisfy a double condition.

First, they have to be *well-designed*, that is to say that they are adapted to the purposes set forth. This is a matter or relevance*:* to what extent do these objectives adequately address the 'needs' of the issue or problem? This first condition is not easy to fulfil in the environmental field. Due to a lack of knowledge or a lack of will/consensus, environmental objectives or methods are not always expressed clearly. Environmental issues need to be well defined and understood. This level of thinking leads beyond the frontiers of law when it comes to finding an answer, on the basis of a substantive analysis, to this question: can the quality of the environment or the condition of the resource be improved by a treaty, law, regulation or rule? This assumes that the "needs" of the environment or the resource are known and that meeting them is possible, something which is easier to determine in some circumstances than it is in others.

Second, instruments have to be *well-implemented*. Does it result in, prove capable of, a behavioural change? The discussion goes beyond an implementation in its narrow connotation, to cover the ability of the legal rule in influencing the behaviour of its recipients in the sense desired by the rule maker.[20] We can say, with Pierre Bourdieu, that: "le jeu avec la règle fait partie de la règle du jeu".[21] For François Ost and Michel Van de Kerchove, "est effective la règle utilisée par ses destinataires comme modèle pour orienter leur pratique", whether they are primary recipients (people to whom the law is addressed), or administrative and judicial authorities (in charge of its implementation). However, what works in one case may not work in others.

Furthermore, an instrument could be well-designed, but not well-implemented. In this case, the problem will not be solved and, vice versa, an instrument could be well-implemented, but if it has not been well-designed, the problem will not be solved.

These are two separate, but cumulative, conditions by which to get an impact in terms of problem-solving. *A priori,* if these two tests are met – *a well-designed* and *well-implemented tool* – in the final analysis, the quality of the environment or the state of the resource will be improved thanks to the tool in question.

---

19 K. Raustiala, "Compliance & Effectiveness In International Regulatory Cooperation", *op. cit.*, p. 410.

20 F. Ost et M. Van de Kerchove, *De la pyramide au réseau. Pour une théorie dialectique du droit*, Bruxelles, Publications des Facultés universitaires Saint-Louis, 2002, p. 329.

21 P. Bourdieu, "Droit et passe-droit. Le champ des pouvoirs territoriaux et la mise en œuvre des règlements", *Actes de la recherche en sciences sociales*, 81/82, 1990, p. 89.

However, very few rules or instruments cumulatively satisfy these two aspects of effectiveness. Most often, a rule/instrument is only effective with respect to one of them.[22]

At this point, I need to add that the effectiveness is rarely total, but is more generally partial. We could have some signs of effectiveness, but not full compliance; this is usually the case. The reality is rarely black or white. Total effectiveness is a kind of utopic dream. Ineffectiveness is more natural in social systems characterized by compromises, indulgence and the quest for the least amount of effort. As Jean Carbonnier has said: "C'est défigurer la réalité humaine et sociale qui s'exprime dans les systèmes juridiques modernes, que de n'en retenir qu'un besoin d'ordre, de régularité, partant de ponctuelle et totale effectivité des règles de droit. Il s'y rencontre des intérêts antagonistes: la propension au compromis, l'indulgence, et même la recherche du moindre effort, qui inclinent les règles de droit à une ineffectivité tout aussi naturelle".[23]

Conversely, we could find laws that are totally ineffective. But in that case, there is a risk that it falls into disuse. This further highlights the importance of effectiveness.

Having said that, effectiveness is not only difficult to circumscribe, but also to assess.

3. DIFFICULTIES IN ASSESSING EFFECTIVENESS

Apart from the polysemic characteristic of the word, the evaluation of effectiveness is not easy.

To go back to the three levels of effectiveness, the first one, legal effectiveness, is fairly easy to measure. But a regime or instrument can be legally effective without solving the problem that led to its creation.[24]

Behavioural effectiveness is less easy to measure, in particular for a lawyer and without any input from other social sciences.

Problem solving effectiveness is even less easy to measure, but it is the most important. As Lawrence Susskind suggests, "it would be a mistake to measure success in terms of anything less than tangible environmental improvements."[25]

---

22 K. Von Moltke, "Research on the Effectiveness of International Environmental Agreements: Lessons for Policy Makers", *Paper prepared for the Final Conference of the EU Concerted Action on Regime Effectiveness*. IDEC, 9-12 November 2000, Barcelona; O. Young, *The Effectiveness of International Environmental Regimes. Causal Connections and Behavioral Mechanisms*. Cambridge: MIT Press, 1999.

23 J. Carbonnier, "Effectivité et ineffectivité de la règle de droit", *L'année sociologique*, vol. 9, 1957-58, p. 13.

24 O. Young, *The Effectiveness of International Environmental Regimes. Causal Connections and Behavioral Mechanisms*, *op. cit.*

25 L.E. Susskind, *Environmental Diplomacy: Negotiating More Effective Global Agreements* (Oxford University Press, Oxford, 1994), p 40.

Even where objectives are clearly articulated, assessments of effectiveness are difficult due to the complexity of social and political structures, the perpetual evolution of ecological systems and gaps of information

Appropriate effectiveness indicators and adequate benchmarks are still lacking; reflection remains extremely theoretical and the problems of establishing causal links between the legal rule or instrument and the observed results also remain.[26] The chain of actions linking the rules, policies and persons to the natural environment is complex, uncertain and discontinuous in a context where many overlapping policies and programs with similar intended outcomes exist.[27] Assessing effectiveness involves a multi-disciplinary task requiring the integration of environmental science and law. Much depends on the criteria used. Ultimately, "whether the protection offered to the (...) environment by law is 'adequate' in scope and stringency is of course a value judgment, which will depend on the weight given to the whole range of competing social, economic and political considerations".[28]

4. HOW TO IMPROVE THE EFFECTIVENESS OF ENVIRONMENTAL LAW

I need to make three preliminary remarks here. The first remark is that there are actually many instruments in the field of the environment that do not meet their objectives. To improve their effectiveness, we have to take the causes of their ineffectiveness into account. These causes can relate to the design or the implementation of a law, regulation or treaty. But they can also depend on political, social or cultural factors. Or course, as a lawyer, it is more difficult to face the latter. However, better legislation should try to take political, social and cultural deadlocks into account.

The second remark is that the issue of effectiveness is posed in very different terms depending on the level of regulation: if it is international law, European law or domestic law.

The third remark is that better legislation and better implementation are two matters that are interlinked. Better legislation can lead to better implementation. An "efficient, cost-effective, equitable, politically acceptable, and 'optimal'" environmental legal system should be quite effective.[29]

26 K. von Moltke, *Research on the Effectiveness of International Environmental Agreements: Lessons for Policy Makers*, Paper prepared for the Final Conference of the EU Concerted Action on Regime Effectiveness, IDEC, 9-12 November 2000, Barcelona, 4-5.

27 *Idem*, p. 4.

28 P. Birnie, A. Boyle, *International Law & the Environment* (2nd ed, Oxford University Press, Oxford, 2002), pp 1-10, quoted by C. McGrath, *Does environmental law work?*, Lambert Academic Pub, 2010, p. 13.

29 C. McGrath, *Does environmental law work?*, Lambert Academic Pub, 2010, p. 13.

Having said that, we can identify two avenues by which to improve effectiveness: better legislation and better implementation.

4.1. BETTER LEGISLATION

The lack of implementation comes from various factors.

Firstly, the threats to the environment are complex, difficult to identify and to deal with. For instance, protecting biodiversity presents a serious challenge. Our law is poorly tailored to face it. Law is traditionally governed by the principle of legal certainty, and always seeks to simplify and categorize reality, whereas biodiversity is a complex, dynamic, evolving and still widely unknown reality.

To go even further, the current environmental crisis is multi-dimensional, with permanent interaction between the different dimensions. Recently, the interdependence of planetary boundaries has been highlighted: planetary boundaries are closely interconnected, because transgressing one may both shift the position of other boundaries or cause them to be transgressed.[30]

Hence, for example, climate change has a profound impact on biodiversity. According to the Millennium Ecosystem Assessment, climate change is to become one of the most severe drivers of biodiversity loss by the end of the century. This statement is even supported by the IPCC reports. Climate change could eventually claim one sixth of the world's species.[31] On the other hand, the loss of biodiversity has consequences on climate change: the significant loss of marine biodiversity weakens marine ecosystems, for example, and consequently the climate and the biosystems of the entire planet, because seas and oceans are vital to biochemical cycles such as that of oxygen.

These interplays clearly complicate the governance of the Earth's system.[32] They have been dealt with by law.

Secondly, the lack of implementation comes from the intrinsic quality of the law. Due to various factors, rules in this field are soft; they are often vague, indeterminate, open-textured, non-quantified and, for a lot of international norms and some European norms, non-self-executing. When it is the case, it opens a wide margin of appreciation in their application. Moreover, their implementation is difficult to monitor and to assess. Ultimately, their enforcement is rather impossible.

For instance, the effectiveness of multilateral environmental agreements (MEAs) is neither easily measured nor plausibly met. MEAs rarely have clear

---

30 See *supra* footnote 1.

31 S. Perkins, "Climate change could eventually claim a sixth of the world's species", *Science*, 30 April 2015.

32 M. Nillsson, A. Persson, "Can Earth system interactions be governed? Governance functions for linking climate change mitigation with land use, freshwater and biodiversity protection", *Ecological Economics*, vol. 81, September 2012, pp. 10-20.

articulations of their principal objectives or the methods to achieve them. This could be due to the inadequate state of the science at the time the agreement was drafted or due to a lack of political consensus among states on how rigorous and precise the objective should be. In the absence of this agreement, objectives tend to be ambiguous, qualified and reflective of the least common denominator among states.[33] It is difficult, then, to monitor their implementation and to sanction non-compliance.

Indeed, designing "good" environmental norms is not easy. They have to be flexible but not too soft, evolving but not fluctuating. They have to combine incitative and coercive tools, general regulations and market-based approaches, public and private mechanisms and so on. One of this century's major challenges (in terms of environmental law) will be to determine the best mix, the best combination between those different tools and approaches on a case by case basis. This challenge will also require the development of new ways of law-making, to strengthen expertise and the interface between experts and policy makers, or even new approaches such as participatory approaches.

However, better regulation should not be an excuse to deregulate. For instance, the EU "fitness check" that the European Commission is carrying out under its Regulatory Fitness and Performance Programme (REFIT) is an important building block in the "better regulation package".[34] Officially, it serves to "make EU law simpler and to reduce regulatory costs, thus contributing to a clear, stable and predictable regulatory framework supporting growth and jobs"[35] In actual fact, the consequence is a loosening of environmental law. A lot of countries – France, for instance – are moving in the same direction. We have to be careful.

To quote Montesquieu, "La loi souffre de trop de maux, qui nuisent à sa compréhension et à son respect. Trop détaillée, alors qu'elle devrait être centrée sur l'essentiel, elle en devient incompréhensible. Trop déclarative, alors qu'elle devrait être normative, elle se dévalorise".[36]

4.2. BETTER IMPLEMENTATION

How might we improve the implementation of environmental law? This is also a very complex issue. The implementation of environmental law evolves with changes occurring in the design of environmental law. The problem is not the

33 See for instance, United Nations Framework Convention on Climate Change, Article 2; Convention on Biological Diversity, Article 6.

34 See for example: Communication from the Commission to the European Parliament, the Council, the European Economic and social committee and the committee of the Regions, *Better regulation for better results – An EU agenda*, Strasbourg, 19.5.2015 COM(2015) 215 final.

35 Http://ec.europa.eu/smart-regulation/refit/index_en.htm [July 4 2016].

36 Montesquieu, *Lettres persanes*, Lettres CXXIX.

same if we talk about a classical tool (command and control) or a more innovative one (incitative tools, market-based mechanisms, voluntary tools, private law …). We have to forget an approach that is only imperative and repressive of law and implementation. On the one hand, a legal norm is not necessarily a mandatory rule of conduct that can be only respected or violated. A lot of norms are supplementary/suppletive. On the other hand, the sanction is not always the best tool of implementation. Sanctions are not always well-tailored, not always possible, not always decided upon. In fact, the likelihood that a violation ends up in court and is sanctioned is extremely low.[37]

Actual incentives will often provide better incentives to prevention/implementation. In some cases, the cooperation model, whereby the agency tries to bring the polluter to compliance through persuasion and by providing information, has proven to be more efficacious than the deterrence one, whereby authorities are hard on polluters and prosecute all cases.[38]

Effectiveness also has a symbolic or even a psychologic dimension, which contributes to maintaining its aura of mystery. According to an often-quoted old American survey, in front of an unexpected red light, car drivers can be divided into three categories: those who stop, those who do not stop, those who slow down. We can divide people into conformists, non-conformists, and superior conformists (those who take the matter into consideration before acting).[39] The possibility of sanctions is obviously not the sole driver of effectiveness. The acceptance of the norm, the recognition of its legitimacy, the existence of incentives are also some of effectiveness's important drivers. They could have a more preventive and deterrent effect.

Furthermore, in a case by case analysis, depending upon the specific context, type of pollutant regulated, institutional design, etc., we need to figure out the optimal combination of incentive and sanction. Seeing the concept of enforcement as an imposition of legal sanctions, or penalties, is too narrow. It is a far more multi-faceted concept than is often assumed. It encompasses a wide spectrum of means for "compelling compliance" with law.[40]

As international lawyers, and even as the most resolute positivists, we know very well that enforcement is not the critical factor and: "at any rate, does not account for a law's binding effect".[41] Because of the complex ways in which the law is made meaningful in the life of its subjects, "the law is … not external, coercive

---

37 M. Faure, *The effectiveness of environmental law: what does the evidence tell us?*, *op. cit.*, p. 321.

38 *Ibid.*, p. 327.

39 W. Allport, "The Curve hypothesis of conforming behavior", *Journal of Social Psychology*, May 1934, p. 141 et s. Cit. J. Carbonnier, op. cit., p. 18.

40 J. Brunnée, "Enforcement Mechanisms in International Law and International Environmental Law", in Ulrich Beyerlin et al, eds., *Ensuring Compliance with Multilateral Environmental Agreements: A Dialogue Between Practitioners and Academia* (2005).

41 *Ibidem*.

and alien but internal, logically necessary and familiar", as it has been stressed by Sir Ian Brownlie.[42]

This is why the following chapters will go from classical tools (control, criminal, administrative, civil sanctions, liability rules, strengthening of the regulatory structure and the role of judges ...), classical but still necessary, to more innovative ones (public participation, effectiveness of instrument mixes, collaborative governance, hybrid governance and private environmental enforcement ...).

As I come to the end of this brief introduction to the book's topic, I realize that I have highlighted many difficulties and obstacles. We have to face them and we have to propose solutions to the shortcomings identified together. Comparative law can be very helpful in achieving this end. I also hope that this book, in the aftermath of the successful Third EELF conference in Aix-en-Provence, will serve this fundamental objective by bringing together practitioners and academics, from varied countries and varied fields, combining empirical and theoretical approaches.

42 I. Brownlie, "The Reality and Efficacity of International Law", *British Yearbook of International Law*, 55 (1981), p. 1, quoted by J. Brunnée, "Enforcement Mechanisms in International Law and International Environmental Law", *op.cit.*

PART 1

MEASURING AND ASSESSING EFFECTIVENESS

CHAPTER 1

THE CLIMATE RESILIENCE OF CRITICAL INFRASTRUCTURAL NETWORK SECTORS

An Interdisciplinary Method for Assessing Formal Responsibilities for Climate Adaptation in Critical Infrastructural Network Sectors

Herman Kasper GILISSEN
Utrecht Centre for Water, Oceans and Sustainability Law of Utrecht University

Peter DRIESSEN
Copernicus Institute of Sustainable Development of Utrecht University

Heleen MEES
Copernicus Institute of Sustainable Development of Utrecht University

Marleen VAN RIJSWICK
Utrecht Centre for Water, Oceans and Sustainability Law of Utrecht University

Hens RUNHAAR
Copernicus Institute of Sustainable Development of Utrecht University, Special Professor of Management of Biodiversity in Agricultural Landscapes at Wageningen University and Research Centre

Caroline UITTENBROEK
Copernicus Institute of Sustainable Development of Utrecht University

Rebecca WÖRNER
*Utrecht Centre for Water, Oceans and Sustainability Law of Utrecht University**

Herman Kasper Gilissen, Peter Driessen, Heleen Mees, Marleen van Rijswick,
Hens Runhaar, Caroline Uittenbroek and Rebecca Wörner

ABSTRACT

This chapter presents and applies an interdisciplinary (law & governance) method for the assessment of the climate resilience of critical infrastructural network sectors. Broadly applicable, this methodological framework comprises three phases, within which six logically arranged steps are set out. The central assessment criterion for climate resilience, the 'expected effectiveness' of responsibilities for climate adaptation, is operationalized through six indicators. These are: awareness, proactivity, appropriateness, explicitness, transparency and legitimacy. Apart from academic purposes, this assessment framework can prove useful to law and policy makers in assessing and (re)developing the relevant arrangements that govern critical infrastructural network sectors. To give examples of the functioning of the assessment framework, this framework is applied in two case studies that address the Dutch electricity and internet sectors. These case studies show a rather low level of expected effectiveness of responsibilities for climate adaptation in both sectors. Apart from their exemplary purpose, these case studies provide insights into potential pitfalls which can be relevant for increasing the climate resilience of other network sectors in the Netherlands, in other EU Member States and abroad.

1. INTRODUCTION

Modern societies and key societal functions, such as emergency management and health care, depend largely upon the smooth-functioning of critical infrastructural networks, such as energy, ICT, drinking water and transportation networks. The collapse of such networks can cause an array of societal disruption and damage. Critical infrastructural networks are particularly prone to external influences, such as floods and other water-related events. The expected climate change increases the chance of such events, thus also increasing the infrastructural networks' vulnerability. International, EU and domestic climate change scenarios display rather clear trends.[1] Focusing on the EU and its Member States, increases in the duration, probability and intensity of weather extremes (e.g. heavy rainfall and extreme droughts) are already being perceived throughout the continent and are expected to increase

* This chapter builds upon research commissioned by the Netherlands Environmental Assessment Agency and the National Research Programme 'Knowledge for Climate' within the framework of the establishment of the Dutch National Adaptation Strategy.

1 See *Intergovernmental Panel on Climate Change*, Climate Change 2014: Impacts, Adaptation, and Vulnerability, IPCC Working Group II contribution to AR5; *European Commission*, An EU strategy on adaptation to climate change (COM(2013) 216); and *Koninklijk Nederlands Meteorologisch Instituut*, KNMI'14-klimaatscenario's voor Nederland – Leidraad voor professionals in klimaatadaptatie, De Bilt 2014.

even further.[2] The associated risks, in this chapter, are referred to as climate risks. The question arises how the responsibilities to combat climate risks for critical infrastructural networks are divided in the EU and in its Member States particularly, and to what extent these responsibilities, and the division thereof, are expected to be effective.[3]

This question is at the heart of this chapter; however, it cannot be addressed to its fullest extent. Therefore, we focus on the second part of this question, or in other words, on the assessment of vulnerable critical infrastructural network sectors' climate resilience.[4] Adopting an interdisciplinary methodological approach, combining insights and experiences from both the disciplines of (environmental) law and governance, we first present a comprehensive and broadly applicable framework for the ex-ante assessment of the 'expected effectiveness' of formal responsibilities for climate adaptation and the division thereof between relevant public and private actors (Section 2). Through this assessment framework, we intend to provide a tool for both academics and law and policy makers to evaluate, compare and (re)develop relevant domestic arrangements that govern critical infrastructural network sectors from an integrated 'law & governance' perspective.[5] After having operationalized the central criterion of expected effectiveness, and having identified a number of indicators in Section 3, we apply this framework to two infrastructural network sectors in the Netherlands; namely, the electricity sector and the internet sector (Section 4). These case studies are mainly meant to show the functioning of the framework, and thus have an exemplary and explanatory role. We conclude with general remarks about the application of

---

2 See *European Commission*, An EU strategy on adaptation to climate change (COM(2013) 216), pp. 2-4.

3 See *P.P.J. Driessen & H.F.M.W. van Rijswick*, Normative aspects of climate adaptation policies, Climate Law 2011 (2), pp. 559-581; *H.L.P. Mees, P.P.J. Driessen & H.A.C. Runhaar*, Exploring the scope of public and private responsibilities for climate adaptation, Journal of Environmental Planning Policy and Management 2012 (3), pp. 305-330; and *A.M. Keessen et al.*, The concept of resilience from a normative perspective: examples from Dutch adaptation strategies, Ecology & Society 2013 (2), pp. 45-56.

4 This chapter builds upon previous studies; see *H.A.C. Runhaar et al.*, Publieke en/of private verantwoordelijkheden voor klimaatadaptatie – Een juridisch-bestuurlijke analyse en eerste beoordeling, Copernicus Institute of Sustainable Development/Utrecht Centre for Water, Oceans and Sustainability Law, Utrecht 2014; *H.A.C. Runhaar et al.*, Prepared for climate change? A method for the ex-ante assessment of formal responsibilities for climate adaptation in specific sectors, Regional Environmental Change 2016 (in press), accepted and published online in 2015 (http://link.springer.com/article/10.1007/s10113-015-0866-2), pp. 1-12 (in this chapter, we refer to the page numbers of the 2015 online publication); and *H.K. Gilissen et al.*, De klimaatbestendigheid van de vitale infrastructuur beoordeeld van juridisch-bestuurlijk perspectief – Over de verwachte effectiviteit van de verdeling van verantwoordelijkheden voor de beheersing van klimaatrisico's in de elektriciteits- en de internetsector, Nederland Juristenblad 2015 (25), pp. 1640-1648.

5 We define such 'arrangements' as coherent sets of distinguishable actors, rules and policies governing a specific sector.

the assessment framework and potential (transferable) lessons to be learnt from the case studies (Section 5).

Here, we first seize upon the opportunity to briefly outline some backgrounds relevant to this chapter. Adaptation is a key strategy in combatting the adverse effects of climate change in EU policies, formally since 2005.[6] Since that time, the concept has developed, along a policy track by and large[7], resulting in the adoption of the European Adaptation Strategy (EAS) in 2013[8], encouraging the Member States to adopt and implement comprehensive adaptation policies (National Adaptation Strategies; NASs) by 2017 at the latest and to 'mainstream' the concept into their relevant sectoral governance domains, among which are those governing critical network sectors.[9] Although the adaptation approach was integrated into sectoral EU legislation on, for instance, flood risk management (i.e. the Floods Directive)[10], it has to be kept in mind that this concept, as far as it is relevant for this work, is mainly rooted in soft law documents at the EU level.[11] There is, to date, no formal obligation stemming from EU law for the Member States to mainstream the adaptation approach into their sectoral law and policies regarding infrastructural network sectors.

Focusing on vulnerable infrastructural network sectors, the absence of explicit and targeted EU legislation does not necessarily mean that the Member States have not adopted explicit or implicit responsibilities for combatting climate risks into their relevant domestic legislation or policies. These responsibilities could, for instance, aim at limiting the *chance* of network failure (and consequently limiting the chance of societal disruption) caused

---

6 See *European Commission*, Winning the Battle Against Global Climate Change (COM(2005) 35), pp. 7-8. About that time, a number of Member States had already adopted National Adaptation Strategies; see *R. Swart et al.*, Europe adapts to climate change – Comparing national adaptation strategies, PEER Report no. 1, Partnership for European Environmental Research, Helsinki 2009, and *G.R. Biesbroek et al.*, Europe adapts to climate change: Comparing National Adaptation Strategies, Global Environmental Change 2010 (20), pp. 440-450.

7 See *European Commission*, Adapting to climate change in Europe – options for EU action (Green Paper; COM(2007) 354); and *European Commission*, Adapting to climate change: Towards a European framework for action (White Paper; COM(2009) 147). Also see *H.K. Gilissen*, The integration of the adaptation approach into EU and Dutch legislation on flood risk management, Journal of Water Law 2014 (3/4), pp. 159-160.

8 See *European Commission*, An EU strategy on adaptation to climate change (COM(2013) 216).

9 See, for instance, *D. McEvoy et al.*, Adaptation and Mainstreaming of EU Climate Change Policy: An Actor-Based Perspective, Centre for European Policy Studies, nr. 149, January 2008; and *C.J. Uittenbroek*, How mainstream is mainstreaming? – The integration of climate adaptation into urban policy (diss. UU), Utrecht 2014.

10 See *H.K. Gilissen*, The integration of the adaptation approach into EU and Dutch legislation on flood risk management, Journal of Water Law 2014 (3/4), pp. 162-163.

11 Further formalization (e.g. the adoption of an 'Adaptation Directive') will be taken into consideration in case the Member States have not adequately fulfilled the objectives of the European Adaptation Strategy by 2017. See *European Commission*, An EU strategy on adaptation to climate change (COM(2013) 216), p. 6.

by climate-related events, they could aim to limit the *consequences* of network failures and mitigate the impact on society of such failure, or at *repairing* possible damage to a network as quickly as possible in order to limit societal disruption and to prevent deterioration. Such formal responsibilities (i.e. legal responsibilities generating a degree of accountability)[12] are the subject of this chapter, regardless of whether these are explicitly aimed at combatting climate risks or are only implicitly relevant through their general applicability in this respect. Whereas the assessment framework comprises aspects of different disciplines (law and governance), the 'objects' to which it is meant to be applied – i.e. formal responsibilities – are legal in nature.

2. A METHODOLOGICAL FRAMEWORK FOR THE ASSESSMENT OF CLIMATE RESILIENCE

The assessment framework to be presented in this section aims to assess the extent to which the current (division of) responsibilities for climate adaptation within network sectors fosters an adequate adaptation to climate change. In that sense, it is a helpful tool for the identification of potential weaknesses in the sectors selected for assessment, as well as for the formulation of recommendations and the development of strategies to eliminate these weaknesses through legal or other means. The method comprises three phases, within which six logically arranged steps have been set out (see Table 1).[13] It concerns the phase of preparation (i.e. delineation, justification, exploration and legal analysis; steps 1 to 4), the assessment phase (step 5) and the phase of reflection and recommendations (step 6).[14] In this section, we briefly address the different phases and steps, followed by an operationalization of our assessment criteria in Section 3. The assessment framework will be applied to two case studies in Section 4 in order to show the functioning of the method and its potential results.

12 With Bovens et al. we define accountability as "an evaluative concept that is used to positively qualify a state of affairs or the performance of an actor". See *M. Bovens et al.*, "Does public accountability work?" An assessment tool, Public Administration 2008 (1), pp. 225-242.

13 For the development of this methodological framework the authors drew inspiration from *I. Curry-Sumner et al.*, Research skills – Instruction for lawyers, Ars Aequi Libri, Nijmegen 2010; and *P. Verschuren & H. Doorewaard*, Designing a research project, Eleven International Publishing, The Hague 2010.

14 The framework presented here largely builds upon and further refines the one presented in *H.A.C. Runhaar et al.*, Prepared for climate change? A method for the ex-ante assessment of formal responsibilities for climate adaptation in specific sectors, Regional Environmental Change 2016 (in press), online version 2015, pp. 4-6.

Table 1. Phases and steps within the framework for assessing the climate resilience of critical infrastructural network sectors

Phase	Step	Description
Phase 1 'Preparation'	Step 1	Delineation of the object (sector) of analysis and a justification for this selection
	Step 2	Identification and description of the major climate-risks risk for the sector selected for assessment
	Step 3	Description of main sectoral characteristics and recent developments within the sector
	Step 4	Analysis of sectoral formal responsibilities in relevant legislation, policies and case law
Phase 2 'Assessment'	Step 5	Ex-ante assessment of the expected effectiveness of sectoral responsibilities for climate adaptation following six indicators
Phase 3 'Reflection'	Step 6	Reflection on the assessment results and the functioning of the assessment framework; formulation of recommendations for systemic improvements

2.1. PHASE 1: PREPARATION

The main aim of the first phase is to 'set the scene' through the collection and analysis of relevant information in preparation of, and needed for, the actual assessment in phase 2. During this preparatory phase, the object of the analysis (i.e. one or more specific infrastructural network sectors or sub-sectors) is selected and narrowed down, followed by a justification of the choice of these specific (sub-) sectors and any further delineations (step 1). Subsequently, the most important climate-related risks to the concerning sector(s) are set out, where needed, on the basis of (technical) information provided by other disciplines (step 2), and the characteristics and most important developments within a given sector are briefly explained (step 3). As a final and key step in the preparatory phase, an overview is given of the formal responsibilities and competences of the public and private actors within a certain sector on the basis of an analysis of the relevant legal and policy framework(s) and, if applicable, relevant case law (step 4).

2.2. PHASE 2: ASSESSMENT

The second phase (step 5) encompasses the actual assessment of the sectoral (division of) responsibilities for adaptation to climate change, based on the information gathered during the first phase. The central criterion within this assessment framework is the 'expected effectiveness' of such responsibilities and the division thereof. It should be kept in mind that the assessment has an ex-ante character and aims to draw *expectations* about the effectiveness of the sectoral responsibilities. The question, thus, is to what extent the system – on the basis of a set of objective indicators – can be expected to be effective. The framework does not aim at assessing the *factual* effectiveness of responsibilities, which can merely be assessed ex-post, after a climate-related event. The question of the extent to which the system has actually proven to be effective will not be addressed through this framework.

The assessment of the expected effectiveness is conducted following six predetermined indicators. Firstly, the explicitness, transparency and legitimacy of the responsibilities concerned are selected as benchmarks for the effectiveness expected.[15] Furthermore, factors such as awareness, a sense of urgency and the type of responsibility (proactive or reactive) play a role in the assessment, just as the question of the extent to which responsibilities and competences are appropriate and appropriately divided amongst the relevant actors does (by reflecting the notions of subsidiarity and proportionality). These indicators are of a mixed nature, comprising legal and governance aspects, and will be further operationalized in Section 3 below. The results of the assessment help to identify potential points for improvement within the arrangements governing relevant infrastructural network sectors. Moreover, they can be a rich source of cross-country comparisons and serve as a good entry point in the search for (transferable) good practices and potential common pitfalls.

2.3. PHASE 3: REFLECTION AND RECOMMENDATIONS

The final phase (step 6), first encompasses an analysis of, and reflection on, the assessment results. In the event that the results show that the expected effectiveness of the selected sector is insufficient, because of a lack of transparency or clarity about the division of responsibilities for instance, targeted recommendations for improvement can be put forward. These can, for instance, entail the adoption, clarification or explication of such responsibilities in legislation or in explanatory/ policy documents. The second aim of the reflection addresses the assessment framework itself, in particular the potential difficulties or imperfections encountered in the application thereof. These may include both imperfections regarding the successive steps or the indicators selected for assessing the expected effectiveness. In case of imperfections, recommendations should be made for the improvement of the assessment framework, be it through the rearrangement or addition of specific steps, or through the introduction of new indicators or the reconsideration of those in place.[16]

15 See also *H.L.P. Mees*, Responsible Climate Change Adaptation – Exploring, analysing, and evaluating public and private responsibilities for urban adaptation to climate change (diss. UU), Utrecht 2014.

16 The application of earlier 'versions' of this assessment framework, for instance, resulted in the adoption of new, additional indicators. The indicator 'explicitness' was first adopted in

3. SIX INDICATORS FOR ASSESSING CLIMATE RESILIENCE

As mentioned above, we consider the expected effectiveness of sectoral responsibilities for climate adaptation to be a central criterion for the assessment of critical infrastructural network sectors' climate resilience. For the purposes of this contribution expected effectiveness is understood as the probability that actors, who are involved in a certain sector, are inclined to adjust their activities to the adverse effects of climate change proactively in order to reduce climate risks to an acceptable level. This probability has to be seen in the light of the current division of responsibilities within those sectors. More specifically, it concerns the extent to which actors internalize climate-related risks in their operational management and the related decisions they make about the implementation of their responsibilities and competences.

The determination of what is an 'acceptable level' depends on the nature of the sector selected for assessment. As far as the critical infrastructure is merely being used for the individual (economic) interests of the involved actors, these actors could determine the acceptable level themselves. However, if the critical network serves a public interest mainly (e.g. electricity, communication, drinking water), it is evident that an external party or mechanism determines the acceptable level, through a democratic legislative process, parliamentary involvement and close (market) supervision for example. This is especially important with regards to the question of whether governmental regulatory or supervisory action – or another form of public intervention – is deemed necessary, since the failure of critical infrastructure can lead to disruptions that have consequences for the society as a whole.

There are multiple indicators for expected effectiveness. In this section, we discuss a selection of six key indicators: (a) the extent of problem recognition (awareness/sense of urgency); (b) the type of the responsibilities (proactive/reactive); and (c) the appropriateness, (d) the explicitness, (e) the transparency, and (f) the legitimacy of the responsibilities and the division thereof. These indicators comprise both objective (responsibility-based) and more subjective (actor-based) elements, because the degree of the effectiveness expected depends not only on the way in which responsibilities are allocated and formulated, but also on the way in which these are perceived by their addressees and by others who are interested. We have selected these specific indicators, because these, in our view, address the main factors that are potentially influential to the expected

H.K. Gilissen et al., De klimaatbestendigheid van de vitale infrastructuur beoordeeld van juridisch-bestuurlijk perspectief – Over de verwachte effectiviteit van de verdeling van verantwoordelijkheden voor de beheersing van klimaatrisico's in de elektriciteits- en de internetsector, Nederland Juristenblad 2015 (25), p. 1643, whereas in the current chapter, the indicator 'appropriateness' is introduced (see Section 3).

effectiveness of responsibilities relating to the adverse effects of climate change for network sectors. More indicators, from other disciplines, can also be added to this framework in future research if deemed fruitful and necessary.

It should be borne in mind that these indicators are closely interrelated. Ambiguously formulated responsibilities can, for instance, cause a misinterpretation thereof; this means that a lack of explicitness can, at the same time, generate a lack of transparency. Moreover, it has to be noted that they are meant to assess a selected arrangement from an interdisciplinary (i.e. an integrated law & governance) perspective, so they comprise both legal and governance aspects. Even though the indicators have a certain normative tenor, in the sense that these indicators *should* be complied with in order to optimize expected effectiveness, these are not in the first place meant to draw strict conclusions about the lawfulness of the arrangements governing infrastructural networks. They are instead meant to identify strengths and weaknesses within such arrangements and formulate recommendations for their improvement by means of legal or extra-legal instruments.

Problem recognition: Those who are not aware of certain risks are not likely to take them into account in daily life. The awareness of climate risks can, therefore, be considered to be a condition for risk-minimizing behaviour.[17] For such behaviour, it is not necessary that the actors involved have a complete knowledge of the risks and their potential adverse effects; incentives can be generated to minimize the risks even if there are uncertainties.[18] However, in such cases the relevant actors, whether public or private, need to be sufficiently convinced that proactive action is already needed at that point, instead of taking a passive and observant demeanour. In other words, there also needs to be a sufficient sense of urgency regarding the implementation of adaptive measures.[19] Both climate risk awareness and a sense of urgency can be stimulated, for example, through awareness raising campaigns, through addressing climate risks and potential adaptive potentials in policies and other relevant documents or, if necessary, through the reinforcement of responsibilities in legislation.

Proactivity: Uncertainty about climate risks requires a proactive approach.[20] There is certainly a need for clarity on the responsibilities to repair or, if necessary,

17 See *H.A.C. Runhaar et al.*, Adaptation to climate change-related risks in Dutch urban areas: stimuli and barriers, Regional Environmental Change 2012 (12), p. 778.

18 See, for instance, *N.A. Marshall et al.*, Climate change awareness is associated with enhanced adaptive capacity, Agricultural Systems 2013, pp. 30-34.

19 See *H.A.C. Runhaar et al.*, Adaptation to climate change-related risks in Dutch urban areas: stimuli and barriers, Regional Environmental Change 2012 (12), p. 780.

20 See, for instance, *J. Spier, Shaping the Law for Global Crises*, The Hague 2011; *E.R. de Jong*, Regulating Uncertain Risks in an Innovative Society: A Liability Law Perspective, in: E. Hilgendorf & J.P. Günther (ed.), *Robotik und Recht Band I*, Baden-Baden 2013, pp. 163-183; *E.R. de Jong & J. Spier*, Climate Change. A Major Challenge and a Serious Threat to

compensate for potential damage in reaction to climate-related events, but there should be at least as much emphasis on minimizing both the probability and consequences of the potential effects of such events. A merely reactive approach to risks, in terms of this assessment framework, will thus be detrimental to the expected effectiveness of climate adaptation. This implies that responsibilities for the minimization of the probability of climate-related damage to networks, and the mitigation of the related consequences of network failure, should also be allocated within the arrangements governing specific network sectors.[21] In our view, though, this should not be of a too informal and non-committal nature. Giving these responsibilities an appropriate, explicit and clear legal basis could increase the expected effectiveness (see also the following paragraphs).[22] This could, moreover, confirm, clarify and secure the rights of those who are dependent upon specific network services, increasing legal certainty and creating possibilities for legal actions, regardless of whether such rights are also safeguarded as fundamental rights under domestic Constitutions.[23]

Appropriateness: Given the need for the allocation of both proactive and reactive responsibilities, another factor influential in the effective implementation thereof is the extent to which these are 'appropriately' allocated.[24] This indicator touches upon the notion of subsidiarity (in a broad sense)[25], which for the purposes of

Enterprises, *Dovenschmidt Quaterly* 2013 *(1)*, pp. 34 – 40; and *H.K. Gilissen*, The integration of the adaptation approach into EU and Dutch legislation on flood risk management, Journal of Water Law 2014 (3/4), p. 157.

21 We refer to 'minimizing risks' in the context of implementing measures in order to minimize the risk of damage or a disruption of services due to climate-related disasters. An example of such a measure is, for instance, refraining from building fragile infrastructure on a location that is prone to flooding or to design the infrastructure in a way that it is more resistant against floods or water-related disasters. 'Mitigating consequences' in this context refers to the implementation of measures in order to minimize the consequences of disasters that are related to climate change. This can be achieved by building a back-up network which can be used in case of failure of the primary network. In practice, this is referred to as creating 'redundancy' or 'back-up capacity'.

22 See *H.A.C. Runhaar et al.*, Prepared for climate change? A method for the ex-ante assessment of formal responsibilities for climate adaptation in specific sectors, Regional Environmental Change 2016 (in press), online version 2015, p. 4.

23 In some EU Member States (e.g. Germany) access to specific network services, such as access to the internet and energy supply, are explicitly formulated as fundamental rights under domestic Constitutions.

24 See *J.G. March & J.P. Olsen*, The logic of appropriateness, ARENA Centre for European Studies, Oslo 2004; and *H.K. Gilissen*, The integration of the adaptation approach into EU and Dutch legislation on flood risk management, Journal of Water Law 2014 (3/4), p. 157.

25 The term 'notion of subsidiarity', in this chapter, is used in a broader sense than the subsidiarity *principle* underpinning EU law is commonly conceived. Whereas the principle is commonly strictly interpreted as a form of 'vertical' subsidiarity (determining the level of government at which specific responsibilities and competences should be implemented), our approach also covers a 'horizontal' dimension, regarding the question of whether certain responsibilities should be imposed on public or private actors. See, for instance, *A. Maltoni*, The Principle of Subsidiarity in Italy: Its Meaning as A "Horizontal" Principle and Its Recent Constitutional Recognition, The International Journal of Not-for-Profit Law 2002 (4), available at

this chapter comprises two key elements. At first, the responsibilities should be imposed upon the actors and at the level best suited for implementing such responsibilities, keeping in mind the specific domestic polity and the manner in which critical network sectors are organized. Furthermore, the actors on which specific responsibilities are imposed, should also have the powers, competences and resources relevant for the effective implementation thereof. In other words, the expected effectiveness ought not to be considered optimal if an actor is responsible for the implementation of a specific responsibility, but lacks the potential for its actual implementation, because of legal impediments or a lack of (financial) means for instance. Through the lens of appropriateness, the responsibilities should, moreover, be proportional from a twofold perspective; they should not unnecessarily put an insuperably excessive burden on the responsible actors, and their desired implementation should not excessively and unnecessarily infringe on other societal or individual interests.

Explicitness: The more general, more vaguely or more broadly a responsibility is formulated, the more uncertainties can arise about their specific objectives. In objective terms, this can be detrimental to the level of legal certainty such responsibilities provide, both to addressees and others interested, potentially affecting the level of expected effectiveness.[26] A highly general responsibility to 'minimize external risks' moreover gives the addressees much discretion to determine which risks to prioritize and which (kinds of) measures to choose in order to minimize these risks. Especially in cases where the awareness of climate risks is low, it is likely that the management of these risks would be given low priority and would be/remain of a reactive nature. Making both the risks and the related proactive and reactive responsibilities more explicit, could benefit the expected effectiveness thereof and could, moreover, increase their legal enforceability if needed. Furthermore, this could increase risk awareness and sense of urgency. There are various ways in which risks and responsibilities can be made more explicit, ranging from 'soft' measures, such as drawing involved actors' attention to their responsibilities by a letter or brochure or by campaigning to raise awareness, to more profound legal measures, such as adopting explicitly formulated and targeted responsibilities in legislation or rules of conduct.

Transparency: A lack of transparency is often related to a lack of explicitness. Whereas the criterion of explicitness mainly addresses the formulation of relevant responsibilities from an objective perspective, transparency in this

www.icnl.org/research/library/files/Italy/The%20Principle%20of%20Subsidiarity%20in%20Italy.pdf; and *A. Colombo*, The Principle of Subsidiarity and European Citizenship, Milano 2004, pp. 16-19 (available at www.academia.edu/2293646/The_Principle_of_Subsidiarity_and_European_Citizenship).

26 See *T. Tridimas*, The General Principles of EU Law, Oxford 2007, p. 242; and *A.W.G.J. Buijze*, The Principle of Transparency in EU Law (diss. UU), Utrecht 2013, pp. 134-135.

chapter is understood, from a more subjective perspective, as the way in which responsibilities are perceived by their addressees. Do they consider these responsibilities as clear and accessible, or in other words: do they know that they are responsible, and do they know and understand what they are exactly responsible and accountable for? In this view, a high level of explicitness does not yet guarantee that also addressees will consider their responsibilities as clear and transparent, regardless of the question whether the responsibilities could and therefore should have been perceived as such following more objective (legal) standards.[27] This could negatively affect the expected effectiveness of such responsibilities. A perceived lack of transparency can be abated through an explication of responsibilities and a clarification of their exact purposes. Any ambiguities and uncertainty about the question who is responsible and what this responsibility entails should be avoided.

Legitimacy: Legitimacy, in this work, comprises two interrelated aspects. These concern the extent to which relevant actors play or (could) have played a role in the actual development and division of their responsibilities and, subsequently, the extent to which these actors consider their responsibilities and the division thereof as reasonable and acceptable.[28] The first (formal) component mainly addresses the question to which extent the responsibilities and their division are the result of a democratic/public decision-making process or other type of public debate or process in which relevant actors and others interested were invited to actively participate and have actually participated. The absence of such a process/debate is not only detrimental to the creation of a legitimate basis for the division of responsibilities for climate adaptation, but can also hamper raising awareness of climate risks and the related creation of sense of urgency in a broader sense. The second component is more subjective in nature and addresses the question how relevant actors perceive their responsibilities in terms of reasonableness and acceptability, given that they are aware of these responsibilities. A low level of support can be detrimental to the expected effectiveness of responsibilities for climate adaptation, as it is assumed that the ones who do not accept their responsibilities and the way they are divided, will be less likely to take them seriously and might neglect them or at best will constantly seek to re-discuss them, generating systemic imbalances.[29]

---

27 In that latter respect, see *A.W.G.J. Buijze*, The Principle of Transparency in EU Law (diss. UU), Utrecht 2013; and *M. van den Broek*, Preventing money laundering – A legal study on the effectiveness of supervision in the European Union (diss. UU), Eleven International Publishing, Den Haag 2015, p. 134.

28 Also see *D. Curtin & A.J. Meijer*, Does transparency strengthen legitimacy? A critical analysis of European Union policy documents, Information Polity 2006 (11), pp. 111-113; *K.O. Lindgren & T. Persson*, Output and input legitimacy: synergy or trade-off? Empirical evidence from an EU survey, Journal of European Public Policy 2010 (4), pp. 450-453; and *F. Biermann*, Earth System Governance – World Politics in the Anthropocene, The MIT Press, Cambridge 2014, pp. 121-144.

29 See *H.A.C. Runhaar et al.*, Prepared for climate change? A method for the ex-ante assessment of formal responsibilities for climate adaptation in specific sectors, Regional Environmental Change 2016 (in press), online version 2015, p. 4.

4. APPLICATION OF THE ASSESSMENT FRAMEWORK: TWO CASE STUDIES FROM THE NETHERLANDS

Having presented our assessment framework, this assessment framework, by way of example, is applied to two Dutch network sectors (i.e. the electricity sector and the internet sector) in the following sections. The results of these case studies are presented following the discerned methodological steps and largely build upon data resulting from empirical research previously conducted by the authors.[30]

4.1. STEPS 1 AND 2: JUSTIFICATION OF THE SELECTION AND THE CLIMATE RISKS PER SECTOR

For the purposes of this work, two Dutch critical infrastructural network sectors have been selected as case studies. These two sectors – the electricity sector and the internet sector – are in fact sub-sectors within the broader energy and ICT sectors respectively. The choice of these sub-sectors is mainly based on the results of research conducted by the Dutch *Organisatie voor Toegepast Natuurwetenschappelijk Onderzoek* (TNO; the Dutch Organization for Applied Scientific Research) on climate risks within the overarching sectors. This research was conducted in the framework of the preparation of the Dutch National Adaption Strategy (NAS) and was commissioned by the Netherlands Environmental Assessment Agency.[31] TNO has indicated these two sub-sectors

---

30 See *H.A.C. Runhaar et al.*, Publieke en/of private verantwoordelijkheden voor klimaatadaptatie – Een juridisch-bestuurlijke analyse en eerste beoordeling, Copernicus Institute of Sustainable Development/Utrecht Centre for Water, Oceans and Sustainability Law, Utrecht 2014; *H.A.C. Runhaar et al.*, Prepared for climate change? A method for the ex-ante assessment of formal responsibilities for climate adaptation in specific sectors', Regional Environmental Change 2016 (in press), online version 2015, pp. 1-12; and *H.K. Gilissen et al.*, De klimaatbestendigheid van de vitale infrastructuur beoordeeld van juridisch-bestuurlijk perspectief – Over de verwachte effectiviteit van de verdeling van verantwoordelijkheden voor de beheersing van klimaatrisico's in de elektriciteits- en de internetsector, Nederland Juristenblad 2015 (25), pp. 1640-1648.

31 See *Nederlandse Organisatie voor toegepast-natuurwetenschappelijk onderzoek*, Klimaatverandering en energie-infrastructuur – Actualisatie van de risico's en kansen voor klimaatadaptatiebeleid, Projectnummer 060.06852, 25 juni 2014; and *Nederlandse Organisatie voor toegepast-natuurwetenschappelijk onderzoek*, Klimaatverandering en de sector Informatie- en Communicatietechnologie (ICT) – Actualisatie van de risico's en kansen voor klimaatadaptatiebeleid, Projectnummer 060.06852, 25 juni 2014. TNO has furthermore made an overview of the most important climate risks for the transport sector (*Nederlandse Organisatie voor toegepast-natuurwetenschappelijk onderzoek*, Klimaatverandering en transport en infrastructuur – Actualisatie van de risico's en kansen voor klimaatadaptatiebeleid, Projectnummer 060.06852, 25 juni 2014). This has brought forward interesting insights, but we have chosen to leave this sector out, considering the space and the special nature of this sector compared to the other two sectors. See *O.E. Jonkeren*, Adaptation to climate change in inland

as being the most critical amongst a selection of other (sub-)sectors. Below, some key results of the TNO studies are presented.

Climate risks for the energy sector: Even though the climate risks within the energy sectors are not estimated to be very significant in general, the risks within the electricity sector stand out. The flooding of interconnectors, transformer stations, electrical substations and power stations specifically through extreme rainfall and other severe weather conditions are considered to be major climate risks. Power failures can have serious consequences for society, since almost all facets of society highly depend on a power supply. Whereas the risk of fluvial flooding is rather small, pluvial flood risks especially have increased considerably over the last decades and are still increasing. The potential consequences of such risks (with possible domino or cascade effects)[32] are great, giving these risks an ever more imminent character.[33]

Climate risks for the ICT sector: TNO has indicated flooding of physical infrastructure, through heavy rainfall or surface water as being the most important climate risk within the ICT sector. Data centres, interconnectors, network cables, street electrical boxes and transformer boxes, as part of the internet infrastructure, are characterized as especially vulnerable objects. Moreover, heat waves can negatively influence the power supply and cooling potential, thereby hindering the proper functioning of servers in data centres. A long-lasting failure of ICT infrastructure can cause societal unrest, as well as serious economic damage and security risks, given that many societally and economically relevant processes are strongly automatized and depend on well-functioning infrastructural communication networks.[34]

---

waterway transport (diss. VU), Amsterdam 2009; and *O. Jonkeren et al.*, Climate change and economic consequences for inland waterway transport in Europe, Regional Environmental Change 2014 (3), pp. 953-965.

32 See *H.A.C. Runhaar et al.*, Publieke en/of private verantwoordelijkheden voor klimaatadaptatie – Een juridisch-bestuurlijke analyse en eerste beoordeling, Copernicus Institute of Sustainable Development/Utrecht Centre for Water, Oceans and Sustainability Law, Utrecht 2014, pp. 121-134. We explicitly recommend to include so-called 'cascade effects' as a component of the future adaption policy. The research in this field should be intensified. In this chapter, we will not discuss the possible cascade effects (and the responsibilities to constrain the risks related thereto).

33 See for more detailed information *Nederlandse Organisatie voor toegepast-natuurwetenschappelijk onderzoek*, Klimaatverandering en energie-infrastructuur – Actualisatie van de risico's en kansen voor klimaatadaptatiebeleid, Projectnummer 060.06852, 25 juni 2014, especially the graphs on p. 23 and pp. 49-50.

34 See for further information *Nederlandse Organisatie voor toegepast-natuurwetenschappelijk onderzoek*, Klimaatverandering en de sector Informatie- en Communicatietechnologie (ICT) – Actualisatie van de risico's en kansen voor klimaatadaptatiebeleid, Projectnummer 060.06852, 25 juni 2014, especially the graph on p. 24.

4.2. STEPS 3 AND 4: OVERVIEW OF SECTORAL CHARACTERISTICS AND CURRENT RESPONSIBILITIES

The electricity sector: The Dutch electricity sector was gradually liberalized since the end of the last century and, therefore, has developed a strong business-oriented character. The current legal framework governing this sector (i.e. the Electricity Act 1998 and its accompanying decrees and regulations; *Elektriciteitswet 1998*)[35] illustrates this well. There is no fundamental right to energy/electricity included in the Dutch Constitution, but a notion of this right is one of the pillars under the Electricity Act 1998.[36] Private actors play a central role within the electricity sector; the State –the Ministry of Economic Affairs and the Energy Department of the Dutch Authority for Consumers and Markets in particular – plays a regulatory and supervisory role. Key private actors are, on the one hand, the distributional network operators and, on the other hand, the producers, distributors and suppliers of energy.[37] The most important infrastructure for the transport and the distribution of electricity comprises the national electricity grid and the regional grids, including their numerous interconnectors, transformer stations, electrical substations, low voltage cables and distribution boxes.[38] As the TNO studies point out, regional distributional networks are especially vulnerable to the adverse effects of climate change (to flooding through heavy rainfall in particular). For this reason, the main focus of this case study lies on these regional networks.

The critical infrastructure within these networks is (economically) owned by regional distributional network operators[39], who are responsible for their day-to-day management and maintenance. These responsibilities *inter alia* include the obligation to keep the grids working, to maintain them and – if necessary – to repair them.[40] A specific responsibility concerns the protection of the grids against 'potential external influences'[41], among which climate related events can

---

35 A full text of the Electricity Act 1998 is available at http://wetten.overheid.nl/BWBR0009755/2016-04-01.

36 See, for instance, Articles 23 and 95b(7) and (8) Electricity Act 1998.

37 See Article 1(1) Electricity Act 1998 for definitions. Network operators are to be considered as semi-public actors; they are appointed by the state as legal persons regulated under private law, of which the Dutch government acts as the only stakeholder (see Article 10 and 10a Electricity Act 1998). Based on the 'Splitsingswet', network operators cannot be producers, suppliers or distributors at the same time (and vice versa; see art. 10b(1) and 11(1) Electricity Act 1998).

38 See for more technical information: http://eduweb.eeni.tbm.tudelft.nl/TB141E/print.php?systemen-ketens-netwerken.

39 The regional network operators are appointed for a period of ten years by the legal owner of a regional network. The appointment needs the approval of the Minister of Economic Affairs. See Article 10(9) and Article 10 and Article 12(2) Electricity Act 1998.

40 For a list of tasks of the network operators, among which the above mentioned, see Article 16(1) Electricity Act 1998.

41 See Article 16(1)(q) Electricity Act 1998. The Minister of Economic Affairs can give instructions to a network operator on basis of Article 16(d)(a) Electricity Act 1998 in the context of 'external

also be understood. Other responsibilities of distributional network operators include the obligatory establishment and implementation of emergency plans and risk analyses.[42] Such plans and analyses can also address climate-related risks, but these are not explicitly mentioned. On the basis of this legal framework, distributional network operators have a relatively large amount of discretion in the interpretation and implementation of their operational and planning responsibilities. In that sense, they can prioritize risks, meaning that they can determine to what extent they will anticipate the expected effects of climate change themselves to a large extent.[43] Regarding these aspects, the State only plays a marginal role.

The internet sector: Just like the right to energy, the right to access to the internet is also not considered to be a fundamental right under the Dutch Constitution.[44] Within the internet sector, private actors play a primary role; the State (i.e. the Ministry of Economic Affairs, the Authority for Consumers and Markets, and the Telecommunication Agency) mainly plays a regulatory and supervisory role. The most important private actors within this sector are the 'suppliers of public electronic communication networks and services' (hereinafter referred to as 'suppliers'), as stated in the Telecommunications Act.[45] The critical infrastructure of this sector consists of the so-called 'backbone' (i.e. the central network of glass fibre cables and internet exchanges), nodes (i.e. servers and data centres) and local network cables, street electrical boxes and transformer boxes. The 'constructed' parts of the network (e.g. data centres and electrical substations) were pointed out by TNO as being particularly vulnerable to the adverse effects of climate change. Therefore, this case study focuses on these 'constructed' parts, mainly data centres.

On the basis of the Telecommunications Act, suppliers are generally obliged to repair any damage to their networks. They, moreover, have a duty of care regarding the continuity of service, which includes the obligatory drafting of business continuity plans.[46] Just like the network operators in the electricity

influences'. Enforcement of the responsibilities takes place via the minister and not via Article 77h and 77i of the Electricity Act 1998 (non-compliance penalty and administrative fine).

42 See art. 16d lid 1 Electricity Act 1998 jo. art. 20a '*Regeling kwaliteitsaspecten netbeheer elektriciteit en gas*', as well as art. 15 en 21 *Regeling kwaliteitsaspecten netbeheer elektriciteit en gas*.

43 See *H.A.C. Runhaar et al.*, Publieke en/of private verantwoordelijkheden voor klimaatadaptatie – Een juridisch-bestuurlijke analyse en eerste beoordeling, Copernicus Institute of Sustainable Development/Utrecht Centre for Water, Oceans and Sustainability Law, Utrecht 2014, pp. 49-56.

44 However, recently (early 2016) a public debate is (re-)initiated about whether access to the internet should be considered to be a fundamental right.

45 See art. 1.1 Telecommunications Act for definitions. A full text of this Act is available at http://wetten.overheid.nl/BWBR0009950/2016-01-01.

46 See art. 11a.1 and 11a.2 Telecommunications Act. See also Section 3 of the *Besluit continuïteit openbare elektronische communicatienetwerken en -diensten*. For more information, consult

sector, suppliers within the internet sector have a great deal of discretion in interpreting and implementing their responsibilities.[47] These provisions, however, are not applicable to services that are not fully or principally concerned with data transmission. For instance, data storage is not covered by this legislation. This implies that the duty of care for business continuity does not apply to data centres, insofar as they confine themselves to data storage and do not offer public access to the internet.[48] An important part of the market, from the perspective of the continuity and quality of services, is therefore not regulated. Incentives for continuous services, thus, are only generated through economic self-interest of the involved actors. Within this context, they fully determine themselves to which extent they will anticipate in their business management to the expected adverse effects of climate change. In this respect, the State does not interfere to a great extent.

4.3. STEPS 5 AND 6: ASSESSMENT, REFLECTION AND RECOMMENDATIONS

In Section 3 above, the concept of 'expected effectiveness' – as a central criterion for the assessment of the climate resilience of infrastructural network sectors – was operationalized through the identification and elaboration of six indicators. In this section, the electricity and the internet sectors' climate resilience will be assessed following these indicators. We present the most important findings per indicator, in order to highlight sectoral differences and similarities and to sketch a view of the climate resilience in both sectors. Where needed, we formulate recommendations for improvement.

Awareness/Sense of Urgency: In both sectors, the levels of awareness and sense of urgency prove less than satisfactory, especially amongst private actors. This is not to say that climate risks are being denied structurally or consciously ignored, but there is an observed lack of structural anticipation in strategic decision-making in operational management.[49] Climate adaptation, in other words, has

---

the following website: www.agentschaptelecom.nl/onderwerpen/openbare-netwerken/continuiteit-en-veiligheid/zorg-en-meldplicht-continuiteit.

47 See *H.A.C. Runhaar et al.*, Publieke en/of private verantwoordelijkheden voor klimaatadaptatie – Een juridisch-bestuurlijke analyse en eerste beoordeling, Copernicus Institute of Sustainable Development/Utrecht Centre for Water, Oceans and Sustainability Law, Utrecht 2014, pp. 26-32.

48 See *H.A.C. Runhaar et al.*, Publieke en/of private verantwoordelijkheden voor klimaatadaptatie – Een juridisch-bestuurlijke analyse en eerste beoordeling, Copernicus Institute of Sustainable Development/Utrecht Centre for Water, Oceans and Sustainability Law, Utrecht 2014, pp. 27-28.

49 See *Planbureau voor de Leefomgeving*, Aanpassen aan klimaatverandering – Kwetsbaarheden zien, kansen grijpen, Den Haag 2015, pp. 79-80.

not yet sufficiently been 'mainstreamed' within these sectors' decision-making frameworks. In the internet sector particularly, climate risks seem to almost completely be set aside for the benefit of other relevant factors, such as optimizing economic benefit. In the electricity sector, on the other hand, there is a positive development: climate risks are increasingly being recognized as threats, as a result of which they are being increasingly taken into account in risk analyses, especially in cases of new network investment.[50] At the level of government, specific policy developments, especially those in the framework of the Dutch Delta Program[51] and the National Adaptation Strategy[52], show an increasing amount of attention being paid to climate risks and their adverse effects for network sectors. These developments, however, have not yet resulted in concrete sectoral policies, guidelines or regulations. As we consider raising awareness and creating a sense of urgency to be primarily a task for the State (both on the central and decentralized level), especially where major public interests are involved, the State should engage further in such efforts, preferably in close cooperation with private actors and their branch organizations.[53]

Proactivity: In the electricity sector, as well as in the internet sector, there are clear and concrete responsibilities for private actors to repair their network infrastructure as soon as possible after calamities. Apart from such reactive responsibilities, also proactive responsibilities in anticipation of risks are adopted in legislation in the electricity sector, albeit these are very generally formulated and not specifically focused on climate-related risks (also see the paragraphs below about 'explicitness' and 'transparency').[54] In the internet sector, and for data centre operators in particular, no such statutory proactive responsibilities exist. Any incentives for proactive behaviour have to be generated through their economic self-interest by and large. In practice, in the electricity sector (where risk awareness seems to increase; see above), climate-related risks are increasingly taken into account in operational planning and anticipatory decision-making. This has not been observed to be the case in the internet sector, arguably due to a lack of statutory proactive responsibilities in combination with a low level of risk awareness. Despite positive developments in the electricity sector, the general attitude towards climate-related risks in both sectors is still of a very reactive

---

50 See *H.A.C. Runhaar et al.*, Publieke en/of private verantwoordelijkheden voor klimaatadaptatie – Een juridisch-bestuurlijke analyse en eerste beoordeling, Copernicus Institute of Sustainable Development/Utrecht Centre for Water, Oceans and Sustainability Law, Utrecht 2014, pp. 40 and 65.

51 See www.deltacommissaris.nl/deltaprogramma/inhoud/deltaprogramma-2016.

52 See www.ruimtelijkeadaptatie.nl/en/nas2016.

53 Also see *Planbureau voor de Leefomgeving*, Aanpassen aan klimaatverandering – Kwetsbaarheden zien, kansen grijpen, Den Haag 2015, pp. 101-104.

54 Network operators must put effort into '*protecting their networks against external effects*', carry out risk analyses, and establish emergency plans based thereon. Also see Section 4.2.

nature.[55] The expected effectiveness could be increased through adopting concrete proactive responsibilities in the internet sector, and to draw more attention to such responsibilities in both sectors. The State plays a clear role in this respect, but so too do key actors within the sectors and the sectors' branch organizations who can support in generating an attitudinal shift towards greater proactivity.[56]

Explicitness: As stated above, there is an absence of concrete proactive responsibilities in the internet sector, whereas such responsibilities do exist in the electricity sector, albeit these are very generally formulated. The level of explicitness, therefore, is to be considered rather low in both sectors. This can be detrimental to the expected effectiveness of climate adaptation within these sectors, both from the perspective of the likelihood that relevant actors will adopt a proactive approach in their planning and operational management, as well as from the perspective of the enforceability of such responsibilities if and where needed.[57] The explication of responsibilities could both increase this likelihood and enforceability. This could, moreover, benefit the legal certainty of both addressees of these responsibilities and those dependent upon the specific network services. Explication, in other terms, could make clear for network operators that they have certain responsibilities, and what is actually expected from them in that respect, and thus what others can reasonably expect and, if necessary, even require. This can be achieved through the adoption of more concretely formulated responsibilities in relevant legislation – which is worth considering, especially for the internet sector – and through the explication and substantiation thereof in explanatory memoranda or other documents.

Transparency: As stated above, a lack of transparency is often closely related to a lack of explicitness. Explicitness has been operationalized from a more objective perspective, whereas transparency in this chapter is understood as the way in which responsibilities are substantively perceived by their addressees. Do they consider these responsibilities to be clear and accessible, or in other words: do they know that they are responsible, and do they know and understand what they are exactly responsible and accountable for? Empirical studies have revealed that most actors within both sectors are aware of their responsibilities or at least assume they (might) have certain responsibilities in relation to climate

55 See *H.A.C. Runhaar et al.*, Publieke en/of private verantwoordelijkheden voor klimaatadaptatie – Een juridisch-bestuurlijke analyse en eerste beoordeling, Copernicus Institute of Sustainable Development/Utrecht Centre for Water, Oceans and Sustainability Law, Utrecht 2014, pp. 41 and 66.

56 See, in a more general sense, *Planbureau voor de Leefomgeving*, Aanpassen aan klimaatverandering – Kwetsbaarheden zien, kansen grijpen, Den Haag 2015, pp. 86-87.

57 See *H.K. Gilissen et al.*, De klimaatbestendigheid van de vitale infrastructuur beoordeeld van juridisch-bestuurlijk perspectief – Over de verwachte effectiviteit van de verdeling van verantwoordelijkheden voor de beheersing van klimaatrisico's in de elektriciteits- en de internetsector, Nederland Juristenblad 2015 (25), pp. 1646-1647.

adaptation, but that most actors – especially 'smaller' actors with less significant market-power – consider their responsibilities to be rather unclear, both as to the concrete division thereof, as well as to their substance.[58] This could arguably be the case due to a lack of statutory responsibilities as such (internet sector), or the rather general and broad formulation of responsibilities (electricity sector). This perceived lack of transparency can be remedied through explication of the responsibilities as described above, and through an actor-oriented, unambiguous and explicit clarification of their exact purposes.

Legitimacy: In the absence of clear, transparent and explicitly formulated responsibilities in both sectors, it is yet too early – and, to a certain extent, also rather pointless – to assess their legitimacy. The legitimacy of the implicit unwritten responsibilities in the internet sector can be questioned from a legal perspective, even though network operators might not consider these to be unreasonable and inacceptable per se. Given that our recommendations address the adoption of new statutory responsibilities for climate adaptation and/or the explication of already existing ones, encouraging public debate about these responsibilities and the division thereof is of greater importance at this stage, from the perspective of legitimacy, but also for the purpose of raising awareness of climate-related risks from a broader perspective. Although there are already early incentives for such a debate, the debate has only come on stream slowly and takes place largely at a rather abstract level away from the public and relevant market actors. In this respect, the debate should be intensified and the range of participants should be broadened. This is the first step in building a legitimate basis under concrete responsibilities for climate adaptation in infrastructural network sectors. Nonetheless, empirical studies show that there are no direct indications that network actors, from a more subjective perspective, consider any responsibilities for climate adaptation as unreasonable or inacceptable and, thus, illegitimate; it is rather their perceived lack of transparency about their (future) responsibilities that concerns them.[59] Without the debate and the related explication of responsibilities (i.e. the current situation), mentioned above, the level of legitimacy thereof is to be considered rather low.

---

58 See *H.A.C. Runhaar et al.*, Publieke en/of private verantwoordelijkheden voor klimaatadaptatie – Een juridisch-bestuurlijke analyse en eerste beoordeling, Copernicus Institute of Sustainable Development/Utrecht Centre for Water, Oceans and Sustainability Law, Utrecht 2014, pp. 40 and 65; and *Planbureau voor de Leefomgeving*, Aanpassen aan klimaatverandering – Kwetsbaarheden zien, kansen grijpen, Den Haag 2015, pp. 78-79.

59 See *H.A.C. Runhaar et al.*, Publieke en/of private verantwoordelijkheden voor klimaatadaptatie – Een juridisch-bestuurlijke analyse en eerste beoordeling, Copernicus Institute of Sustainable Development/Utrecht Centre for Water, Oceans and Sustainability Law, Utrecht 2014, pp. 41-42 and 66-67; and *Planbureau voor de Leefomgeving*, Aanpassen aan klimaatverandering – Kwetsbaarheden zien, kansen grijpen, Den Haag 2015, pp. 78-80.

Appropriateness: As stated above, responsibilities for climate adaptation should be imposed upon actors that are best suited for the implementation thereof, keeping the specific domestic polity and the manner in which critical network sectors are organized firmly in mind. Furthermore, the actors upon which specific responsibilities are imposed should have the powers, competences and resources relevant for the effective implementation thereof, and the responsibilities should, as such, be proportional. Under the current circumstances, there are no direct and concrete indications that the responsibilities and the division thereof do not meet such requirements. Given the Dutch organization of the electricity and internet markets, it is not to be considered unreasonable that responsibilities for climate adaptation are imposed upon key market actors. The State plays a regulatory, supervisory and coordinating/stimulating role, and should take an active attitude in this respect, despite the fact that access to energy supply and the internet are not considered fundamental rights under the Dutch Constitution. The State should, moreover, guarantee that relevant actors will not unnecessarily face legal impediments in the implementation of their responsibilities imposed upon them by law, and it should make use of its arsenal of tools and competences, in the domain of spatial planning for instance, to foster an effective implementation of such responsibilities. If necessary, it can financially support actors in implementing their responsibilities if the public interest gives proper reasons thereto. It should, finally, be stated that the requirements mentioned should be at the basis of any future (re)formulation of responsibilities in order to prevent that such developments will become detrimental to the expected effectiveness of climate adaptation in infrastructural network sectors.

5. CONCLUSIONS

In this chapter, we presented and applied a novel interdisciplinary method for the assessment of the climate resilience of critical infrastructural network sectors through the lens of the criterion of 'expected effectiveness' of formal responsibilities for climate adaptation. This central criterion was further operationalized through six indicators: awareness, proactivity, appropriateness, explicitness, transparency and legitimacy. These indicators comprise legal and governance aspects, thus aiming to draw out expectations about the effectiveness of sectoral responsibilities for climate adaptation from an integrated perspective. This is of added value, given that the climate issue – and in particular its relevance for infrastructural network sectors – is a multi-facetted issue, requiring an integrated multi-disciplinary approach, instead of a parallel set of mono-disciplinary approaches. The assessment framework is designed in such a way that it can easily be applied to a wide range of network sectors, that also gain insights from other disciplines and can be easily integrated into it, and that it can easily be adapted to experiences with its application. This has resulted, for instance, in the recent addition of the indicator of appropriateness, adding more legal aspects stemming from the notions of subsidiarity and proportionality. Apart from its academic purposes of evaluating and comparing domestic sectoral responsibilities for climate adaptation, this framework is also well-suited to more practical applications, such as the assessment and (re)development of domestic arrangements governing critical network sectors within the EU and abroad.

The application of this assessment framework to two Dutch case studies (focusing on the electricity and the internet sectors) shows a rather low degree of climate resilience in both sectors. Although there are sectoral differences in performance, the likelihood that relevant network actors will adequately anticipate climate-related risks in their operational planning and decision-making is considered to be sub-optimal. This is mainly due to a lack of climate risk awareness and a sense of urgency, a lack of explicit and transparent responsibilities (both regarding their formulation, and the way in which these are perceived by their addressees), and a related reactive, instead of a proactive, sectoral attitude towards such risks. Expected effectiveness of sectoral responsibilities for climate adaptation can be increased through awareness raising and the explicitation and clarification of these responsibilities in legislation or other formal documents. The need for an attitudinal shift towards a more proactive approach to climate-related risks of relevant actors within these sectors themselves notwithstanding, the State and other public actors also play a clear role in this respect through their agenda-setting, regulatory and supervisory competences and tasks. These public responsibilities should also be emphasized more and should be taken seriously in order to make climate adaptation more successful overall. These, and other results from our case studies and their related recommendations, can provide valuable lessons for other sectors and/or other countries, facing similar issues. More in-depth evaluations and cross-country comparisons could lead to more concrete and more broadly relevant recommendations and to the identification of potentially transferable good practices.

PART 2
IMPROVING EFFECTIVENESS

2.1. BETTER LEGISLATION

CHAPTER 2

THE EFFECTIVENESS OF PAYMENT FOR ECOSYSTEM SERVICES: A MIX BETWEEN A GRADIENT MODEL OF PUBLIC INTERVENTION AND AN EFFECTIVE NORMATIVE FRAMEWORK

Adélie Pomade
PhD in Law, HDR, Visiting Professor, FURG (Brazil)
Associate Researcher CEDRE (USL-B) (Belgium)

ABSTRACT

This contribution suggests that the binary distinction between purely "public" and "private" PES is not relevant from a legal point of view. A gradient model of public intervention seems more accurate, from private PES mostly, in which the whole process is voluntary and mainly governed by private contracts between the beneficiary and producers, to mainly public-driven PES, based on subsidies paid for predefined sustainable farming practices. Within this gradient, three factors may influence the performance of the instrument and ensure its effectiveness, efficacy or efficiency: actors, knowledge and monitoring. Another correlation with the success of PES seems to lie in the intensity and the quality of the mechanism's normative framework, whatever the public or private nature of the regulation. This should take three kinds of factors into account: ecological concerns, social concerns and economical concerns.

1. INTRODUCTION

This contribution will present the results of a legal study made for a European collective project called "Invaluable". This study deals with the question of the place of Law in market-based instruments (MBI), in Payments for Ecosystem Services (PES) specifically.

Ecosystem services were presented in 1997 by Gretchen Daily as "the conditions and processes through which natural ecosystems and species that build support and enable human life".[1] A simplified definition, subject to a relative consensus, was proposed in the 2005 Millennium Ecosystem Assessment (MEA): services here refer to "benefits provided by ecosystems to human well-being".[2] These benefits can be goods (food, wood, vegetable fats …) but also services (air purification, pollination …). Their preservation refers to the expression of societal needs that can be associated with basic needs (food, the need to breathe …), energy, or welfare or cultural identity (tradition …).[3] In order to maintain these services, Market-based instruments were then developed outside of the law. Some of them are called Payments for Environmental Services (PES).

PES has not received a standard definition, but globally they consist in remunerating someone for the continuation or the implementation of a virtuous practice with regards to biodiversity and ecosystem services. They tend to be considered in terms of market-based instruments in the economic literature.[4] If we analyse PES through a legal approach, we should introduce the notion of "agreement". Consequently, in this present study, we will analyse this mechanism: a landowner concludes an agreement with a third party and receives payment for a virtuous practice with regards to biodiversity and ecosystem services. Even with this conception of PES, we noticed the heterogeneity of processes: the design and implementation of PES are as diverse as contexts in which they are developed.

The PES mechanisms are built on the basis of legal regulation. Some of these instruments are subject to extensive public regulation. Public regulation refers to unilateral norms enacted by a public authority (such as through legislation). Some of the PES could also be subjected to private regulation. Private regulation can be considered to be any voluntary norm negotiated and adopted by private and/or public parties to a PES (such as in private contracts). In all, combinations of public and private regulation can be observed to differing degrees.

According to the growing literature and case studies on the topic, actual PES schemes seem to show various degrees of effectiveness. This means that their ability to reach their biological and economical goals are quite different, depending on their specific context. Environmental goals do not depend on the public or private nature of the organization that establishes the PES; however, they do depend on the reason why the PES mechanism was set up in the first place (preservation of a forest ecosystem, improving water quality in a given territory …). In this

---

1 *G. Daily, Nature's Services: Societal Dependence on Natural Ecosystems,* Washington, Island Press, 1997, 392 p.

2 Millennium Ecosystem Assessment, *Ecosystem Wealth and Human Well-Being*, Island Press, 2005, 155 p.

3 *D. Schröter (et al.),* Ecosystem service supply and human vulnerability to global change in Europe, *Science*, 2007, pp. 1333-1337.

4 *A. Karsenty (et al.),* Du Sud au Nord: regards croisés sur les Paiements pour Services environnementaux, Cahiers de Biodiv'2050: Initiatives, 2014, n° 2.

sense, the mechanism put in place has to be distinguished from the agreement that is concluded. For instance, the mechanism can present precise and targeted objectives (*French case – see below*) or broad and ambitious goals (*Belgian case -see below*). However, each PES agreement concluded with an actor offering a specific objective that is adjusted with the actor's behaviour. In this sense, the goal of any given PES mechanism can have a very targeted and precise objective and the PES agreement, implemented with actors, can request specific objectives, and be set up by a private organization (French case). Similarly, the goal of a PES mechanism can have a very broad objective; the PES agreement implemented with actors can have specific individual goals, and be set up by public organization (Belgian case). Economic and social objectives should be understood as "accessories" of the PES because, by definition, a PES aims at preserving ecosystem services. In this sense, they are not the main goal of the PES, but they constitute an added value to the mechanism. If their primary objective is basically to help those who wish to engage themselves, through an environmentally responsible approach, to change their techniques or behaviours, they can also be a factor in the social development of individuals and families.

Consequently, to analyse the effectiveness of a PES, two methods are available. The first one consists in studying similar kinds of cases that concern PES with similar targeted goal to show some results of a specific type of PES. The second method consists in analysing different kinds of PES, from the more targeted goal to the broadest one possible, to highlight a more systemic approach and to obtain more global conclusions, which could then be conceptualized or could involve thinking with legal concepts. Here, we have chosen the second issue.

Our study consisted in analysing the place and the role of public and private regulation in the effectiveness of PES. Two main results emerged from our study. First, the legal analysis suggests that a "pure" public regulation does not ensure the effectiveness of PES as well as a "pure" private regulation does. In that way, the intervention of the public authority in the design and implementation of PES can only partly contribute to their success. It seems that a gradient model of public intervention, as a "more or less" intervention of public authority, could have a positive effect on the success of PES. Moreover, we noticed that a mix between public and private regulation does not allow PES to be rendered fully effective. We noticed that other factors, which do not depend on public authority, may influence their performance. The second result has shown that an important factor of effectiveness of PES schemes seems to reside in the intensity and the quality of the normative framework of the mechanism, rather than in the public or private nature of the regulation.

To present these results it is necessary to briefly describe three case studies: the Vittel case in France, the agro-environmental scheme in Belgium and Costa Rica's PES program. Finally, this work covers three main issues: the hypothesis of a gradient model of public intervention, the balance between public and private regulation within PES schemes (and more generally market-based instruments), the link between normative frameworks and effectiveness.

2. CASES STUDIES

2.1. FRENCH VITTEL CASE

To understand the PES mechanism put in place in the Vittel Case, it is necessary to explain its context. In France, the legislation for selling "natural mineral water" is very strict. Vittel waters are labelled "natural mineral waters". This implies that water must come from a well-protected specific underground source, the composition of the water must be stable and the water must be bottled at the source.[5] According to French legislation, apart from the elimination of natural unstable elements such as iron and manganese, no treatment is allowed for "natural mineral water" and stability has to be achieved naturally. Water quality is so crucial to business operations that over 300 tests of water quality are carried out in the central laboratory of the Product Technology Center in Vittel every day.[6]

In the early 1980s, the owners of the Vittel brand realized that the intensification of agriculture in the Vittel catchment posed a risk to the nitrate and pesticides levels in the Source and consequently to the Vittel brand. The increased nitrate rate was caused primarily by the heavy leaching of fertilizers from the maize fields in the winter, when fields are barren, overstocking and the poor management of animal waste. Consequently, to continue to operate the water source, the Vittel Company had to find a solution to the pollution generated upstream. One alternative was chosen by Vittel. It had to convince farmers to change their farming practices, and develop a system of incentives attractive enough for them to want to do so. Consequently, in 1989, Vittel, in partnership with the French National Agronomic Institute (INRA), launched a four-year multidisciplinary action research program called Agriculture-Environnement-Vittel (AGREV). The objective was threefold. First, to understand the relationship between actual farming practices and the nitrate rate in the aquifer. Then, to identify and test the practices necessary to reducing and maintaining the rate of nitrates at the desired level rate. Finally, to identify the necessary incentives for farmers to change their practices.

The mechanism proposed and put in place by Vittel is based on a private initiative. According to the mechanism, it is a contractual relationship between

---

5 *D. Perrot-Maître*, The Vittel payments for Ecosystem Service: "Perfect" PES Case,", Report, International Institute for Environment and Development, London, UK, 2006.

6 *J.L. Croville*, Water Resources and Environment Group, Nestlé Waters MT, Face to face interview, Report, July 2006.

two private actors: a Company and farmers. There are two kinds of contracts here: contracts with farmers who are owners and usufruct contracts. Private regulation is over-dominant, whatever the identity of the contracting party is. The private regulation developed between Vittel and farmers is interesting because it supposed the intervention of lots of stakeholders without any previous legal framework. Indeed, there was no public regulation that required putting a mechanism, such as a PES, in place. The conclusion of the contract, called the "package", was the result of a long discursive process between farmers, research actors and the private sector and was based on a scientific study which would enable them to be informed about ecological and agronomic factors and made it possible to reach Vittel's goals. Moreover, the participation of institutionalized intermediaries was important because they had a strong awareness-raising policy, dialogue between stakeholders and took farmers' interests into account. The Vittel case is a perfect example of the degree of negotiation and regulation put in place. Contracts offer financial advantages and technical assistance. Furthermore, a significant place was given to intermediaries who negotiated the contracts, monitored, helped farmers and who communicated about the PES scheme. Finally, the process supposed a strong monitoring of practices and the evolution of the quality of water.

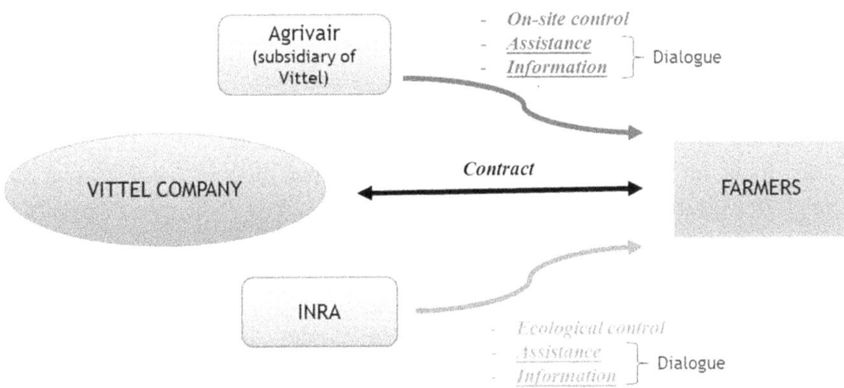

The mechanism of PES in the Vittel case presents strong characteristics that certainly lead to the success of the PES. First, the contracts are differentiated according to the cost structure and location of the individual farms. Second, the link between ecosystem services, *i.e.* water filtration, the maintenance of adequate levels of nitrate in the plant sub-root system and management practices has been established scientifically at the sub-basin and plot levels. Third, payments are not conditional upon the change in nitrate rates in the aquifers, given that the contribution of individual farms to water quality in the spring is impossible to establish. Rather, they are based rather on new farm investment and the cost of adoption of new farming practices. Fourth, to fine tune recommendations made to farmers, INRA monitors the nitrate rates at 17 sites across four soil types and two types of farming systems all year round.

However, the mechanism is limited. In terms of sustainability of the program's results, once farmers have undertaken the transition, the farming system is sustainable, since it was designed to maintain farm income at all times. A few farmers decided to switch to organic milk production to increase the profitability of their operation, but they found themselves unable to market the milk on the organic market. The reason for this is that in France, whenever milk producers have a contract with a cooperative, the milk belongs to both the producer and the cooperative and, regardless of its quality, cannot be marketed independently of the cooperative. Perhaps the presence of more public regulation would allow to link these situations.

The Vittel case study is also very interesting in the field of the flow of knowledge (from the most scientific data to the experiences on the ground) because the whole process, from the design of PES to its implementation, is based on it. Furthermore, it brings together ecological, economic and social aspects.

The strong relationship with the scientific sector have led in depth work on knowledge: scientific data and study to determine polluted lands, high priority areas, and assess (upstream and downstream) the rate of nitrates and other dangerous substances. Knowledge of experience was also taken into account at the time of the dialogue with farmers. It concerned their practices, their expectations and their capacity of adaptability.

Knowledge was taking into account beforehand the implementation of PES. To achieve this, a four-step methodology was developed and was based on ecological, economic and social aspects.[7] Unlike conventional approaches to agriculture, which focus on the agronomic aspects of practices, the methodology focused initially on understanding the history, the geography and the sociology of the area and of its people. Scientific and economic research was only introduced later, after a dialogue had been successfully established between Vittel and the farmers, compatibility between the farmers' and Vittel's objectives had been demonstrated and the idea of a mutually beneficial partnership had been accepted.

Knowledge was also taken into account after the implementation of the PES. To achieve this, a strong monitoring was put in place to evaluate the adequation between practices and ecological change (more exactly, the link between ecosystem service such as water filtration and the maintenance of adequate levels of nitrate in the plant sub-root system and management practices).

---

[7] First, it tended to understand the farming systems and why farmers did what they did. This is farmers' knowledge through their experience and goals based on their experience. Second, it aimed at analyzing conditions under which farmers would accept to change their practices. This aspect deals with economic and ecological aspects. Third, it aimed at identifying, testing and validating the management practices necessary to reducing the nitrate threat in farmers' fields. This is a practice-ecological ratio. It involves bringing together farmers' knowledge and ecological hypothesis and data. The fourth step was to provide financial and technical support to farmers willing to enter the program. This supposes bringing enough data, information and explanation to farmers to organize the changing practices themselves.

As a conclusion on this case study, it is important to underline that the ecological and economic advantages from the PES scheme are predominant. Furthermore, from a social perspective, the dialogue brought about trust and proximity between stakeholders.

In the Vittel case, the public regulation was absent, other than the legislation on bottled water specifically. In that case, then, we can note that the flow of knowledge does not depend on law, but on the dialogue between the actors. The whole process of PES, from its design to its implementation, is based on the flow of knowledge. Upstream, the implementation of PES, the exchange of data, willingness and experiences constituted the main part of the process. The aim was to adapt the farmers' activity and practices without changing them in a way they will not accept. This case-by-case approach plays an important part in a successful outcome.

Ecological and economic consequences were both taken into account in light of the sensitivity of each farmer to establishing mutual agreements and mutual enrichment between them and Vittel. But unlike conventional approaches in agriculture, the methodology focused initially on understanding the history, the geography and the sociology of the area and its people. Scientific and economic research was only introduced later, after a dialogue had been successfully set up.

The role played by intermediaries, such as AGREV or INRA, was also very important to convince farmers of the opportunity, for them, of the operation. It has also contributed to confidence-building between farmers and Vittel.

2.2. BELGIUM AGRO-ENVIRONMENTAL MEASURES

In Belgium, measures have been taken on the basis of agro-environmental measures implemented by the European Union (EU). The provision of agri-environmental measures, called AEM, established by the EU in the framework of the Common Agricultural Policy (CAP), was clarified by Regulation 1698/2005. According to this text, the AEM consists of annual payments to farmers who adopt a voluntary approach. These payments shall cover additional costs and income foregone or the costs incurred resulting from the implementation of new practices. It is, therefore, a financial compensation to farmers and is an economic instrument to protect the environment.[8]

In Belgium, the development of the European rural policy is the responsibility of the regions. In this contribution, we take the Walloon Region case into account. The Region relied on a set of pre-existing, general and not specific to this type of agricultural aid legislation. Indeed, the rules on rural development in Wallonia, referring to AEM, is based on the laws of 1961 and 1975. At that stage, AEM did

8 *C.H. Born*, Le régime de subventions agro-environnementales en Région Wallonne: un choix pertinent et efficient pour promouvoir une agriculture durable?, CDPK, 2011, n° 2, pp. 155-202.

not fall under the pillar of the CAP. Therefore, the reference to rural development is not envisaged in this legislation. The lack of updating and enriching of these two texts' meaning creates an ambiguity in the system and in the nature of the measures developed in Wallonia. This creates a legal regime exposed to hybridization and opening the possibility of an original legal instrument. It was not until the decree of 8 December 1994, revised in 1999 and in 2004, and especially the Order of the Walloon Government (called AGW) of 24 April 2008 on agro-environmental that subsidies were considered in the implementation of EAM in the Walloon region.

In parallel, in accordance with the request of the EU, Belgium has adopted a national strategic plan, consisting of Flemish, Walloon and national components. In Wallonia, the plan is implemented by the regional rural development program, called Pwdr 2007-2013. Under this program, the Walloon government has designated as a managing authority called "Département des aides de la DG03". This is the only accredited paying agency. It is responsible for scheduling, the execution and the accounting of payments and administrative control on site, although delegation in detail is possible.

The whole process is governed by legally binding provisions from EU, national and Wallonian regulations and soft law (such as a National Strategic Plan). It seems to be a very clear process because there is no intermediary, no groups of farmers or leaders, and the payer is the societal community through the State.

Consequently, the mechanism is built on public regulation. As suggested by the title of the AGW, the regime of the AEM implemented in Walloon law is analysed as a subsidy mechanism, *i.e.* as an allowance funds lost, granted by the government to legal entities under public and private law as well as individuals to support the development of activities considered relevant to the general interest.[9]

Generally, grants are awarded through a unilateral administrative act and are often the subject of a regulatory framework. In the Walloon Region, law does not provide any explicit authorization to the Government to conclude agreements with farmers[10], but they do not prohibit it either. Indeed, the AGW qualifies agri-environmental measures as "subsidies". However, on closer examination, the granting of AEM in Walloon Region is not completely devoid of similarities to the contractual tool.[11] In this particular case, there is an agreement between the parties in the transaction: farmers have to take the initiative and accept the grant award. Just as with any subsidy system, the farmer freely takes the initiative to

9 *D. Renders, Th. Bombois & L. Vansnick,* La définition de la subvention et ses rapports avec la notion d'aide d'Etat, in D. Renders (ed.), Les subventions, 2011, pp. 11-161.

10 *C.H. Born,* Le régime de subventions agro-environnementales en Région Wallonne: un choix pertinent et efficient pour promouvoir une agriculture durable?, *supra note 3.*

11 French definition: «*L'accord de volonté (manifesté) entre deux ou plusieurs personnes, destiné à produire des effets de droit, qu'il s'agisse de donner naissance à des obligations, de transférer un droit subjectif, de modifier ou d'éteindre un droit ou une convention préexistant*": *P. Wery,* Droit des obligations, Vol. I, Théorie générale du contrat, 2nd ed., 2011, p. 60.

engage himself in an AEM and must accept its conditions. It is the principle of contractual freedom[12], even if specifications are defined statutorily and are not subject to negotiation. It is the same as a pre-formulated standard contract.

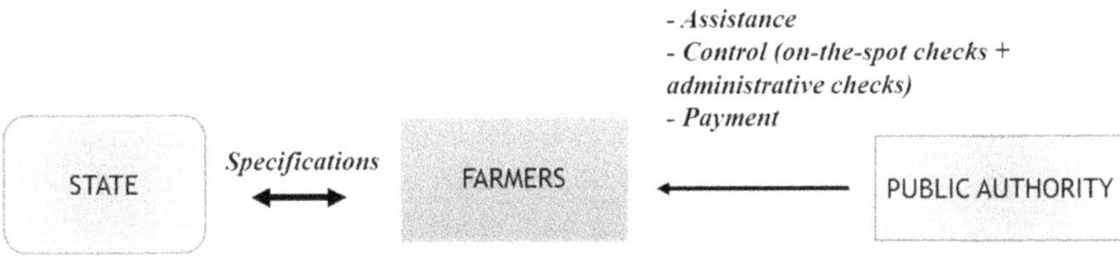

Different types of control are exercised by relevant authorities to ensure compliance with the conditions of eligibility for aid commitments and the compliance by farmers. Two types of control must be exercised annually. On the one hand, administrative checks are carried out for all aid applications and cover all elements that it is possible and appropriate to control by administrative means.[13] On the other hand, on-the-spot checks must be made each year on a sample of 5% of farms engaged in AEM.[14] In this case, they cover all of the commitments and obligations of the beneficiary that can be checked at the time of the visit. However, only 1% of farms applying for grants (including AEM) are subjected to such control.[15] This low-pressure control partly acts to the detriment of the effectiveness of the tool.

For those reasons, the effectiveness of such a mechanism is quite different from the Vittel mechanism and is less satisfactory. Furthermore, the effectiveness of the mechanism is considered through several modalities of implementation. First, assistance given to farmers by the DG03 ensures support, transparency of information, communication and sufficient dialogue to allow farmers not only to be informed about the required method, but also to determine the best ways to reach the goals stated. The assistance allows the adhesion of farmers to be arrived at and control permits to guarantee the respect of specifications. Today, AEM generates massive support from the Walloon farmers. The awareness of farmers, especially younger ones, and their willingness to participate in the collective effort for the environment also contribute thereto. This creates a positive attitude toward the environment. This is not the case of the command and control approach.[16] Second, the effectiveness is considered through the mobilization of farmers. Despite massive support for PES, some reluctance is

---

12 Article 1134, alinea 1er, Code Civil.

13 Article 11.1, Regulation (CE) n° 65/2011.

14 *Id.*

15 *C.H. Born*, Le régime de subventions agro-environnementales en Région Wallonne: un choix pertinent et efficient pour promouvoir une agriculture durable?, *supra note 3*.

16 *European Commission*, Agri-Environment Measures. Overview on General Principles, Types of Measures, and Application, Report, March 2005, p. 9, http://ec.europa.eu/agriculture/publi/reports/.

persistent because of payment delays from the administration, the complexity of the procedure, the control pressure or simply because of a lack of information.[17] Moreover, the irregularity of the monitoring and the limited period of subsidies neither encourage farmers to respect their obligation, nor encourages them to get involved in the scheme after the first period of implementation. It creates a risk of ineffectiveness of the tool. At the very least, the effectiveness is measured through the methods adopted by farmers. Indeed, even if the PES tool is voluntary, once farmers are involved in the relationship, then they must respect specific methods required by public regulation. We note an unequal adhesion to methods: the less stringent ones are preferred.[18] This has an impact on the effectiveness of the tool.

Consequently, we can conclude that sometimes, the positive impact on the environment results from the cumulative effect of a large number of commitments, even if they are not very binding. Sometimes, the impact directly results from the practical implementation of targeted measures, ones with a high environmental value. The appreciation of this impact is very difficult. It requires putting clear and measurable objectives and the establishment of a regular scientific monitoring, based on pertinent agri-environmental indicators.[19] It appears that, in the Walloon system at least, subsidies would be more effective and efficient if they were more focused on some practices and/or geographic areas or environments that have specific environmental problems.[20] The Walloon region has funded many scientific studies on the environmental impact of AEM.[21] This appears largely positive. From an environmental point of view, quantitative and qualitative targets set in Pwdr for methods are difficult to assess because they require a range of criteria which combine regular scientific assessment and a calculation of the efficiency of the measure. Nevertheless, results seem positive.

---

17 *C.H. Born*, Le régime de subventions agro-environnementales en Région Wallonne: un choix pertinent et efficient pour promouvoir une agriculture durable?, *supra note 3*.

18 Adhesion to mechanism differs from methods requested. It strongly influences the overall environmental impact of the program. It seems that the most successful AEM in the Walloon Region is hedges, winter soil cover, grassy headlands and natural grasslands. Furthermore, there is a growing success of AEM for the protection of surface waters (rivers) in areas of large cultures. It is noted that the participation is actually very strong for some undemanding measures (called "green light"), such as the maintenance and upkeep of hedges or winter soil cover, and significantly lower for other more stringent measures (called "deep green"), such as the environmental Action Plan. For some methods, the objectives of Pwdr 2007-2013 in terms of rate of commitment were fulfilled; for others they were not.

19 *European Commission*, Development of agri-environmental indicators for monitoring the integration of environmental concerns into the common agricultural policy, (COM(2006)508 final), 15th September 2006.

20 *C.H. Born*, Quelques réflexions juridiques sur le régime de mesures agro-environnementales en Région wallonne, in C.H. Born & F. Haumont (eds.), Actualités du droit rural. Vers une gestion plus durable des espaces ruraux?, 2011, pp. 255-275.

21 *C.H. Born*, Le régime de subventions agro-environnementales en Région Wallonne: un choix pertinent et efficient pour promouvoir une agriculture durable?, *supra note 3*.

2.3. COSTA RICA'S PES PROGRAM

The Program for Payments for Ecosystem Services (PPES)[22] in Costa Rica was established in 1996 and was based on several legal texts. First, is the 7575 Forest Act 1996, which is the legal basis of payment for environmental services.[23] Then, there is the Law of the Regulatory Authority for Public Services that provides the institutional framework and, finally, the Biodiversity Law that establishes the contribution of Costa Rica to the conservation of biodiversity in accordance with the decisions of the United Nations Conference on Environment and Development in 1992. It is also based on various international agreements, such as the United Nation Framework Convention on Climate Change which allows Costa Rica to take a central role in the prevention of global climate change through project management and the conservation of natural forests and forest plantations.

In the late 1990s, FONAFIFO, created by the Forest Act of 1996, established the PPES with its own management structure and board. Its objective was to promote a rational use of natural resources, with limited deforestation and maintaining of forest ecosystem services (like carbon sequestration, watershed protection, biodiversity and landscape beauty).[24]

The PES mechanism is based on public and private regulation. Its hybrid nature makes the instrument interesting. PPES implementation is regulated by two primary legal instruments that are updated annually. First, an annual decree is signed by the Ministry of Environment, which defines the eligible PES modalities and the total budget allocation for each of them. Second, there is the procedure manual that defines the PES access conditions, requisites, priority criteria and administrative rules. These documents are revised annually by FONAFIFO's executive management and are submitted for comment to three main actors: SINAC (the forestry public administration representative), ONF (the forestry private sector representative) and the Board of Agronomy Engineering that supervises the forestry regent's activities. After consultation, the decree and procedure manual are approved by FONAFIFO's board and are signed by the Minister of Environment.[25]

The PPES program proposes payments to landowners according to their land uses (forest conservation, reforestation, sustainable management, *etc.*) with the justification that these lands uses generate ecosystem services either locally or

---

22 Official website: www.fonafifo.com/paginas_espanol/servicios_ambientales/servicios_ambientales.htm.

23 They are defined as "*services provided by forests and forest plantations to protect and improve the environment*".

24 *R. Pirard & E. Broughton*, What's in a Name? Market-Based Instruments for Biodiversity, Analyses, IDDRI, Sc. Po, IFRI, n° 3, May 2011, pp. 4-31.

25 *J.F. Le Coq (et al.)*, The Governance of Costa Rica's Programme of Payments for Environmental Services: A Stakeholder's Perspective, in R. Muradian & L. Rival, Governing the Provision of Ecosystem Services, 2013.

globally.[26] These payments vary with land uses, probably assuming that services have different values.[27] The financial resources for the program are collected from several sources, among them the hydrocarbon industry, multilateral cooperation (World Bank loans, Global Environment Facility grants) and voluntary contributions by private hydroelectric producers.[28] So, for the moment, beneficiaries do not pay for services they have received. FONAFIFO oversees making the payments, but it is also responsible for the management of the whole scheme. Contracts are signed between FONAFIFO and landowners for various periods of time, depending on the land use.[29]

To participate in the program, landowners must present a sustainable forest management plan prepared by a licensed forester called, in Spanish, a "*regente*". These plans describe the land use proposed, and include information on land tenure and physical access; topography, soils, climate, drainage, actual land use and carrying capacity with respect to land use; plans for preventing forest fires, *and so on*. Once their plans have been approved, landowners begin adopting the specified practices, and receive payments.[30] The initial payment can be requested at contract signing, but subsequent annual payments are made after verification of compliance (by the *regentes*, with a sample being audited). The establishment of trustworthy contract monitoring and verification systems is an important part of this system of payments. Monitoring can be undertaken by the *regentes*, with regular audits to verify the accuracy of monitoring. Noncomplying participants forfeit further payments, and *regentes* who incorrectly certify compliance can lose their license. If landowners are paid, the net value of the payment is lower than its face value, given that landowners must pay the *regentes* for the initial management plan and for monitoring (these fees comprise about 15% of payments).

The following figure illustrates the mechanism.[31]

---

26 *G.A. Sanchez-Azofeifa (et al.)*, Costa Rica's Payment for Environmental Services program: Intention, implementation and impact, Conservation Biology, vol. 21, n° 5, 2007, pp. 1165-73.

27 *R. Pirard & E. Broughton*, What's in a Name? Market-Based Instruments for Biodiversity, *supra note 24*.

28 The hydrocarbon industry was originally targeted through the consumer tax on fossil fuels, but due to unsatisfactory money transfers by the Ministry of Finance to the institution in charge of making the payments to land owners, a share of this tax on fossil fuels was assigned formally to the PES program.

29 This being the duration applied to reforestation since the plantation has to be maintained long enough to ensure that it is done properly.

30 For information, additionality is not explicitly part of Costa Rica's PES design and is nowhere part of the Forestry Law 7575. Instead, this criterion is externally-imposed, evolving along with the international climate change policy dialogue.

31 Source: *J.F. Le Coq (et al.), supra note 25*.

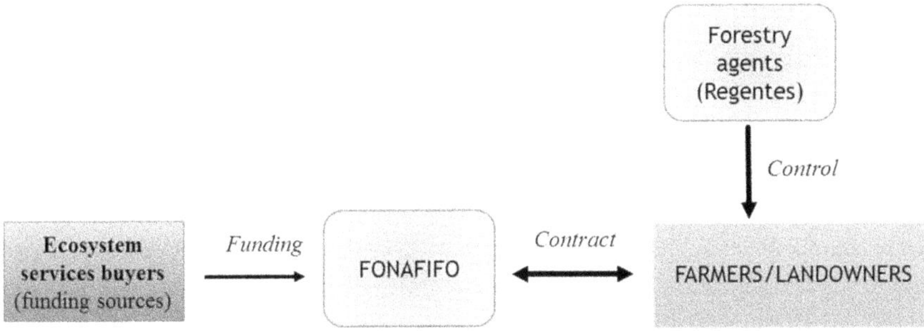

There were several generations of PES in Costa Rica. First considered to be an alternative to the command and control approach, they become increasingly framed by public regulation. The balance between public and private regulation is interesting, regarding the passage of time: a negotiated framework, an exclusively "contractualised" one, was gradually legalized under the creation and organization of the FONAFIFO. Furthermore, the private regulation framed by a hybrid regulation (self-regulation made by an independent authority, the FONAFIFO), then become public regulation. Whether the contractual instrument still exists (it was first negotiated and concluded between a landowner and a beneficiary), it is now non-negotiable[32] and takes place in a complex scheme that implies a partly state-owned institution.

The mechanism presents quite economically and ecologically perverse effects. The PPES program has been very popular with landowners, with requests to participate far outstripping available financing.[33] Nonetheless, the PPES suffers from various kinds of gaps[34], linked with actors involved therein. First, offering payments that are insufficient to inducing the adoption of socially-desirable land uses, thereby causing socially-undesirable land uses to remain in use.

Second, the PPES seeks to generate environmental services through forest land uses solely. The introduction of an agroforestry contract marks a small move away from pure forest land uses. Nevertheless, it is unfortunately impossible to determine the extent to which the PPES has successfully generated environmental services.[35] Although the PPES has established a strong system to monitor land user compliance with payment contracts, the program remains weak in monitoring its effectiveness in generating the services desired.

Third, and something which is considered to be the other major weakness in the PPES, is the lack of data on the extent to which activities have generated environmental services. It is interesting to note that the legal framework made

32 That is why this system is sometimes qualified as a subsidy one: *R. Pirard & E. Broughton*, What's in a Name? Market-Based Instruments for Biodiversity, *supra note 24*.

33 *S. Pagiola*, Payments for Environmental Services in Costa Rica", MPRA Paper n° 2010, December 2006. http://mpra.ub.uni-muenchen.de/2010/.

34 *Id.*

35 *Id.*

for the PES did not concern the field of knowledge. In other words, the nature of knowledge and data mobilized to determine the opportunity, the place, modalities and efficacy of PES are not contained in public regulation. Knowledge mobilized within PES comes from other mechanisms. It is the example of the *regentes* which are documents required to participate to PES programs. Apart from these pieces of information (often few in number and poor), no economic, socio-economic or social data are required. Downstream, there are ecological and economical valuations. The problem is not the collection of data, but the fact that an analysis is not undertaken. FONAFIFO could do that, but there is a lack of dialogue within the institution and a non-sharing of knowledge between it and landowners (partly because contracts built on plans validated by *regentes* are non-negotiable). Lastly, in all these aspects, the law is absent. The mechanism is based on practice; the weak role of public regulation in the flow of knowledge must be adjusted within PES, at the stage of their collection, introduction and circulation.

Despite these criticisms, we can underline some virtuous effects, the flexibility and adaptability of the PPES programs, for example. This comes from the lack of command and control regulation and is due to the decree and the manual discussed and approved each year. This form of public regulation does not seem to be a barrier to the evolution of PPES. On the contrary, it is a source of adaptability in regards to economics and ecological and social contexts.

On the basis of this first part of our study, we can draw two tables that resume the respective presence of influence of public and private regulation on the effectiveness of PES. This table represents a global observation of the PESs studied:

PES	Public regulation	Private regulation	Effect[36]
PES Costa Rica	Low	High	Low
PES France	Low	Very high	High
PES Belgium	High	Low	Medium

The second table illuminates the relation between public and private regulation and normative framework and their effects on the PES. This refers to the degree of obligations created within the mechanism:

PES	Public regulation	Private regulation	Normative framework	Effects[37]
PES Costa Rica	Low	High	Low	Low
PES France	Low	Very high	Very High	High
PES Belgium	High	Low	High	Medium

36 Economic, Social and Ecological effects.
37 Economic, Social and Ecological effects.

This second table leads to some observations: low public regulation and low normative framework lead to low effects for the PES, and high public regulation and high normative framework seems to lead to high effects for the PES.

Crossing this table with the first one, another observation arises: high private regulation and high normative framework can lead to high effects of the PES.

Consequently, the success of PESs seem not only to depend on a balance between public and private regulation, but also to depend on a strong normative framework.

These comments allow us to study the PES scheme deeper, through a more theoretical approach.

3. RESULTS

3.1. THE BALANCE BETWEEN PUBLIC AND PRIVATE REGULATION WITHIN PES

This study has led to the first result dealing with the legal analysis of PES. We have highlighted that a "pure" public regulation does not ensure the effectiveness of PES or of "pure" private regulation. In that way, the intervention of the public authority in the design and implementation of PES can only partly contribute to its success. It seems that a gradient model of public intervention, as a "more or less" intervention of public authority, could have a positive effect on the success of PES. Moreover, we noticed that a mix between public and private regulation does not make the PES fully effective. We noted that other factors, which do not depend on public authority, may also influence their performance.

As stated previously, we can notice a heterogeneity of PES's processes.[38] In Costa Rica, we observed a mix of regulation, even if the public one was quite absent. In contrast, we noticed two extreme cases. On the one hand, we presented the French Vittel case which perfectly shows the success of a PES without any public intervention, and on the other hand, we developed the Belgian case which illustrates a subsidies mechanism based on public regulation. These case studies show that the binary logic that classified PES in "public PES" and "private PES" is no longer relevant.[39]

To solve this ambiguity, it appears to be necessary to cross over this binary logic which opposes private and public PES and to think according to a gradient logic. In this perspective, the gradient represents the magnitude (from the lowest to the highest) of the public authority's intervention on the process put in place

---

38 *A. Karsenty (et al. Supra note 42.*

39 *R. Pirard & E. Broughton*, What's in a Name? Market-Based Instruments for Biodiversity, *supra note 24.*

within the PES. The next figure gives an example of what could be the better public regulation for any given case:

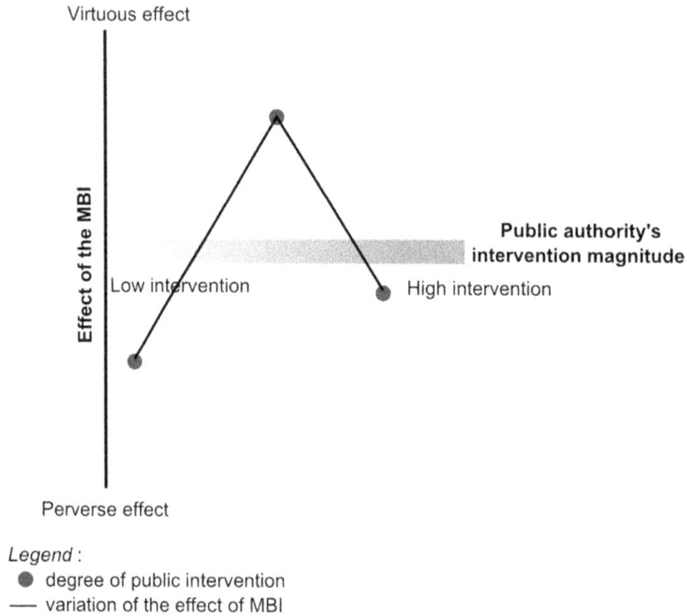

In a theoretical perspective, this variability refers to the emerging concept of normative densification. This concept is not defined exactly[40], but it still has sufficient features to greatly distinguish it from any other legal phenomenon and it is best known as a legislative inflation, for example.[41] The normative densification relativized the public normativity as unique normativity. This is precisely the case for the PES case studies analysed in the report. In principle, the normative nature of the law allows the public authority to organise and sanction life in society. Whether soft law challenges this principle, the normative densification increases the phenomenon because it tends to recognize other natures of normativity (scientific, social ...). This situation refers, in particular, to self-regulation which means that people can self-organize their private or professional relationship on the basis of standards they have determined themselves.[42] The design and implementation of PES, observed in the different case studies, reflects this trend in favour of a withdrawal of the law in the relationship or, at least, in favour of a reorganization of the place of law in the relationship. Actually, we notice several normative phenomena that tend to relativize the place and the role of law

40 *C. Thibierge (et al.)*, Densification normative. La naissance d'un processus, 2013.

41 *R. Savatier*, L'inflation législation et l'indigestion du corps social, Dalloz 1977, n° 43.

42 *J. Chevallier*, L'Etat régulateur, Revue française d'administration publique, 2004, n° 3, p. 200; *G. Timsit*, La régulation. La notion et le phénomène, Revue française d'administration publique, 2004, n° 1, p. 206.

in regulating human activity.[43] This sometimes takes the shape of competition normativities.[44] From our study's perspective, it is illustrated by the balance between public regulation and private regulation to organize a transaction and relationships. It relates to a new way of governing by "instruments"[45], whatever they may be. This new form of regulating behaviour is observed in PES through the use of a contractual instrument and the involvement of a growing number of private or semi-private actors in the payment mechanism. However, the contractual approach promotes a new governance to the benefit of private actors, because it questions the role of the State and its public regulation in the relationship.[46]

The interest and the originality of such a model, one based on a gradient, seems to be the potential of the law's adaptability. Indeed, this way of public authority action does not consist of framing a tool or its process as a whole, but in intervening on specific aspects (*i.e. "factors". See next paragraph*) to ensure the success of the MBI. The objective is to find the better ratio of public intervention/ private intervention, according to local needs, contexts and socio-ecosystem practices. Whether this gradient logic emerges from the analysis of case studies, we can wonder if it would not emphasise the emergence of a new form of law intervention.[47]

Moreover, we noticed that a mix between public and private regulation does not make it possible to make the PES fully effective. In that sense, other factors may influence the performance of the instrument and public regulation could act upon them.

All throughout the legal analysis of case studies, some key elements of the PES mechanism stand out. Their particularity is that they strongly influence the success of the instrument. Some of them act in anticipation of the implementation of PES and others after, and they are linked to actors (stakeholders), knowledge and monitoring of the tool.

Actors are the first key factor of a PES's success. In Costa Rican and French PES case studies, we noticed the presence of intermediaries: either directly in the contractual agreement between payer and beneficiary (Costa Rica), or at the heart of the relation in order to guarantee its well-functioning (France). The action developed by them in the Vittel case has proven extremely profitable to the contractual relation and has played a key role in the tool's success. Those case studies also highlighted different levels of collaboration between stakeholders,

---

43 *C. Thibierge*, Conclusion, in C. Thibierge (*et al.*), Densification normative. La naissance d'un processus, 2013, p. 1143.

44 *B. Frydman*, Comment penser le droit global?, in, J.Y. Chérot & B. Frydman (eds.), La science du droit dans la globalisation 2012, pp. 46 et ss.

45 *P. Lascoumes & Y. Le Galès*, Gouverner par les instruments, 2004.

46 A. Langlais, Jeux et enjeux juridiques autour des PSE, International workshop PESMIX, 11th-13th July 2014, Montpellier (Sum up in *A. Karsenty (et al.), supra note 4)*.

47 A. Pomade, Les paiements pour services environnementaux contribuent-ils à l'émergence d'un «gradient de juridicité»?, (*under evaluation*).

from an open dialogue (France) to an institutional dialogue (Costa Rica). The analysis of actors' intervention and the implication of stakeholders in the process put in place within PES revealed profound effects on the efficacy, effectiveness and efficiency of the tool. For this reason, we can now suggest that the public authority should intervene with respect to both the intermediaries engaged in the process (to define their role and their assistance mission) and in the dialogue that takes place between stakeholders (through the strengthening of science policy interfaces, ensuring transparency of information, ensuring negotiations ...).

Knowledge is the second key factor. In PES case studies in France and Costa Rica, we noticed a significant difference in the awareness of knowledge in its broadest definition (scientific knowledge and the experience on the ground ...). The PES observed in Costa Rica highlighted a lack of knowledge, and the PES studied in France showed the key example of the perfect pairing of useful knowledge, be it scientific data or experiential knowledge. The place of knowledge is important because it plays a considerable role, beforehand, in the choice of spaces that can be the subject of a PES, or in the choice of stakeholders or in specific issues. It enables us to assess the effectiveness of PES and the need to adjust practices at a later time. The public authority could act on the flow of information (knowledge mobilized ...), data collection (through science policy interface ...) and the exploitation of data (crossing knowledge ...) to ensure that all of the knowledge necessary to assess a case is mobilized. Consequently, public regulation would not frame the mechanism, but ensures, punishes and controls the compliance of conditions of design and the implementation of PES. This mixed knowledge, when taken into account, finds its theoretical justification in the conceptual tool of internormativity. This concept is defined in two different senses.[48] The first evokes the passage of a standard of a normative system to another, or the inter-influence of different nature of standards (legal, social, economic ...). The second meaning refers to contacts between normative systems, power relationships and the interactions observed between two or more normative systems. Knowledge observation refers to the first meaning of internormativity. The flow of knowledge is considered here in an interdisciplinary perspective, crossing standards and data of different natures (social, scientific, economic ...). We can make two observation here. On the one hand, the different mechanisms do not propose the same degree of internormativity, insofar as the nature of mobilized data is highly variable. On the other hand, the normative influence (understood as the weight of a given standard in the final decision)[49] is also variable. In view

---

48 Sur ces définitions, voir: *A.-J. Arnaud* (dir.), Dictionnaire encyclopédique de théorie et de sociologie du droit, 2ème édition, 1993; *K. Benyekhlef,* Une possible histoire de la norme. Les normativités émergentes de la mondialisation, 2008, p. 797; *J.-G. Belley*, Réactif, activation, phases et produits, in J.-G. Belley (ed.), Le droit soluble. Contributions québécoises à l'étude de l'internormativité, 1996, p. 21.

49 *A. Pomade*, La force normative d'un avant-projet et la force normative de son émetteur: connexion ou dissociation?, in C. Thibierge (*et al.*), Force normative. Naissance d'un concept,

of the case studies, it appears that the weight of scientific data will depend on the number and nature of the other standards mobilized in the process. This normative influence[50] refers to the concept of normative force, which makes it possible to assess a standard's degree of influence. For instance, in Costa Rica, the flow of knowledge crossed with the concept of internormativity can be analysed in two different ways. During the stage of the design of the PES, knowledge both permits the giving of information on social, economic and ecological context and to give pre-conditions through the regente document. During the step of the implementation of the PES, it permits the building of a database of lessons learnt from the implementation, concerning efficacy, effectiveness and efficiency of both the PES and PPES Program. This permits thinking of the next PES. During the design step, we noted that a major condition by which to conclude a PES was to present a sustainable forest management plan, prepared by a licensed forester called "regente". This describes the land use proposed, including ecological and geographical information (land tenure and physical access, topography, soils, climate, drainage, actual land use and carrying capacity with respect to land use and plans for preventing forest fires, illegal hunting, illegal harvesting and monitoring schedules). The more numerous data are ecological and geographical ones. They prevail over and above all other types of information and for that reason are those which have the most weighting in the process. The concurrence between data is not high, so the weight of data is easy to determine.

During the step of implementation, alongside the ecological evaluation, an economical assessment is completed to determine the economic benefits of biodiversity through PES. In that case, there are at least two different natures of data. The question is to know how each one will be taken into account to build the next PES, a PES which could propose better effectiveness. The advantages of a database collection based on the assessment of the implementation of PES leads to establishing strong archived imagery and/or classified land cover time series at the program's inception. It also leads to having forest land used as the target facilitates cross-site comparisons, relative to more specific site-based criteria like water quality standards, sedimentation rates or stand-based measures of carbon storage.[51] However, it is necessary to make some remarks. The impact of Costa Rica's PES scheme is measured through spatial data considerations, sampling considerations and the effects of institutional path dependency owing to the unique evolution of the PES in the country. Regarding spatial data, explicit criteria and technical procedures for regentes to follow were slow to come about during initial contract establishment and in subsequent monitoring. Since 2004, data collection has changed. Data collected prior to 2004 were recorded in a variety of

2013, pp. 499-515 et ss.

50 *C. Thibierge (et al.),* Force normative. Naissance d'un concept, 2013.

51 *A.E.* Daniels *et al.*, Understanding the impacts of Costa Rica's PES: Are we asking the right questions?, Ecological Economics, 2010, pp. 2116-2126.

incompatible formats, resulting in unnecessary spatial errors when changing the datum and projection in a post-hoc fashion. Only in 2006 and later, regentes were required to map a polygon corresponding to the ground area(s) contracted for PES within the larger farm. The paucity of adequate spatial data made satellite-based monitoring a challenge in the early years of the PES, particularly where it was not coupled with extensive field mapping andverification. Sampling considerations arise from the dynamic and progressive nature of conservation in Costa Rica, and are further exacerbated by uncertainty in spatial data. Regardless of the approach taken to evaluating the PES, any assessment hinges on knowing what area corresponds to PES contracts, what area does not and what area is ineligible for PES, such as the land in national parks. Even with all of this information, the state of the science or lack of monitoring practice implies a non-measured or measurable impact of the PES implemented in most cases. In fact, uncertainty often prevails. This situation highlights the difficulty of finding reliable information, mixing them and measuring the weight of each of them in the PES's effectiveness. The analysis of the internormativity observed within a PES, at the stage of its implementation, is very difficult because there is no certainty and no specific organization or network that can bring together information. During the first part of this chapter, we described the French process through the Vittel case. This case well-illustrated the weight of social and environmental data in the process. By presenting the Costa Rican's situation now, we better understand the complexity of sharing knowledge within the PES, leading to its effectiveness.

Monitoring is the third key factor. French and Belgian case studies related to PES account for an unequal monitoring on the implementation of the tool. Whereas the French case study shows an ongoing monitoring from the design to the implementation of the tool, the Belgian case presented an insufficiency in the monitoring scheme at the stage of implementation. In this last case, monitoring is insufficient and sanctions appear to have been applied only very rarely. This situation does not seem to be the result of those responsible for the monitoring; in the French case it is a private authority and in the Belgian case it is a public one. The element the most important concerns the organization of an ongoing monitoring that makes it possible to adjust the effectiveness of PES, as and when required.

The analysis of the role of law towards the knowledge used in such PES was less intermediate, even if the French Vittel case appears as an exception. In general, case studies have shown that a strong intervention of public regulation in the collection, the circulation and the introduction of knowledge throughout the process developed within PES can be useful to ensure the success of the tool, but is not enough. For that reason, we can add some remarks about the relation between public and private regulation in practice. The lack of public regulation does not necessarily entail the failure of the PES. The Vittel case is particularly indicative of this observation. However, because this case study is quite accurate, it would probably be wrong to assert a general principle. In addition, we may assume that public regulation could intervene to contribute to the success of the PES in order to recreate the conditions for success. Consequently, public regulation would not have framed the mechanism, but could ensure, punish and control the compliance of conditions of design and implementation of PES. This will conduct to several initiatives from public authority. We can make recommendations that highlight how the relation between public and private regulation might be thinking, operating and how public regulation could act to facilitate these relations. Concerning the mixed regulation, we can suggest:

Favouring regulating diversity, by promoting a framework made by public regulation in order to determine each stage of the design (knowledge mobilization, stakeholders and conduct-exchanges) and the implementation of the PES (plurality of administrative checks on the application of the instrument, evaluation and exploitation of ecological, economic and social results).

Providing a public regulation that determine terms which must be considered by private regulation (casuistry and contextual approach related to the co-contractors). Concerning the governance and the involvement of actors, we can propose that public regulation could:

Strengthen the presence of independent intermediaries in the design and implementation process of PES.

Determine the role of independent intermediaries accurately: mediator, negotiator, assistance, control.

Delete any form of intermediary in the contractual relationship (limit direct relation supplier-beneficiary).

Concerning mobilized knowledge, we suggest that the public authority could take measures which permit to:

Adopt an integrated approach (science, local knowledge, field experience ...) during the implementation of PES.

Evaluate and cross the evolution of knowledge in the implementation of PES (social, economic, ecological in their reports to practices perpetrated ...).

3.2. THE INTENSITY AND QUALITY OF THE NORMATIVE FRAMEWORK OF THE MECHANISM

The second result of our study has shown that an important factor of the effectiveness of PES schemes seems to lay in the intensity and the quality of the mechanism's normative framework, rather than in the public or private nature of the regulation.

In that way, the intensity represents the magnitude (from the poorly regulated to the highly regulated one) of the normative framework observed within the process put in place within PES. This means that public and private regulation, mobilized by public and private actors, have to organize their field of intervention to ensure that all aspects of the mechanism are framed and controlled (steps of the process, knowledge taken into account, stakeholders …).

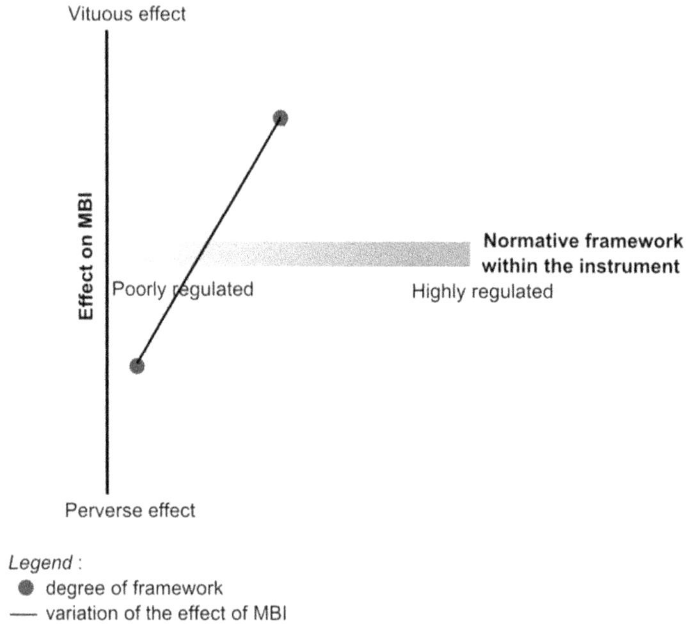

To ensure this framework, actors have to take three kinds of factors into account. The first one is the ecological concerns. The PES Vittel case in France shows that a more positive and nature conservation-oriented approach is possible from stakeholders and plays a part in the success of the tool. The second factor is the economic concerns. This factor is linked to stakeholders' economic situation. Clearly, it refers to their financial needs. In that way, a good payment can encourage them to get involved in the implementation of the tool. The third factor is social concerns. The Belgian case study illustrates the role of PES in stakeholders' education, socialization and the collateral impact that it could produce on their family. This aspect is very important in the success of PES because it constitutes an extra motivation to join the MBI tool.

The involvement of all actors in the mechanism of PES is in line with the current new way of thinking "public action", which is defined as the actions of public institutions and of a plurality of public and private actors from civil society which act jointly in multiple interdependencies to produce forms of the regulation of collective activities.[52] This means that a concerted and collective action generates successful decision-making.

52 *J. Commaille*, Sociologie de l'action publique, in L. Boussaguet, S. Jacquet & P. Ravinet (eds.), Dictionnaire des politiques publiques, 3ème édition, 2009, p. 519.

Furthermore, this collective action, built to self-regulate or co-regulate activities and practices, also refers to an emerging concept in law, well known in political science and management: empowerment.[53] Some authors have developed definitions of this concept of empowerment.[54] Depending on the context, it can refer to a theory, a framework, a plan, a goal, an ideology, a process, a result[55] or a consequence.[56] At an individual level, empowerment is defined as the capacity of people to promote self-esteem, self-confidence, initiative and control.[57] Some authors speak about a "social recognition processes", or the capacity of people to meet their needs, to solve their problems and to mobilize the necessary resources to feel in control of their own lives.[58] In the PES analysis, we could say that empowerment refers to the awareness of stakeholders of a PES to have a crucial role to play in the administration of the tool. In a collective sense, empowerment refers to a process which implements cooperation, synergy, transparency and flow of information. It is the result of a strong participation in political and collective actions and requires the active involvement of people. *A priori*, PES case studies do not reflect a form of successful empowerment. However, they highlight the potential thereof. By the lack of public regulation, the Vittel case corresponds to the characterization of empowerment. In contrast, the Costa Rican case tends towards another vision of empowerment, one more focused on a mix of public-private perspective. In the latter, empowerment allows us to change the current structures and power relations between the various public and private bodies, stakeholders and individuals.[59]

At least, this study of PES success factors should be linked with a reflection on governance. Having appeared in the wake of the globalization of the economy, the concept of governance show the need to renew the relationship between civil society and decision-making powers.[60] In the case of PES, the concept is used, especially in Belgium and Costa Rica, as the implementation process of environmental policy whose purpose is to ensure the management of natural resources by

53 *M.H. Bacqué & C. Biewener*, L'empowerment, une pratqiue émancipatrice, 2013; *M.H. Bacqué*, Empowerment et politiques urbaines aux Etats-Unis, Géographie, économie, société, 2006, n° 1, Vol. 8, pp. 107-124; *A.G. Gagnon & P. May*, Empowerment et diversité culturelle: quelques prolégomènes, Métropoles, 2010, n° 7; *J. Friedmann*, Empowerment: the politics of alternative development, 1992.

54 *J. Rappapont, Studies in Empowerment: introduction to the Issues, Prevention in Human Services, 1984, pp. 1-17.*

55 E. Hawley Mc Whirther, Empowerment in counselling, Journal of Counselling & Development, 1991, pp. 222-227.

56 *C.H. Gibson*, A concept analysis of empowerment, Journal of Advanced Nursing, 1991, pp. 354-361.

57 *A. Eisen*, Survey of neighborhood-based, comprehensive community empowerment initiatives, Health Education Quarterly, 1994, pp. 235-252.

58 *C.H. Gibson, supra note 56.*

59 *S. Sherwin*, No Longer Patient: Feminist Ethics and health Care, 1992.

60 *D. Bourcier*, Comment s'accorder sur les normes?, Le Droit et la Gouvernance face à Internet, Lex Electronica, 2006, Vol.10, n° 3.

the actors concerned[61] and to inform on methods of land management.[62] The governance of biodiversity has evolved over the past decades. First, it was seen in terms of nature reserves considered as tools of governance.[63] Later, questions about the role of the capitalist system in the degradation of the environment questioned the organization of biodiversity conservation in the 1970s and 1980s. Biodiversity has become closely linked to socio-economic issues, thereafter being incorporated into a perspective on sustainable development.[64] Today, there are many illustrations of the governance of biodiversity, such as bioprospection[65], and it generally refers to the rational use of resources by humans.[66] Whatever the design of PES, they are an illustration of the renewed governance of biodiversity.

Local governance is an important factor in the success of the PES. The social acceptability of conservation programs depends on the place given to the collective organization of governance.[67] For better environmental and social performance, factors of success PES are identified as a participatory approach, deliberative strategies to reduce conflicts[68], the ability to make compromises on the full compliance of payments[69], the negotiation about what you are going to do[70] and a trustworthy relationship.[71] It is necessary to think of ways to improve the involvement of stakeholders in the decision-making process and the recognition of values and identities associated with ecosystems. It is also important to question how an adaptive approach to PES governance can be built, focusing on the best participation.[72] This involves finding the best balance between flexibility

---

61 *C. Eberhard* (dir.), Droit, gouvernance et développement durable, 2005.

62 H. Rey-Valette H., *et al.*, Guide pour la mise en œuvre de la gouvernance en appui au développement durable des territoires,© Cemagref, CNRS, Geyser, Inra, Supagro, Université Montpellier 1. Diffusion INRA-Montpellier, 2011.

63 *D. Dumoulin-Kervan*, Les politiques de conservation de la nature au cœur de l'internationalisation et de la convergence des ordres politiques, Revista de la CEPAL, 2005, pp. 71-86.

64 *E. Rodary*, La gouvernance de la biodiversité et le développement, in P. Jacquet & L. Tubiana (eds.), Regards sur la Terre, 2008, Chapter 4.

65 *F. Thomas*, Biodiversité, biotechnologies et savoirs traditionnels. Du patrimoine commun aux ABS, Revue Tiers Monde, 2006, n° 188, pp. 825-842; *T. Dedeuwaerdere*, Bioprospection, gouvernance de la biodiversité et mondialisation, Les Carnets du Centre de Phylosophie du Droit, 2003, n° 104.

66 *J.P. Raffin*, De la protection de la nature à la gouvernance de la biodiversité, Ecologie et Politique, 2005, n°30, pp. 97-109.

67 *U. Pascual*, Social equity matters in Payments for Ecosystem Services, International workshop PESMIX, 11th-13th June 2014, Montpellier (Sum up in *A. Karsenty (et al.), supra note 4).*

68 *Id.*

69 *S. Engel*, What have we learnt on designing PES? A critical economist's view, International workshop PESMIX, 11th-13th June 2014, Montpellier (Sum up in *A. Karsenty (et al.), supra note 4).*

70 *M. Antona*, Round Table «Les PSE: des instruments environnementaux ou de développement?», International workshop PESMIX, 11th-13th June 2014, Montpellier (Sum up in *A. Karsenty (et al.), supra note 4).*

71 *B. Landreau*, Programme gouvernemental 'Socio Bosque' en Équateur – Présentation et analyse de la première initiative de PES national en Amérique du Sud, International workshop PESMIX, 11th-13th June 2014, Montpellier (Sum up in *A. Karsenty (et al.), supra note 4).*

72 *A. Karsenty (et al.), supra note 4.*

and legal certainty. This conception of local governance, which involves civil society in the management of biodiversity, can certainly impact on conservation modes of ordinary biodiversity, beyond the PES. On the one hand, the PES can be considered to be a transitional step towards a reconfiguration of agricultural production methods or forest management methods, one that will not be based on the existence of a payment but, instead, on an empathetic and voluntary approach, an awareness of the impact of his personal or professional behaviour on biodiversity and ecosystems. On the other hand, the PES can be seen as a catalyst for local initiatives (collective initiatives of farmers ...) possibly based on another model than that of the PES as it is currently conceived, and for which modalities and mechanisms remain to be created. The strength of ecosystem services is to focus on the relationship between man and his environment. Ecosystem services do not consider biodiversity and ecosystems in a disconnected way, from the unique angle of the species or habitats. The human dimension envisaged in ecosystem services, and the link between human behaviour and environmental impact, is probably what contributes to the success of the PES because the mechanism has a "direct" human benefit.

From an economic point of view, one might think about the coming terms and conditions of the cost of conservation, but from a legal point of view, the issue of the cost of conservation must be linked with the issue of responsibility and with the agreement concluded through the PES. With PES, responsibility for the good ecological status of the environment seems to remain up to those who pay and those who are paid to ensure the conservation of ecosystems. This approach excludes the rest of civil society, who are not involved in a PES mechanism. The monetization of this mechanism tends to spread the cost and environmental responsibility among a certain category of actors. To the extent that ecosystem services are considered as profits produced for human well-being, without a distinction being made between humans, the PES model is not completely satisfactory. It is also for this reason that one can think that the PES mechanism is only a transitional step, because it creates a kind of inequality based on economic criteria.

4. CONCLUSION

Regarding the balance between public and private regulation within PES, our legal study shows that a binary conception of such a tool is not relevant. Instead of a categorization between public PES and private PES, we proposed instead to integrate all forms of PES mechanisms into a gradient model of public intervention. In this perspective, the gradient represents the magnitude, from the lowest to the highest, of the public authority's intervention on the process put in place within PES. This mixed approach is more adequate to reality and will contribute to the success of the tool. Regarding the intensity and the quality of the normative framework of the mechanism, we conclude that the nature of regulation is not the key to success. On the contrary, the concept's importance can be found in the strong framework of all mechanisms and processes, rather than in the public or private nature of the regulation.

CHAPTER 3

THE EFFECTIVENESS OF ENVIRONMENTAL LAW THROUGH CONTRACTS

Mathilde Hautereau-Boutonnet
Professeur at Jean Moulin Lyon III University
(Institute of Environmental Law/ CNRS, UMR 5600 EVS)

When referring to the effectiveness of the law in a traditional sense, at first "contracts" seem to have little to do with the topic envisaged here; namely, "the effectiveness of environmental law". The concept of effectiveness, "*effectivité*" in French, described by the Doyen Carbonnier as "the effective application" of legal rules, primarily invites us to look at whether the law is in fact applied and, in order to achieve this, to question the process of implementation, which involves both obligations and sanctions.[1] Given that contracts are voluntary legal instruments, which, by an agreement of two or more willing parties, lead to the performance of various obligations[2], it seems that they cannot contribute to this process of the implementation of environmental law. Indeed, in addition to the fact that contracts relate mostly to interpersonal dealings that are only a little focused on the general environmental interest, given that they are solely based on the will of the parties, it could seem at first glance that they would afford little support to environmental law with regards to its implementation.

Yet, when we take a closer look at positive law, contracts now play a significant role in environmental law. Various studies have focused on contracts[3] and have

---

1 See his famous article on effectiveness and non-effectiveness of the rule of law, «Effectivité et ineffectivité de la règle de droit», *Flexible droit, pour une sociologie du droit sans rigueur*, Paris LGDJ, 9e éd., 1998, p. 133. On the concept of effectiveness, see J. Commaille, *Dictionnaire de la culture juridique*, (dir.) D. Alland et S. Rials, PUF.

2 See in particular the French definition arising from the recent reform of contract law, ordinance no. 2016-131 dated 10 Feb. 2016 on the reform of contract law, the general regime and the proof of obligations, art. 1101, "A contract is an agreement between two or more willing parties intended to create, amend, transfer or extinguish obligations".

3 See *Environmental Contracts, Comparative approaches to regulatory innovation in the United States and Europe*, E. W. Orts et K. Deketelaere, Kluwer Law International, 2001; C. Giraudel (dir.), *La protection conventionnelle des espaces naturels*, Préf. M. Prieur, PULIM 2000; M.

shown that they are becoming an essential regulation tool for environmental policies at the domestic, international or European levels, given that they can replace, anticipate, supplement or implement the law or can even make up for its shortcomings. In fact, a large and diverse range of contracts has been revealed: Natura 2000 contracts, carbon contracts, contracts for the sale of contaminated land, insurance contracts relating to environmental damage, waste disposal agreements, neighbourhood protection contracts, bioprospecting contracts, implementation contracts related to the international REDD system, rural leases with environmental clauses, energy performance contracts, agri-environmental contracts, conservation easements, ecological compensation agreements, provision of environmental services, public or private sustainable procurement, etc.

This list is long and not exhaustive and it does, in fact, relate to the effectiveness of environmental law. Indeed, all of these examples reveal the same dimension of effectiveness: the implementation of the objectives of environmental law, from the prevention to the remediation of damage. This is relevant here as it can be noted that a number of these contracts are prescribed by the legislator. They relate to frameworks which, in an incidental or in a direct way, rely on contracts in order to ensure that environmental law is actually effective. They demonstrate how contracts are used as a tool for the application of environmental law. Take, for example, the Natura 2000 contract, a way to protect biodiversity which is directly prescribed by the legislator.[4] There are other types of contracts that are certainly guided by the great objectives of environmental law and contribute to the protection of the environment, but they are mainly entered into on a voluntary basis and, therefore, arise mostly from contractual practices which, day after day, tend to give certain contracts an environmental dimension, in particular among businesses which tend to include environmental elements in their commercial policy. They show that contracts are also a tool that enable parties to make environmental law effective through a creative act.

This should, in no way, come as a surprise if one recalls the normative originality of contracts. Contracts are not just a legal instrument; they are also an individual norm[5] which is included in the hierarchy of norms. Given that they are subject to objective law, contracts may then be the vehicle for the implementation of general norms and, ultimately, give rise to another norm at the individual level. Thus, by

Hautereau-Boutonnet (dir.), *Le contrat et l'environnement, Etude de droit interne, international et européen*, PUAM, Coll. Droit(s) de l'environnement, Préface G. J. Martin, 2014; *Le Contrat et l'environnement, Etude de droit comparé*, Bruylant 2015.

4 E. Truilhé-Marengo, Contractualisation et réglementation, quelle articulation entre les outils de gestion des sites Natura 2000, *RJE* 2005/30, p. 131.

5 C. Thibierge, Libres propos sur les sources du droit, *Mélanges en l'honneur de Ph. Jestaz*, p. 545; H. Kelsen, *La théorie juridique de la convention*, Sirey, Archives de Philosophie du Droit et de sociologie juridique, 1940, p. 33; D. de Béchillon, *Qu'est-ce qu'une règle de droit?*, O. Jacob, 1997, p. 28 s.; J. Ghestin, Les données positives du droit, *RTD civ.* 2002, p. 11.

applying environmental law, contracts have the ability to achieve the transition from a general norm to an individual norm and to facilitate the achievement of environmental objectives at a social level. Contracts apply environmental law and, at the same time, create an individual norm. Environmental law applies to contracts and, thereafter through contractual freedom and the binding effect of contracts, contracts create environmental law.

These two aspects of contracts, implementation and the creation of environmental law, reveal two poles of effectiveness that deserve to be looked at separately as they open different suggestions for discussion[6]: on the one hand, the traditional understanding of effectiveness[7], which consists in limiting the concept to the idea of the "implementation of environmental law" in a vertical manner. In this case, the idea is to demonstrate that contracts are a tool to implement the objectives or the frameworks related to environmental law, by observing a normative movement from top to bottom or from a general norm to an individual norm. On the other hand, a less typical understanding of this concept, one that is more sociological in nature and which focuses on the review of stakeholders' actual conducts, is quite close in fact to the second part of the definition chosen in the Vocabulaire juridique produced by Association Henri Capitant and which states that effectiveness is also the "nature of a situation which exists in fact, in reality" (a definition which is well-known in international public law). In this case, with regards to contracts, the idea is to focus on what they are as a tool that can actually be used in real life by the relevant people and on the effects that they produce. Applied to this topic, the horizontal implementation of environmental law is thus revealed, with contracts being a tool that creates new obligations, thereby implementing the environmental objectives created by individuals.

Involving both "effects" and "facts", the effectiveness of environmental law thereby entails two processes of effectiveness of environmental law through "implementation contracts" as well as "creative contracts": the vertical effectiveness of environmental law in contracts (1) and horizontal effectiveness (2).

1. THE VERTICAL EFFECTIVENESS OF ENVIRONMENTAL LAW THROUGH CONTRACTS

We can already see that contracts are used by legislators as a tool to enforce various environmental frameworks or objectives. Here, the environmental order from the top uses contracts for the purpose of effectiveness at the bottom level.

6 Concerning this idea of various conceptions, see the following article which is particularly informative, Y. Leroy, La notion d'effectivité en droit, *Droit et Société*, 2011/3, n° 79, p. 715-732.

7 See J. Carbonnier, cited above, See also, P. Lascoumes, «Effectivité», in A.-J. Arnaud (dir.), *Dictionnaire encyclopédique de théorie et de sociologie du droit sans rigueur*, LGDJ, 1993, p. 217.

This vertical effectiveness of contracts could be strengthened in the future if we take the fact that the contractual order, and not just the environmental order, has the ability to impose environmental obligations on the contracting parties into account. This second trend deserves to be looked at, given that it opens a world of possibilities on the side of "implementation" contracts. Indeed, extending to more than the various contracts envisaged by the legislator, it could involve a much wider range of contracts. The contractual influence of the environmental legal order (1.1.) would be supplemented by the influence of the contractual legal order (1.2.).

1.1. THE CONTRACTUAL INFLUENCE OF THE ENVIRONMENTAL LEGAL ORDER

The environmental legal order mostly involves the intervention of all the legislators. Over the past few years, we have seen that contracts have become a tool for the effectiveness of environmental objectives prescribed by the various legislators. It is a key instrument for their implementation, one which cannot materialise without the conclusion of a contract, whether this contract is expressly or impliedly envisaged by law. The integration of contracts to environmental law can be noted at two levels: either the legislator imposes a number of environmental obligations on contractual relationships which, in theory, have nothing to do with the environment. The contract is then only incidentally environmental. Or the legislator envisages contracts as being a real tool that implements an environmental framework: contracts are then directly environmental.[8]

In the first case, the example of contracts for the sale of contaminated land is particularly relevant here. While it is primarily an exchange agreement focused on the economic interests of the parties, as a result of the legislator's intervention, it may also include an environmental dimension favourable both to the right to environmental information and to the remediation of environmental damage. Indeed, in addition to the fact that various legislators are ensuring that buyers are fully informed as to the extent of any contamination that exists on a piece of land at the time of a sale, others go even further by requiring the seller to put things right prior to the conclusion of the sale agreement. In both cases, sales of land become an opportunity to achieve environmental objectives. To give a number of examples, French law requires the disclosure of environmental information in this regard (Article L. 514-1 of the Environmental code and Article L. 125-7 of the same), US law, through the CERCLA legislation (*Comprehensive Environmental Response Compensation and Liability Act*), incidentally requires buyers to carry

8 Concerning this distinction between contracts, directly or incidentally environmental, M. Hautereau-Boutonnet, *in Le contrat et l'environnement, Etude de droit interne …*, cited above, p. 443 et seq.

out an environmental audit, these buyers are potentially held liable for the decontamination if they are aware of its existence[9], but also Belgian law, and more specifically Walloon law, according to which sales have become an event that creates due diligence and intervention obligations imposed on the seller of a real right.[10]

In the second case, we must highlight the wide variety of relevant environmental frameworks and contracts. On the one hand, frameworks that relate to the protection of biodiversity, the reduction of greenhouse gas emissions and the fight against deforestation or to the protection of the marine environment, can be prescribed by domestic, European or international law and can directly or incidentally create new contracts. On the other hand, these contracts can be internal or transnational, private or administrative, relating to real or personal rights, involving arrangements that go from investments to sales. In all cases, contracts enable the effective achievement of environmental objectives prescribed by the legislator when designing these frameworks. They facilitate the transition from a general environmental norm to an individual environmental norm.

This can be demonstrated by examining the following three examples:

- First of all, there are the conservation easements that are directly prescribed by various national legislations (for example, Canada, Australia, the US)[11] and which are currently in the process of being adopted by French law.[12] Generally speaking, they involve a contract between a landowner and a legal entity, such as an NGO, pursuant to which the former creates a number of environmental charges over his or her property in favour, in particular, of a more eco-friendly management of the land, which will have to be carried out by the other party and be complied with by the successive owners. These contracts enable the implementation of the objectives at an interpersonal level and materialise the objectives related to the protection of biodiversity in dealings between private persons.
- Second of all, carbon contracts. While the effectiveness of the various markets for the exchange of greenhouse gas quotas in Europe and elsewhere is subject to the conclusion of moveable property sale agreements enabling

9 Concerning this reminder, see the thesis by S. Lavallée and its INCURSIONS in comparative law, La réhabilitation des terrains contaminés et le droit québécois: un droit négocié, éd. Y. Blais, p. 57 et s. See also, regarding Quebec law, S. Lavallée, Le terrain contaminé, une fatalité historique pour le contrat?, perspective québécoise, in *Le contrat et l'environnement, Etude de droit comparé*, cited above, p. 69.

10 J. Van Ypersel, *in Le contrat et l'environnement* cited above, p. 251; see also Entretien, Le propriétaire, acteur essentiel de la dépollution, *Environnement et Développement Durable* 2014/7, Entretien 4.

11 C. de Klemm, Approche comparative et critique, in *La protection conventionnelle des espaces naturels*, PULIM.

12 See the draft bill of law for the restoration of biodiversity, of nature and landscapes, new reading of the text forwarded to the French Assemblée Nationale on 25 May 2016, no. 641.

the circulation of quotas, we can also point out that the Clean Development Mechanism (CDM), established by Article 12 of the Kyoto Protocol on climate change as part of the flexibility instruments enabling the States to fulfil their obligations to reduce greenhouse gas emissions, gives rise to the conclusion of transnational investment contracts.[13] Indeed, it enables the Northern States, in exchange for the allocation of certified emission reduction units (CERs), to establish investment projects supporting the fight against climate change in Southern countries and, to this end, involves the conclusion of contracts governing both the performance of the economic activity and the allocation of the CERs. Without the conclusion of such contracts, the CDM would be without effect.

- Thirdly, Natura 2000 contracts, which are administrative contracts. The European directive dated 21 May 1992 on the conservation of natural habitats and of wild fauna and flora[14] has set the goal for Member States to set up "coherent European ecological networks of special areas of conservation under the title Natura 2000" (Article 3). Once a site is registered as a special area of conservation, the State must then take protective measures. An objectives document, referred to as "DOCOB", sets out the conservation and restoration measures, as well as the manner in which they are implemented, and is prepared for each site. The directive provides that the management may be carried out using various methods, including contracts, and French law has chosen to use the latter, Article L. 414-3-I of the Environmental code stating that " for the application of the *document d'objectifs*, the holders of real and personal rights to the land included in the site as well as the professionals and users of the marine areas located on the site can sign, with the administrative authority, contracts entitled "Natura 2000 contracts"". This example, thus, shows that contracts are clearly envisaged by the European Union as a tool for the effectiveness of environmental law.

Ultimately, whether in domestic, European or international environmental law, contracts are used as a tool to contribute to the effectiveness of various environmental objectives or frameworks prescribed by the law at the top. The latter is materialised at an interpersonal level. However, this effectiveness of environmental law through contracts is still relative, given that it is prescribed by the legislator in very specific cases. Implementation contracts are still a matter of "special" law. Yet, going further, a decompartmentalisation of effectiveness could very well take place and implementation contracts could be extended to other

13 M. Lemoine, «Le recours au contrat dans le cadre du MDP du protocole de Kyoto sur les changements climatiques», *in Le contrat et l'environnement, Etude de droit interne, international et européen* (dir. M. Hautereau-Boutonnet), PUAM, 2014, p. 217.

14 E. Truilhé-Marengo, L. 206, 22 juillet 1992.

situations, under the environmental influence of the contractual legal order. This is where the verticality of the contractual order would play a role.

1.2. THE ENVIRONMENTAL INFLUENCE OF THE CONTRACTUAL LEGAL ORDER

According to a strict definition, the "contractual legal order" means all of the general norms that are imposed upon contracting parties and, thus, govern contracts.[15] While our discussion here is solely prospective, we wish to show that the role played by contracts in the effectiveness of environmental law could be increased in the future, based on the normative strength and content of the various general norms which regulate them, which would impose contractual duties from which environmental obligations could be derived. Here it would be the law of contracts at the top that would impose environmental objectives in order to create an environmental implementation norm.

A number of contractual duties can be found in most domestic legal systems and are also well known in international trade law. First of all, we think of the requirement of good faith in the performance of a contract. Under French law, according to the new Article 1104 of the French Civil code included in the reform of contract law, contracting parties must negotiate, conclude and perform contracts in good faith. The courts have inferred a number of related duties, such as the duty to disclose to the other contracting party prior to the conclusion of a contract various elements which are decisive to its consent or to renegotiate the contract in the case of hardship, or to adopt a consistent conduct during the performance of the contract and to collaborate in the proper performance of the contract.[16] Pursuant to the UNIDROIT principles, to which certain transnational contracts may refer, in their latest 2010 version, the requirement of good faith can be found in Article 1.9 as "good faith in international trade" and may also appear, here as well, in various specific duties such as the prohibition of inconsistent behaviour to the detriment of the other party[17], the obligation to renegotiate in the event of a hardship[18] as well as the duty to cooperate during the performance of a contract.[19] As for the principles and customs of international trade, legal academics include therein the binding effect of contracts and good faith in particular.[20]

---

15 Here we are using the expression used by D. Mazeaud, "*nouvel ordre contractuel*" or "new contractual order", in Ruptures et permanence dans le droit des contrats, RDC 2003-1, p. 295.

16 Concerning this French law reminder, see M. Fabre-Magnan, *Droit des obligations 1. Contrat et engagement unilatéral*, PUF, 2e éd. 2012, p. 78, which discusses all these duties.

17 Article 1.8 included in the 2004 version.

18 Art. 6.2.1 cited above.

19 Article 5.1.3: "Each party shall co-operate with the other party when such co-operation may reasonably be expected for the performance of that party's obligations".

20 On this reminder, E. Gaillard, «La distinction des principes généraux du droit et des usages du commerce international», Etudes P. Billet, p. 203, p. 208.

There are two duties that could strengthen the effectiveness of environmental law by imposing that the protection of the environment be taken into account in contractual dealings.

On the one hand, the duty of good faith. One can imagine that, in the future, a number of judges might consider that good faith requires the performance of a contract towards a goal that would also take environment protection into account, where the achievement of personal interests should not harm the environmental interests of the community. Courts could order parties to a contract to comply with a number of environmental objectives. By way of example, the performance of a lease could imply an eco-friendly use of the property, without harm being caused to the environment and ensuring that any environmental damage be put right at the end of the lease. In the consumer sector, any consumer should have the right to be informed, on the basis of good faith, of the environmental consequences of the production of a good or a service. With respect to the climate, one could even imagine that good faith could have consequences on transnational supply agreements and imply the adoption of clauses related to climate change adaptation and mitigation. Thus, a court or an arbitrator could infer therefrom that the parties should communicate to each other information related to the consequences of their activities on global warming, reduce greenhouse gas emissions arising from their activities by following the best available practices, control the climate-related behaviour of sub-contractors, renegotiate contracts based on the evolution of available scientific information for adaptation or mitigation purposes.

We can already find, under French law, one judgment issued by a trial judge, albeit a French and isolated case, is worth highlighting as, relating to the aforementioned supply agreement, it gives us food for thought. This judgement was issued by the Nancy Court of appeal on 26 September 2007.[21] Two companies were bound by a steam supply agreement. One of them, a producer of water steam which used the cogeneration technique, had benefited from the legislation implementing the European Union emissions trading system, as this technique allowed it to receive an excess of quotas which it could sell on the market. The other party, despite using the water steam in a manner that satisfied the environmental conduct of the supplier, did not receive any benefits therefrom. In other words, one party benefited from a financial advantage that had not been contemplated at the time when the contract was concluded and which was achieved as a result of the economic transaction by which the two parties were bound. The user of the water steam, the supplier's client, then asked the court to order a renegotiation of the contract so that it could receive benefits from this environmental effort. The court approved this claim and invited the parties to renegotiate the supply agreement on the basis of good faith, stating that "beyond the inequitable harm

---

[21] SAS Novacarb c/ SNC Socoma, *RLDC* 2008/49, n° 2969 O. Cachard, *RTD civ.* 2008, p. 295, B. Fages. *JCP* 2008. II. 10091, M. Lamoureux.

to the individual interests of the SAS Novacarb, which could already be grounds for a renegotiation of the agreement (supporting this, Com. 3 Nov. 1992, Bull. civ. IV, n° 338), the economy of the disputed contract and the concerted practice of the parties were also aimed at reducing the emissions of polluting gas, which of course benefits the general interest, not only at the national level but most importantly at the global level, at least in the current state of scientific knowledge as approved by a majority".[22] Most importantly, the court specified that "in order to rectify the contractual imbalance described above – be it only temporary and currently without vital consequences for SAS Novacarb – and in the general interest of the reduction of greenhouse gas emissions, the obligation- arising out of Articles 1134 paragraph 3 and 1135 of the French Civil code, to perform the contract in good faith, and including therein "all the consequences imposed by equity … impose upon the obligation according to its nature" – should encourage the parties, now both fully aware, to resume the disrupted negotiations". Despite the lack of a "win-win" clause, and thanks to the use of the theory of hardship, this solution allows the court to impose a renegotiation of the supply agreement so that the parties can share the benefits of green growth. Most of all, this decision shows that a court can impose new obligations in the name of an environmental cause and can, thus, insert elements into the contract environmental goals in the name of a key contractual duty: the duty of good faith. Under the influence of the contractual order at the top, contracts are moving towards the application of the bottom-level environmental law.

Another duty could also attract the attention of the courts. The duty of contractual consistency or, according to the UNIDROIT principles, the impossibility for a party "to act inconsistently with an understanding it has caused the other party to have and upon which that other party reasonably has acted in reliance to its detriment". This duty could lead the courts to request a behaviour consistent with certain undertakings of a business favourable to the protection of the environment. For instance, let us assume that a supplier publicly exposes the fact that it undertakes, in the context of its commercial dealings, to adopt a conduct supporting the fight against environmental degradation or, more specifically, the reduction of greenhouse gas emissions, in particular through compliance with international referential (the UN global compact) or with climate standardisation systems. This business could, thus, lead the other contracting party to believe that it is taking concrete measures to achieve this. An arbitrator or a court may here be lead to remind this business of its duty to be consistent and not to act inconsistently by ordering such a party to comply

22 The court went on to say: "that legal academics have, in fact, given to the obligation to perform agreements in good faith a new dimension by considering that "beyond the individual interest of each party, contracting parties should keep in mind the common interest (or even of the common good)" and that "the individualistic ethics must partially give way to contractual justice, based on solidarity" (*Rép. civ. Dalloz*, v° Bonne foi, n° 44; along the same lines B. Oppetit, "Ethique et vie des affaires", *Mél. A. Colomer*, 1993, Litec, p. 319 s.) …».

with certain obligations, such as the obligation to carry out its business in a more eco-friendly manner. Here as well, there is no doubt that the court would be using the contract as a tool to diffuse therein an environmental dimension and would, thus, demonstrate how environmental law can be effective through a contract "implementing it". Most importantly, this effectiveness would be even more remarkable as, while implementing environmental law, contracts would necessarily then become a creative source thereof. This would be the horizontal effectiveness of environmental law.

2. THE HORIZONTAL EFFECTIVENESS OF ENVIRONMENTAL LAW THROUGH CONTRACTS

The dual nature of contracts must be looked at through the lens of our subject: a contract is a norm that implements various environmental objectives sometimes contemplated by the legislator, but it is also a norm that creates a legal situation; namely, an individual norm which is, in itself, the source of environmental effects chosen pursuant to contractual freedom and guaranteed by the binding effect of contracts. Through its effects, namely the environmental obligations that must be complied with, contracts achieve a horizontal effectiveness of environmental law by implementing it within contractual dealings. Here it is the creation of contractual environmental obligations (2.1.), but also their prescription (2.2.), that contribute to the effectiveness of environmental law.

2.1. THE CREATION OF CONTRACTUAL ENVIRONMENTAL OBLIGATIONS

Generally speaking, the effectiveness lies here in the creation of norms with environmental effects. One advantage of contracts is key here: the contractual freedom to create and include the environmental obligations chosen.

More specifically, this horizontal effectiveness is better understood by looking at the example of the implementation of contracts that create environmental obligations despite there being no legal provisions imposing such obligations. This concerns, for example, businesses which handle environmental protection objectives in contracts governing their various trade relationships. Through what is referred to today as "sustainable procurement"[23], they then insert "environmental clauses" or "sustainable development clauses" in contracts destined to achieve

[23] See «Les achats durables des entreprises», in *Etude de droit interne, international et européen*, dir. M. Hautereau-Boutonnet, PUAM, Coll. Droit(s) de l'environnement, Préface G. J. Martin, 2014, p. 305.

their own economic interests primarily.[24] While some clauses lead businesses to adopt conduct that is favourable to the protection of the environment through compliance with a standardisation system, a code of good conduct or with the most favourable legislation, others require them to produce their goods in a certain way, using techniques that do no harm the environment.[25] In any case, they contribute to the effectiveness of the main environmental principles, the avoidance of environmental harm in particular, through the "greening" of the individual norms they create.

An even more specific example can be described to demonstrate this horizontal effectiveness phenomenon: the example of climate change issues. Indeed, transnational businesses of the Northern countries, in order to preserve their economic interests and to avoid any future liability on their part[26], will be increasingly lead to insert obligations relating to climate, in the supply agreements that bind them to suppliers and sub-contractors located in vulnerable Southern countries. The objectives set by international law on climate change, namely adaptation to the effects of climate change and its mitigation, are inserted into contracts and give rise to the creation of individual obligations.

In practical terms, regarding adaptation, with respect to these environmental obligations, contracts could include clauses in order to anticipate the economic consequences they might suffer if climate events do occur, but also if any changes are made to national legislations that would be likely to disrupt their trade relations. This would include clauses for the termination of contracts, for the incurrence of liability, but also index clauses and hardship clauses which will contribute to the effectiveness of the objective of adaptation to climate change. As for mitigation, businesses could go even further by engaging in the fight against climate change. Contracts could give rise to obligations requiring suppliers to use production techniques supporting the reduction of greenhouse gas emissions or to comply with the most favourable legislation in this field for instance. In both cases, what must be noted is that businesses contribute to the effectiveness of environmental law, by not only applying the objectives of international law related to the fight against climate change, but also by bringing them to life within horizontal relationships.

However, effectiveness will only be fully achieved when these environmental obligations are actually applied This is where the binding effect of contracts has a significant role to play.

---

24 M. Boutonnet, «Des obligations environnementales spéciales à l'obligation environnementale générale en droit des contrats», *D.* 2012 chron. p. 372.

25 Id.

26 On this argument, M. Hautereau-Boutonnet, «Le potentiel climatique du contrat d'approvisionnement climatique», *Revue Environnement – Energie – Infrastructures*, juin 2016.

2.2. THE PRESCRIPTION OF CONTRACTUAL ENVIRONMENTAL OBLIGATIONS

The horizontal effectiveness of environmental law benefits from the second advantage of contracts: their binding effect. Given that contracting parties must comply with contracts, the effectiveness of environmental covenants can be guaranteed by the possibility of a sanction by a judge in the event of a breach. Most importantly, this prescription could be strengthened in the future, thanks to the role of two players in the law of contracts: the court or the arbitrator, and contractual practices, given how the latter can impose new obligations on the relevant contracting parties, without them consenting thereto. Despite the lack of obligations willingly created by the parties, they could be deemed to be bound by such obligations.

Indeed, first of all, in contract law, new duties can be found by courts or arbitrators. Under French law, as in other domestic legal systems, courts already have the ability to "insert" obligations into contracts[27] and, in the name of the binding effect of contracts, order the parties to comply with agreements which "create obligations not only as to what is expressed therein, but also as to all the consequences imposed by equity, usage or law".[28] Pursuant to the UNIDROIT principles[29], to which the parties may refer in a transnational contract, in their latest 2010 version, contracts are binding as to their express obligations but also as to the "implied" obligations resulting in particular from the nature and the purpose of a contract, the practices established as between the parties and usages, from good faith and what is reasonable.[30] Furthermore, pursuant to the *lex mercatoria* and even where the parties are silent, arbitrators may find principles and usages that apply to a dispute.[31]

There is nothing to stop us, then, from imagining that these courts or arbitrators will find and then prescribe, based on the binding effect of contracts, contractual obligations favourable to environmental protection in the future. Admittedly, it will be necessary for them to decide that they are faced with an implied obligation. For now, we will point out that as for French law, and these are admittedly very relative examples, courts have not hesitated, at the beginning

---

27 L. Josserand, *Le forçage du contrat*, Etudes Gény, T. 2, Sirey, 1934, p. 340. Concerning this reminder, in p. M. Fabre-Magnan, cited above, p. 496.

28 Art. 1194 of the French Civil code, previously Article 1135.

29 Concerning these principles, see in particular P. Deumier, «Les principes UNIDROIT ont 10 ans, un bilan en demi-teinte», *RDC* 2004/3, p. 774; D. Mazeaud, «A propos du droit virtuel des contrats, Réflexion sur les principes d'UNIDROIT et la Commission Lando», *Mélanges M. Cabrillac*, Litec, 1999, p. 125.

30 Articles 5.1.1 and 5.1.2 of the UNIDROIT principles.

31 Concerning this reminder, E. Gaillard, «La distinction des principes généraux du droit et des usages du commerce international», *Etudes P. Billet*, p. 203; B. Goldman, «Frontières du droit et *lex mercatoria*", *APD*, T. IX, 1964, p. 177; «La *lex mercatoria* dans les contrats et l'arbitrage international: réalités et perspectives», *JDI* 1979, p. 475.

of the century, to include a safety obligation in transport agreements[32] before extending it to a large number of contracts and even granting the benefit thereof to third parties. Given that they are mindful of environmental protection, they could tomorrow be tempted to insert into certain contracts, such as leases, sale agreements, construction or o supply agreements, environmental obligations guaranteeing a form of environmental safety. These obligations would be in addition to the obligations deriving directly from the inclusion of environmental law in contracts and would then be a creative source of environmental law.

Going even further, secondly, in a number of legal systems, contractual practices can lead to the emergence of a usage that must be followed. For example, under Article 1.9 of the UNIDROIT Principles, the parties are bound by a usage that is widely known and observed regularly in international trade by parties in the particular trade concerned, except where the application of such a usage would be unreasonable. Similarly, usages, which derive in particular from a repeated contractual practice that is deemed to be mandatory, are looked upon as norms constituting the *lex mercatoria*.[33] Ultimately, courts or arbitrators could, thus, decide that the need to carry out operations that are clean and compatible with the objectives set out by environmental law, such as the reduction of greenhouse gas, constitutes a usage and implies compliance with a number of obligations at the time when a contract is entered into or when it is carried out.

These are, of course, only prospective thoughts. Courts will still have to find usages that amount to obligations to be complied with in contractual practices. However, from a theoretical perspective, this is significant. Indeed, it may also be seen as a general norm with a binding effect.[34] Therefore, if an environmental usage were to be recognised in contractual dealings, this would mean that a new general norm within the contractual order would govern contracts and give them an environmental dimension. Through a feedback effect, the horizontal effectiveness of environmental law would enhance the contractual order and would ultimately open, once again, a vast range of possibilities for its vertical effectiveness. Thus, we can see how contracts could become an indispensable tool for the effectiveness of environmental law in the future.

---

32 Civ. 21 nov. 1911, S. 1912.I.73, note Lyon-Caen. Concerning this reminder, M. Fabre-Magnan, publication cited above, p. 474.

33 See B. Goldman above.

34 P. Deumier, *Le droit spontané*, Economica, 2002, p. 156 et s.

CHAPTER 4

LEGAL WEAKNESSES AND WINDOWS OF OPPORTUNITY IN TRANSNATIONAL BIODIVERSITY PROTECTION: AS SEEN THROUGH THE LENS OF AN ECOSYSTEM APPROACH-BASED PARADIGM

Elina Raitanen
Doctoral Candidate, Faculty of Law, University of Turku (Finland)

ABSTRACT

This chapter reflects upon the weaknesses of transnational environmental law to protect biodiversity – stemming from fragmentation and anthropocentrism. The study employs an ecosystem approach-based paradigm as a perspective of legal research, given that it seeks to overcome the fragmentation of natural resources law and the rigidity of a legal decision-making structure, which arguably reflect the old semantics of the environment as merely a set of resources to be consumed. These features of the contemporary legal architecture are ill-matched with the socio-ecological realities and, thereby, are predisposed to environmental degradation. I propose that the fragmentation and rigidity of law could be mitigated through the adoption of an ecosystem approach-based framework in law via further integration and adaptation. From a transnational law perspective, the integration of biodiversity drivers are perhaps best facilitated through institutional linkages in and between regimes, and through contractual arrangements. The adaptation, on the other hand, could arguably be fostered via the operationalization of the precautionary principle on lower governance levels through adaptive law methods and processes.

1. INTRODUCTION

Biodiversity has an intrinsic value[1], but since it can also have an indirect impact on internationally acknowledged human rights[2], it is also no less than vital from an anthropocentric perspective to protect biodiversity.[3] Despite several multilateral environmental agreement regimes dedicated wholly or primarily to tackling aspects of biodiversity loss, human activity keeps causing massive extinctions to biodiversity and biodiversity loss continues to occur at an unacceptably high rate.[4] Arguably, one major reason why the regulatory attempts have failed in halting biodiversity loss is the contemporary positive regulatory structure, which was originally built on anthropocentric premises to exploit and commodify nature.[5] Consequently, the laws to protect interconnected and uncertain environmental matters have been formulated under a sector-based, rigorous approach taking technical data into account – without a full understanding of the environmental problematic and of ecology.[6] From the perspective of biodiversity, this means that there are many other laws than just those specifically known as "biodiversity laws" whose goal achievement is essentially connected to biodiversity preservation. Therefore, this artificial fragmentation often leads to inefficiencies[7] and problem-shifting.[8] Additionally, contemporary ecological understanding emphasizes constant transformations in – and various inter-linkages and interdependencies between – ecosystems, whereupon the rigid, front-end built laws show significant inconsistency with their object.

My suggestion is that these two major legal challenges need to be dealt with – not only to succeed in halting the continuing biodiversity loss, but also to contribute to the ongoing debate about the maturity of environmental law.[9] Since the contemporary ecological paradigm shows fundamental inconsistency with the legal one, this study also seeks to consolidate the tension by proposing the

1 The preamble of the Convention on Biological Diversity, adopted in Rio in 1992, acknowledges inter alia, the scientific, educational, cultural, recreational and aesthetic value of biodiversity.

2 International law entails obligations to act cooperatively to protect and advance fundamental human rights. These human rights include, but are not limited to, the right to life, the rights to health, water, food, a clean environment, and other social, economic and cultural rights.

3 *S. Turner,* A Global Environmental Right, 2014, p. 16.

4 *S. H. M. Butchart et al.*, Global Biodiversity: Indicators of Recent Declines, Science 2010 (28), pp.1164-1168.

5 *C. Cullinan,* Wild Law: Governing People for Earth, 2002.

6 *N. Y. Turgut,* The Influence of Ecology on Environmental Law: Challenges to the Concept of Traditional Law, Environmental Law Review, 2008 (2), p. 119.

7 *O. R. Young,* (eds.), The Effectiveness of International Environmental Regimes: Causal Connections and Behavioral Mechanisms, 1999; *E. Louka,* International Environmental Law: Fairness, Effectiveness, and World Order, 2006.

8 *P. Sands & J. Peel,* Principles of International Environmental Law, 2012, p. 893.

9 See e.g. *E. Fisher et al.*, Maturity and Methodology: Starting a Debate about Environmental Law Scholarship, 2009 (2), pp. 213 – 250.

operationalization of the ecosystem approach-based paradigm in laws related to natural resources governance. Accordingly, an increase of the adaptive capacity and precaution in laws, and the further creation of linkages in and between regimes, could contribute to a more coherent, adaptive and effective management of natural resources. Therefore, the goal of this chapter is to find out what kind of restrictions and opportunities these developments need to face within the contemporary legal framework.

In analysing the opportunities and restrictions to operationalize the ecosystem approach-based paradigm to answer the two major challenges discussed above, this study adopts an 'environmental law methodology'.[10] The analysis is critical in a sense that it questions the tenets of the existing framework and instead seeks to understand how law influences – or fails to influence – the environment.[11] I will begin with a short examination over the normative basis of the ecosystem approach. I then discuss how this approach embodies the socio-ecological paradigm and how this understanding is already reflected in environmental law and discipline. In the third chapter I will scrutinize how the regulatory failures to halt biodiversity loss could be combatted by operationalizing an ecosystem approach-based paradigm in germane laws. This will be done from two aspects: first, by outlining the opportunities to battle fragmentation through linkage creation within and between law regimes, and second, by searching for possibilities to achieve more adaptability in natural resources governance through the means of existing legal framework – especially the precautionary principle. Finally, the conclusions are drawn in the fourth chapter. Since the environmental issues are, more or less, of a transboundary nature the analysis is made from the perspective of transnational law.[12]

2. ECOSYSTEM APPROACH-BASED PARADIGM – NORMATIVE BASIS AND THE RATIONALE

While acknowledging that there is no single way to implement the ecosystem approach[13], this chapter primarily adopts the formulation of the Conference of

---

10 Environmental law methodology seeks to find out how ecological sustainability is to be achieved through the work of law as a control system. *S. Westerlund*, Theory for Sustainable Development: Towards or Against?, in *H.C. Bugge & C. Voigt* (eds.), Sustainable Development in International and National Law, 2008.

11 *A. Jóhannsdóttir, I. Cresswell & P. Bridgewater*, The Current Framework for International Governance of Biodiversity: Is It Doing More Harm Than Good?, Review of European Community and International Environmental Law, 2010 (2), p. 141.

12 The term "transnational" here refers to actions that transcend national frontiers – whether involving state or non-state actors. See more in e.g. in *C. Scott*, "Transnational Law" as Proto-Concept: Three Conceptions, 2009, pp. 859 – 876.

13 See e.g. *De Lucia* who highlights the competing narratives and genealogies of the ecosystem approach in his in depth examination of the ecosystem approach by distinguishing the

the Parties to the Convention on Biological Diversity.[14] The goal is, however, not to explore the explicit content of this formulation, but merely to utilize the approach as a perspective for research. I also use the term 'ecosystem approach-based paradigm' to demonstrate a desirable framework for natural resources governance, reflecting the timely socio-ecological narrative.[15] I think this paradigm is legitimate, since the complex nature of socio-ecological systems leads us necessarily to the need for interdisciplinary and holistic approaches and the redefinition of the relationship between humans and nature.

As is defined in the Decision of the Conference of the Parties, the ecosystem approach is "a strategy for the integrated management of land, water and living resources that promotes conservation and sustainable use in an equitable way". The Decision furthermore suggests that in order to maintain ecosystem services, the conservation of ecosystem structure and functioning – also described as the maintenance of ecosystem integrity[16] or resilience[17] – should be a priority target of the ecosystem approach.[18] From the perspective of biodiversity protection, this means that the conservation of ecosystem resilience is of greater significance for the long-term maintenance of biological diversity than the protection of single species.

While the ecosystem itself may not be managed, the human activities which interact with – and impact upon the ecosystem – may be managed with a view to conserving biodiversity and ensuring sustainable development.[19] In short, the idea of an ecosystem approach involves focusing on ecosystems – implying that the management should also be holistic and reflective – looking at human activities and their cumulative impacts in an integrated, as opposed to sectoral,

---

concept in anthropocentric and eco-centric aspects. *V. De Lucia*, Competing Narratives and Complex Genealogies: The Ecosystem Approach in International Environmental Law, Journal of Environmental Law, 2014 (28).

14 CBD Decision V/6 'Ecosystem Approach', Doc. UNEP/COP/5/23 (2000); CBD Decision VII/11 'Ecosystem Approach', Doc. UNEP/CBD/COP/7/21 (2004).

15 The idea is to identify the main unifying framework of shared concepts and unfamiliar principles and possibly even contrast with the concept of traditional law. Here, this framework is set under the concept of 'the ecosystem approach-based paradigm'. The principles of coherence and precaution alongside related themes such as general interest and the holistic approach are among the major features of this framework. About the common framework – or roof, see *Turgut, supra*, note 7, pp. 124 – 128.

16 According to the definition of strong sustainability ecological 'integrity' means the ability of an ecosystem to recover from disturbance and reestablish its stability, diversity and resilience. See more in Phase2 Strong Sustainability Think Tank at: http://nz.phase2.org/what-is-strong-sustainability. Last visited on 20th April 2016.

17 According to *Holling*, 'resilience' is the capacity of an ecosystem to withstand disturbance and maintain the same basic processes and structures. *C. S. Holling*, Resilience and Stability of Ecological Systems, Annual Review of Ecology and Systematics, 1973 (4).

18 CBD Decision V/6, *supra*, note 15, Principle 5.

19 *R. Long*, EU Law and the Ecosystems Approach: Making it Work in the Marine Environment, Conference Paper for the 6th ABLOS Conference Contentious Issues in the Law of the Sea- Surely Not!", 2010.

and adaptive, as opposed to front-end manner. This requires a governance approach that is based on the ecological boundaries of the ecosystem, rather than jurisdictional boundaries.[20]

The ecosystem approach also suggests that human beings are to be included as an integral component of all of the world's ecosystems.[21] Indeed, while social systems are inherently linked to the ecological systems, they should be conceived as one social-ecological system.[22] Hence, the ecosystem approach promotes conservation and the sustainable use of natural resources in an equitable way – implying that interested communities must be involved through the development of efficient and effective structures and processes for decision-making and management.[23]

The ecosystem approach is also adopted here as a paradigm to express the contemporary understanding of the environment, constituted through the socio-ecological narrative, which emphasizes the relationships and interactions between things. As *Philippopoulos-Mihalopouloulos* observes: "[m]odern environmental understanding has emerged through the application of technical scientific knowledge, rendered more meaningful through various interpretive frameworks of 'environmental sensibility', which treat the environment, not as a thing, but as dynamic process of which humans are a part, which has a history, an economy, and a power to transform and be transformed."[24] This pace and magnitude of ecological and social change are, consequently, creating pressures for environmental law to evolve further.[25] The fundamental challenge is that the legal system is not yet ecosystem-based[26], but instead regulates different components of ecosystems in a fragmented and rigid (front-end) manner.

The narrative discussed above, however, is nascent in the recent development of environmental law and policy. For instance, concrete regulatory measures

---

20 *F. M. Platjouw,* The need to recognize a coherent legal system as an important element of the ecosystem approach, in: *C. Voigt* (eds.), Rule of Law for Nature – New Dimensions and Ideas in Environmental Law, 2013, pp. 158 – 174.

21 CBD Decision V/6, *supra*, note 15, para 2.

22 "This means that in our globalized society, there are virtually no ecosystems that are not shaped by people and no people without the need for ecosystems and the services they provide". The definition of the resilience by the Stockholm Resilience Centre at: www.stockholmresilience.org/21/research/research-news/2-19-2015-what-is-resilience.html. Last visited on 20th April 2016.

23 CBD Decision X/29, Marine and Coastal Biodiversity, UNEP/CBD/COP/10/27 (2011), para. 13(h) & Annex, para. d.

24 *J. Goodie,* The Ecological Narrative of Risk and the Emergence of Toxic Tort Litigation, in: *Philippopoulos-Mihalopouloulos* (eds.), Law and Ecology – New Environmental Foundations, 2011, p. 66.

25 *C. A. Arnold*, Fourth Generation Environmental Law: Integrationist and Multimodal, William & Mary Environmental Law and Policy Review, 2011 (3), p. 774.

26 *Platjouw, supra*, note 21, p. 161.

have been adopted at the EU[27] and national[28] levels, which provide a legal basis for the implementation of the ecosystem approach.[29] Moreover, the rapid recent development of international environmental law[30] – especially the three-dimensional shift initiated at the Rio conference towards diversification and pluralism[31] – can be linked to a more fundamental paradigm shift in post-modern socio-ecological theory. *Sand* describes this evolvement as a move "from the stereotype of a presumed balance of nature towards a holistic/biocentric 'new ecology' based on dynamic non-equilibrium". The approach, he continues, is only open to natural change, but is ready to control the risks of excessive anthropocentric interference. This 'informational regulation' that enforces the transparency of decision-making, rather than on traditional 'command and control' instruments, has also been defined in terms of 'reflexive environmental law'[32] as a self-organizing process (autopoiesis).[33]

In the following section, the operationalization of the ecosystem approach rationale will be further scrutinized from a legal point of view. The particular interest here is in finding out what kind of general restrictions and opportunities the current legal framework offers for the operationalization of the ecosystem approach-based paradigm to combat the regulatory weaknesses of transnational biodiversity protection. As noted by the Conference of the Parties, an ecosystem

27 Council Directive 2008/56/EC on establishing a framework for community action in the field of marine environmental policy (Marine Strategy Framework Directive), OJ 2008 L 164/19; Council Regulations 1380/2013/EC OJ 2013 L 354/22 & 2015/812/EC 2015 L 133/1 on European Common Fisheries Policy; Council Directives 92/43/EEC on the conservation of natural habitats and of wild fauna and flora OJ 1992 L 206 and 2009/147/EC on the conservation of wild birds OJ 2009 L 20/7 (obtained through the establishment of the NATURA 2000 network); Council Directive 2014/89/EU on establishing a framework for maritime spatial planning, OJ 2014 L 257/135; and Council Directive 2004/35/CE on environmental liability with regards to the prevention and remedying of environmental damage, OJ 2014 L 143.

28 Norway's Act of 19 June 2009 No. 100 Relating to the Management of Biological, Geological and Landscape Diversity.

29 Although the approach was present already in marine related treaties adopted over 30 years ago it gained ultimately wider support when adopted as the primary implementation framework of the Convention on Biological Diversity.

30 Most descriptions of the historical evolution of international environmental law distinguish three or four major 'periods' or 'phases': the traditional era until the 1972 UN Stockholm Conference on the Human Environment; the modern era from Stockholm to the 1992 UN Conference on the Environment and Development (UNCED) in Rio Janeiro; and the post-modern era after Rio. *P. H. Sand*, Evolution of International Law, in: *Bodansky, Brunnèe & Hey* (eds.), The Oxford Handbook of International Environmental Law, 2007, pp. 29 – 43.

31 This three-dimensional shift refers to "[t]he UNCED concept of 'common but differentiated responsibilities' acknowledging the breakdown of traditional egalitarian fictions and the emergence of a new legal poly-centricity; the inter-generational dimension of the 'sustainable development'; and the 'participatory revolution' at Rio preparing the ground not only for subsequent reforms in UN accreditation rules, but also for the public-private partnerships eventually formalized at the Johannesburg World Summit on Sustainable Development". *Sand*, *supra*, note 31, pp. 29 – 43.

32 About 'reflexive law', see note 95.

33 *Sand*, *supra*, note 31, pp. 29 – 43.

is a functioning unit that can operate at any scale, depending upon the problem or issue being addressed.[34] Therefore, this understanding should define the appropriate level for management decisions and actions. This approach will often imply decentralization to the level of local communities.[35] Some issues may, however, require action at higher levels via, for example, transboundary cooperation, or even cooperation at the global level. Since biodiversity loss is an issue that spans national borders, this analysis employs a transnational law perspective.

3. OPERATIONALIZING THE ECOSYSTEM APPROACH-BASED PARADIGM TO COMBAT THE REGULATORY WEAKNESSES OF BIODIVERSITY PROTECTION

3.1. TOWARDS COHERENT LAWS – CREATING LINKAGES

In the case of biodiversity protection, the drivers of change[36] must first be defined to be able to regulate the activities causing biodiversity loss. Although many of these drivers are already being regulated, it is made in an uncoordinated and fragmented manner. Therefore, we need a coherent legal system in order to ensure the integrated management of land, water and living resources to maintain the ecosystem resilience.[37] While the national level coordination is essential for successful governance[38], the role of national policy coordination in promoting regime interaction in natural resources governance should not be overstated. This is especially due to the nature of environmental problems as collective issues between states and states' varying resources.[39] Therefore, this analysis is mainly interested in transnational measures.

---

34 CBD Decision V/6, *supra*, note 15, Principle 11.

35 *Id.*, Principle 2.

36 The major drivers of biodiversity loss have been described with the acronym 'HIPPO' for habitat loss, invasive species, pollution, population (human overpopulation), and overharvesting. *E.O. Wilson*, The Future of Life, 2002, pp. 51 – 51. In addition to these drivers of biodiversity loss, climate change is becoming an increasingly important threat to biodiversity.

37 According to *Platjouw*, a coherent and integrated legal system calls for integration of the governance sectors, the regulatory subject-matters and the governance interests. *Supra*, note 21, pp. 161 – 162.

38 According to the UN's Under-Secretary-General for Legal Affairs "coordinated and strategic national government actions and initiatives in different international forums are crucial for the development of the required interlinkages and synergies", UN Doc A/55/274 (2000), Annex I, para 15.

39 *M. A. Young*, Regime Interaction in Creating, Implementing and Enforcing International Law, in: *M. A. Young*, (eds.) Regime Interaction in International Law – Facing Fragmentation, 2012, pp. 85 – 110.

To begin with, despite the common focus of various multilateral environmental agreements (MEAs) and the unifying principles of international environmental law, the often uncoordinated, *ad hoc* manner development of modern international environmental law has sometimes led to a structural incoherence in the form of duplication, divergence and even conflict between environmental standards and obligations.[40] An example of a conflict between obligations can be found when the Kyoto Protocol[41] promotes planting homogenous young trees at the expense of managing old growth forests – leading to a conflict with obligations established under the Biodiversity Convention.[42, 43] There are also hundreds of MEAs currently in force, dealing with various environmental issues – six of these focused on biodiversity affairs solely.[44] Additionally, it should be borne in mind that biodiversity preservation is essential to the achievement of the goals articulated in various international regimes[45] and that the drivers of ecosystem degradation and biodiversity loss are regulated many times, even outside of the actual environmental agreements. *Caddell*, for instance, criticizes the inefficient convention structures, with diverse institutional priorities noting that a great many other regimes than those, expressly called "biodiversity related", relate to biodiversity.[46]

The fragmentation of the connected issues into several separate agreements leads to "regulatory inefficiencies stemming from overlapping provisions in agreements, inconsistencies in obligations, significant gaps in coverage, and duplication of goals and responsibilities".[47] In this way, modern environmental law disregards the cumulative environmental impact created by all human activity. Instead, as *Pardy* argues, human actions are regulated as isolated events: "Environmental law consists of different regulatory regimes that apply

40 E.g. *K. N. Scott*, International Environmental Governance: Managing Fragmentation through Institutional Connection, Melbourne Journal of International Law, 2011 (1), p. 180; *R. Caddell*, The Integration of Multilateral Environmental Agreements: Lessons from the Biodiversity-Related Conventions, Yearbook of International Environmental Law, 2011 (11), p. 37.

41 Kyoto Protocol to the Framework Convention on Climate Change, opened for signature 11 December 1997, 2303 UNTS.

42 Convention on Biological Diversity, opened for signature 5 June 1992, 1760 UNTS.

43 *K. N. Scott*, *supra*, note 41, p.180.

44 The Convention on Biological Diversity (1992); the Convention on Conservation of Migratory Species; the Convention on International Trade in Endangered Species of Wild Fauna and Flora (1975); the International Treaty on Plant Genetic Resources for Food and Agriculture (2004); the Ramsar Convention on Wetlands (1971); the World Heritage Convention (1972); and International Treaty on Plant Genetic resources for Food and Agriculture (ITPGRFA) (2001). More at: www.cbd.int/brc/.

45 Biodiversity is especially crucial to the adaptation to climate change under the UN Framework Convention on Climate Change (1992). The biodiversity preservation is also fundamentally connected to the realization of human rights. See e.g. *E. Louka*, Biodiversity and Human Rights: The International Rules for the Protection of Biodiversity, 2002.

46 *Caddell, supra*, note 41, p. 74.

47 *E. B. Weiss*, International environmental Law: Contemporary Issues and the Emergence of a New World Order, Georgetown Law Journal, 1993 (3), p. 699.

to different kinds of environmental hazards or natural resources – containing fact-specific standards that are applied (or not) to one situation at a time."[48] As some scholars suggest, the fragmentation of international environmental law into multiple MEA regimes is one crucial reason behind the continuing biodiversity loss.[49] As an example, *Long* points out the problem of invasive species, which is widely regarded as the second most important driver of biodiversity loss: The haphazard coverage of this driver highlights a gap in international legal coverage of biodiversity issues and suggests that the fragmentation of the issues embracing biodiversity loss works against an effective response to the problem.[50] The drawing of functional connections between biodiversity preservation and other environmental concerns in law have, thus, been seen to play an important part in the solution. This requires not only the internal linking of environmental laws – but also linking biodiversity preservation with other overlapping areas of law.[51]

Since there is no internationally binding environmental integration principle[52], solutions for managing potentially inconsistent obligations and other regulatory inefficiencies between different regimes are often pursued by creating cooperative arrangements or other institutional linkages between agreements.[53] However, despite the increased recognition of these connections by, the CBD institutions

---

48 *B. Pardy,* In Search of the Holy Grail of Environmental Law: A Rule to Solve the Problem, JSDLP – RDPDD, 2005 (1), p. 38.

49 Compared to fundamental market failures, fragmentation may still be a relatively minor cause of continuing biodiversity loss. Nonetheless, international legal responses are fragmented and issue-based according to the objective of individual treaty systems, resulting in differing or even contradictory positions adopted across or within various treaty bodies. *E. K. Rakhyun & K. Bosselmann,* International Environmental Law in the Anthropocene: Towards a Purposive System of Multilateral Environmental Agreements. Transnational Environmental Law, 2013 (2), p. 286. The inconsistencies have also increased the risk of problem shifting by improving the performance on one system by degrading another e.g. M. *Nilsson & Å. Persson,* Can Earth System Interactions be Governed? Governance Functions for Linking Climate Change Mitigation With Land Use, Freshwater and Biodiversity Protection, Ecological Economics, 2012, pp. 61-71. See also *Long*, who categorizes international legal instruments to demonstrate that the fragmentation in international environmental law is problematic for the global effort to protect biodiversity. *A. Long,* Developing Linkages to Preserve Biodiversity, Yearbook of International Environmental Law, 2011.

50 *Long* suggests that invasive species would likely be the subject of an MEA if the biodiversity regimes resulted from a comprehensive assessment of biodiversity protection needs. Instead, the problem is now addressed to some extent by several conventions. *Long, supra,* note 50, p.53.

51 *Long, supra,* note 50, p. 42.

52 By comparison, in the European Union the environmental integration principle (11 TFEU) has quite an established role in granting the Union the competence to take legally binding measures to ensure that protection of the environment is at least taken into consideration when decisions are being taken in other fields. However, *Jans* criticizes the Lisbon version of the integration principle for no longer having the special status of a "general principle of EC law". *J. H. Jans,* Stop the Integration Principle?, Fordham International Law Journal, 2011, pp. 1533 – 1547.

53 *Caddell, supra,* note 41, p. 38 – 39; *Scott, supra,* note 13, p. 2.

for instance[54], policy implementation has allegedly too rarely been affected by this recognition and linkages between biodiversity and other priorities are often left outside the scope of law.[55] One fundamental reason for this is the inherent fragmentation of international law, resulting from the diversity of national legal systems that participate in it.[56] Indeed, states′ sovereignty over their natural resources comprises a momentous obstacle to transnational environmental governance. What also appears to be problematic is the legal autonomy of the treaties. Many conventions also claim to be inward-looking and either averse or unable to give away part of what they perceive to be their sovereignty[57], which can be seen to reflect a translation of the national sovereignty of states into institutional sovereignty of treaty regimes.[58] Indeed, the states' lack of parallel membership of the regimes, whose interlinking is desirable, or unwillingness to agree to allow normative and institutional interplay gives rise to questions of legitimacy – thereby severely hampering the regime's interaction.[59] The problem is, as *Johansdottir* observes, that if a treaty contains no specific duties around ecological sustainability, then the default position is state sovereignty, with its right to exploit natural resources.[60] Consequently, the lack of global commitment contributes to the favour of national sovereignty, which is the equivalent to exclusive private property.[61]

---

54 The CBD regime has established institutional linkages with other biodiversity conventions (especially through the Biodiversity Liaison Group), non-biodiversity centered multilateral environmental agreements (the CBD works with the UNFCCC, and the Desertification Convention through the Joint Liaison Group) and non-environmental international regimes that affect behavior driving biodiversity loss (partnership with the FAO in the implementation of its agricultural biodiversity work program).

55 "Although the regimes aimed at climate change, pollution, biodiversity loss, and degradation of land all embrace fundamental international environmental law precepts and all aim to improve the human relationship with the natural world, each does so through a shattered manner". *Long, supra*, note 50, p. 47.

56 International Law Commission, Fragmentation of international law: difficulties arising from the diversification and expansion of international law, A/CN.4/L.702 (2006), p. 6.

57 U.N. Multilateral Environmental Agreements: A Summary, doc. UNEP/IGM/1/INF/1, (2001), para. 42.

58 *J. Bartelson,* The Concept of Sovereignty Revisited, European Journal of International Law, 2006 (2), pp. 463-74.

59 *M. A. Young*, Regime Interaction in Creating, Implementing and Enforcing International Law, in *M. A. Young* (eds.) Regime Interaction in International Law – Facing Fragmentation, 2012, pp.85 – 110.

60 There is also little incentive for states to be serious about global responsibilities if they can rely on their fault position. *A. Johannsdottir,* The Significance of the Default – A Study in Environmental Law Methodology with Emphasis on Ecological Sustainability and International Biodiversity Law, 2009.

61 *K. Bosselmann*, Property Rights and Sustainability: Can They Be Reconciled?, in *D. Grinlinton, & P. Taylor* (eds.) Property Rights and Sustainability: The Evolution of Property Rights to Meet Ecological Challenges, 2011, pp. 23 – 42.

Significant challenges currently exist for the formation and maintenance of effective linkages between the biodiversity-related conventions.[62] Inter alia, when it comes to the coordination of climate and biodiversity regimes, *Hodas* reminds us that "a broad mandate for the climate regime's treaty or administrative bodies to cooperate with the CBD could lead to the perception that state sovereignty is eroded by "importing" concepts or rules from the CBD".[63] A classic barrier to this kind of cooperation between the United Nations Framework Convention on Climate Change (UNFCCC) and the Convention on Biological Diversity (CBD) is that the US is party to the former, but not to the latter.[64] Moreover, if an MEA regime seeks to extend its scope to link with other agreements or organizations, "due care needs to be exercised to ensure it is not seen as an attempt to intrude on the work of other bodies".[65]

Therefore, according to *Long*, in considering the role of institutional linkages, we must consider where and how far institutional linkages should be pursued given resource and political constraints. Moreover, institutional linkage should not be considered as a necessary requirement to issue-linkage, because "political and bureaucratic delays and qualification may, indeed, prevent programs from fully and rapidly embracing issue-linked program elements".[66] *Long* also notes, that "while the extensive development of multiple biodiversity-related regimes provides a rather obvious example of institutional fragmentation, the root cause of this situation is the fragmentation of the issue area into separate treaties".[67] Hence, he proposes that we should start developing programs that target "spaces" of particularly significant issue linkage[68] that affects biodiversity. These programs, according to him, may be developed between or within regimes.[69] Accordingly,

---

62 According to *Caddell* this results in particular for three reasons, namely: strategic uncertainty (the precise objective of synergy arrangements has been little explored); disparate working practices (the working practices of many conventions are not conducive to promoting co-operation between them; and resource implications (resource constraints continue to undermine the capacity of MEAs to maintain effective linkages. He thus proposes that smaller synergy projects that are adequately supported, and provide clarity of purpose, objective, and responsibility should be adopted as the optimal model if inter-treaty co-operation in the biodiversity sector. *Supra*, note 41, p. 68 – 74.

63 "Any effort by actors in one regime to influence rule development in another will be limited by the extent to which memberships are congruent". *H. van Asselt,* Managing the Fragmentation of International Environmental Law: Forests at the Intersection of the Climate and Biodiversity Regimes, New York University Journal of International Law and Politics, 2012 (4), pp. 1205-78.

64 In its submission to the UNFCCC, the US noted that the CBD and the UNFCCC have a distinct legal character, mandate and membership, and insisted that biodiversity issues be dealt with outside the UNFCCC. *Rakhyun & Bosselmann, supra*, note 50, p. 297.

65 *Id.*, at p. 298.

66 *Long, supra*, note 50, p. 61.

67 *Id.*, at p. 50.

68 By 'issue linkage' *Long* refers to measures that respond to the artificial separation of ecologically connected issues according to legal authority. *Id.*, at p. 48.

69 *Id.*, at p. 43.

there is a clear potential in developing linked programs to provide multiple benefits.[70]

Perhaps the greatest development opportunity for this kind of issue linkage is, as *Long* suggests, within the program of 'reducing emissions from deforestation and forest degradation in developing countries; and the role of conservation, sustainable management of forests and enhancement of forest carbon stocks in developing countries' (REDD+).[71] The primary focus of REDD+ is climate regulation through reducing greenhouse gas emissions and increasing carbon sequestration by forests, but Parties to the UNFCCC have also agreed that REDD+ actions should take the multiple functions of forests and other ecosystems into account.[72] REDD+ has the potential to achieve important benefits for biodiversity conservation and to secure the provision of ecosystem services, such as water regulation, soil erosion prevention and the provision of timber and non-timber forest products. Hence, different contract-based mechanisms should be seen as a potential way to integrate the multiple drivers of biodiversity loss and ecosystem degradation.

While the REDD+ can be criticized for also posing certain risks to biodiversity[73], and as a financial carbon offset mechanism it also gives rise to ethically and morally dubious arguments[74], it does not seem likely to achieve genuine coherence in natural resources` management by mere command model mechanisms either. Even the ecosystem approach recognizes a need to understand and manage the ecosystem in an economic context, emphasizing that: "[a]lignment of incentives allows those who control the resource to benefit and ensures that those who generate environmental costs will pay".[75] Different contract-based mechanisms also possess the potential to fill certain regulatory gaps, involve traditionally non-contracting parties and to introduce innovative monitoring institutions. However, as the experience confirms, these gains cannot be realized through sole contractual instruments either, but there seems to be a clear call here for multiple mechanisms.[76]

---

70 *Id.*, at p. 73.

71 *Id.*, at p. 69.

72 U.N. FCCC/CP/2010/7/Add.1: Decision 1/CP.16.

73 For example, if forests are protected from conversion to agriculture, but the drivers of conversion are not tackled, other ecosystems are likely to be threatened instead. More on problem shifting in *Nilsson & Persson*, *supra*, note 50.

74 REDD+ has been criticized for being a new form of colonialism in which industrialized Northern countries use the natural resources of developing countries as sponges for their pollution, instead of reducing greenhouse gas emissions at the source. E.g. *J. Cabello & T. Gilbertson*, A Colonial Mechanism to Enclose Lands: A Critical Review of two REDD+-Focused Special Issues, Ephemera Theory & Politics in Organization, 2012, pp. 162-180. About the criticism on commodification of nature see also the discussion on the two paradigms of sustainable development in e.g. *E. Neumeyer*, Weak Versus Strong Sustainability: Exploring the Limits of Two Opposing Paradigms, 3rd ed., 2010.

75 CBD Decision V/6, *supra*, note 15, Principle 4.

76 *N. A. Affolder*, The Private Life of Environmental Treaties, The American Journal of International Law, 2009 (3), pp. 510 – 525.

3.2. TOWARDS ADAPTIVE LAW – THE PRECAUTIONARY PRINCIPLE REVISITED

There is yet another important flaw in the contemporary laws, in addition to their structural incoherence; namely, their incompatibility with uncertainty. Indeed, the functions of the dynamic and complex socio-ecological systems are often poorly understood. There is also uncertainty over the value of certain ecosystems and their services, and uncertainty about the potential effects of certain policies and projects on the functioning of ecosystems.[77]

In ecology, the equilibrium paradigm has long been replaced with a complex, stochastic non-equilibrium one.[78] This is to say that ecologists have developed examples indicating that ecosystems and natural resources exist in a variety of stable states, instead of returning to equilibrium. The feature that mediates transition among these states is called resilience.[79] Resilience – or the ability of a system to cope with inevitable changes – is, thus, the precondition for the health of that system.[80]

Under the non-equilibrium paradigm, all natural resources management is an ongoing experiment instead of a series of discrete, final decisions.[81] The challenge is that the law demands certainty. Accordingly, there is a requirement for eliminating randomness from the legal decision-making activity and to protect legitimate expectations.[82] In other words, whereas human actions in modern democracies adhere to the rule of law, the prerequisites for ecological resilience depend on the laws of nature. While sustaining certainty in resource allocation in society[83], the current legal framework consequently assumes a globally stable

---

77 See more in *D. B. Botkin*, Discordant Harmonies: a New Ecology for the Twenty-first Century, 1990; *L. H. Gunderson & C. S. Holling* (eds.), Panarchy: Understanding Transformations in Human and Natural Systems, 2002; *L. H. Gunderson & L. Pritchard* (eds.), Resilience and the Behavior of Large-Scale Systems, 2002; *L. H. Gunderson et al.*, Foundations of Ecological Resilience, 2009; *B. Walker & D. Salt*, Resilience Thinking: Sustaining Ecosystems and People in a Changing World, 2006.

78 *A. D. Tarlock*, The Nonequilibrium Paradigm in Ecology and the Partial Unraveling of Environmental Law, Loyola of Los Angeles Law Review, 1994 (3), p. 1123.

79 Scientists speak of a panarchy, as a nested set of adaptive cycles. Because adaptive cycles operate over specific ranges of scale, a system's resilience is dependent upon the interactions between structure and dynamics at multiple scales. See e.g. *L. H. Gunderson & C. S. Holling* (eds.), Panarchy: Understanding Transformations in Human and Natural Systems, 2002.

80 This study considers ecosystem resilience closely comparable with ecosystem integrity, see *supra*, notes 17 and 18.

81 Committee on Scientific and Technical Criteria for Fed: Acquisition of Lands for Conservation, National Research Council, Setting Priorities for Land Conservation, 1993, pp. 113 – 138.

82 "The process of deciding environmental regulations has flexibility, but once regulations are agreed upon, regulations are rigid in nature ("front-end"). By setting environmental regulations at the front-end, the legal process guarantees certainty for legal and economic interests". *A. S. Garmestani, C. R. Allen & M. H. Benson*, Can Law Foster Social-Ecological Resilience? Ecology and Society, 2013 (2), p. 37.

83 Legal institutions are prone to give primary value to the resilience of, especially, economic institutions, such as production of and transactions in consumer goods and private property

nature of the environment.[84] Indeed, there has been a tendency in the past to manage components of biodiversity either as protected or non-protected.[85] While the traditional, "bean counter" mentality-based method of measuring the performance of environmental law is useful to the command-and-control regime, it does not contribute to adaptive approaches.[86] Also, while a formalized legal process is important for enforceability, it very much complicates the management of resilience, which in light of our current understanding, is the prerequisite for the functioning of ecosystems and, therefore, for the maintenance of biodiversity. Indeed, rigid legal rules prevent the flexibility needed to adapt to changing and unpredictable conditions and place pressure on the legal system to allow means of flexibility through the non-enforcement or invalidation of the rules. The complex and uncertain dynamics of interconnected ecosystems and social systems, on the other hand, require that resource regulators and managers have a certain amount of discretion.[87]

An unfortunate consequence of the tension between legal and socio-ecological systems is that nature and human relationships are regulated and managed, based on historic conditions and linear patterns of change. This arguably makes the law ill-suited for many of the urgent environmental issues.[88] One could even claim that the inability of law to the account for uncertainty in the management process indicates that the law is at odds with science.[89] In addition, it is unlikely that the principle of sustainability can be realized through the rigid command-and-control regimes.[90] Indeed, environmental policy is challenged by the fact that there are often no discrete sources or clearly traced lines of causation. Complex adaptive systems are, as *Ruhl* puts it, "excruciatingly hard for researchers to understand, and thus even harder for law to wrestle under control".[91] However,

---

rights. *C. A. Arnold & L. H. Gunderson,* Adaptive Law and Resilience, Legal Studies Research Paper Series Paper, 2013, p. 10429.

84 *J. B. Ruhl,* Climate Change and the Endangered Species Act: Building Bridges to the No-Analog Future, Boston University Law Review, 2008 (1); *R. K Craig,* "Stationarity Is Dead" – Long Live Transformation: Five Principles for Climate Change Adaptation Law, Harvard Environmental Law Review, 2010 (9).

85 CBD Decision V/6, *supra*, note 15, Principle 9.

86 *J. B. Ruhl,* Thinking of Environmental Law as a Complex Adaptive System: How to Clean up the Environment by Making a Mess of Environmental Law, Houston Law Review, 1997 (4), p. 997.

87 *Arnold & Gunderson, supra*, note 84, p. 10436.

88 *J. B. Ruhl,* Regulation by Adaptive Management – is it Possible?, Minnesota Journal of Law, Science & Technology, 2006, pp. 21 – 57.; *A. S. Garmestani et al.,* Panarchy, Adaptive Management and Governance: Policy Options for Building Resilience, Nebraska Law Review, 2009. See also *Tarlock*, who observes that "environmental law is, to a greater extent than other areas of law, a product of external values not rooted in the environment of human dignity and thus it is difficult to integrate into our legal system". *Supra*, note 79, p. 1134.

89 *B. Karkkainen,* Panarchy and adaptive change: around the loop and back again. Minnesota Journal of Law, Science & Technology, 2005 (7), 59 – 77.

90 *Ruhl, supra*, note 87, p. 996.

91 *J. B. Ruhl, supra*, note 89, pp. 22 – 24.

McDonald & Styles note that the incorporation of uncertainty into decisions about resource allocation, development approvals and the land management of these mechanisms in statutory regimes involves fairly minor legislative amendment. It is arguably their effective implementation and enforcement that will require more fundamental, political and institutional change.[92]

The paradigm shift in ecology towards non-equilibrium affects the fundamental justifications for environmental and natural resources law, the relationship between law and scientific research, the strategies to promote environmental values and the rules that structure environmental decision making.[93] *Bosselmann* further encourages us to reclaim the full meaning of the rule of law by insisting on its moral basis, given that: "[a] rule of law without any content is not worth having". Since the core content of the rule of law has always been defined around human dignity and security, *Bosselmann* rightfully claims the integrity of ecological systems as being the single most important imperative.[94]

Resilience-based adaptive governance will require organizational learning, cross-scale linkages and adaptive capacity to govern in a more flexible, iterative and adaptive manner.[95] Whereas administrative decisions are traditionally made at the beginning of a project, making it practically difficult to change course where new information or problems are identified, adaptive law[96] recognizes uncertainty

---

92 *J. McDonald & M. C. Styles*, Legal Strategies for Adaptive Management under Climate Change, Journal of Environmental Law, 2014 (1), pp. 51 – 52. See also *Karkkainen*, who notes that it does not seem very difficult to reduce the adaptive management procedures and modes of justification to a set of administrative law principles aimed at providing the transparency, accountability, and objective boundaries that are currently lacking. *B. Karkkainen*, *supra*, note 90, p. 75.

93 *Tarlock*, *supra*, note 79, pp. 1134-37.

94 *K. Bosselmann*, The Rule of Law Grounded in the Earth – Ecological Integrity as a Grundnorm, in *M. Vestra & M. Vilela* (eds.), The Earth Charter, Ecological Integrity and Social Movements 2014 p. 10.

95 Historically, the idea of adaptive governance can be linked to reflexive law: The concept of reflexive law arises from both systems and critical theories, more specifically the systems theory of *Niklas Luhmann* and the discourse theory of *Jürgen Habermas*. It shifts theoretical focus from the level of norms to the level of communication and provides a procedural process with room for innovation. See more in *A. S. Garmestani & M. H. Benson*, A Framework for Resilience-based Governance of Social-ecological Systems. Ecology and Society, 2013 (1), p. 9.

96 As a response to the maladaptive features of U.S. legal system *Arnold & Garmestani* have drafted an adaptive law framework featuring the following categories: 1) multiplicity of articulated goals; 2) polycentric, multimodal, and integrationist structure; 3) adaptive methods based on standards, flexibility, discretion, and regard for context; and 4) iterative legal-pluralist processes with feedback loops, learning, and accountability. *Arnold & Gunderson*, *supra*, note 84, p. 10428. *Garmestani, Allen & Benson* call for an "adaptive law" approach and suggest we: utilize adaptive management and adaptive governance; reform administrative law: "front-end" to "backend"; require communication, monitoring and intermediaries; and account for scale to integrate law and social-ecological resilience. *Garmestani, Allen & Benson*, *supra*, note 83, p. 37.

as an inherent feature in natural systems.[97] Adaptive law also acknowledges the limitations of science to make accurate predictions about future environmental impacts. It further recognises that the 'front loading' of decisions is a critical weakness, given that it leads to decisions that are inevitably based on incomplete information.[98]

As for the adaptive capacity in law, it increases discretion when value judgments need to be performed concerning socio-ecological systems.[99] Therefore, there is a need for appropriate and relevant standards to govern the exercise of discretion. The standards should focus the decision makers on maintaining the resilience of ecosystems and social systems. An adaptive law favours incremental and gradual changes that transition experimentally to new standards or arrangements, while monitoring, assessing and adjusting these changes and their effects.[100] Instead of seeking "maximum" and "high-level" sustainable yields, law- and policy-makers should, therefore, consider the alternative of "clearly sustainable" standards that require revisions as better information becomes available (principled flexibility).[101] In short, resilience science informed adaptive legal system calls for adaptive *methods*, methods based on context-regarding standards, tolerance for uncertainty and flexible discretionary decision making. It also favours adaptive *processes* based on iterative legal-pluralist actions with feedback loops, learning and accountability.[102]

With regards to the adaptive resilience governance there is a strong linkage to an internationally acknowledged principle; namely, the precautionary principle. *Craig* argues that due to the ecological uncertainties, natural resources laws should promote resilience by re-envisioning management rules to more precautionary ones than have been employed in the past.[103] Indeed, the precautionary principle entails taking the vulnerability of the environment, the limitations of science, the availability of alternatives and the need for long-term, holistic environmental considerations into account – thereby operating

97 "The ecosystem approach requires adaptive management to deal with the complex and dynamic nature of ecosystems and the absence of complete knowledge or understanding of their functioning." CBD Decision V/6, *supra*, note 15, para. A) 4.

98 E.g. *S. A. Shapiro & R. L. Glicksman*, The APA and the back-end of regulation: procedures for informal adjudication, Administrative Law Review, 2004, pp. 1159 – 1178.

99 *Platjouw, supra* 21, note, pp. 164 – 172.

100 *Arnold & Gunderson, supra*, note 84, p. 10,438. As an example, Professor *John Dernbach* notes that several of the processes in the Paris Agreement (Paris Climate Conference (COP21) in December 2015) may be understood in terms of reflexive law and governance: Also, reflexive approaches improve the capacity of governmental institutions and other entities to learn about themselves and their actions and also stimulate them to use this information to make appropriate changes. Paris to Earth: Act Locally Within a Global Framework, December 13th 2015, available on the Internet at: http://johndernbach.com/2015/12/470/. Last visited on 20th April 2016.

101 *R. K. Craig*, 'Stationarity is Dead' – Long Live Transformation: Five Principles for Climate Change Adaptation Law, Harvard Environmental Law Review, 2010 (1), pp. 46 – 48.

102 *Arnold & Gunderson, supra*, note 84, p. 10428. See also note 97.

103 *Craig, supra*, note 102, p. 48.

as a safeguard against asymmetric information and imperfect monitoring.[104] Hence, the ecosystem approach-based understanding seems to be closely linked to the rationale of the precautionary measures. *Trouwborst* observes that both the ecosystem approach and the precautionary principle are part of a recent trend in international law – striving away from reactive and fragmented environmental policies. He further suggests that the ecosystem approach and the precautionary principle both represent a more holistic and proactive response to the failure of ad hoc approaches to environmental management. Both can also be considered to be the basic features of a sustainable use of natural resources and bring similar significance to scientific information. In addition, they mandate similar implementing measures, calling for a diminution of the stress of anthropocentric causes on ecosystems.[105] However, it should be noted, that despite the above resemblances, the precautionary principle and the ecosystem approach cannot be equated; they do possess certain similar characteristics and can, thus, be used to complement each other.

While the precautionary principle already has extensive support by states in legal and policy instruments[106] and in international case law[107], the legal status of the ecosystem approach still seems somewhat unspecified.[108] Therefore, by possessing many converging features with the ecosystem approach and its management strategies, the precautionary principle is perhaps the key element in legitimizing more adaptive natural resources governance at the transnational law

104 *W. Burns*, Potential Causes of Action for Climate Impacts under the United Nations Fish Stocks Agreement, Climate Law Reporter, 2007 (7).

105 *A. Trouwborst*, The Precautionary Principle and the Ecosystem Approach in International Law: Differences, Similarities and Linkages, RECIEL, 2009 (1), pp. 26 – 37.

106 The precautionary principle can be found in a great variety of intergovernmental declarations, resolutions and action programs and more than sixty multilateral treaties covering multiple environmental issues. It has also become an important tenet of EU environmental law and policy. A growing number of states are also implementing the precautionary principle in their domestic environmental laws and policies.

107 The principle has been "incorporated into a growing number of international treaties and other instruments [which in turn] has initiated a trend towards making this approach part of customary international law". See the ITLOS, Seabed Disputes Chamber, Responsibilities and Obligations of States Sponsoring Persons and Entities with Respect to Activities in the Area, Advisory Opinion of 1 Feb. 2011, at para. 135.

108 Despite the uncertainties of the precautionary principle`s legal status (e.g. due to the differing views between the EU and the USA) *Birnie and Boyle* suggest that its wide international adoption shows that it "does have a legally important core on which there is international consensus – that in performing their obligations of environmental protection and sustainable use of natural resources states cannot rely on scientific uncertainty to justify inaction when there is enough evidence to establish the possibility of a risk of serious harm, even if there is as yet no proof of harm. In this sense the precautionary principle is a principle of international law on which decision makers and courts may rely in the same way that they may be influenced by the principle of sustainable development". *P. Birnie & A. Boyle*, International Law & the Environment, 2002, pp. 118 – 120. According to *Trouwborst*, the precautionary principle not only is a standard feature of modern environmental treaties but also must be deemed part of customary international law. The ecosystem approach is neither". *Supra*, note 106, p. 26, 36.

level. Indeed, as *Trouwborst* argues, "[t]he ecosystem approach should be taken into account in the application of the precautionary principle".[109] However, regardless of the wide recognition of the legal status of the precautionary principle, it is still a rather complex and controversial concept.[110] It has, among other things, been criticized for being ill-defined and, thus, too vacuous to offer any useful guidance for decision-making.[111]

I, therefore, suggest that adaptive law methods and processes be used as regulative tools to operationalize the precautionary principle – thereby also helping to mitigate the problems related to an excess of discretion[112] and equipping the principle with value-based aspects.[113] This decision framework would enable what I call 'cautious learning'. Accordingly, "clearly sustainable" standards (that require revisions where better information becomes available)[114] would allow decisions, with not so a lot of precaution involved, when the uncertainty in question is not particularly high. When, again, the uncertainty is considered to be high – but inaction is undesirable – then it would be best to act incrementally. This would include acting, while at the same time being open for change, if improved knowledge or gathered experience implies that actions need to be altered.[115]

---

109 *Trouwborst* continues, that the precautionary principle is also to be regarded as an integral component of applying the ecosystem approach. *Trouwborst, supra*, note 106, p. 36.

110 *P. Kelly*, The Twilight of Customary International Law, Virginia Journal of International Law, 2000 (2), pp. 227 – 233.

111 E.g. *Bodansky* argues that the precautionary principle cannot serve as a regulatory standard because it does not specify how much (pre)caution should be taken. *D. Bodansky*, Scientific Uncertainty and the Precautionary Principle. Environment, 1991 p. 5.

112 The interplay between the precautionary principle and adaptive management has indeed been discussed before. For instance, *Tarlock* points, that the adaptive management corrects the bias of the precautionary principle towards no action in the face of uncertainty and the opposite bias for immediate fixes. *D. Tarlock*, Ecosystems, in D. *Bodansky, J. Brunée & E. Hey* (eds.), The Oxford Handbook of International Environmental Law, 2014, pp. 581 – 582. *McDonald & Styles* observe, that current approaches to fisheries management in Australia are premised on adaptive management being used as a tool to give effect to the precautionary principle, and that courts in Canada and Australia have taken same kind of approach in several cases. In some judgments, they claim, "the two concepts are used interchangeably, as if they operate in the same way. In others, adaptive management is the mechanism used to control for the margin of error in relation to uncertain impacts and to achieve proportionality and cost-effectiveness as required under the precautionary principle". *J. McDonald & M. C. Styles, supra*, note 93, p. 39.

113 This would be important since the normative underpinnings of the precautionary principle have received only little attention albeit the degree to which we are prepared to take precautions is related to the values which we attach to the nature and human wellbeing. *M. Ahteensuu & P. Sandin*, The Precautionary Principle, in *S. Roeser et. al.* (eds.), Handbook of Risk Theory, 2012, p. 974.

114 *Craig, supra*, note 102, pp. 46 – 48.

115 This idea comes straight from *Doremus*, who only uses the term 'structured learning'. *H. Doremus*, Precaution, Science, and Learning While Doing in Natural Resource Management, Washington Law review, 2007, pp. 547 – 579.

4. CONCLUSIONS

The notion of an ecosystem approach is repeatedly referred to in legal and political international documents and its components are supported by an increasing number of legal scholars. Therefore, its rationale has unquestionably claimed a place in natural resources law. In this chapter, the ecosystem approach has been used as a method of research to frame the important legal weak points of the transboundary governance of biodiversity – and to shed some light on how to overcome them. Firstly, there is an urgent need for the increasingly efficient addressing of the drivers of ecosystem degradation and biodiversity loss; these drivers often do not exist within a single regime. From the perspective of an ecosystem approach-paradigm, it would thus be accordant to create linkages in and between different regimes, given that a social-ecological system with many redundant connections is in all likelihood more resilient than a system that has few connections.[116] While the fragmentation of law is not *the* problem, as such, but merely a character of modern law[117], the failure of regimes to communicate has led to inefficient and deficient natural resource management.

Contemporary law also evidences a tension concerning the operationalization of the ecosystem approach by limiting the execution of cross-sectoral connections. This justifiably brings forth a question about the dogmatic values behind contemporary legal architecture. As the land health depends upon the integrity of the ecological whole, the operationalization of this premise requires a new understanding of sovereignty – tantamount to private property. This means that within the legal architecture the reflection on the "old semantics of environment as resource and of the human as center" – would need to change.[118]

There is also a clear need to break down the modern dichotomy between public and private, state and non-state, international and domestic, hard law and soft law, etc. and to call for more flexible mechanisms. The best changes often contribute to ecologically informed inter-linkages by being based on institutional informative cooperation and, increasingly so, on contractual mechanisms. Moreover, the private sector is also getting involved in treaty implementation. Indeed, the efforts made by private corporations, aiming at complying with e.g. environmental treaties, is an ever-increasing phenomenon, which highlights environmental treaties and their becoming linked in a new way.[119]

---

116 This applies not only for ecological systems but also for social institutions. *B. Walker et. al.*, Resilience, Adaptability and Transformability in Social-ecological Systems. Ecology and Society, 2004 (2), p. 5.

117 Also, tolerance and pluralism are not only compatible with institutional fragmentation, but its best justification. *M. Koskenniemi & P. Leino*, Fragmentation of International Law? Postmodern Anxieties, Leiden Journal of International Law, 2002, p. 579.

118 See e.g. *Turner, supra*, note 4, p. 68.

119 For instance, using the UNESCO World Heritage Convention as an example, *Affolder* highlights the phenomenon of corporations conforming their behavior to environmental treaty requirements in *Affolder, supra*, note 77.

As for the paradigm shift to non-equilibrium and resilience science, the legal system seems to be at odds with the ecological ones in many ways. Since the uncertain future of ecological systems will require cautious management measures, it is up to the social systems – including the legal one – to adapt. This calls on us to adopt a central argument of environmental ethics; namely, the need to collapse the modern dichotomy between fact and value in order to develop new resource management principles. Accordingly, *Tarlock* concludes that "through science, simple and sophisticated, we have increasingly come to see natural processes as phenomena to be respected rather than manipulated".[120] Moreover, in the words of *Cullinan*, "the crucial question is not how to use the rule of law to protect the environment but how to align legal systems with Earth`s laws".[121] Therefore, we might have to revise the tenets of natural resources law.

An adaptive legal system provides us with the much-needed humility and responsibility necessary for constant learning, something required in order to further sustainable development. Indeed, it calls for adaptive methods – based on tolerance of uncertainty, flexible discretionary decision making standards and iterative, learning based processes.[122] Given that governance requires the guidance of a legal principle and enforcement by the judicial branch[123], I suggest that the precautionary principle serve here as a good reference point for legal reasoning and interpretation. We are, after all, witnessing the rise of a complex, stochastic non-equilibrium paradigm in ecology, and until – if ever – the scientific absence is replaced by scientific presence, it is the precautionary principle specifically that safeguards the ecological space for the future.[124] On the basis of the above, the precautionary principle seems like the most compatible presentee to legitimize the existing socio-ecological paradigm in the transboundary context. If it were to be further enriched with adaptive law methods and processes, then it could more effectively contribute to adaptive law strategies on different governance levels.

---

120 *Tarlock, supra*, note 79, p. 1137.

121 *C. Cullinan*, The Rule of Nature`s Law, in *C. Voigt*, *C.* (eds.): Rule of Law for Nature – New Dimensions and Ideas in Environmental Law, 2013, p. 108.

122 *Arnold & Gunderson, supra*, note 84, p. 10428.

123 *L. H. M. de Lima Demange*, The Principle of Resilience, Pace Environmental Law Review, 2013 (2), p. 711.

124 *A. Philippopoulos-Mihalopoulos,* Absent Environments – Theorising Environmental Law and the City, 2007, p. 133. Environmental law is also intensively connected to science, and "we need more science to avert risks, but more science breeds more risks". Therefore, the precautionary principle has potentially indispensable importance in the ever more technical world. *A. Philippopoulos-Mihalopoulos,* The Silence of the Sirens: Environmental Risk and the Precautionary Principle, Law and Critique, 1999 (2), pp. 175-97.

CHAPTER 5
BETTER EXPERTISE THROUGH INSTITUTIONAL LINKAGES*
The Case of the Mediterranean Basin

Guillaume Futhazar
Ph.D Candidate in Public Law - OT-Med /Aix Marseille Univ, Univ Toulon, CNRS, DICE, CERIC

1. INTRODUCTION

The Mediterranean Basin encapsulates all of the global issues of international environmental law. Identified as a hot spot for biodiversity[1], its environment is under constant anthropic pressure, resulting from the urbanization of coastlines, intense marine traffic, land-based pollution, overfishing or invasive alien species.[2] Additionally, despite the strong involvement of the scientific community in these issues, there are still numerous questions left unanswered, be they about the state of the Mediterranean environment or on the exact impact of human activities.[3]

In light of these various threats and uncertainties – that are not exclusive to the Mediterranean Basin –, States have sought, from early on, to co-operate in order to mitigate their impact on the environment.[4] As a result, the region is nowadays characterized by the existence of numerous international multilateral

---

* This study is a contribution to two different initiatives: The Circulex project (ANR-12-GLOB-0001-03 CIRCULEX), funded by the French National Agency for Research, and the Labex OT-Med (no. ANR-11-LABX-0061) funded by the French Government 'Investissements d'Avenir' program of the French National Research Agency (ANR) through the A*MIDEX project (Doc ANR-11-IDEX-0001-02).
The author wishes to thank all the other Ph.D candidates of the CERIC whose inputs and ideas were essential to the drafting of this article. Particular thanks go to Clio Bouillard whose help and comments were especially valuable.

1 *A. Cuttelod, N. García, D. Abdul Malak, et al.*, The Mediterranean: A Biodiversity Hotspot Under Threat. In: J.-C. Vié, C. Hilton-Taylor and S.N. Stuart (eds). The 2008 Review of The IUCN Red List of Threatened Species, 2008, pp.1-13.

2 *UNEP/MAP*, State of the Mediterranean Marine and Coastal Environment, 2012, 92 p.

3 *Id.*, pp. 84s.

4 *P. Haas*, Saving the Mediterranean The Politics of International Environmental Cooperation, 1990, 303 p.

legal instruments.[5] Both specialized Mediterranean agreements and global conventions coexist and overlap, thus creating a Mediterranean "*regime complex*"[6] for the environment in which countries with various economic and technical capacities have to co-operate (see figure 1). Still, despite this regional legal density, there is no clear sign of improvement of the Mediterranean environment, thus highlighting the lack of effectiveness of this whole regime complex.

Figure 1. Partial list of legal instruments relevant to the Mediterranean environment[7]

Mediterranean agreements	Regional agreements of Mediterranean relevance (RAMER)	Global agreements
General Fisheries Commission for the Mediterranean Barcelona Convention - Dumping Protocol - Prevention and emergency Protocol - LBS Protocol - SPA and Biodiversity Protocol - Offshore Protocol - Hazardous waste Protocol - ICZM Protocol ACCOBAMS Ramoge Agreement Pelagos Sanctuary Union for the Mediterranean	International Commission for the Conservation of Atlantic Tunas European Union's Legislation - Marine Strategy Framework Directive - Common Fisheries Policy - Water Directive - Habitat Directive Council of Europe's environmental treaties - Bern Convention - European Landscape Convention The Convention on the Protection of the Black Sea Against Pollution	World Heritage Convention Ramsar Convention CITES Convention on Migratory Species United Nations Convention on the Law of the Seas International Maritime Organization's conventions - Marpol Convention - Ballast Water Convention Convention on Biological Diversity United Nations Convention to Combat Desertification United Nations Framework Convention on Climate Change

5 *RAC/SPA*, International Legal Instruments Applied to the Conservation of Marine Biodiversity in the Mediterranean Region and Actors Responsible for their Implementation and Enforcement, 2010, 35p.

6 *A. Orsini, J-F. Morin & O. Young*, Regime Complexes: A Buzz, A Boom or A Boost for Global Governance, Global Governance 2013 (19), p. 29. The authors define the notion of regime complex as "*a network of three or more international regimes that relate to a common subject matter; exhibit overlapping membership; and generate substantive, normative, or operative interactions recognized as potentially problematic whether or not they are managed effectively*".

7 This list is based on the agreements listed in, *UNEP/MAP*, State of the Mediterranean Marine and Coastal Environment, *supra* note 3, pp. 81-82 and *RAC/SPA*, International Legal Instruments Applied to the Conservation of Marine Biodiversity in the Mediterranean Region and Actors Responsible for their Implementation and Enforcement, *supra* note 6. As the list goes on, it appears that, as the environment is an inherently transversal issue, precisely delimiting what concerns the Mediterranean environment and what does not is difficult and open to debate.

All in all, in this relatively small patch of land and sea, most of the common traits of international environmental law are apparent; namely: irreplaceable environment, scientific uncertainty, anthropic threats, high legal density, South/North divide and a lack of effectiveness. This makes the Mediterranean Basin a particularly relevant case study with regards to international environmental law's effectiveness.

This chapter will focus on the relation that exists between law and science as a prerequisite, among others, for the effectiveness of international environmental law in the Mediterranean Basin. In order to examine this relationship, we will analyse the activities of Mediterranean Technical Bodies (MTBs) and try to determine if they match specific criteria. But, before doing so, we must first explain the concept of technical bodies (1.1) and specify the relevant criteria we seek to identify. (1.2). The relevance of legal instruments in this field also has to be clarified (1.3).

1.1. TECHNICAL BODIES: A BROAD CATEGORY

In the context of this chapter, we understand technical bodies as being institutions that work on scientific and technical matters in order to promote better designs for environmental regulations and laws and assist actors in implementing existing legal frameworks. These bodies are also set within a specific conventional framework (*i.e.* they do not exist independently therefrom). Admittedly, this definition is very broad, but it allows us to take into account the wide typology of institutions whose activities fall into this category without creating confusions with other concepts used by the doctrine.

For instance, authors have referred to "Transnational Scientific Institutions" in order to describe regulatory institutions that exist at an international level.[8] In his paper, Oren Perez refers to the Intergovernmental Panel on Climate Change (IPCC) as an example of Transnational Scientific Institution. However, given that the IPCC exists independently from any conventional frameworks[9], it does not qualify as a technical body in our understanding of the concept (though it does work on similar issues for a similar purpose).

The concept of "Science-Policy Interface" is also frequently used; however, it is not to describe an institution, but to describe a social process in which scientists and decision-makers co-produce knowledge.[10] This social process can, nevertheless, be set within an institution, such as the (IPCC) or the Intergovernmental Platform

8 *O. Perez*, The Hybrid Legal-Scientific Dynamic of Transnational Scientific Institutions, EJIL 2015 (26).

9 Though it does evidently have close ties with the United Nations Framework Convention on Climate Change.

10 *S. Van Den Hove*, A rationale for Science Policy Interfaces, Futures 2007 (39), p. 824, "*[Science-Policy Interfaces] are social processes which encompass relations between scientists and other*

on Biodiversity and Ecosystem Services (IPBES). This case goes to show that the concepts of Transnational Scientific Institutions and Science-Policy Interfaces can overlap, as demonstrated by the IPCC, which illustrates them both. Yet, a technical body may not necessarily fit into the Science Policy Interface category as it does not always establish a social process that brings together both scientists and decision-makers.

This simple definition also allows us to take into account not only the expertise process of such bodies – even though it is often the most publicized activity – but also activities such as research priorities identification, environmental data harmonization, information sharing or even capacity-building (activities that are of paramount importance for the effectiveness of environmental law).

In the context of our chapter, our analysis will differ slightly from previous analyses by legal scholars concerning expertise. While there is a vast body of literature that discusses the role of expertise and science in the design and implementation of laws and regulations[11], our focus will be less on the impact and nature of the activities led by the Mediterranean technical bodies[12] and more on the different legal means that exist to frame their work. In other words, our focus is on the impact of law on technical bodies, rather than on the impact of technical bodies on law.

Indeed, we seek to determine whether or not the existing legal framework applicable to the activities of MTBs guarantees the existence of specific criteria.

1.2. CRITERIA FOR TECHNICAL BODIES

Social scientists have engaged in a thorough analysis of the subtle dynamic that exists between law and science that contributed to deconstructing the common assumption of a linear relation between two completely distinct objects with clear boundaries: science and society (and by extension, law).[13] In the wake of this

---

actors in the policy process, and which allow for exchanges, co-evolution, and joint construction of knowledge with the aim of enriching decision-making".

11 See for instance, *E. Truilhé Marengo (ed.)*, Preuve scientifique, preuve juridique, 2012, 358p.; *B. Simma*, The International Court of Justice and Scientific Expertise, American Society of International Law Proceedings 2012 (106); *R. Encinas de Munagorri*, Expertise scientifique et décision de précaution, RJE 2000 (25); *E. Naim*-Gesbert, Les dimensions scientifiques du droit de l'environnement – Contribution à l'étude des rapports de la science et du droit, 1999, 808 p.; *M.A. Hermitte*, L'expertise scientifique à finalité politique, réflexions sur l'organisation et la responsabilité des experts, Justices 1997 (8).

12 On Regional Fisheries Management Organizations in the Mediterranean, see *S. Gambardella*, L'expert scientifique et l'exemple des commissions régionales de pêche: un acteur aux multiples visages du processus décisionnel, Journal International de Bioéthique 2014 (25).

13 Most notably, the work of Sheila Jasanoff is extremely relevant on this topic. See for instance S. Jasanoff, The Fifth Branch Science Advisers as Policymakers, 1990, 302 p. and S. *Jasanoff*, States of Knowledge: the Coproduction of Science and Social Order, 2004, 317p. For a compiled version of her work in French, see *O. Leclerc*, Le Droit et La Science en Action, 2013, 208 p. For

realization, academics then sought to identify the appropriate frameworks that could lead to an appropriate relation between scientists and decision-makers in order to promote better decision-making. The concept of Science-Policy Interface (SPI) came about in this way.[14]

However, in order for SPIs to have an impact, specific conditions have to be fulfilled.

The general consensus is that SPIs are likely to exert influence on the decision-making as long as they are perceived as being credible, relevant and legitimate.[15] Credibility is the perceived validity of information, methods and procedures provided and applied in an SPI.[16] For instance, an interface relying on objectively unqualified experts will lack credibility. Relevance is the extent to which the work carried out within an interface is responsive to the conditions and needs of the policy process.[17] A report on the effects of one chemical on the marine environment, when end-users are waiting for clarifications on the combined effects of several chemicals, will lack relevance. Finally, legitimacy is the perceived fairness, balance and political acceptability of the output.[18] An interface that only takes inputs from developed countries into account is likely to be perceived as being illegitimate by developing countries.

We believe that these three characteristics are as relevant for an SPI as they are for any technical body. Indeed, due to the varying nature of technical bodies, their recommendations will not necessarily be legally binding. Even if a technical body is not an SPI, as it does not promote co-production of knowledge or exchanges, its work will nevertheless be perceived and assessed by end-users associated with the regime in which it exists (States, NGOs, experts, individuals and so on). Therefore, the probability of a technical body effectively having an impact on its regime is highly dependent upon its perceived credibility, legitimacy and relevance.

1.3. THE ROLE OF LAW

It is possible to ensure the existence of these three criteria through the implementation of legal means. For instance, credibility and legitimacy can be preserved with the adoption of precise rules of procedure concerning the

---

a short introduction to these various concepts, see *C. Bonneuil, P-B. Joly*, Sciences, techniques et société, 2013, 128 p.

14 *S. Van den Hove, supra*, note 10.

15 *T. Koetz, K. Farrell & P. Bridgewater*, Building Better Science-Policy Interfaces for International Environmental Governance: Assessing Potential within the Intergovernmental Platform for Biodiversity and Ecosystem Services, International Environmental Agreements 2011 (original paper), p.3.; *J.C. Young, A.D. Watt, S. Van Den Hove, S. et al*, The SPIRAL synthesis report: A resource book on science-policy interfaces, 2013, p. 61.

16 *T. Koetz, K. Farrell & P. Bridgewater, supra* note 15, p.3.

17 *Id.*

18 *Id.*

nomination of experts within a technical body.[19] Drawing on this idea, this chapter aims to study the existing legal and institutional framework in the Mediterranean Basin in order to determine whether or not it contributes to the credibility, relevance and legitimacy of MTBs. If the MTBs benefit from the appropriate framework, in order to achieve credibility, relevance and legitimacy, then it can then be argued that the interfaces are able to contribute to the effectiveness of the Mediterranean regime complex.[20]

However, this chapter will focus on an aspect that has hitherto drawn little attention: the legal framework for the interaction between MTBs and how these interactions can promote credibility, relevance and legitimacy.

In order to do so, we will analyse three different aspects of the Mediterranean framework. Firstly, by studying the architecture of the technical network of the Mediterranean Basin, we highlight the wide typology of MTBs and how they already engage in joint activities (2) Secondly, we analyse how the existence of "shared objects" can enhance the credibility and relevance of MTB (3). Thirdly, we discuss the existence of contractual linkages between MTBs (4). These contractual linkages raise various questions that are of great consequence for the general theory of sources in international public law.

Throughout this analysis, we also hope to illustrate how MTBs can act as bridges between their regimes and allow for progressive defragmentation.

All of these aspects are concrete ways through which to promote credibility and relevance, given that they prevent discordant or redundant messages that would hinder the implementation of multilateral environmental agreements. They also promote credibility by allowing exchanges between specialized technical bodies. However, as far as legitimacy in concerned, interaction between MTBs is not necessarily an appropriate tool for improvement.

2. THE MEDITERRANEAN INSTITUTIONAL LANDSCAPE

Establishing a list of all of the multilateral agreements relevant to the Mediterranean environment highlights how important the issue of harmonization and co-operation is. More than 25 treaties and protocols are implemented in the

19 For instance, this topic has been debated thoroughly in the context of the recently established IPBES. See Decision IPBES-2/3: Procedures for the preparation of the Platform's deliverables.

20 It is important to stress that effectiveness is the result of cumulative components. For instance, if States do not implement their international obligations, then effectiveness will not be achieved, even though institutions benefit from the appropriate framework. Consequently, our analysis does not try to illustrate whether or not the Mediterranean regime complex is effective, but rather if its institutions have the capacity to contribute to its effectiveness.

region[21] and most of these agreements rely on specific institutions and technical bodies in order to assist their implementation.

For instance, the establishment of a Secretariat is a common institutional feature of these agreements. Secretariats, given that they often represent the institutional memory of these agreements[22], can also act as technical bodies thanks to their technical and political expertise in the fields linked to the agreements they manage. Moreover, Secretariats are frequently asked to draft reports on technical matters.[23] This type of activity can even be specifically called upon in the text of the agreement establishing the Secretariat, as is the case for the CITES.[24] Additionally, when the Secretariat acts as a conveyor of the recommendations of its associated technical body within another regime, it arguably acts as a technical body.[25] Still, this does not mean that all Secretariats fit this broad category as their activities will often depend on how flexible their mandate is and will involve the implication of their staff.

Several specialized bodies have also been created on an *ad hoc* basis to assist members with regards to scientific and technical aspects linked to the implementation of their obligations. For example, the member of the CITES formally established an Animal committee and Plant committee during the 1980s in order to benefit from technical and scientific support in the decision-making process.[26] Other agreements provide for the creation of Science-Policy Interfaces in their initial texts. This is the case of the Subsidiary Body on Scientific Technical

---

21 See *supra*, figure 1 and note 7.

22 On this topic see *F. Biermann & B. Sibenhüner* (eds.), Managers of Global Change: The Influence of International Environmental Bureaucracies, 2009, 367 p. and *S. Jinnah*, Post-treaty Politics: Secretariat Influence in Global Environmental Governance, 2014, 245 p. Earlier works also acknowledge this unique role of Secretariats, see *J-M Lavieille* (eds), Conventions de Protection de l'Environnement. Secrétariats, Conférence des Parties, Comités d'Experts, 1999, 502 p., pp. 419-429.

23 It is fairly common that States request from their Secretariat reports on technical and scientific matters. For instance, the ACCOBAMS Secretariat together with the Scientific Committee is frequently asked, via COP resolutions, to work on specific matters. See *ACCOBAMS*, Resolution 4.9 Fisheries interaction with cetaceans, p.2, "*invites the Agreement Secretariat and the Scientific Committee to pursue the collaboration with relevant Organizations and Bodies to consider further the relations between prey depletion and increasing interactions between cetaceans and fishing activities, proposing remedial solutions where possible*".

24 CITES, Article XII The Secretariat: *The function of the Secretariat shall be [...] to undertake scientific and technical studies in accordance with programmes authorized by the Conference of the Parties as will contribute to the implementation of the present Convention, including studies concerning standards for appropriate preparation and shipment of living specimens and the means of identifying specimens.*

25 We further develop this notion in the fourth section of this Article.

26 For a detailed chronology and analysis of these committees, see *M-P. Lanfranchi*, Le Traitement de la Connaissance Scientifique dans le Cadre de la CITES, Journal International de Bioéthique 2014 (25).

and Technological Advice (SBSTTA) of the Convention of Biological Diversity, which is described in Article 25 of the Treaty.[27]

Following this rationale, this consideration allows us to illustrate what a technical body does not constitute; Conference of the Parties, even though they will consider technical and scientific matters, do not fall into this category as their primary function is decisional. Neither do Standing Committees nor Bureaus that manage administrative issues during intersessional periods. Compliance Committees are also not technical bodies, given that they are only concerned with issues of implementation.[28]

Unfortunately, describing the existing dynamic between all of these different technical bodies goes far beyond the scope of a simple book chapter.[29] Consequently, for the purposes of our analysis, we will focus on the bodies linked to Mediterranean Agreements.[30] Namely: the Barcelona Convention and its protocols, the General Fisheries Council for the Mediterranean (GFCM), the Agreement on the Conservation of Cetaceans in the Black Sea Mediterranean Sea and Contiguous Atlantic Area (ACCOBAMS), the Pelagos Agreement, the Ramoge Agreement and the Union for the Mediterranean (UFM).

In the context of this part, we will firstly describe the institutional landscape of the region (2.1) and secondly will give examples of the different joint activities that have been undertaken (2.2). In so doing, we aim to illustrate the threats of redundancy or contradiction and the subsequent management needs they entail.

2.1. THE MEDITERRANEAN TECHNICAL BODIES

The typology of the MTBs is highly diversified, most notably concerning the bodies related to the Barcelona Convention and the GFCM.

The Barcelona Convention, as the legal component of the Mediterranean Action Plan (MAP), relies on a complex institutional structure, which evolved

27 For an analysis of this body in its science-policy interface role, see *T.Koetz, P.Bridgewater, S. van den Hove, B. Siebenhüner*, The role of the Subsidiary Body on Scientific, Technical and Technological Advice to the Convention on Biological Diversity as science–policy interface, environmental science & policy 2008 (11).

28 Nevertheless, drawing a line between what is technical or scientific and what is not is a perilous exercise that raises serious philosophical questions. See for instance *S. Jasanoff, op. cit. supra*, note 13 or *B. Latour*, Nous n'avons jamais été modernes, 1991, 210 p.

29 The "gap analysis" prepared by UNEP for the IPBES negotiation process appears to be an attempt to conduct such an analysis although it is focused on a very specific topic: the science policy interfaces for biodiversity and ecosystem governance. UNEP/IPBES/2/INF/1, Gap analysis for the purposes of facilitating the discussions on how to improve and strengthen the science-policy interface on biodiversity and ecosystem services.

30 By Mediterranean agreements, we refer to legal instruments whose primary focus is the Mediterranean environment. The members to these agreements are also mainly Mediterranean actors.

and grew over time and was fairly recently clarified during the 17th Meeting of the Parties of Barcelona Convention.[31] The Coordination Unit, which acts as the Secretariat for the MAP, is responsible for the supervision of the other main component of the MAP; namely, the Regional Activity Centres (RAC), the Mediterranean Commission on Sustainable Development (MCSD) and the Programme for the Assessment and Control of Marine Pollution in the Mediterranean Region (MED-POL). The following table provides a description of these components' various mandates and their establishment date.

	Mandate[32]
MED-POL (1975)	To contribute to the prevention and elimination of land-based pollution of the Mediterranean.
Regional Marine Pollution Emergency Response Centre (REMPEC) (1976)	To contribute to preventing and reducing pollution from ships and combating pollution in case of emergency.
Blue Plan/RAC (BP) (1984)	To contribute to raising awareness of Mediterranean stakeholders and decision-makers concerning environment and sustainable development issues in the region, by providing scenarios to assist in decision-making
Priority Action Programme/ RAC (PAP) (1980)	To contribute to sustainable development of coastal zones and sustainable use of their natural resources.
Specially Protected Areas / RAC (SPA) (1985)	To contribute to the protection and preservation and sustainable management of marine and coastal areas of particular natural and cultural value and threatened and endangered species of flora and fauna.
Centre for Cleaner Production/ RAC (CP) (1996)	To contribute to pollution prevention and sustainable and efficient management of services, products and resources based on the sustainable production and consumption integrated approach adopted by UNEP.
Info / RAC (1993)	To contribute to collecting and sharing information, raising public awareness and participation and enhancing decision-making processes at the regional, national and local levels.
MCSD (1996)	To make relevant proposals and recommendations to the contracting parties based on the assessment of major sustainable development issues of common concern to the countries of the region or set out in international and regional agendas. It is made up of government representatives and members of the wider community (NGOs, scientific community, international organizations).

31 Barcelona Convention, Decision IG.19/5 Mandates of the Components of MAP.

32 *Ibid.*, except for the description of the MCSD which is based on the MAP website: www.unepmap.org/index.php?module=content2&catid=001017002 (last accessed: 20/04/2016).

In achieving their mandate, the MED-POL and the six RACs undertake assessments (MED-POL), engage in capacity-building activities (REMPEC), catalyse research (SPA/RAC) or create knowledge for decision-makers (CP/RAC), improve data flows (INFO/RAC), draft scenarios as an aid to decision-making (Blue Plan/RAC) and foster discussions among decision-makers and the scientific community (MCSD).[33] Relying on this vast field of institutional expertise, and supported by relevant synergies, the MAP ensures a holistic approach is adopted for environmental stakes in the region.[34]

The GFCM also has a complex institutional structure. Its activities are implemented through its Secretariat and several committees have been established so as to conduct the intersessional activities. Two different committees specialize in scientific and technical matters, the Scientific Advisory Committee and the Committee on Aquaculture. These committees are composed of several sub-committees and working groups, all of whom are working on specific aspects linked to their mandate. The following table gives a general overview of these different bodies.

	Components
Scientific Advisory Committee (1997)	Subcommittee on Stock Assessments (1999) Subcommittee on Marine Environment and Ecosystem (1999) Subcommittee on Economic and Social Sciences (1999) Subcommittee on Statistics and Information (1999)
Committee Aquaculture (1995)	Working Group on Marketing (2007) Working Group on Sustainability (2007) Working Group on Sitting and Carrying Capacity (2007)

Similar to the MAP, albeit on a more focused subject, these bodies provide their expertise to members of the GFCM, but also promote research and engage in capacity-building activities.

Finally, concerning ACCOBAMS, the Pelagos agreement and the Ramoge agreement, the existing framework for their technical bodies can be described as being rather straightforward with the existence of a Secretariat and a permanent scientific and technical body. Where the UFM is concerned, it only relies on a Secretariat staffed with experts qualified in various fields.

33 The MCSD, as it engages both scientists and decision-makers in a specific process falls into the Science-Policy Interface category described by Sybille Van den Hove (see *supra*, note 10).

34 While a structural overview may lead to this conclusion, authors have on several occasions highlighted the institutional shortcomings of the MAP. For instance, see *S. Frantzi*, What Determines the Institutional Performance of Environmental Regimes? A Case Study of the Mediterranean Action Plan, Marine Policy 2008 (32) and *S. Frantzi & J-C. Lovett*, Is Science the Driving Force in the Operation of Environmental Regimes? A Case Study of the Mediterranean Action Plan, Ocean and Coastal Management 2008 (51).

With such a dense framework, there is an obvious risk of duplication or contradiction between the different activities conducted within the MTBs.[35] This risk is only a part of the different threats that are linked with the fragmentation or international environmental law, where obligations and rights can be redundant or contradictory.[36]

Accordingly, the activities led by the different MTBs are not done in complete isolation from one another and there are several cases of joint activities that illustrate how the different technical bodies have increased their credibility and relevance through collaboration.

2.2. JOINT ACTIVITIES

The Pelagos Sanctuary and ACCOBAMS have collaborated on several projects concerning whale watching activities.[37] In so doing, the technical bodies of both regimes have pooled their common expertise in order to produce recommendations for all parties.

In the MAP context, the involvement of ACCOBAMS is even more remarkable. Currently, the MAP is working on the definition of "ecological objectives" in order to achieve a Good Environmental Status (GES) for the Mediterranean and the ACCOBAMS bodies were explicitly involved in the determination of the objectives relevant to cetaceans.[38] This ensures the greatest relevance and credibility for all cetacean-related objectives that will eventually be agreed upon by Member States of the Barcelona Convention.

The GFCM and the PAM have also collaborated on several occasions. For instance, in 2007, the RAC/SPA and GFCM held a "Transversal Workshop on Marine Protected Areas (MPAs)".[39] During this meeting, States' representatives as well as experts from the different Mediterranean technical bodies and NGOs discussed the different perception they had of the notion of marine protected areas in the Mediterranean regimes. This type of workshop is a necessary tool for increasing the effectiveness of protected areas by disseminating shared understandings across regimes and States.

---

35 Concerning Science Policy Interfaces for biodiversity, this threat was highlighted several times in the gap analysis for the IPBES see *supra*, note 29.

36 On this topic, see the seminal report of the International Law Commission, *ILC*, Fragmentation of International Law: Difficulties Arising from Diversification and Expansion of International Law, 2006, 256p.

37 *ACCOBAMS*, Guidelines for implementing a Pelagos/ACCOBAMS label for commercial whale watching activities, 2010, 21p.

38 *ACCOBAMS*, ACCOBAMS-MOP5/2013/Doc10, ACCOBAMS contribution to the ecosystem approach process in the Mediterranean.

39 Report of the Transversal Workshop on Marine Protected Areas (MPAs) (GFCM & RAC/SPA), available on line: www.fao.org/fishery/nems/36147/en (last accessed: 20/04/2016).

Though this type of joint activities can contribute to enhancing the characteristics of the MTBs involved, it only does so in a limited scope and timeframe. Consequently, in order to set these partnerships in a more durable framework, other means are used, such as "shared objects" and contractual relations.

3. "SHARED OBJECTS" AS A MEANS FOR COORDINATION BETWEEN TECHNICAL BODIES AND REGIMES

After years of legal densification in international environmental law, it can only come as a rational approach to seek harmonization between regimes, rather than to establish new ones. This theme has mobilized numerous authors[40] and institutions[41] and several means of regime interaction have been identified and discussed.[42] In the context of this section, we argue that harmonization between environmental regimes can be enhanced through the existence of "shared objects".

We understand "shared objects" as being any type of regime interaction that relies on the mutualisation of institutions, norms, concepts and goals. For instance, a technical body that is operating in two different regimes is a shared object. Similarly, purposes and goals that are enshrined in several regimes, and which frame the work of their technical bodies, are also shared objects.[43] Shared objects can, thus, be the result of different processes, such as the circulation of norms and actors between regimes or the rationalization of overlapping processes (*i.e.* the omnibus decision of the Chemical Cluster).[44]

While, in our context at least, this harmonization can only be partial, as it will mostly concern technical and scientific aspects, it is nevertheless a necessary step towards effectiveness. By using technical bodies as bridges between regimes, the relevance and credibility of these bodies are also necessarily increased by erasing duplications and contradictions and by fostering co-operation.

---

40 *S. Oberthür, O. Stokke*, Managing Institutional Complexity Regime Interplay and Global Environmental Change, 2011, 353 p.

41 *UNEP-WCMC*, Promoting Synergies within the Cluster of Biodiversity-related Multilateral Environmental Agreements, 2012, 95 p.

42 For instance the Basel Convention, Rotterdam Convention and Stockholm Convention, now referred as the "chemical cluster" have joint COPs and even adopt "omnibus decision". This decision was made possible by the strong overlap of the objects and purposes of these conventions. On this topic see *K. Scott*, International Environmental Governance: Managing Fragmentation through Institutional Connection, MelbourneJIL 2011 (12).

43 It is important to stress the fact that we use the term "object" in its broadest sense, thus moving away from its usual meaning in law.

44 See note 42.

Studying the different ways in which shared objects can influence the work of MTBs reveals two types of interaction. Firstly, we witness a form of vertical harmonization[45], in which common goals, strategies and frameworks are set, thereby fostering coherence between the works of the different MTBs (3.1). On a horizontal level, the co-operation between regimes can be achieved through the transformation of technical bodies into shared objects (3.2).

3.1. COMMON GOALS AND FRAMEWORKS

The diffusion of general concepts, goals and frameworks generated at the global level or within the Regional Agreements of Mediterranean Relevance (particularly the European Union in our context) appears to be a widely used means of harmonization across regimes. The tendency is a well-documented phenomenon in international relations[46] and is starting to get attention in the legal field.[47] We argue that the establishment of common frameworks and goals is an efficient means of coordinating the activities of MTBs in order to prevent contradictions.

Though the diffusion of norms and concepts in other regimes do not impose direct legal obligation on their members systematically, it nevertheless influences the institutions attached to the regime which can, in time, influence their legal framework.[48] For instance, the "Ecosystem Approach", promoted by the CBD in its 2000 resolution[49], was incorporated in the normative corpus of the Barcelona convention in 2008[50] and has been a central component of the activities of the MAP technical bodies ever since.[51] It has also been incorporated as a reference in the ACCOBAMS work programme[52] and is being considered more and more

45 In this context, the adjective "vertical" does not necessarily imply that global instruments are influencing regional ones, or that there is a legal hierarchy between the different agreements implemented in the region. We use this term in order to stress that, by setting a common goal or framework, actors tend to work towards a higher and commonly agreed objective.

46 For instance, *A. Ovodenko, R. Keohane*, Institutional Diffusion in International Environmental Affairs, International Affairs 2012 (3).

47 For instance, *H. Van Asselt*, Integrating Biodiversity in the Climate Regime's Forest Rules: Option and Trade-offs in greening REDD design, RECIEL 2011 (20) and *G. Futhazar*, The Diffusion of the Strategic Plan for Biodiversity and Its Aichi Biodiversity Targets within the Biodiversity Cluster: An Illustration of Current Trends in the Global Governance of Biodiversity and Ecosystems, YIEL 2015 (25).

48 *F. Biermann et al.*, Studying the Influence of International Bureaucracies in F. Biermann & B. Sibenhüner (eds.) *supra* note 22, p. 48.

49 CBD, Decision VI/12. Ecosystem Approach.

50 Barcelona Convention, Decision IG 17/6: Implementation of the ecosystem approach to the management of human activities that may affect the Mediterranean marine and coastal environment.

51 The sheer number of meetings on this topic conducted within the MAP context illustrate how central this concept is. See www.unepmap.org/ (last accessed: 10/01/2016) in the "meeting documents" section.

52 *ACCOBAMS*, Resolution 5.2 Work Programme 2014-2016.

within the GFCM.[53] The case of the EU Marine Strategy Framework Directive (MSFD)[54], adopted in 2008, is even more salient as a diffusion case and highlights the high degree of influence the EU has in the environmental governance of the region, both legally and politically. Several reports and decisions by the MAP[55], ACCOBAMS[56] and GFCM[57] highlight the importance of the MSFD in their activities. Considering that the MSFD calls for regional co-operation within the relevant institution for its implementation[58], the fact that it has become predominant as an objective within the Mediterranean regimes may come as an indication of its success in this respect.

However, simply setting up a common strategy or agreeing on precise goals is not sufficient to fully erase redundancy or contradictions. Horizontal interaction between regimes via their institutions is a necessary complementary step to the vertical harmonization described above. The following section will analyse how shared technical bodies – as one possible type of horizontal interaction – can act as bridges between regimes.

3.2. SHARED TECHNICAL BODIES

Shared technical bodies are institutions that are formally linked to two or more regimes and whose activities benefit all regimes. The existence of these shared bodies is particularly relevant when there is a significant overlap between regimes as illustrated by the following examples.

The REMPEC, established in 1976 under the initial name of Regional Oil Combating Centre, is administered by both the International Maritime Organization (IMO) and the UNEP/MAP. This shared "parenthood" facilitates the roles of the REMPEC as a technical body contributing to both the implementation of the legal components of the MAP (the 1976 Emergency Protocol and Prevention and the 2002 Emergency Protocol) and of the OMI (most notably the MARPOL convention) by Mediterranean States. This central role in the implementation

53 *GFCM*, GFCM: XXXVIII/2014/2, Report on fisheries intersessional activities in 2013-2014, recommendations and work plan for 2014-2015, p. 27.

54 Directive 2008/56/EC of the European Parliament and of the Council of 17 June 2008 establishing a framework for community action in the field of marine environmental policy, OJ L 164/19.

55 *Barcelona Convention*, UNEP(DEPI)/MED IG.21/Inf.9, Reports of the meetings of the Ecosystem Approach Coordination Group during the 2012-2013 biennium.

56 *ACCOBAMS*, Resolution 4.3 Contribution from ACCOBAMS to the implementation of the Marine Strategy Framework Directive.

57 The GFCM has signed a Memorandum with the International Council for the Exploration of the Sea in order to contribute to the implementation of the Marine Strategy Framework Directive. See GFCM, GFCM: XXXVIII/2014/Inf.9, GFCM framework for co-operation and arrangements with party organizations, p.3.

58 Directive 2008/56/EC *supra* note 54, art. 6 "Regional Cooperation".

of both regimes is highlighted in the 2005 Regional Strategy for Prevention of and Response to Marine Pollution from Ships[59] where REMPEC is requested to provide assistance to members of the PAM for the ratification of international agreements, with specific reference being made to the MARPOL convention.[60] This co-administration of REMPEC is also apparent in the way the meetings of its focal points areis organized. Reports on the relevant activities of the IMO are presented to the focal points on a biannual basis. Moreover, IMO representatives attend every focal point meeting as observers and present the documents related to the IMO to the participants.

Institutional links can be established through other legal means, as was the case for the CP/RAC in 2009. During the 4th CoP of the Stockholm Convention on Persistent Organic Pollutants, the convention members nominated the CP/RAC as a regional centre for capacity-building and the transfer of technology.[61] This nomination was the end result of a process in which precise terms of reference and rigorous selection criteria were set.[62] As a result of this nomination, the CP/RAC now has to submit reports and work plans for the Stockholm Convention's Secretariat on a regular basis. This link increases coherence between the different regimes through the mutualisation of an existing technical body. This prevents, concerning the specific issue of capacity building and technology transfer, inconsistencies that would otherwise hinder the implementation of both the Barcelona protocols relevant to chemicals and the Stockholm convention. Similarly, the RAC-SPA was designated as a coordination unit for ACCOBAMS during it's first MOP (Resolution 1.4).

For these three examples, it is important to stress that, while they are at the crossroads of different regimes, they do remain "at the service" of Mediterranean States. Their activities do not directly benefit other members of the global regimes, but at least they contribute to preventing discordance. However, these "shared" technical bodies remain somewhat of an exception within the Mediterranean framework, be it through a COP decision or joint administrative parenthood. Other than the REMPEC and the two RACs, no other MTBs seems to act in a similar way and regime interaction through MTBs appear to be mainly the result of the implementation of other instruments, most notably the Memoranda of Understanding (MoUs).

59 Barcelona Convention, UNEP(DEC)/MED IG.16/10, Regional Strategy for Prevention of and Response to Marine Pollution from Ships.

60 *Idid.*, § 4.1, p. 5.

61 Stockholm Convention, decision SC-4/23, Regional and subregional centres for capacity-building and transfer of technology.

62 Stockholm Convention, Doc COP. 4/22, Selection of regional and subregional centres for capacity-building and transfer of environmentally sound technologies under the Stockholm Convention.

4. MEMORANDA OF UNDERSTANDING

Several different MoUs are currently being implemented within the Mediterranean Basin. Used as a means of formalizing pre-existing relations, these memoranda establish bridges between the agreements implemented in the Mediterranean region via their Secretariats. The Memoranda existing between the Secretariats of the GFCM, the MAP and ACCOBAMS are fairly representative of the structure and scope of existing MoUs in the region and, as such, constitute an appropriate focus for our study. To present them, we will first highlight their purpose (4.1) and then discuss their possible legal nature (4.2)

4.1. THE PURPOSE OF THE MEDITERRANEAN MoUs

The GFCM adopted a series of memoranda in 2012 as a stepping-stone in a broader reflexive process concerning its co-operation with other organizations.[63] The co-operation agreements with the GFCM and ACCOBAMS give a clear view of how they can contribute to enhancing the relevance and credibility of their respective technical bodies. For instance, ACCOBAMS and GFCM are in agreement in their memorandum on areas of co-operation, such as in the collection of information, assessment, research and monitoring, dissemination of information and the development of capacity-building activities.[64] With regards to the collaboration between the GFCM and the MAP, both parties have agreed to co-operate on the identification, protection and management of marine areas of particular importance and on the promotion of an ecosystem-based approach for the conservation of marine environment and ecosystems and the sustainable use of marine living resources. Finally, the MAP and ACCOBAMS have recently (February 2016) adopted an MoU in which both Secretariats have agreed to co-operate on themes such as the collection and assessment of information relating to the conservation of cetaceans or the development of capacity-building activities.[65]

For all of these memoranda, their organizational arrangements call for the implementation of joint activities and convening of meetings as deemed relevant by both parties. A duty of information is also called for, so that each party can be kept up to date on its partner's relevant activities.

All in all, these agreements do not radically change the way the Mediterranean institutions co-operate. However, because they take on the form of precise

63 *GFCM*, GFCM: XXXVI/2012/Inf.5(Rev.1), GFCM Framework for Cooperation with Party Organizations – Memoranda of Understanding. The appendixes of this document contain the Memoranda currently being implemented by the Commission.

64 *Id.*, p. 20.

65 Barcelona Convention, Decision IG.22/18 Cooperation Partners, annex II.

contracts, they do ensure predictability and clarity in future co-operation.[66] Even though their widespread use has been noticed by authors[67], these instruments have not, to our knowledge, been precisely defined from a legal perspective.[68] As such, their legal nature remains somewhat of an enigma.

4.2. THE LEGAL NATURE OF MEDITERRANEAN MoUs

To try and determine the legal nature of these objects, we will first list the "hints" (process, signatories, wording and provisions) that could help us in this task (4.2.1.) and then try to propose different answers, while at the same time discussing their possible implications (4.2.2.).

4.2.1. Instruments with several legal indicators

In our specific case, it is not entirely clear whether or not the signatories of these Memoranda have the international legal capacity to enter in agreements with other international institutions. Indeed, for the ACCOBAMS and the MAP, it was the different heads of Secretariats who signed the memoranda with the GFCM. Similarly, in 2013, the MAP Secretariat signed a MoU with the Secretariat of the UFM.[69] Moreover, while these agreements may, in some cases, be presented to the Member States of the regimes they are linking for their acknowledgment[70], or even subject to the review of legal offices[71], the condition for their coming into effect depends on the signature of the authorized representatives[72]; namely, the Head of the Secretariats.

---

66 Predictability and clarity are two important characteristics of legal security. See, *Conseil d'État*, Sécurité Juridique et Complexité du Droit, 2005, pp. 281s. Other authors have identified accessibility, stability and predictability as being the components of legal security. See, *T. Piazzon*, La Sécurité Juridique, 2009. In any case, the memorandums ensure all of these different components.

67 *K. Scott*, International Environmental Governance: Managing Fragmentation through Institutional Connection, *supra*, note 43 and *L. Boisson de Chazourne*, The Global Environment Facility: On Linkages Among Institutions, Max Planck Yearbook of United Nations Law 1999 (3).

68 However, MoUs between States have been the subject of doctrinal discussions. See *A. Aust*, Modern Treaty Law and Practice, 3rd edition, 2013, pp. 28-54.

69 Barcelona Convention, Decision IG.21/14 Cooperation Agreements, Annex I.

70 *Ibid.* The parties only "welcomed" the different MoUs. As such, it does not clearly constitute an approval by States.

71 *Supra* note 63 in the context of the GFCM. § 2 "*As far as GFCM is concerned, the finalized draft MoUs were transmitted to the FAO Legal Office which reviewed their provisions and ensured their compatibility with the rules of the Organization. As a further step, and after the clearance from the FAO Legal Office, the draft MoUs were sent to the competent ADG to get an additional clearance*".

72 *Supra*, note 69. "*Art. 14 Duration: This MoU will be effective upon the last date of signature of the authorized representatives and remain in force for three years from this date.*"

While it is commonly agreed upon that Secretariats of International Organization have the legal capacity to enter into binding agreements[73], the situation is not entirely clear concerning Secretariats of MEAs. Though some influential authors have expressed the opinion that their international legal capacity should be considered as a prerequisite for the realization of their mandate[74], there is still no clear authoritative statement providing a definitive answer to this question. This uncertain situation notwithstanding, the choice of the term Memorandum for these agreements could indicate that it was not necessarily the intention of the signatories to establish a formal and legally binding agreement, thus adding more uncertainty to this convoluted legal question.[75]

Yet, these agreements, drafted as contracts, have clauses that show all of the characteristics of legally binding instruments. For instance, amendments and termination procedures are formulated in clear and precise terms with requirements similar to what one would expect to find in an international bilateral agreement between States.[76] They even provide for the adoption of supplementary agreements within their own context.[77] Admittedly, the degree of precision and obligation of MoUs varies greatly and depends on the general purpose of the instrument. While some MoUs exist as the simple manifestation of a political partnership and provide only vague and general principles of co-operation[78], others, such as the one existing between the MAP and ACCOBAMS, even have a dispute settlement clause relying on the intervention of an arbitral tribunal.[79] All in all, in the context of our study, the Memoranda bear a significant degree

---

73 *O. Corten & P. Klein*, Les Conventions de Vienne sur le Droit des Traités Commentaire Article par Article, 2006, vol.1, p. 238.

74 *R. Churchill & G. Ulfstein*, Autonomous Institutional Arrangements in Multilateral Environmental Agreements: A Little-noticed Phenomenon in International Law, AJIL 2000 (94), p. 655 and *B. Desai*, Multilateral Environmental Agreements: Legal Status of the Secretariats, 2010, pp. 165-166.

75 *United Nations*, Treaty Handbook, 2012, p. 68, "*The term memorandum of understanding (M.O.U.) is often used to denote a less formal international instrument than a typical treaty or international agreement*". On the other hand, formal treaties exist under the name of Memorandum. On this aspect see *J. Gant, J Barker*, Encyclopaedic Dictionary of International Law, 3rd edition, 2009, p.375. The authors highlight the fact that a MoU between several States concerning Trieste was later officially published as a treaty (Memorandum of Understanding (with annexes and exchange of notes) regarding the Free Territory of Trieste, U.N.T.S. vol. 235 p.99).

76 See for instance Clause 8 and Clause 10 of the GFCM/MAP Memorandum, *supra*, note 63, appendix B, pp. 12-17.

77 See for instance Article 3.4 of the MAP/UFM Memorandum, *supra*, note 69.

78 For instance, the CBD/IPBES Memorandum is significantly less detailed than the ones being currently implemented in the Mediterranean Region. Memorandum of Cooperation between the Secretariat of the Convention on Biological Diversity and the Secretariat of the Intergovernmental Science Policy Platform on Biodiversity and Ecosystem Services. Available on line: www.cbd.int/doc/agreements/agmt-ipbes-2014-10-09-mou-en.pdf (last accessed: 20/04/2016).

79 *Supra*, note 65, Annex II, art. 13 Dispute Settlement.

of precision, obligation (at least in the choice of the wording)[80] and, in some cases, delegation.[81] Therefore, we face a situation in which an instrument of an uncertain legal nature nevertheless shows the characteristics and functions one can expect of a law.

Finally, according to the GFCM's official documentation, these instruments are implemented and are subject to frequent reviews of effectiveness.[82] If so, this adds another layer to the legal understanding of these instruments. Not only do they show the function (predictability and clarity) and characteristics (obligation, precision, delegation) of law, they are also implemented and reviewed. In light of all of these elements, two different conclusions can be reached.

4.2.2. The possible different legal natures of the Mediterranean MoUs

Two different scenarios are conceivable.

Firstly, following the doctrine on the international legal capacity of Secretariat and the legal nature of COPs[83], it is realistic to consider that these Memorandum are, in fact, international treaties between International Organizations (IOs), given that they show all of the cumulative characteristics of one. This situation is made even more salient by analysing actual treaties between IOs. For instance, the Agreement between the United Nations and the United Nations Educational, Scientific and Cultural Organization[84] or the Agreement between the United Nations and the International Labour Organization[85] have similar dispositions to the MoUs we have discussed in the previous section. For instance, both call for the exchange of information and public information. The major difference with the MoU is that both agreements have provisions concerning administrative and financial alignment.

While this outcome is plausible, based on a theoretical analysis, it is less likely than in practice States agree to such a situation that would imply a loss of control

---

80 On the wording of treaties in comparison to MoUs, See *A. Aust*, *supra* note 68, p. 429. The MoUs studied in this section contain wording categorized by the author as being typical of formal treaties rather than MoUs. For instance: "shall"; "enter in force"; "parties".

81 These three components have been described as the characteristics of "legalization". See *K. Abbott, R. Keohane, A. Moravcsik et al.*, The concept of legalization, International Organization 2000 (54), p. 401, "*Obligation means that states or other actors are bound by a rule or commitment or by a set of rules or commitments. [...]Precision means that rules unambiguously define the conduct they require, authorize, or proscribe. Delegation means that third parties have been granted authority to implement, interpret, and apply the rules; to resolve disputes; and (possibly) to make further rules*".

82 *GCFM*, GFCM:XXXVIII/2014/Inf.9, GFCM framework for co-operation and arrangements with party organizations, pp. 1-5.

83 See note 74.

84 *UNESCO*, Basic Texts 2014, p. 171.

85 Official Bulletin of the ILO, Vol. XXIX, 15 November 1946, No. 4.

over the institutions they have established.[86] Even more than States, on at least one occasion, other IOs have refused to consider Secretariats as also being IOs. This was the case for the Secretariat of the CITES, whose request for a website domain (".int"), usually associated with IOs, was declined by the Internet Assigned Numbers Authority (a body of the Internet Corporation for Assigned Names and Numbers) on the basis of the absence of independent legal personality.[87] Acknowledging such a situation would also cause another explosion of IOs in an already crowded institutional environment.[88]

Secondly, if we consider that Secretariats of Conventions, in the absence of a clear authoritative statement, do not possess the legal capacity required, then these MoUs can be seen as "pseudo" legal objects. The use of the term "pseudo" is here used as way of conveying the fact that while these MoUs do not fit in with the classical sources of international law, they achieve the same results as formal legal instruments. And, despite this "pseudo" nature, they still contribute to effectively bridging regimes through their technical bodies. We argue that this effectiveness is achieved because the instruments show all of the functions and characteristics of law, regardless of the initial intent of the Secretariats.

Indeed, two different situations can be considered with regards to the perception of the Secretariats involved in these agreements.

Firstly, it is plausible that even though the term "Memorandum" was chosen, the Secretariats perceive them as being legally binding instruments. Considering the way in which they are written, and the fact that they go through the review of the legal offices, it can very well be the case that they are perceived of as full-fledged contracts. Metaphorically speaking, this can be compared to batesian mimicry, "*a form of biological resemblance in which a noxious, or dangerous, organism (the model), equipped with a warning system such as conspicuous colouration, is mimicked by a harmless organism (the mimic)*".[89] In so doing, the mimic achieves the same end result as the model: predators are kept at bay. Following this rationale, we believe that the effectiveness of these Memoranda is in great part due to the fact that they are so similar to valid legal agreements, while still being unfit to be classified in existing international public law. They

---

86 See *S. Bauer*, Does Bureaucracy Really Matters? The Authority of Intergovernmental Secretariats in Global Environmental Politics, Global Environmental Politics 2006 (6). This article illustrate how the Secretariat of the CCD had to face the dissatisfaction of Member States after it had overstepped the boundaries set by them (see pp. 40s). Also, see *A. Guzman*, International Organizations and the Frankenstein Problem, EJIL 2013 (24). This article highlights the different ways in which States try to restrict the powers of the international organizations they create in order to preserve control over these new entities.

87 CITES, SC54 Doc.8, Legal Personality of the Convention and the Secretariat. Yet, to add even more to this confusing dilemma, the Convention on Biological Diversity's web site has the ".int" domain name.

88 See *P. Daillier, M. Forteau, A. Pellet*, Droit International Public, 8th edition (2009), pp. 637- 708; *M. Shaw*, International Law, 6th edition (2008), pp. 1282-1331.

89 Encyclopedia Britannica on line: http://global.britannica.com/science/Batesian-mimicry (emphasis added). Last accessed: 17/05/2016.

can, at best, be qualified as soft law. But the fact that they produce practical effects is an illustration of their "normative strength".[90] Following the metaphor, the "venom" of the model is its legally binding characteristic while its "conspicuous colouration" are the functions and characteristics of law. In sum, institutions, be they Secretariats or Scientific Bodies, respect these instruments as a result of their careful elaboration[91] and formulation and also because they contribute to the implementation of their mandate. This approach is directly in line with the theories of law as "belief"[92] where, all in all, "*what makes something international law may well be the belief that it is such*" and where "*as soon as enough people accept and believe that something is law, it becomes law*".

Secondly, even if the Secretariats chose to rely on Memoranda in order to avoid unnecessary legal heaviness in their co-operation[93], their subsequent practice with regards to these agreements illustrate that they nevertheless act as if they were bound by a binding contract. Here again, the characteristic of the Memoranda and the fact that they contribute in achieving the mandate of both signatories are key elements in explaining their implementation.

In any case, it is highly likely that the staff of the Secretariats being linked by these instruments do not even consider the legal questions raised by these Memoranda. As their only purpose is to achieve their respective mandate, they simply use whatever tool is best suited to help them in doing so. The question of the legal nature of these memoranda may very well be relevant only in front of an arbitrator or judge.

It seems that the use of MoUs will be more and more frequent, as suggested by the recent "hints" given by the MAP[94] or GFCM.[95] It is plausible that these agreements, for the above reasons, will "*supersede all prior communications and representations between the Parties*"[96] and become the usual means of co-operation between the different elements of the Mediterranean regime complex. For instance, as indicated by the MAP Secretariat, discussions are ongoing on memoranda with the CBD and during the last COP of the Barcelona convention,

---

90 *C. Thibierge et alii*, La Force Normative – Naissance d'un Concept, 2009.

91 In some cases, the elaboration of a Memorandum can take several years and be the source of tensions. On this type of occurrence, see *S. Jinnah, op. cit. note* 21, pp. 147-177. In this chapter the authors analyses the negotiation process between the CITES and the FAO that led to the adoption of a Memorandum in the context of a controversy concerning the Bluefin tuna.

92 *J. Pauwelyn*, Is it International Law or not, and does it even matter?, *in J. Pauwelyn, R. Wessel, J. Wouters (ed.)*, Informal International Lawmaking, 2012, p.140.

93 On the reliance on informality see, *J. Pauwelyn, R. Wessel, J. Wouters*, When Structures Become Shackles: Stagnation and Dynamics in International Lawmaking, EJIL 2014 (25). This article provides a synthesis of the previously quoted book (note 92).

94 *Supra*, note 70, "*Request the Secretariat to further expand the co-operation with International and Regional Organizations such as the GEF, the WB, the UNDP, the EU, bilateral co-operation agencies and other relevant actors with a view to mobilize as many actors as possible in support of implementing in a coherent, synergistic and effective manner the priorities established by the Contracting Parties to the Barcelona Convention*".

95 *Supra*, note 64, p.4, "Possible future MoU that could be adopted by the Commission".

96 Clause 1 of the ACCOBAMS/GFCM Memorandum. See *supra*, note 63.

a memorandum was also signed with the Secretariat of the Commission on the Protection of the Black Sea against Pollution.[97]

It is hard to appropriately name these instruments and the practices in which they are set. The temptation of simply describing them as being *sui generis* is high, but nevertheless we believe that the term "interinstitutional administrative law" reflects the purposes of these Memoranda in an appropriate way. The question remains, however, if this "interinstitutional administrative law" fits into international public law or not, given that it challenges the classical theory of sources.

The following graph (figure 2) gives a partial overview of the connection between some of the elements of the Mediterranean regime complex. Though it does not provide an exhaustive representation of all of the different connexions, it does illustrate the fact that the different regimes and their respective technical bodies are less and less isolated in their work.

Figure 2. Partial overview of the Mediterranean institutional connexions

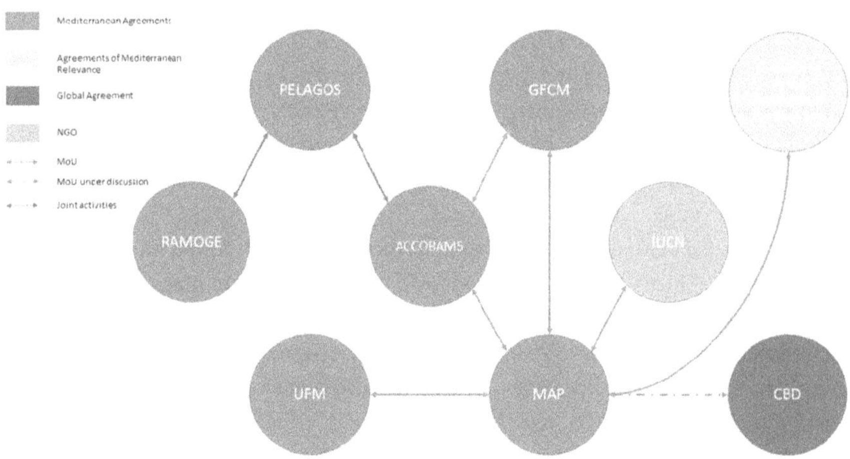

5. CONCLUSION

Through a variety of instruments of a blurry legal nature, the Mediterranean regimes have set up an intricate system that can benefit their technical bodies' credibility and relevance. Simply put, common objectives and frameworks prevent contradictions while collaborative agreements prevent duplications and fosters co-operation.

However, there are limitations to this approach. Firstly, this architecture does not necessarily increase the legitimacy of MTBs. This legitimacy is inherently

97 *Supra*, note 65, annex III. This Mou has the same characteristics as the one previously described. Also, it has provisions concerning the use of an arbitral tribunal in case of disputes.

linked to the very nature and form of the activities undertaken by a technical body. Consequently, a legitimacy crisis might not be resolved by the fact that MTBs benefit from a legal framework increasing their collaboration. For instance, if an MTB's assessment is being conducted by experts from the Global North exclusively, or if there is a suspicion of conflict of interests, inter-connections might not be sufficient to solve this issue. Therefore, this threat to the work of MTBs has to be dealt with within the appropriate regime.

It appears that this process is also being driven by institutions, while States are relatively passive (at best, they give their consent in the final steps of a process led by institutions). We believe that a stronger involvement of Mediterranean States, in order to increase the synergies among institutions and the quality of the work conducted within the different MTBs, would be a significant step in the right direction. This lack of State-involvement in the synergistic push of environmental regimes has been underlined by the UNEP in the context of the biodiversity cluster.[98] Consequently, it is important to demonstrate how synergies and better MTBs are a cost-efficient way of achieving effectiveness. In so doing, we can hope to convince States to take part in this global phenomenon.

Finally, we realize that our analysis is incomplete, given that it is based solely on official documentation. Even if we highlighted what can be seen as innovations within the region[99], their concrete repercussion on the work on MTBs can only be truly assessed by using methods that are usually foreign to the legal discipline (*i.e.* interviews, on-site observation ...). For instance, we still do not know with certainty how the evolution we just described is perceived by the individuals working for the MTBs or by the representatives of Mediterranean States. If there is no change in how Mediterranean participants perceive the regimes in which they are navigating, then the evolution we highlighted in our analysis will likely remain inconsequential. Also, as official documentation is only representative of a fraction of the actual dynamics that exists within regimes, then it may very well be that some of our analysis is simply incomplete or incorrect. If research based on interviews and field work came to completely different conclusions, this would highlight an enormous gap between institutional communication and institutional activities. This goes to show that environmental governance has to be studied from a pluri-disciplinary perspective in order to be fully understood. Only then can cause and effect be identified and explained.

Nevertheless, by investigating the subject of technical bodies in the Mediterranean Basin, we have highlighted innovative legal practices that we hope will be further researched in order to lay down a comprehensive analysis of this rich and fascinating region.

---

98 *Supra* note 41.

99 UNEP refers to MoUs as important steps towards greater collaboration between regimes. *UNEP*, Regional Oceans Governance Making Regional Seas Programmes, Regional Fisheries Bodies and Large Marine Ecosystem Mechanisms Work Better Together (2014).

CHAPTER 6
ENVIRONMENTAL DIGNITY RIGHTS

Erin Daly
Professor of Law, Widener University Delaware Law School (USA)

James R. May
Distinguished Professor of Law, Widener University Delaware Law School
*Chief Sustainability Officer, Widener University (USA)**

ABSTRACT

The threats to human rights caused by environmental degradation – including those caused by climate change – are increasingly evident. And yet, there continues to be confusion and a lack of consensus about how human rights will be affected, as demonstrated at the recent climate talks in Paris. Taking better advantage of the role of constitutionally-instantiated dignity rights can help to diffuse this dissonance. Most of the effects that environmental degradation have on people can be seen in threats to their ability to live in dignity, including the ability to fully develop one's personality, to live in a community and to claim other rights. The right to dignity, though rooted in international law, is recognized in most of the world's constitutions and a robust jurisprudence of dignity rights has been developing in many countries. We conclude that environmental outcomes – including climate change – can and should be informed by dignity rights and corresponding jurisprudence, a synthesis we call "environmental dignity rights."

> "Man has the fundamental right to freedom, equality and adequate conditions of life, in an environment of a quality that permits a life of dignity and well-being, and he bears a solemn responsibility to protect and improve the environment for present and future generations."
> – Stockholm Declaration on the Human Environment[1]

---

* The authors would like to thank Janet Lindenmuth for help with research on the role of dignity in international and domestic (U.S.) environmental law.

1 Stockholm Declaration on the Human Environment, Principle 1 www.unep.org/Documents.Multilingual/Default.asp?documentid=97&articleid=1503.

The importance of dignity as a founding value of the new Constitution cannot be overemphasized. Recognizing a right to dignity is the acknowledgement of the intrinsic worth of human beings: human beings are entitled to be treated as worthy of respect and concern.
– S v. Makwanyane and Another, Constitutional Court of South Africa[2]

1. INTRODUCTION

Environmental outcomes can and should be informed by the concept of dignity. Human dignity is an elemental value that presupposes that every human being has equal worth. It emphasizes the fundamental value and equality of all members of society – humans are not only endowed with dignity, but each is endowed with an equal quantum of dignity.[3] In the words of the United Nation's Declaration on Human Rights, "All human beings are born free and equal in dignity and rights." Where dignity is recognized, each person's dignity is inalienable, irreducible and infinite.[4] In our view, the environmental discourse about environmental outcomes – including climate change – could stand to benefit from a commitment to human dignity, or what we call, "environmental dignity rights."

Environmental dignity rights are individuated and collective. In the modern conception of dignity, each new-born has a special coin that is handed out at birth and carried throughout the course of its life. It can be used as often as one wishes, in a multitude of circumstances, and in all aspects of one's lived experience. Some of us are better reasoners than others, some of us are more morally sensitive than others, but the UDHR is indiscriminate: each of us, just by virtue of having been born human, is endowed with human dignity, and bestowed with equal worth. Dignity as such, then, can only be surrendered or yielded. It can neither be traded

---

2 S v. Makwanyane and Another, 1995 (6) BCLR 665 (CC) at para. 328.

3 See generally, "Dignidade constitucional: direitos e valores em construção" "Constitutional Dignity: Rights and Values in Concert," in "Leituras Constitucionais Contemporâneas" ed. Felipe Dutra Asensi and Daniel Giotti de Paula, (Getulio Vargas Foundation, Brazil) (2014). See also, Daly, E., DIGNITY RIGHTS: COURTS, CONSTITUTIONS, AND THE WORTH OF THE HUMAN PERSON (2011) (evaluating hundreds of dignity rights cases from around the world and arguing that, collectively, that these cases have developed a meaning of human of dignity that is based on the equal value of each member of the human family.); Barak, A., "Human Dignity: The constitutional Value and the Constitutional Right (Cambridge 2015); Dupre, C., The Age of Dignity (Cambridge 2016). For an extended overview of the evolution of dignity as a right, see also D. Townsend, Taking dignity seriously? A dignity approach to environmental disputes before human rights courts, 6 JHRE (2015) 204-225; C. McCrudden, "Human Dignity and Judicial Interpretation of Human Rights," (2008) 19 Eur J Int Law 655.

4 Hannah Arendt called this a "tremendous equalizing of differences which comes from being citizens of some commonwealth." Arendt, "The Perplexities of the Rights of Man," in The Portable Hannah Arendt (Peter Baehr Editor) at 43.

nor lost through folly, nor compounded through wise investment. It cannot be captured or conquered. And it is communal.

The internationalization of human dignity stands as a precursor to the modern environmental movement. Indeed, most commentators place the origins of the modern conception of dignity in the opening lines of 1948's Universal Declaration of Human Rights (UNDR) which categorically asserts that "the inherent dignity and [] the equal and inalienable rights of all members of the human family [are] the foundation of freedom, justice and peace in the world".[5] Similar language has since found its way into almost every significant international human rights document, from the International Covenant of Civil and Political Rights and the International Covenant of Economic, Social and Cultural Rights, on down. The relatively recent affirmation in international law that every person has human dignity did not change the fact that every person has always had, and always will have, human dignity; it did not create dignity where it had not previously existed. But it does change our *knowledge* about it. And once we know that dignity inheres in each member of the human family, we can never un-know it. This marks an important shift in how we think about what it is to be human in an environmentally-stressed planet.

Dignity can play a larger role in imagining how to respond to environmental stressors. International law's categorical recognition of the "inherent dignity" of "each member of the human family" reflects the specialness of humanity and of each member of that group, just by virtue of being born human. The UDHR makes this explicit, by resting the recognition of human dignity on the fact that human beings "are endowed with reason and conscience and should act towards one another in a spirit of brotherhood." Both parts of this phrase are elucidating. The first clause indicates that for the drafters of the UDHR, human dignity is compelled by our unique capacity to reason, though the UDHR goes further in also grounding it on the fact of human conscientiousness. That we have the capacity to make decisions, and to understand the morality of our decisions, makes us different and special. The second part of the sentence imposes a moral obligation on each of us to recognize the dignity, "the specialness", of each other person. Human dignity is not just a descriptor; it is precatory. The UDHR's declaration that we are all "equal in dignity" simply by virtue of being born human established a new moral paradigm that requires that each of us treat every other person with respect, including in our response to environmental challenges.

Comparative constitutionalism is a key component in imagining environmental dignity rights. The majority of countries on the planet have taken the next step of constitutionalizing the concept of human dignity. Over the last 50 years, dignity has become entrenched in constitutional systems throughout

5 UN General Assembly, Universal Declaration of Human Rights, 10 December 1948, 217 A (III), available at: www.unhcr.org/refworld/docid/3ae6b3712c.html [accessed 3 May 2016].

the world, in several forms: it can be a fundamental value[6], a stand-alone right[7], or a right associated with particular interests (e.g. work[8]) or segments of the population (women, disabled people, people in state custody, etc.[9]). More than 160 nations include dignity, in some form, in their constitutional texts and hardly a new constitution is adopted or amended without it.[10]

As a result, a robust global jurisprudence of dignity in constitutional systems around the world has developed. Drawing on textually based constitutional rights to dignity, this set of domestic cases is informed by, but distinct from, the case law developed at the international and regional levels that interprets and applies international and regional instruments. Although the cases come from every region of the world and every constitutional culture, and although they involve vast areas of human experience, the courts' understanding of human dignity and the role it plays in constitutional governance has coalesced around a small number of central features.

At the heart of dignity jurisprudence is the recognition that governments must respect people's capacity to fully develop their personalities and to control the course of their lives. We plan for ourselves and our progeny, as we seek to conserve the dignity of future generations. This set of fundamental values has many implications that are broadly felt throughout constitutional law. First, the capacity to fully develop one's personality is manifest in a broad spectrum of other constitutionally recognized rights, from civil and political rights like free speech and equality and voting to social rights like education and housing, to reproductive rights, to capital and other forms of punishment, and more. Dignity thus informs the scope of the rights that people enjoy under their constitutions. Another corollary of the government's obligation to respect people's need to control the course of their lives is the recognition that dignity is experienced not only individually but always in community with others. That is, one indispensable aspect of self-fulfilment is the ability to participate fully in one's social environment. There are scores of other implications of dignity's promise

---

6 Constitution of the Dominican Republic, Art. 38: "The State bases itself on respect for the **dignity** of the person and organizes itself for the real and effective protection of the fundamental rights that are inherent to it. The **dignity** of the human being is sacred, innate, and inviolable; its respect and protection constitute an essential responsibility of the public powers." See also e.g. Constitution of Albania, Preamble.

7 Constitution of Kenya, Art. 28: "Every person has inherent **dignity** and the right to have that **dignity** respected and protected."

8 Constitution of Nepal, Article 51(i)(2): "Guaranteeing social security by ensuring the basic rights of all laborers in accordance with the concept of **dignity** of labor."

9 Constitution of Haiti, Art. 44-1: "Prisons must be operated in accordance with standards reflecting respect for human **dignity** according to the law on this subject."

10 Pin, Andrea, The Arab Road to Dignity: The Goal of the 'Arab Spring' (April 12, 2016). Kellogg Institute for International Studies Working Paper Series No. 408, 2016. Available at SSRN: http://ssrn.com/abstract=2765366.

of full development of the personality but these two seem to us to be particularly pertinent to environmental rights, especially in the context of climate change.[11]

Despite dignity's emergence as a norm in international law and a right in constitutional texts, it remains largely invisible in advancing environmental protection at the international and domestic levels. There are more than 250 multilateral environmental agreements currently in force.[12] Yet – as far as we can tell – none of them recognizes or even mentions "dignity," save for one since-expired trade agreement.[13]

Likewise, domestic environmental laws seem to overlook dignity as well. Our survey of more than two-dozen environmental and natural resources laws in the United States, for example, yielded no results for "dignity."[14] A search of subnational environmental laws also yielded no results for "dignity."[15] Moreover, little if any scholarship discusses the linkages between the two realms. For example, much has been written about the linkages between human rights and the environment[16], human and environmental rights[17] and whether or not there is a fundamental right to a quality environment.[18] There is also a growing

---

11 Other lessons to be learned from the global dignity jurisprudence include the obligation to respect the equal worth of each person, to ensure a quantum of material comfort, obligations with respect to custody and dependence, and so on. We address some of these issues elsewhere.

12 www.wto.org/english/tratop_e/envir_e/envir_neg_mea_e.htm (accessed May 4, 2016).

13 The Lomé Convention is a trade and aid agreement between the European Economic Community and 71 African, Caribbean, and Pacific countries, primarily consisting of former colonies of the principal powers of Western Europe. While it is no longer in force, largely due to development of the European Union, it was for a while the world's sole trade agreement that linked sustainability, environmental outcomes and human dignity: "Support shall be provided in ACP-EEC cooperation for the ACP States' efforts to achieve comprehensive self-reliant and self-sustained development based on their cultural and social values, their human capacities, their natural resources and their economic potential in order to promote the ACP States' social, cultural and economic progress and the well-being of their populations through the satisfaction of their basic needs, the recognition of the role of women and the enhancement of people's capacities, *with respect for their dignity.* This development shall be based on a sustainable balance between its economic objectives, the rational management of the environment and the enhancement of natural and human resources." Article 4, Lomé Convention, available, with commentary, at: http://ec.europa.eu/development/body/cotonou/lome_history_en.htm (last checked May 2, 2016) (emphasis added).

14 Survey conducted using Westlaw databases, federal environmental law statutes, with search term "dignity." (Conducted May 2-5, 2016).

15 Ibid.

16 *See generally* Shelton, Dinah. 'Human Rights and the Environment.' *Yearbook Intl. Envtl. L.* 13 (2002): 199; Bonine, Svitlana Kravchenko and John E. *Human Rights and the Environment: Cases, Law and Policy.* Carolina Academic Press, 2008.

17 *See e.g.*, Gormley, Paul W. *Human Rights and the Environment: The Need for International Co-operation.* Sijthoff, 1976; Thorme, Melissa. 'Establishing Environment as a Human Right.' *Denv. J. Int'l L. & Pol'y* 19 (1991); 301; Merrills, J.G. 'Environmental Protection and Human Rights: Conceptual Aspects.' In *Human Rights Approaches to Environmental Protection*, by Alan E. Boyle & Michael R. Anderson, 25. Oxford University Press, 1996 (reconciling environmental and human rights).

18 *See generally* Turner, Stephen J. *A Substantive Environmental Right: An Examination of the Legal Obligations of Decision-makers Towards the Environment.* Kluwer Law International,

corpus of scholarship about embodying environmental rights constitutionally[19] and the emergence of such rights in the global order of environmental law.[20] The discussion about environmental rights also internalizes related concepts of intergenerational equity and the precautionary principle.[21] Yet, with few exceptions, there is very little written about the connection between dignity and environmental outcomes.[22]

Moreover, despite the broad scope of dignity cases, and their importance for understanding the scope of human freedom within constitutional structures, few cases have even touched on environmental rights and fewer still have engaged seriously with the challenges that environmental problems pose for human dignity. As a legal matter, this is not entirely surprising because of the different lineages of environmental and human – and dignity in particular – rights. Legal protection for the environment has traditionally fallen within the purview of local ordinances on the one hand and international law on the other. Human rights, by contrast, while influenced by developments at the international level, find their fullest and most readily enforceable expression in the domestic constitutions of the world's nations. It is only recently – as exemplified by the appointment in 2015 of the United Nations' first Special Rapporteur for Human Rights and the Environment – that legal scholars and practitioners are focusing on the relationship between environmental and human rights.

As a matter of lived experience, however, the near-absence of a dialogue between environmental and dignity rights is surprising and disappointing because of the many ways in which environmental conditions impact human dignity. As the world's climate changes, the pressures on human dignity will exacerbate. The

2008; Bruch, Carl. *Constitutional Environmental Law: Giving Force to Fundamental Principles in Africa*. 2, Environmental Law Institute Research Report, 2000; Hayward, Tim. *Constitutional Environmental Rights*. 12-13. Oxford University Press, 2005; Pallemaerts, Marc. 'The Human Right to a Healthy Environmeny as a Substantive Right.' In *Human Rights and the Environment*, by Maguelonne Déjeant-Pons & Marc Pallemaerts, 11-21. Oxford University Press, 2002 (discussing the extent to which international law recognizes the existence of a substantive individual right to a healthy environment).

19 *See, e.g.*, Brandl, Hartwin Bungert and Ernest. 'Constitutional Entrenchment of Environmental Protection: A Comparative Analysis of Experiences Abroad.' *Harv. Envtl. L. Rev.* 16 (1992):1; Shelton, Dinah. 'Human Rights, Environmental Rights, and the Right to Environment.' *Stan. J. Int'l L.* 28 (1991): 103 [hereinafter Shelton I]; Symposium. 'Earth Rights and Responsibilities: Human Rights and Environmental Protection.' *Yale J. Int'l L.* 18 (1993): 18; Sax, Joseph L. 'The Search for Environmental Rights.' *J. Land Use & Envtl L. (1990): 93; Cf.* Fernandez, José L., 'State Constitutions, Environmental Rights Provisions, and the Doctrine of Self-Execution: A Political Question?' *Harv. Envtl. L. Rev.* 17 (1993): 333 (objecting to enforcement of constitutional environmental rights).

20 Percival, Tseming Yang and Robert V. 'The Emergence of Global Environmental Law.' *Ecology L. Q.* 36 (2009): page.

21 Hiskes, *supra* at 130.

22 But see M Düwell "Human Dignity and Future Generations," in M Düwell, J Braarvig, R Brownsword and D Mieth (eds), *The Cambridge Handbook of Human Dignity* (Cambridge 2014) 551-558. See also D. Townsend, Taking dignity seriously? A dignity approach to environmental disputes before human rights courts, 6 JHRE (2015) 204-225.

multitudinous ways in which the natural environment impacts human dignity notwithstanding, constitutional courts have not yet fully appreciated the link.

The opportunity for deploying dignity as a means to improve environmental outcomes, we conclude, lies in growing jurisprudence concerning constitutionalized dignity rights. We believe that the well-developed global body of dignity cases could inform nascent environmental rights jurisprudence in many ways, given the breadth of each area of law and of lived experience at the intersection of human dignity and the natural environment. In this chapter, we focus on two contributions – one substantive and the other procedural – that constitutional dignity rights cases could make to environmental protection, each one flowing from the attributes of the dignity cases described above. First, the promise of the full development of the personality could help provide definition, content and boundaries to emerging environmental rights if it were used as a measure of their violation. Dignity, as a measure of environmental rights, could affect threshold matters such as standing, as well as questions of interpretation and application and the scope of remedies. A second contribution of dignity jurisprudence to environmental rights is the recognition that full respect for human dignity requires governments to accord, not only with substantive rights, but also with procedural rights to democratic engagement in community decisions.

We focus on these two aspects of dignity jurisprudence for several reasons. First, these two examples illustrate both the substantive and the procedural dimensions of dignity rights as they relate to environmental protection. We also note that these aspects of environmental dignity jurisprudence are particularly pronounced in the context of climate change and, therefore, demand that particular attention be paid: as the effects of climate change exacerbate, the threats to people's ability to live to their full capacities, individually and collectively, will increase. Finally, these two aspects of this body of law touch on some of dignity's most important attributes – its essential connection to our ability to control our own lives, its ability to link to other rights, its social aspect and its roots in deeply held and arguably universal values. Thus, we believe that the contribution that these particular aspects of dignity rights could make to environmental outcomes are significant. At the same time, the failure of litigants and courts to recognize the link between dignity rights and environmental outcomes suggests that further investigation is needed.

The issues addressed here lie at the intersection of two potentially vast areas of legal inquiry and experience. Environmental law encompasses both anthropocentric and eco-centric orientations and has been the subject of extensive jurisprudence, codification and commentary in all spheres from the local to the global.[23] The dignity jurisprudence, for its part, is vast, comprising cases from

23 This jurisprudence is discussed more fully in Part I, below; see also generally, Daly, E., Dignity Rights Courts, Constitutions, and the Worth of the Human Person (University of Pennsylvania

national tribunals with constitutional jurisdiction from all around the globe. In this chapter, we engage primarily in a comparative constitutional analysis that is global in geographic scope; while regional and international tribunals have much to contribute to this discussion, they are beyond the scope of our present analysis.

This chapter has five parts. Part I provides an overview of dignity rights, including scope and applications, considering dignity both as a measure of a constitutional violation and as a right to engage in a political community. Part II provides an overview of environmental rights, noting that while environmental constitutionalism is growing in countries around the world, it is not yet as developed as the global constitutional jurisprudence relating to human dignity. Part III explains the relationship between human dignity and environmental protection. Part IV then posits two principal ways in which dignity rights, as understood by constitutional tribunals, could inform and enhance environmental outcomes. We conclude that taking human dignity rights seriously would help to nourish more rational environmental outcomes, including in the context of climate change.

2. DIGNITY RIGHTS IN COMPARATIVE CONSTITUTIONAL PERSPECTIVE

Although originally a philosophical and religious concept, dignity now is considered a legal right that is enforceable in courts around the world. The first, most important recognition of human dignity in a legal instrument can be found in the 1948 Universal Declaration of Human Rights, whose preamble begins with an acknowledgment of every person's dignity: "Whereas recognition of the inherent dignity and of the equal and inalienable rights of all members of the human family is the foundation of freedom, justice and peace in the world."[24] Like a dominant gene, human dignity descended into the following generation of international law in the common language of both International Covenants, which begin by recognizing that the rights enumerated therein "derive from the inherent dignity of the human person."[25] It is the common ancestor to all

Press, 2013); Barak, A., "Human Dignity: The constitutional Value and the Constitutional Right (Cambridge 2015); C. McCrudden, "Human Dignity and Judicial Interpretation of Human Rights", EJIL, 2008, vol. 19, n°4, pp. 655-724; D. Kretzmer et E. Klein (dir.), The Concept of Human Dignity in Human Rights Discourse, La Haye: Kluwer Law International, 2002, 324.

24 Universal Declaration of Human Rights, Preamble.

25 ICCPR, Preamble and ICESCR, Preamble. "Dignity" appears twice in the preambles in both covenants, and one additional time in each. In the ICCPR, it appears in connection with liberty: "All persons deprived of their liberty shall be treated with humanity and with respect for the inherent dignity of the human person." (Art. 10 (1)). In the ICESCR, it appears in connection with education: "The States Parties to the present Covenant recognize the right of everyone to education. They agree that education shall be directed to the full development of the human personality and the sense of its dignity, and shall strengthen the respect for human

modern human rights, informing and implicating most other human rights at the international and national levels.[26]

From these common international sources, which characterized dignity principally as the source for other rights, many of the world's constitutions have incorporated dignity not only as a foundational value but also as a right; by now, hardly a new constitution is adopted without reference to the right to dignity. It can be a stand-alone right that is eternal[27], foundational[28], implied in life[29], or a mother right whose progeny has constitutional status.[30] Oftentimes, it is associated with other important rights of vulnerable groups, such as the rights of prisoners[31], of women and children[32], of the disabled[33], and so on. It can be conceptualized simply, but profoundly, as the right to have rights.

Over the last sixty years, courts in Latin America, Europe, Asia, Africa, the Middle East and North America have developed a robust jurisprudence of dignity

---

rights and fundamental freedoms. They further agree that education shall enable all persons to participate effectively in a free society, promote understanding, tolerance and friendship among all nations and all racial, ethnic or religious groups, and further the activities of the United Nations for the maintenance of peace." (Art. 13).

26 Iain Currien & Johon De Waal, Bill of Rights Handbook, 526 (Juta & Co. 2005). See also Cheadle MH, Davis DH & Haysom NRL South African Constitutional Law: The Bill of Rights (2014) LexisNexis (Durban), Section 5.1; see also Section 5.2.2: "The right to dignity, a core value from which other rights derive, is frequently invoked together with the specific enumerated right relied upon to challenge conduct or laws. Dignity, thus, stands as a forensic reinforcement to the other specified rights. Not infrequently, constitutional litigation brought primarily on the grounds of another fundamental right has been decided on the question of the right to dignity. In other instances, the court has referred to or enquired into the impact on the right to dignity of the conduct or law complained of."

27 See Germany, Basic Law, Art. 1. "(1) Human dignity shall be inviolable. To respect and protect it shall be the duty of all state authority. (2) The German people therefore acknowledge inviolable and inalienable human rights as the basis of every community, of peace and of justice in the world." And See Art. 79 (3), prohibiting amendment of Article 1.

28 See South Africa Constitution, Art. 1: " The Republic of South Africa is one, sovereign, democratic state founded on the following values: (a) Human dignity, the achievement of equality and the advancement of human rights and freedoms." And see S v. Makwanyane and Another, 1995 (6) BCLR 665 (CC) at para. 328: ("The importance of dignity as a founding value of the new Constitution cannot be overemphasized. Recognizing a right to dignity is the acknowledgement of the intrinsic worth of human beings: human beings are entitled to be treated as worth of respect and concern. This right therefore is the foundation of many of the other rights that are specifically entrenched.").

29 Danial Latifi & Anor v. Union of India and Other Petitions (2002) 4 LRI 36, citing Olga Tellis v. Bombay Municipal Corp (1985) 3 SCC 545; and Maneka Gandhi v. Union of India (1978) 1 SCC 248.

30 Barak, at 299-300 noting that the rights to due process, education, and labor relations are daughter rights which derive from the mother-right to human dignity. See also Hungary Const. Court, Decision 8/1990 (IV. 23.) AB, ABH 1990, 42, 44, 45.

31 See e.g. Haiti Constitution, Art. 44-1: "Prisons must be operated in accordance with standards reflecting respect for human dignity according to the law on this subject."

32 India Constitution, Arts. 39 and 51(a).

33 Uganda Constitution, Art. 16.

on subjects as diverse as health care, imprisonment, privacy, education, culture, the environment, sexuality and death, among other things.

Civil and political rights, which derive from the Enlightenment-era constitutions such as the French Declaration of the Rights of Man and Citizens and the American Constitution, have been brought into the modern age through the International Covenant of Civil and Political Rights, and into the constitutional traditions that have adopted and adapted them. Chief among those rights are life and liberty, both of which have been identified by constitutional tribunals as sounding in human dignity.[34] The right to dignity has also been recognized in both civil and common law traditions, in the right to vote[35] and to participate in the political process[36], the right to information[37], the right to protect one's reputation[38] and the right to equality and against discrimination[39] among others. These rights – as the French Declaration reminds us – are among the rights of citizenship. They have been recognized not only as rights in and of themselves but also as aspects of the right to dignity; in South Africa, this aspect of dignity is referred to as "civic dignity."[40]

In other political and jurisprudential cultures, dignity rights are relevant to the quality of people's lives. The availability of housing in South Africa[41], the rate of a pension in Peru[42] and Germany[43] the availability of health care in Colombia[44], a decent wage in India[45], the right to marry in South Africa[46] can all be measured by what is required to assure human dignity.

The importance of human dignity to the ability of people to fully control their lives can be seen in the language of some constitutions, including Andorra's which

34 See e.g. S v. Makwanyane and Another, 1995 (6) BCLR 665 (CC) (invalidating the death penalty in South Africa on the ground that it violates human dignity) and see e.g. Miranda v. Arizona, 384 U.S. 436 (1966) (finding the police interrogation may be "destructive of human dignity" at 457).

35 EXP.N..° 0030-2005-PI/TC (Peru Constitutional Tribunal).

36 Doctors for Life International v. Speaker of the National Assembly and Others (CCT12/05) [2006] ZACC 11; 2006 (12) BCLR 1399 (CC); 2006 (6) SA 416 (CC) (17 August 2006).

37 Decision No. 7 of June 4, 1996 on CC No. 1/96, section I (Bulgaria, 1996) and EXP.N..° 02005-2009-PA/TC, Lima ONG, "Acción De Lucha Anticorrupcion, para. 6 (Peru Constitutional Tribunal (2009).

38 Corte Suprema de Justicia [CSJN] [Supreme Court of Justice], 7/7/1992, "Ek- medjian v. Sofovich," Fallos (1992-315-1492) (Arg.).

39 HCJ 4541/94, 49(4) PD 94 [1995] (Isr.) and see R. v. Kapp [2008] 2 SCR 483, 2008 SCC 41 (Can.).

40 August and Another v. The Electoral Commission, Case CCT 8/99 [1999] ZACC 3; 1999 (3) SA 1; 1999 (4) BCLR 363 (1 April 1999), Doctors for Life International v. Speaker of the National Assembly and Others (CCT12/05) [2006] ZACC 11; 2006 (12) BCLR 1399 (CC); 2006 (6) SA 416 (CC) (17 August 2006).

41 Government of the Republic of South Africa and Others v Grootboom and Others [2000] ZACC 19, 2001 (1) SA 46 (CC), 2000 (11) BCLR 1169 (CC), Constitutional Court.

42 EXP.N.° 05913-2007-PA/TC (2009) (Peruvian Constitutional Tribunal).

43 BVerfG, 1 BVL 1/09, 1 BVL 3/09, 1 BVL 409 of 9 Feb. 2010 (Hartz IV).

44 See e.g. Sentencia T-292/09 (Constitutional Court of Colombia).

45 Francis Coralie v. Union of India AIR 1981 SC 746.

46 Minister of Home Affairs v. Fourie and Another, Case CCT 60/04 (2005).

guarantees to all persons a right to education "which shall be oriented towards the dignity and full development of the human personality, thus strengthening the respect for freedom and the fundamental rights."[47] And it can be seen in the case law throughout the world. The Indian Supreme Court has explained that: "These fundamental rights represent the basic values cherished by the people of this country since the Vedic times and they are calculated to protect the dignity of the individual and create conditions in which every human being can develop his personality to the fullest extent. They weave a 'pattern of guarantees on the basic- structure of human rights' and impose negative obligations on the State not to encroach on individual liberty in its various dimensions."[48] The Court went on to explain that the main objective of India's struggle for liberation was "to build a new social order where man will not be *a mere plaything* in the hands of the State or a few privileged persons but there will be full scope and opportunity for him to achieve the maximum development of his personality and the dignity of the individual will be fully assured."[49]

The Constitutional Court of Colombia has developed a shorthand for the human desire "to live as one wishes." This includes some measure of control over both what a person becomes and does. The Canadian Supreme Court has elaborated on this link between dignity and full development of the personality or control over one's life course: "The idea of human dignity finds expression in almost every right and freedom guaranteed in the [Canadian Charter of Rights and Freedoms]. Individuals are afforded the right to choose their own religion and their own philosophy of life, the right to choose with whom they will associate and how they will express themselves, the right to choose where they will and what occupation they will pursue. These are all examples of the basic theory underlying the *Charter*, namely that the state will respect choices made by individuals and, to the greatest extent possible, will avoid subordinating these choices to any one conception of the good life."[50] In Europe, the right to dignity is nothing less than the "essence of European constitutionalism."[51]

Thus, the concept of dignity has had a profound impact on jurisprudence around the globe, animating and informing other constitutionally-recognized individual rights and values. For some, dignity embraces all the other human rights, thrown together in one basket. In this sense, it does not add much to the already unwieldy and ill-defined body of human rights law. Most courts that have engaged with their national constitutional commitment to human

---

47 Const. Andorra, Art. 20.

48 *Maneka Ghandi v. Union of India*, [1978] INSC 17; [1978] 2 SCR 621; [1978] 1 SCC 248; AIR 1978 SC 597 (25 January 1978), 667-68.

49 Maneka Ghandi.

50 74. *R. v. Morgentaler* [1988] 1 SCR 30, 158 (opinion of Wilson, J.).

51 Catherine Dupré, The Age of Dignity: Human Rights and Constitutionalism in Europe (Hart 2015) at 99, quoting SW v. United Kingdom, Application no. 20166/92, ECtHR, 22 November 1995.

dignity have found that it does much more. In some instances, because it informs the obligations that governments owe to individuals in a system of democratic constitutionalism, it constitutes the very measure of protection for other constitutional guarantees, defining what constitutes a violation, the injury and how to remedy it. In other cases, it embodies a distinct human right that is not otherwise covered by constitutional guarantees and one that is peculiarly vulnerable to dramatic environmental harms. This conception of dignity – the right to participate in a political community and to exercise all other rights – is perhaps the least understood, but the most important, of the environmental dignity rights.

3. ENVIRONMENTAL RIGHTS IN COMPARATIVE CONSTITUTIONAL PERSPECTIVE

Global environmental constitutionalism, a relatively recent phenomenon at the confluence of constitutional law, international law, human rights and environmental law that embodies the recognition that the environment is a proper subject for protection in constitutional texts and for vindication by constitutional courts worldwide.[52]

---

52 See generally, James R. May & Erin Daly, GLOBAL ENVIRONMENTAL CONSTITUTIONALISM (Cambridge Press 2015); James R. May & Erin Daly, ENVIRONMENTAL CONSTITUTIONALISM: A RESEARCH COMPENDIUM (Edward Elgar 2016); *Symposium on Global Environmental Constitutionalism: An Introduction and Overview*, 21 Widener L. Rev. 139 (2015); James R. May & Erin Daly, *Robinson Township v. Pennsylvania: A Model for Environmental Constitutionalism*, 21 Widener L. Rev. 151 (2015); Erin Daly & James R. May, *Comparative Environmental Constitutionalism*, Jindal Global Law Review (Special issue on Environmental Law and Governance – Indian and International Perspectives) (2015); *Constitutional Directions in Procedural Environmental Rights*, 28 Jrnl. Envtl. L. & Lit. 101 (2014); James R. May & Erin Daly, Environmental Rights and Liabilities, 3 Eur. J. Env. Lia. 75 (2012); James R. May & Erin Daly, N*ew Directions in Earth Rights, Environmental Rights and Human Rights: Six Facets of Constitutionally Embedded Environmental Rights Worldwide*, IUCN ACADEMY OF ENVIRONMENTAL LAW E-JOURNAL, vol. 1, 2011, posted Feb. 22, 2011; Erin Daly &James R. May, 'Global Constitutional Environmental Rights.' In *Routledge Handbook of International Environmental Law*, by Shawkat Alam, Jahid Hossain Bhuiyan, Tareq M.R. Chowdhury and Erika J. Techera. Routledge, 2012; Erin Daly & James R. May, 'Vindicating Fundamental Environmental Rights Worldwide.' *Ore. Rev. Intl. L.* 11 (2010): 365-440; Daly, James R. May and Erin. 'New Directors in Earth Rights, Environmental Rights and Human Rights: Six Facets of Constitutionally Embedded Environmental Rights Worldwide.' *IUCN Academy of Environmental Law E-Journal* 1 (2011); James R. May & Erin Daly. 'Constitutional Environmental Rights Worldwide.' In *Principles of Constitutional Environmental Law*, by James R. May. ABA Publishing, Environmental Law Institute, 2011; May, James R. 'Constituting Fundamental Environmental Rights Worldwide.' *Pace Envtl. L. Rev.* 23 (2006): 113.See also, Boyd, David R. The Right to a Healthy Environment: Revitalizing Canada's Constitution. UBC Press, 2012: 65. See also Hiskes, Richard P. The Human Right to a Green Future: Environmental Rights and Intergenerational Justice. Cambridge University Press 2008; Hayward, Tim. Constitutional Environmental Rights. Oxford University Press, 2005.

Throughout human history and all over the world, humans have lived in tension with nature and at other times in harmony with it, alternatively reforming and revering the natural environment around them. The constitutional law of nations around the world has recently taken note of this legacy: in one case from Sri Lanka, for example, the court referred "to the irrigation works of ancient Sri Lanka, the Philosophy of not permitting even a drop of water to flow into the sea without benefiting humankind," and emphasized that for several millennia sustainable development had been already consciously practiced with great success in Sri Lanka.[53]

On the other side of the globe, the same sentiment is echoed in the 2008 constitution of Ecuador, which guarantees the rights of nature, by recalling the values of the local indigenous civilizations, referring to nature as *Pacha Mama*, or Mother Earth, in the language of the Achuar people of the Amazon.

What is new, too – at least in the last few decades – is a growing concern about severe and deepening environmental challenges, including increased pollution, loss of speciation and biodiversity, and global climate change, to name just a few. And with it, greater attention to how to protect the environment through law, and in particular, through law that is most deeply entrenched in the legal system of nations.

Environmental and dignity rights share common features. As with dignity rights, environmental rights can be coalescent, merging governmental structures and individual rights modalities in furtherance of "an overarching legal-normative framework for directing environmental policy."[54] It can be deployed to protect local concerns, such as access to fresh food, water or air, or global concerns like biodiversity and climate change that share elements of both human rights and environmental protection. Environmental constitutionalism offers a way forward when other legal mechanisms fall short.

Environmental rights, like dignity rights, implicate most matters affecting the human condition, including life, health, food, housing, education, work, socio-economic status, culture, non-discrimination, peace, children's health and general well-being – as well as the quality of the earth's water, ground, and air.[55] It

53 *Bulankulama and Six Others v. Ministry of Industrial Development and Seven Others* S.C. Application No 884/99 (F.R) (Supreme Court of the Democratic Socialist Republica of Sri Lanka).

54 Hawyard, Tim. *Constitutional Environmental Rights*. Oxford University Press, 2005.

55 *See* United Nations Comm'n on Human Rights, Sub-Comm'n on Prevention of Discrimination & Protection of Minorities, Human Rights and the Environment, prepared by Fatma Zohra Ksentini, U.N. Doc. E/CN.4/Sub.2/1994/9 at ¶ 248 (July 6. 1994), concluding: Environmental damage has direct effects on the enjoyment of a series of human rights, such as the right to life, to health, to a satisfactory standard of living, to sufficient food, to housing, to education, to work, to culture, to non-discrimination, to dignity and the harmonious development of one's personality, to security of person and family, to development, to peace, etc. *See also* MacDonald, Karen E. 'Sustaining the Environmental Rights of Children: An Exploratory Critique.' *Fordham Envtl. L. Rev.* 18 (2006): 5. 'Others have even argued that environmental harm can result in a breach of the right to security of the person (non-intervention).'

encompasses both human and non-human phenomena and, therefore, draws from both environmental rights movements and human rights movements, both of which have ballooned over the last few decades. The grand scope of environmental constitutionalism suggests that it offers complex and multi-layered constitutional value. But environmental constitutionalism's ambition may also be its greatest weakness: the nearly limitless application of human and environmental rights makes it difficult for constitutional drafters to choose an appropriate language through which to protect the environment and may dampen judicial enthusiasm for their vindication.

The constitutions of about three-quarters of nations worldwide address environmental matters in some fashion. About 76 aim to grant a basic environmental right explicitly, with more than a dozen more doing so implicitly through attendant a right to life, dignity or health. Dozens of others impose reciprocal duties, commit to environmental stewardship or policies. Dozens of others still ensure a right to information, participation and justice in environmental matters. Moreover, many subnational governments have followed suit. Indeed, most people on earth now live under constitutions that protect environmental rights in some way. And environmental constitutionalism continues to emerge and evolve in courts all around the globe, although many constitutionally-embedded environmental rights provisions have yet to be energetically engaged.

4. IMAGINING ENVIRONMENTAL DIGNITY RIGHTS

The role (or lack thereof) of dignity rights in the most recent climate change negotiations may help to illustrate the current tenuous relationship between dignity and environmental protection, particularly in the context of climate change. At the COP21 talks in Paris at the end of 2015, negotiators wrangled over the relationship between human rights and climate change; the issue proved so divisive that references to human rights were included in the preamble but not in the substantive provisions of the document.[56] This confusion and lack of consensus reflect a failure to appreciate the important and varied ways that climate change threatens human rights throughout the world and to the right to human dignity in particular.

Climate change – and environmental degradation more generally – affect the full spectrum of recognized human rights. Climate change "directly and

56 FCCC/CP/2015/L.9/Rev.1: "Acknowledging that climate change is a common concern of humankind, Parties should, when taking action to address climate change, respect, promote and consider their respective obligations on human rights, the right to health, the rights of indigenous peoples, local communities, migrants, children, persons with disabilities and people in vulnerable situations and the right to development, as well as gender equality, empowerment of women and intergenerational equity, …."

indirectly implicates" important human rights responsibilities because it "connects the many dangerous climate impacts to the human rights commitments states have already undertaken."[57] The right to life is increasingly threatened as floods, landslides and fires become more common and more severe; the right to health is impacted when droughts makes access to food less secure or when pollution makes potable water less available; rights relating to property (including agricultural, inheritance, and development) are threatened when rising sea levels erode land; cultural rights may be threatened by reckless logging, overfishing, or mining, as labour and employment rights might be – to give just a few examples. And, as is so often the case, people who are already vulnerable to human rights abuses are made more so by environmental degradation: those who are less likely to be politically protected and who have fewer resources to protect themselves – including women, poor people, ethnic minorities and children – are most likely to be subject to this panoply of environmentally-generated human rights abuses. They have fewer options to avoid the effects of climate change, and fewer means with which to combat them. When land erodes, or ceases to be fertile, they move to cities, where their communities are diminished and where they may or may not find employment, shelter and services and where they are more likely to find themselves physically and psychologically in danger. If they have no cities to move to, like the former residents of the Cataret Islands, they become climate refugees, sometimes for generations. The ways that environmental degradation, including climate change impacts, affects the lives of people throughout the world and threatens their human rights are varied in scope, infinite in number, and profound in meaning.

And yet, of all the national constitutions that reference dignity or environmental rights, only Belgium's explicitly binds the two together: "Everyone has the right to lead a life worthy of human dignity ... [including] the right to enjoy the protection of a healthy environment."[58] South Africa's constitution provides that "everyone has the right to an environment that is not harmful to their health or well-being ..."[59] suggesting a link between environmental health and human psychological health, particularly when read in light of the constitution's transformative commitment to human dignity. But given the significant number of constitutions that link dignity to other aspects of human experience, combined

57 Maxine Burkett, A Justice Paradox: On Climate Change, Small Island Developing States, and the Quest for Effective Legal Remedy, 35 Haw. L. Rev. 633, 646-47 (2013).

58 Belgium Const., Title II, Article 23(4).

59 Section 24 of the Constitution of the Republic of South Africa, Act 108 of 1998 provides that "everyone has the right to an environment that is not harmful to their health or well-being; and to have the environment protected, for the benefit of present and future generations, through reasonable legislative and other measures that:
(i) prevent pollution and ecological degradation;
(ii) promote conservation and
(iii) secure ecologically sustainable development and use of natural resources while promoting justifiable economic and social development.

with those that protect a wide variety of environmental values, it is surprising that constitutions are so reticent on the link between human dignity and a healthy environment.

Decisions from national courts that recognize the interrelationship between dignity and environment are also rare, though some leading examples come from environmental ("green") courts: Kenya's Environmental and Land Court in Nairobi acknowledged that environmental rights must be read in light of the constitutional commitment to human dignity[60]: "The Preamble to the Constitution ... proclaims that the people of Kenya, when making the Constitution were committed to nurturing and protecting the well-being of the individual, the family, communities and the nation. Likewise, the national values and principles that bind this Court ... include human dignity, equity, social justice, human rights, non-discrimination, protection of the marginalized and sustainable development."[61]

Facing the calamitous threats of climate change, the Lahore High Court Green Bench in Pakistan went further, acknowledging the interrelationship between dignity rights and environmental rights. In creating a climate change commission, the Bench bound the two together under the auspices of the right to life: "Fundamental rights, like the right to life (Article 9) which includes the right to a healthy and clean environment and right to human dignity (Article 14)."[62] Impatient with the lack of progress on climate change issues, the court continued: "From Environmental Justice, which was largely localized and limited to our own ecosystems and biodiversity, we need to move to Climate Change Justice. Fundamental rights lay at the foundation of these two overlapping justice systems. Right to life, right to human dignity, right to property and right to information under Articles 9, 14, 23 and 19A of the Constitution read with the constitutional values of political, economic and social justice provide the necessary judicial toolkit to address and monitor the Government's response to climate change."[63] It is precisely the constitutional value of human dignity (along with others) that compels a serious governmental response to climate change.

---

60 Kenya Constitution, Art. 10(2) (b) and (2)(d).

61 Friends of Lake Turkana Trust v Attorney General & 2 others [2014] eKLR, IN THE ENVIRONMENT AND LAND COURT AT NAIROBI ELC SUIT NO. 825 OF 2012 (finding insufficient evidence of actual violations of the right to dignity, life, livelihood and cultural and environmental heritage by the Gibe III hydroelectric project at the planning and implementation stages, but finding that the risks "that the harnessing of such electricity in Ethiopia is likely to affect its right to life and a livelihood and its cultural and environmental heritage ... imposes a positive duty upon the Respondents and Interested Party to provide the Petitioner with the all relevant information in relation to importation and/or purchase and transmission of electric power from Ethiopia."

62 Ashgar Leghari v. Federation of Pakistan (W.P. No. 25501/2015) Lahore High Court Green Bench para 7.

63 Ashgar Leghari v. Federation of Pakistan (W.P. No. 25501/2015) Lahore High Court Green Bench para 7.

A rare example of a constitutional court recognizing the relationship between dignity and the environment comes from the Israeli Supreme Court, which has been at the forefront of global dignity jurisprudence. In one case involving the right to water for those living in illegal settlements in the desert, the Court tried to "find the balance between the demand for keeping the law and its appropriate enforcement and the concern for a person's basic and existential need for water ..."[64]

While there are other examples of national tribunals recognizing the dignity implications of environmental challenges, it is fair to say that they are few and far between. And none, so far, engages in the type of meaningful analysis that could instruct or inspire other courts.

5. INVOKING ENVIRONMENTAL DIGNITY RIGHTS

Most of the effects that environmental degradation has on people can be seen in threats to their ability to live in dignity: the ability to be self-reliant is challenged when land is no longer fertile, when people are uprooted and resources are no longer available to support the full development of personality, when growing inequalities between those who can protect themselves from the environment and climate change and those who cannot compromise the ability of increasing numbers of people to control the course of their own lives. As we've seen, constitutional courts around the world have described the right to human dignity in a variety of factual settings outside the context of environmental protection. Bringing this jurisprudence into the realm of the natural environment will help to inform environmental outcomes.

Human dignity can be used to advance environmental outcomes primarily in two ways. The first is substantive: guaranteeing that each person may fully develop his or her own personality can be used as a measure of environmental rights in threshold matters, as a measure of violation and in fashioning a remedy. The second is procedural: full respect for human dignity requires governments to accord procedural rights to information and participation in community decisions.

---

64 Abu Masad v. Water Commissioner (Israel Supreme Court, 2011) (access to water in illegal settlements, where neither party disputed that the rights of Bedouins to water was part of their basic right to live in dignity and that this imposed on the state an affirmative obligation to provide some potable water).

5.1. DIGNITY AS THE MEASURE OF ENVIRONMENTAL VIOLATIONS

One way in which the already developed dignity jurisprudence of the world's constitutional courts could contribute to environmental rights discourse is for courts to use human dignity as a measure of environmental rights. Understanding how environmental rights are affected by human rights and, in particular, dignity rights, would ameliorate one of the biggest obstacles to the vindication of environmental rights. Most substantive environmental rights provisions are written in remarkably vague terms, where the content and boundaries of both nouns and adjectives are ill-defined and amorphous. This can deter judicial officers from applying the provisions and vindicating the rights guaranteed therein: judges are often unwilling to make judgments about what a "quality environment" or a "healthy environment,"[65] a "sound" environment[66], or a "healthy and ecologically balanced human environment" is.[67] The problem is only marginally alleviated when the rights are procedural, allowing "everyone" to "be informed about the status of the environment and its protection"[68] or to "participate in the making of public decisions which have an impact on the environment."[69] Bringing dignity into environmental rights jurisprudence requires reconfiguring a host of jurisprudential issues.

Bringing dignity to environmental rights cases can also provide some definition to the capacious and uncertain terms in which constitutional environmental rights are typically written. The most palpable harm of a permit for a hydroelectric dam, for instance, may be seen in the destruction of the communities that thrive on the river's banks, which in turn impairs the dignity of those who would live within those communities. Water pollution and the concomitant inadequacy of clean water may be actionable because they impair human dignity whether or not they can also be shown to violate a right to health, to life, or even to water. The minimum amount of water necessary to comply with the right would be determined by reference to plaintiffs' ability to live with dignity, for example.

In enforcing constitutional environmental rights, courts could look to dignity to determine whether the right to a quality (or healthy or balanced) environment has been violated. Permits for mining exploration and exploitation could be deemed to violate human and environmental rights when the dignity of those who work in mines or live in nearby communities was impaired. Timber licenses could be challenged if clearcutting threatened the right of people to live with

65 See e.g. Nicaragua Const.,Title IV, Chapter 3, Article 60, Colombia Const. Title II, Ch. 3, Art. 79.

66 Montenegro Const., Art. 23.

67 See e.g. Portugal Const., Part I, Section 3, Chapter 2, Article 66(1), Dominican Republic Const., Art. 67(1), Costa Rica Const., Title V, Art. 50.

68 Albania Const., Art. 56.

69 France, Charter of the Environment, Article 7.

dignity among trees for the resources and protection they provide. Dams could be built to provide electricity, but not if flooding displaces people and diminishes their communal and individual dignity. Information about environmental policies would have to be provided and opportunities for participation assured so that people can exercise their civic dignity.

Socio-economic environmental rights clearly implicate human dignity. Insofar as socio-economic rights affect the quality of life of individuals and communities, they are particularly vulnerable to environmental degradation and those threats are heightened by the effects of climate change. Housing, medical care and education are all more precarious in conditions of environmental hardship due to climate change: rising temperatures can impair the ability to learn and to work, flooding can force separation, flight, and repatriation which in turn threatens rights relating to family, culture and community. When victims and survivors of such abuses raise constitutional claims, the measure for violation can be the point at which government action or inaction has infringed upon human dignity.

Environmental civic and political rights also implicate human dignity. The Aarhus Convention is widely viewed as the most innovative and important international accord in support of procedural rights in environmental matters.[70] It stands procedural rights on three pillars – access to information, right to participation and access to justice – all of which have been incorporated into many of the world's constitutions. About three dozen incorporate one or more of these pillars, in environmental matters specifically, and many more provide these rights generally and in ways that are applicable to environmental matters.[71] Almost all of the constitutions that provide for procedural environmental rights also guarantee substantive environmental rights, so that the former can be seen to support and to ensure the efficacy of the latter.

Because these rights implicate citizens' decision-making authority, they implicate both civic and personal dignity, although few constitutions explicitly state how procedural rights enhance individual and community decision-making and, therefore, dignity. Finland's constitutional provision shows how this can be done: "The public authorities shall endeavour to guarantee … for everyone the possibility to influence the decisions that concern their own living environment."[72] Zambia's constitution is also illustrative: "The people shall have access to environmental information to enable them to preserve, protect and conserve the environment."[73] Or Ethiopia's: "People have the right to full consultation and to the expression of views in the planning and implementation of environmental

70 Aarhus Convention on Access to Information, Public Participation in Decision-Making and Access to Justice in Environmental Matters, June 25, 1998, 38 ILM 517 (entered into force on October 30, 2001).

71 See May & Daly, Global Environmental Constitutionalism (Cambridge U. Press 2015), ch. 8.

72 Finland Const., Chapter 2, Section 20.

73 Zambia Const., Section 302.

policies and projects that affect them directly."[74] In each of these, the purpose for which procedural rights are guaranteed is explicit and stated in terms that fuse together environmental and dignity interests: to exert decisional authority and control over their environment.

Most of these provisions, just like most substantive environmental rights provisions, are severely under-enforced, whether because of the overall state of rule of law in the country, restrictions on constitutional review, or ineffective enforcement mechanisms. To the extent that national courts are willing and able to vindicate substantive and procedural environmental rights, they may be deterred by the openness of the language, which creates a judicial obligation to fill in the textual lacunae. Dignity can help to fill in those gaps. It ensures that, when we evaluate a claim, whether sounding in environmental or human rights, attention remains on the human person asserting his or her rights.

Accepting dignity claims could reduce the burden and the costs borne by plaintiffs who would otherwise be expected to proffer extensive and expensive scientific evidence of causation and injury just to have their claims considered. Maintaining the focus on dignity could also reorient the remedial outcome of litigation.

5.2. STANDING

Judicial insistence on narrow conceptions of standing that require plaintiffs to show specific, individual and readily cognizable harms caused by the challenged environmental degradation is one of the major obstacles to the vindication of environmental rights. When the impact on human dignity has been taken into account, courts should be more willing to accept claims that draw attention to the ways in which environmental degradation hampers human dignity, whether or not it also harms other specifically identified human or constitutional rights or the environment itself.

Dignity can provide a benchmark to a claim to help courts and litigants identify the standard by which a violation or a remedy should be judged: a healthy or clean or balanced environment can be defined by whether human dignity can flourish or is compromised. In so doing, it can produce an added benefit of shifting the focus of the claim back to the plaintiff's actual injury: plaintiffs bring claims not just to get the information or to stop an environmentally threatening project, but because the government's action violates their right to dignity including their right to full development of the personality. This can open up standing by allowing plaintiffs to assert their interest in the litigation when their dignity is threatened, whether or not health or other interests can also be shown to have been compromised.

---

74 Ethiopia Const., Chapter 10, Article 92(3).

5.3. RIGHTS TO INCLUSION

The procedural environmental rights cases suggest yet another way to think about human dignity – one that has been under-appreciated in both the dignity and the environmental literature and jurisprudence.

In addition to helping to define the violation of other rights, dignity has an independent significance that arises from its dual nature: it concerns both how we feel and how we are seen by and relate to others. Dignity's social aspect compels the right to be a part of a community. Inclusion and acceptance are the hallmarks of the recognition of another person's dignity; conversely, exile, excommunication and exclusion are the ultimate denigrators of human dignity. Think of solitary confinement as the worst punishment short of death. This communal aspect is recognized in a few constitutions, including Italy's, whose constitution recognizes that: "All citizens have equal social dignity and are equal before the law, without distinction of sex, race, language, religion, political opinion, personal and social conditions"[75] and that of Belize, whose preamble protects "the identity, dignity and social and cultural values of Belizeans, including Belize's indigenous peoples."[76]

In a political community, dignity is the right to make decisions that contribute to the common good as the constitutional repudiation of the Apartheid regime in South Africa suggests, dignity denied some is dignity denied to all.[77] In a cultural community, it is the right to participate in and perpetuate the community's norms.[78] In a legal or juridic community, it is the right to have and claim rights.[79] As the South African Constitutional Court has said in a case about housing: "Affording socio-economic rights to all people therefore enables them to enjoy the other rights enshrined in [the Constitution]."[80] And in an Indian case about education, the Supreme Court said that human development "allows individuals to lead a life with dignity with a view to participate in the Governmental process

---

75 Constitution of Italy, Art. 3.

76 Constitution of Belize, Preamble.

77 S v. Makwanyane and Another, 1995 (6) BCLR 665 (CC): "Respect for dignity of all human beings is particularly important in South Africa. For apartheid was a denial of a common dignity. Black people were refused respect and dignity and thereby the dignity of all South Africans was diminished. The new Constitution rejects this past and affirms the equal worth of all South Africans. Thus, recognition and protection of human dignity is the touchstone of the new political order and is fundamental to the new Constitution."

78 See e.g. Luis Alejandro Lobatón Donayre y más de cinco mil ciudadanos contra el Poder Ejecutivo, EXP.N.° 0042-2004-AI/TC: «"el hecho que la Constitución de 1993 reconozca el derecho fundamental de las personas a su identidad étnica y cultural, así como la pluralidad de las mismas, supone que el Estado social y democrático de Derecho está en la obligación de respetar, reafirmar y promover aquellas costumbres y manifestaciones culturales que forman parte de esa diversidad y pluralismo cultural."

79 Arendt, Arendt, "The Perplexities of the Rights of Man," in The Portable Hannah Arendt, ed. Peter Baehr (New York: Penguin, 2000), 37; John Helis, "Hannah Arendt and Human Dignity: Theoretical Foundations and Constitutional Protection of Human Rights," Journal of Politics and Law 1, 3 (September 2008). See also Daly, Dignity Rights 132-137.

80 Republic of South Africa v. Grootboom, 2000 (11) BCLR 1169 (CC), 23 (S. Afr.).

so as to enable them to preserve their identity and culture."[81] Dignity's social aspect is, thus, self-reinforcing: communities foster human dignity by nurturing the conditions in which people can develop their personalities, and by exercising their rights of participation, the experience of human dignity strengthens communities.

The problem of climate change helps to contextualize some of the ways in which the consideration of dignity can advance environmental outcomes. As climate change changes the land and land usage, communities that live on, and off, the land are certain to be impacted and the relationship that people, and entire communities and cultures, have to the land is put under pressure. In particular, as land offers less protection to people, as they are forced off their land, compelled to move to cities or other communities where they are outsiders, their ability to participate in democratic decision-making, to claim rights, to maintain and perpetuate cultural norms are all challenged. Many principles of public participation are based on connection to real property including ownership or at least stable residency; without such locatedness, people become marginalized, disenfranchised and ultimately stateless. And, conversely, as communities break down by the increased competition for scarce resources and by the uprootedness of the population, they are less able to foster the human dignity on which communities themselves depend. The very experience of human dignity in a community becomes diminished, as does the ability to assert rights and to secure protection against governmental or other authorities.

Compounding the problems, environmental refugees are unlikely to find stability in new places to live or inclusion in new communities. Thus, the insult to both the individual and communal dimensions of human dignity, forged by climate change and environmental degradation, may well be visited not only upon the present generation, but also upon "generations yet to come."[82] Environmental dignity rights, just like other environmental rights, transcend both time and space.

6. CONCLUSION

Legal protection for environmental health and human rights have different genealogies that are only now beginning to converge as legal experts, at both

---

81 Islamic Academy of Educ. & Anr v. Vs (2003) INSC 361, 189. See also Soobramoney v. Minister of Health, KwaZulu-Natal 1997 (12) BCLR 1696, para. 8: "We live in a society in which there are great disparities in wealth. Millions of people are living in deplorable conditions and in great poverty. There is a high level of unemployment, inadequate social security, and many do not have access to clean water or to adequate health services. These conditions already existed when the Constitution was adopted and a commitment to address them, and to transform our society into one in constitutional order. For as long as these conditions continue to exist that aspiration will have a hollow ring."

82 Pennsylvania Const., Art. I, s. 27.

domestic and international levels, are recognizing the human rights impact of environmental degradation, including the climate.

With environmental dignity rights in mind, we witness increasing recognition that governments may be violating human rights when they fail to protect the environment. The human right to dignity is among the most vulnerable to environmental degradation and the effects of climate change. Dignity has come not only to define specific interests like the right to humane treatment or to earn a living wage, but also to protect the basic rights of a person to control his or her own life, to live in society with others, to claim other rights and, importantly, to live in an environment that is conducive to those principles. Respect for human dignity would require protecting the environment to permit people to live in harmony with their surroundings. It may even require us to take measures to protect against the worst ravages of climate change and, in turn, could help improve the environment.

Understanding how the environment affects the enjoyment of rights and the capacity to claim them will produce better advocacy and better judicial decision-making. The interconnections between human dignity and the environment are deep and multifaceted, and they run in both directions, as environmental degradation threatens human dignity and the failure to protect human dignity can, in turn, increase environmental precarity. For instance, poverty forces people to use trees, the only natural resources that are available to them, as fuel for cooking or heating or to keep malarial bugs away or to pay for their children's education. But the resulting deforestation produces more environmental vulnerability, in the form of more widespread landslides and storms that sweep further inland, which in turn threatens the housing, lives, and livelihood – that is, the very dignity – of more and more people. At the same time, the healthier the natural environments around people – the cleaner the air, the purer the water, the more robust the forests, the more likely people are to live with dignity, in intact communities that thrive in balance with nature. And the more the built environment around people is clean and healthy, the more likely people are to be able to fully develop their personalities – a key determinant of human dignity. Sustainable development is necessary to preserving the human dignity of present and future generations.

The imperatives of climate change may bring the environmental impacts on human dignity to the fore. Catastrophic climate events implicate "rights to life, dignity, and personal security-core civil and political rights."[83] Drought and desertification, for example, endanger food security, which diminishes dignity.[84] This, then, necessarily implicates a right to food, health, healthful living

83 Burkett, 646-47.

84 Graham Frederick Dumas, A Greener Revolution: Using the Right to Food as a Political Weapon Against Climate Change, 43 N.Y.U. J. Int'l L. & Pol. 107 (2010).

conditions, sanitation, water, and adequate housing and, ultimately, to dignity.[85] People living on small island nations are particularly vulnerable to the climate change impacts.[86]

Thus, legal actions associated with climate change are on the rise, primarily under causes of action associated with international human rights or domestic laws or doctrines, such as public trust.[87] Island nations seem especially well suited to pursuing actions against continental countries in North America and large energy-intensive multinational corporations for avoiding, mitigating and adapting to the changed circumstances wrought by climate change.

85 Burkett, 647.

86 Burkett, 645.

87 Rachel Brown, The Rising Tide of Climate Change Cases, The Yale Globalist (Mar. 13, 2013) http://tyglobalist.org/in-the-magazine/theme/the-rising-tide-of-climate-change-cases/ (last visited Jan. 7, 2016).

CHAPTER 7

THE ENVIRONMENTAL PROTECTION OF TRADITIONAL KNOWLEDGE AND THE ACTIVE PARTICIPATION OF INDIGENOUS PEOPLES IN THE PLANNING, MANAGEMENT AND DECISION-MAKING PROCESSES AS MEANS OF IMPROVING THE EFFECTIVENESS OF ENVIRONMENTAL LAW

Priscilla Cardoso Rodrigues
Professor of Indigenous Peoples Law
Federal University of Roraima, Amazonia, Brazil

ABSTRACT

Indigenous traditional knowledge refers to nonmaterial benefits arising from the intrinsic relationship between indigenous peoples and nature, which is responsible for providing livelihood, cultural identity, beliefs, spirituality, knowledge, ethical values, among other important contributions to human well-being. For that reason, it can be recognized as a kind of cultural ecosystem service, one which will enable these peoples to benefit from the ecosystem services theory, its ways of assessment and valuation and the way it can influence the planning, management and decision-making. However, to overcome the failures and gaps left behind by the economic valuation methods in the ecosystem services theory, we propose here a new conceptual and methodological framework for ecosystem services valuation, one which embodies a multimethod and multi-criteria approach, participatory and deliberative techniques and methodologies arising from anthropology, sociology and ethics, in addition to quantitative and qualitative methods analysis, flexible and adaptive management and participation structures.

Extending the active participation of indigenous peoples to the environmental planning, management and decision-making processes, in turn, will provide a more effective, legitimate, democratic and socially acceptable realization of these processes, and, consequently, will significantly improve the effectiveness of the Environmental Law.

1. INTRODUCTION

The regions of the world considered to be the most significant to the conservation of biodiversity are home to approximately 370 million indigenous belonging to 5,000 different indigenous peoples, according to the United Nations. Thanks to their traditional knowledge, these peoples live in a traditional way of life that does not threaten natural resources and environments, which is why their territories show a higher degree of conservation and an increase in local biodiversity, despite their economic, political and historical limitations. For this reason, the present chapter aims to advocate the environmental legal protection of indigenous traditional knowledge (ITK) as well as their active participation in the planning, management and decision-making processes as a means to increase the effectiveness of Environmental Law.

To this end, we have developed our study based on three main objectives. Our first objective has been to consider the environmental legal protection of ITK by recognizing them as cultural ecosystem services, so that it will enable these peoples to benefit from the ecosystem services theory, its ways of assessment and valuation and the way it can influence the planning, management and decision-making process.

The recognition of ITK as cultural ecosystem services stems from the cultural ties between indigenous peoples and the environment surrounding them, as well as from their benefits for human well-being, which can be described as spiritual, inspirational, aesthetic and cultural benefits. Thus, for the same reason why ecosystem services have been used as mechanisms of improvement of the political, economic and administrative decision-making, they can also help to improve decision-making concerning the access and the use of ITK, their traditional territories and especially the ecosystems in which they live and on which they depend for their physical and cultural survival.

However, before we can use the ecosystem services theory for this purpose, it is necessary first to overcome the gaps left by governments, decision-makers, stakeholders and even researchers relating to the cultural ecosystem services valuation, especially with regards to the "monist concept" of economic valuation, which is characterized by the use of quantitative and utilitarian techniques and criteria, founded on monetary and market-based valuations. Because most of the benefits provided by the cultural ecosystem services are nonmaterial benefits (spiritual, inspirational, recreational and aesthetic benefits), they feature intangible and immeasurable values that cannot be assessed by those economic criteria of valuation.

Therefore, our second objective is to demonstrate the inadequacy of the economic and monetary criteria for assessing and evaluating both the cultural ecosystem services and the ITK, and then to reflect on more appropriate mechanisms of valuation, such as the participative and deliberative methods, as well as approaches arising from anthropology, history, sociology and socio-environmentalism.

In many countries, the participation of indigenous peoples and movements in bioprospecting activities has resulted in the formation of a number of partnerships and agreements between the indigenous peoples and researchers, professional associations and companies, in addition to a number of ethical codes, statements and policies whose aim is to set ethical limits to the access and exploitation of traditional knowledge and genetic resources. Extending this participation to environmental planning, management and decision-making processes, and likewise to policies, actions and environmental protection programs, would be a way of overcoming the scientific uncertainties and the inadequacy of some institutions of governance that currently undermine the effectiveness of the actual Environmental Law.

Thus, our third objective is to attempt to demonstrate that, when acting alongside the institutions that make up the current environmental and global governance structure (non-governmental organizations, international organizations, civil society and States), indigenous peoples and movements would play a key role in turning it into a kind of "governance for sustainability".[1] This would ensure greater legitimacy to the decisions on environmental matters and, therefore, a greater effectiveness to Environmental Law.

In order to achieve these objectives, we emphasize the importance of adopting a pluralist approach, regarding the ethical pluralism[2], in addition to methodological and legal pluralism. In this way, we can create a solid research scheme capable of articulating "the ethical dimensions raised by science, economics, politics and law to define the 'environmental law space' ethically founded"[3], and at the same time we can articulate the intercultural and interdisciplinary dimensions involving the production of legal knowledge concerning the rights of indigenous peoples.

---

1 *K. Bosselman* (2008). *The Principle of Sustainability*: Transforming Law and Governance, Ashgate, Hampshire; Burlington.

2 *M.G.F.P.D. Garcia* (2007). *O lugar do direito na protecção do ambiente*. Almedina, Coimbra.

3 Translated from *J.J.G. Canotilho* (2007). O lugar do Direito na protecção do ambiente. *RevCEDOUA*, v. 10. n. 20. p. 163-164, 2007.2, p. 164.

2. INDIGENOUS TRADITIONAL KNOWLEDGE AND ITS RECOGNITION AS CULTURAL ECOSYSTEM SERVICES

2.1. DEFINITION AND LEGAL PROTECTION OF THE INDIGENOUS TRADITIONAL KNOWLEDGE

The ITK is a complex system of knowledge that includes their beliefs, social and cultural practices, spirituality, forms of expression, arts and everything else that pertains to their way of seeing and living in the world. This knowledge results from a cultural heritage collectively developed from generation to generation, which is reproduced and recreated by each indigenous in his/her relationships with the community and the environment. It also enables indigenous peoples to keep their ways of being and living through their own strategies for physical and cultural survival, in addition to enabling them to transmit their culture over generations.[4] It is thanks to their ITK that indigenous languages and cultures have survived until today, even though indigenous peoples have experienced colonial times and centuries of indigenist policies whose goals were their integration and assimilation.[5]

Despite the marked differences among the most diverse indigenous peoples around the world, what identifies all of them in a common sense is the perception that humans and nature are part of an indivisible whole and, therefore, must live and develop themselves in reciprocity. This is the true ethical foundation that underpins the interactions between indigenous peoples and the environment, and which determines not only a way of life focused on environmental conservation, but also the individual and collective identity of indigenous peoples.

Furthermore, the term "traditional" does not mean that the ITK is a static, ancient or backward knowledge. Instead, most of it is part of the cultural dynamics of current indigenous communities, as a result of their evolution over time by incorporating new ideas coming internally from the very community

---

4 It should be clarified that we have no intention to establish a single and closed definition for the wide diversity of knowledge and expressions created and recreated by many different indigenous peoples all over the world, because it would be unfair and inaccurate, as yet stated by the World Intellectual Property Organization (WIPO): "No single definition would do justice fully to the diverse forms of knowledge and expressions that are held and created by indigenous peoples and local communities throughout the world. Their living nature also means that they are not easy to define. There is not, as yet, any generally accepted, formal definition of these terms." (*WIPO* (2015). *Intellectual Property and Genetic Resources, Traditional Knowledge and Traditional Cultural Expressions*: Overview, WIPO, Geneva, p. 13). The intention is to make it easy for the readers to understand the complexity and the dimensions that such knowledge involves.

5 For example, in Brazil, nowadays still are 274 indigenous languages being spoken by indigenous peoples from 305 different nations, according to the 2010 Census of the Brazilian Institute of Geography and Statistics (*IBGE*, Censo Demográfico, 2010).

or externally from their interaction with the environment and the surrounding society. Thus, what characterizes the indigenous knowledge as traditional, is the way it is created, developed and transmitted within a community, because it is responsible for keeping the specific and traditional strategies for physical and cultural survival of indigenous peoples and for the transmission of their culture over generations.

Although the broad term "traditional knowledge" covers both definitions of traditional ecological knowledge and traditional cultural expressions as part of the holistic essence of the indigenous culture, it is very common that they are designed in distinct ways, giving rise to different political and legal approaches: the first under the environmental perspective of access to biodiversity, and the latter under the perspective of intangible cultural heritage.[6]

In this sense, in the international context, traditional ecological knowledge is protected from the perspective of the Environmental Law, by legal instruments such as the Convention on Biological Diversity (1992)[7] and their respective Nagoya Protocol (2010), the International Treaty on Plant Genetic Resources for Food and Agriculture (2002)[8], the International Convention for the Protection of New Varieties of Plants 1961), the UN Convention to Combat Desertification (1995). On the other hand, the traditional cultural expressions are protected mostly by UNESCO's specific system of preservation and safeguarding of cultural heritage, by legal instruments such as the *Convention* Concerning the *Protection of the World Cultural and Natural Heritage* (1972), the Convention for the Safeguarding of the Intangible Cultural Heritage (2003), the *Convention on the Protection and Promotion of the Diversity of Cultural* Expressions (2005)).

---

6 The WIPO usually makes a distinction between the traditional ecological knowledge as kinds of agricultural, environmental or medicinal knowledge, and knowledge associated with genetic resources (such as the traditional medicine, hunting and fishery, animal migration patterns, water management, etc.); and the traditional cultural expressions as ways in which traditional culture is expressed (such as verbal expressions (stories, tales, poetry, riddles, signs, elements of languages, etc.), musical expressions (songs and instrumental music), expressions by actions (dances, plays, artistic forms of rituals, etc.) and tangible expressions (drawings, paintings, carvings, jewelry, metal ware, textiles, designs, carpets, sculptures, pottery, terracotta, crafts, mosaic, needlework, basket weaving, woodwork, costumes, musical instruments, architectural forms, etc.). (*WIPO*, *supra*, note 5, p. 14-16.).

7 Considered the first international instrument to protect the ITK, albeit indirectly when establishing international protocols for the protection and sharing of genetic resources, the Convention on Biological Diversity (CBD) was responsible for promoting deep changes in the legal and political scene of the protection of this knowledge by boosting the realization of intergovernmental agreements and national measures, as well as several agreements, declarations and public policies adopted by indigenous communities, researchers and companies. In this way, when establishing the appropriate access and benefit sharing arising from the utilization of genetic resources, the CBD also supports the intellectual property rights of indigenous peoples.

8 The International Treaty on Plant Genetic Resources for Food and Agriculture of the FAO has provisions relating to prior informed consent, sharing of benefits and protection of traditional knowledge, which in some cases may serve to protect the ITK, albeit indirectly, since it is designed for farmers.

From a more specific approach, the UN Declaration on the Rights of Indigenous Peoples (UNDRIP, 2007) protects the ITK as a whole, by a holistic, multicultural autonomous and non-instrumental perspective and which is, consequently, more appropriate to the complexity of this knowledge, although within the framework of intellectual property, as established in its Article 31.

Specifically, in the framework of intellectual property system, the WIPO has created a specific body for the protection of traditional knowledge as a whole, the WIPO Intergovernmental Committee on Intellectual Property and Genetic Resources, Traditional Knowledge and Folklore (IGC), which has discussed incisively the need of creating a *sui generis* system that would be able to give them the appropriate, legitimate and effective protection they demand.[9]

Indeed, the current intellectual property system has not been able to achieve the fair, equitable, adequate, and effective protection of the ITK, because it is structured by an individualistic and patrimonialistic perspective whose purpose is the protection of a work or invention characterized by its originality and the possibility to identify its authorship. Even though this may be perfectly adequate for Western societies where knowledge is individualized, compartmentalized, and susceptible to appropriation, it has proven to be incompatible with the complex and collectivized nature of the traditional knowledge of indigenous societies.

In fact, we can say that neither the intellectual property system or the protection system of intangible cultural heritage nor the biodiversity protection system have been able to prevent the misappropriation, the unauthorized exploitation and the undesired, unfair and inequitable uses of ITK without the consent of indigenous peoples and without sharing any of the benefits arising from their use by third parties.

2.2. INDIGENOUS TRADITIONAL KNOWLEDGE AS CULTURAL ECOSYSTEM SERVICES

According to the Millennium Ecosystem Assessment (MA)[10], the ecosystem services are defined as material and nonmaterial benefits provided by ecosystems

---

9 In the words of WIPO, that body should be "an international legal instrument would define what is meant by TK and TCEs, who the rights holders would be, how competing claims by communities would be resolved, and what rights and exceptions ought to apply." (*WIPO*, *supra*, note 5, p. 45.).

10 As a result of research developed by the MA in order to assess the consequences of ecosystem changes for human well-being and the necessary actions to assist the conservation and sustainable use of these ecosystems, it is important to highlight the following reports:
Technical Reports:
J. Alcamo et al (2003). Ecosystems and Human Well-Being: a Framework for Assessment. Island Press, Washington.
R. Hassan, R. Scholes & N. Ash (eds.) (2005). Ecosystems and Human Well-Being: Current State and Trends: Findings of the Condition and Trends Working Group. Island Press, Washington.

for humans and their wellbeing, which are systematically divided into four types: provisioning, regulating, cultural and supporting services. Within this fourfold classification, the cultural services are considered nonmaterial benefits resulting from environmental contexts co-produced by the constant interactions between humans and nature, which give rise to cultural goods and benefits that people obtain from ecosystems. They derived from the natural resources and also from the cultural legacy left by societies both past and present.

The ITK, in turn, comprises nonmaterial benefits resulting from the cultural ties between indigenous peoples and nature, which are responsible for their particular forms of social organization, beliefs, spirituality, cultural identity and everything else that refers to their specific ways of being and living in the world, whose effects on human well-being may be intellectual, scientific, spiritual, inspirational, aesthetic, cultural, recreational, amongst others. Therefore, their benefits for human well-being transcend the utilitarian and material ones, since they concern their own identity as individuals, communities and peoples.

In that way, the ITK performs not only the basic function of providing livelihood and food security for those peoples, through the exploration, albeit sustainable, of natural resources available, but also: environmental conservation; enhancement of biodiversity through traditional management of fauna and flora specimens; maintenance of traditional and sustainable ways of living and interacting with nature; maintenance of indigenous values and cultural and spiritual heritage; maintenance of indigenous social relations and territory; and contribution to the entirety of humanity with the knowledge of medicinal and pharmaceutical use of nature resources.[11] This ITK has also provided valuable

---

S. R Carpenter et al. (eds.) (2005). Ecosystems and Human Well-Being: Scenarios: Findings of the Scenarios Working Group, v. 2, Island Press, Washington.

K. Chopra et al (eds.) (2005). Ecosystems and Human Well-Being: Policy Responses: Findings of the Responses Working Group of the MA, v. 3, Island Press, Washington.

D. Capistrano et al (eds.) (2005). Ecosystems and Human Well-Being: Multiscale Assessments: Findings of the Sub-global Assessments Working Group of the MA, v. 4, Island Press, Washington.

MA (2005c). *Our Human Planet*: Summary for Decision-makers. Island Press, Washington.

Synthesis Reports:

MA (2005a). *Ecosystems and Human Well-being: Synthesis.* Island Press, Washington.

MA (2005d). *Ecosystems and Human Well-being*: Biodiversity Synthesis. World Resources Institute, Washington.

MA (2005e). *Ecosystems and Human Well-being*: Desertification Synthesis. World Resources Institute, Washington.

C. Corvalan et al (eds.) (2005) Ecosystems and Human Well-Being: Health Synthesis: a Report of the MA, World Health Organization, Geneva.

MA (2005f). *Ecosystems and Human Well-being*: Wetlands and Water Synthesis: a Report of the MA. World Resources Institute, Washington, DC, USA.

MA (2005g). *Ecosystems and Human Well-being*: Opportunities and Challenges for Business and Industry. World Resources Institute, Washington, DC.

11 It has been estimated that more than 50% of the currently existing medications have been originally discovered in plants because of their use in indigenous traditional medicine. The same logic also extends to the cosmetic industry. D. Pearce & S. Puroshothaman, 1993; G.M.

contributions for the improvement of agriculture, fishing, hunting and the management of plants and forests.

It can also be helpful in environmental management and policy, because it is able to provide a more realistic evaluation of the environment and, therefore, sets more effective management techniques. Furthermore, it can guide processes of environmental education and awareness in society by showing the importance of biodiversity conservation to human existence and the possibility of living in a unified and integrated manner with nature. As values, beliefs and cultural norms may influence the perceptions and behaviours of individuals and societies, the indigenous experiences and ways of living are able, for example, to change both the consumption choices of individuals and the way they interact with the environment.[12]

For all those reasons, recognizing the ITK as cultural ecosystem services can be an important strategy for the preservation of the most different ecosystems around the world. Since this knowledge can provide an integrated management of natural and genetic resources, by promoting their conservation and sustainable use and recognizing humans and their cultural diversity as an important part of many ecosystems, any damage to the integrity of that knowledge would involve immeasurable environmental losses for present and future generations of both indigenous and nonindigenous people.

On the other hand, while this intrinsic relationship between indigenous peoples and nature provides them with a completely sustainable way of life, it also makes them completely dependent on the ecosystems in which they live. This reliance on ecosystems and their services is disproportionally felt by indigenous peoples due to combinations of prejudice, lack of rights or ignored rights, the lack of access to social support or personal resources and also due to the fact that they usually live in remote and inaccessible areas, distant from concentrations of social services and political power[13], which causes them to be more vulnerable to degradation and changes in ecosystems, such as floods, drought, disease, among others.

For that reason, recognizing the ITK as cultural ecosystem services can also ensure adequate, legitimate, fair and effective legal protection, since the ecosystem services theory has been shown to be an important weapon in combating the increasing attacks on the ecosystems on which indigenous peoples and all humankind depend.

Cragg & D. J. Newman, 2004 *apud* A.J. Beattie (coord). New Products and Industries from Biodiversity. In *R. Hassan, R. Scholes & N. Ash* (eds.), *supra*, note 11, p. 276).

12 People's engagement with environment is contingent, context specific, fluid and mutable, since economic, technological, social, political and cultural factors may influence the meanings, values and behaviors relating to human ways of using natural resources (*UK NEA* (2011b). *The UK National Ecosystem Assessment*: Synthesis of the Key Findings. UNEP-WCMC, Cambridge, p. 81). By showing a harmonious way of living with nature, the ITK can influence the behaviors and lifestyles of individuals and communities at large, and therefore improve human well-being as a whole.

13 *R. Hassan, R. Scholes & N. Ash* (eds.), *supra*, note 11, p. 155.

3. THE VALUATION OF INDIGENOUS TRADITIONAL KNOWLEDGE WITHIN THE ECOSYSTEM SERVICES FRAMEWORK

3.1. THE VALUATION OF ECOSYSTEM SERVICES, BENEFITS, AND VALUES

The ecosystem services theory has been widely used to support the planning, management and decision-making by showing how changes in ecosystems can lead to severe consequences in ecosystem services provision and, therefore, for human well-being. For this purpose, ecosystem services research has focused on the interpretation of the benefits provided by the different ecosystems on Earth, in their assessment and in their contribution to human well-being, in addition to their mapping, valuation and valorisation.

The ecosystem services notwithstanding, literature has shown different kinds of value and methods of valuation in practice, and the ecosystem services concept has become largely associated with economic valuation, thanks to its special emphasis on those ecosystem services that provide material benefits and can, therefore, be assessed and valued by economic and monetary criteria. Since 1997, when scholars such as *G. Daily*[14] and *R. Constaza*[15] started to defend the payment of ecosystem services as the main way of protecting the various ecosystems and their services, to today, a vast literature has been developed in order to demonstrate how significant the economic valuation is in preventing the abusive and unrestrained use of ecosystem services by giving visibility to their economic value.

However, in most cases, economic valuation only addresses the valuation of the benefits and values that are market-mediated, leaving the nonmaterial ones aside by using the justification that they are intangible and immeasurable, as in the case of cultural ecosystem services, which is why they often end up being discarded as hidden externalities. In that way, although the economic valuation has played the relevant role of translating ecological concerns into economic arguments[16], thereby internalizing the value of ecosystems and transmitting it to a wide audience, by discarding the nonmaterial contributions of ecosystems, the ecosystem services theory may have closed the door to other social and cultural relevant perspectives to the preservation of the most diverse ecosystems.[17]

---

14 *G. C. Daily* (ed.) (1997). *Nature's Services*: Societal Dependence on Natural Ecosystems. Island Press, Washington.

15 *R. Costanza* et al (1997). The Value of the World's Ecosystem Services and Natural Capital. *Nature*, v. 387, p. 253-260, London.

16 *TEEB* (2009b). *TEEB for National and International Policy Makers*, ch. 8, p. 38.

17 *K. M. A. Chan, T. Satterfield & J. Goldstein* (2012). Rethinking Ecosystem Services to Better Address and Navigate Cultural Values. *Ecological Economics*, v. 74, p. 8.

As a result, in practice, the economic valuation ends up restricted to the services that typically provide material benefits (such as the provisioning ecosystem services), and at the same time, it disregards, as hidden externalities, the ecosystem service category that would typically provide nonmaterial benefits (as the cultural services), since they do not fit into their utilitarian and homogenizing requirements.

However, the question of the plurality of ecosystem services values and benefits is more complex and extensive than the classification into provisioning, regulating, cultural and supporting services. When the contributions of these services are considered from the wide meaning of their importance for life, survival and human well-being, rather than the limited meaning of their market value, it is possible to note that the different categories of ecosystem services can provide different benefits and values (material or nonmaterial)[18], which have an effect on different scales and geographical levels (local, regional, national or international), and leave a huge gap in the theory and evaluation of ecosystem services as a whole. Moreover, not considering the nonmaterial values in the planning, management and decision-making can make their decisions opposed to what matters most to people and, consequently, can make them illegitimate and ineffective in achieving the expected goals.

Therefore, to ensure that the valuations of ecosystem contributions are as complete, adequate and effective as possible, they must consider both their material and nonmaterial dimensions, because the value of an ecosystem service also depends on the marginal value of the benefits from which they are interdependent[19], otherwise it runs the risk of leaving the biodiversity's most important goods and values unprotected.[20]

---

18 In order to demonstrate that other categories of ecosystem services, besides the cultural services, can also provide intangible and immeasurable benefits, *Chan* et al have used the "fishery" as an example. Fishery is a provisioning service par excellence, and thereby it can have their economic value calculated based on their material benefits and values. However, although the food supply is the main and most common benefit derived from fishery, this has also nonmaterial benefits, once it can define a particular way of life for fishermen, including the ethical, political, and spiritual dimensions that may result from it. (*K. M. A Chan* et al (2012). Where Are Cultural and Social in Ecosystem Services? A Framework for Constructive Engagement. *BioScience*, v. 62, n. 8, p. 745.).

19 To illustrate this situation of interdependence, *Chan, Satterfield & Goldstein* cite the case of a shift from traditional fishery to commercial fishery that took place in the Nuxalk First Nation of British Columbia (B.C.). Even though this shift has improved employment, it simultaneously has triggered a loss of subsistence activities, and consequently, the cultural benefits associated with them, like the appreciation of place, cultural heritage, social capital and social cohesion. Such example makes it clear that the intangible and immeasurable dimensions are also present in other types of ES than just the cultural services, and it also makes clear that they are interdependent. Nevertheless, the intangible dimensions of fisheries are rarely reflected in the monetary valuations of their respective goods on the market, which makes this valuation deficient and incomplete. (*Chan, Satterfield & Goldstein*, *supra*, note 18, p. 12-14).

20 The deficiency and risks of using merely economic criteria for valuing the ecosystem services contributions have already been alerted by the most important assessment reports of the ecosystem services framework, as follows:

3.2. VALUING THE INDIGENOUS TRADITIONAL KNOWLEDGE THROUGH AN ECOSYSTEM SERVICES APPROACH

There is no doubt that human beings have always been highly influenced by ecosystems either in knowledge systems, modes of production, forms of consumption or property systems. However, the sociocultural value of an ecosystem depends on the value that each person or community assigns to ecosystems functions, goods and services, which in turn depend on their ethical, religious, cultural and philosophical perceptions of nature. So, while in Western societies these values are defined by the degree of utility an ecosystem can provide, in the indigenous societies, the value of an ecosystem transcends any utilitarian satisfaction, since their connection with nature defines not only their way of living, but mainly their very identity as individuals, communities and peoples.

Thus, a particular ecosystem in which indigenous people live, such as a forest, can define their means of physical survival by providing food, fibre or wood, but it is also responsible for defining their way of life, cultural identity, political and social organization, beliefs, spirituality, knowledge and ethical values. That is the reason why losses and damages in ecosystems like that can lead to an irreversible disruption of social, cultural, religious and economic

---

Among the possible measures that *MA Report* suggested that must be taken to reduce and/or prevent the degradation of ecosystems, it has highlighted the need that the decision-making processes take into account the value of all ecosystem goods and services, not only the market-mediated ones: "Make sure the value of all ecosystem services, not just those bought and sold in the market, are taken into account when making decisions" (*MA* (2005b), *supra*, note 11, p. 21).

Similarly, *TEEB Report* has highlighted the lack of an adequate valuation of ecosystem services among the top biodiversity crisis factors: "The main cause of the biodiversity crisis is unsustainable growth in consumption and production, exacerbated by a tendency to undervalue biodiversity and the ecosystem services it supports. Current decision-making is biased towards short-term economic benefits because the long-term value of ecosystem services is poorly understood. Recognising the value of ecosystem services can lead to better more cost-efficient decisions and avoid inappropriate trade-offs." (*TEEB, supra*, note 17, ch. 4, p. 2). In addition: "This is the case even if markets do not exist or if these values are not expressed in monetary terms: values can also be based on qualitative or semi-quantitative assessments. What we actually measure in monetised form is very often only a share of the total value of ecosystem services and biodiversity. 'True' values are usually much higher." (*TEEB, supra*, note 17, ch. 1, p. 21).

Furthermore, the *UK NEA Report* has highlighted that the omission of valuing ecosystem services and goods that are outside the market in the decision-making processes can lead to negative consequences for the human and social well-being: "An important prerequisite for this is a better grasp of the values of the full range of ecosystem services, including cultural values based on ethical, spiritual and aesthetic principles. The values of most ecosystem services are currently omitted from national economic frameworks and local decision making. Failure to include the valuation of non-market goods in decision making results in a less efficient resource allocation." (*UK NEA, supra*, note 13, p. 13.).

stability, or even the very survival of an entire indigenous community or people, and consequently to corresponding impact that cannot be calculated merely by economic and monetary criteria of valuation. Given this symbiotic relationship between indigenous peoples and the ecosystem in which they live, any planning, management, and decision-making processes that might interfere with or change the vital stability of that ecosystem should take not only the material values it provides, but also, and especially, their nonmaterial values into account.

In the specific case of recognizing the ITK as cultural ecosystem services, this can become even worse, which is why the reparation for a damage, loss, misuse or misappropriation of an ITK must refer to something more important than indemnification or cash compensation. Otherwise, applying an economic valuation and a corresponding economic compensation in those cases would turn the ITK into a commodity and, as a consequence, would trigger unexpected changes in the social interactions and disruptions in the political institutions of that indigenous people, similarly to what has been happening to several indigenous peoples around the world.[21]

Because of situations like those, the current economic methods of valuation based on market estimates and carried out by scientists or economists who do not know and/or ignore the social and cultural reality and the rights of indigenous peoples, urgently need to be reviewed in order to include a more consistent and coherent valuation method, one which is able to valuate nonmaterial benefits and values of the ITK, and which takes the interests and needs of their holders and the community into account, as well as the perspectives of those who cannot express their interests, such as future people and non-human organisms.[22]

---

21 To illustrate situations like that, Paige West ethnographically describes how an environmental conservation policy based on economic valuations ended up turning a good of important cultural value to an indigenous community into a commodity, which has led to serious social consequences. West refers to the Papua New Guinean net string bags (called *Bilum* in TokiPisin). These bags were considered a "source of pride" and a "labor of love" for the women of Maimafu, and it was also an important part of social exchanges, in addition to being the most important local symbol of women's traditional knowledge. After the aforementioned conservation policy, the *Billum* has become a mere commodity with a market value, as well as the women who produce them, with no autonomy and no control over their exchanges, while men have assumed the new control on the trading of such goods. In this way, the social value of the bags and the women has completely changed, causing irreversible social consequences, and aggravating the already existing inequalities between men and women. In West's words: "the value of women's labor is being commodified at the same time that is socially erased". (*P. West* (2006). *Conservation is our government now*: the politics of ecology in Papua New Guinea. Duke University Press, Durham; London. p. 183-214).

22 *Chan, Satterfield & Goldstein*, *supra*, note 18, p. 11.

3.3. A CONCEPTUAL AND METHODOLOGICAL PROPOSAL TO VALUATE THE INDIGENOUS TRADITIONAL KNOWLEDGE THROUGH AN ECOSYSTEM SERVICES APPROACH

As observed above, the use of the ecosystem services approach to understanding the interactions between culture and nature is a relatively new perspective; this is one reason why most of the existing mechanisms and procedures for valuating the ecosystem services are not designed to encompass cultural services and goods.[23]

However, the latest research on the ecosystem services valuation has shown significant advances relating to the establishment of more comprehensive methods of valuation. An important contribution may be found in *Chan, Satterfield & Goldstein* in which the authors suggest a deliberative democratic multimethod, and especially, a multimetric approach in order to adopt choice surveys based on paired comparisons and a subjective scaling (when necessary) as key elements of the valuation process, instead of using the dollar as the only metric, as happens in the current valuation processes.[24]

In the same vein, the *TEEB Report* has contributed by showing the importance of qualitative methods to understand the environmental and social impacts of changes in ecosystems and their services and to avoid the risks of creating a policy bias by focusing on vested interests. In this respect, the TEEB proposes the following pragmatic approach: "always identify impacts qualitatively, then quantify what you can, then monetise (where possible)."[25]

Furthermore, the *UK National Ecosystem Assessment* (*UK NEA*) has also contributed by showing the importance of deliberative tools, such as the participatory multi-criteria analysis, which produces sophisticated descriptive interpretations, based on reasoned arguments and considering different sources of quantitative and qualitative evidence, in order to incorporate the ecosystem services approach and the nature of shared values in the decision-making processes.[26]

Based on those contributions, we can conclude that an adequate conceptual and methodological framework for valuing ecosystem services must put aside the monist concept of economic valuation, given that it is marked by a lack of effective participatory methods and by the primacy of scientific knowledge as a key source to assess and valuate ecosystem services, and introduce instead a multimethod and multi-criteria approach, one which includes: a variety of participatory and deliberative techniques, including the possibility of group analysis and deliberation; an integrated approach that recognizes the diversity of actors involved and the different levels and sectors of influence (local, regional, national, international levels; public and private sectors; etc.); methodologies

23 *UK NEA*, *supra*, note 13, p. 83.
24 *Chan, Satterfield & Goldstein*, *supra*, note 18, p. 15-16.
25 *TEEB*, *supra*, note 17, ch. 4, p. 2-6.
26 *UK NEA*, *supra*, note 13, p. 33.

stemming from the social sciences, from anthropology, sociology, and ethics especially; quantitative and qualitative methods of analysis to make it possible to achieve a more complete and comprehensive set of values; and flexible and adaptable management and participatory structures.[27]

Moreover, for such a structure to be effectively and formally incorporated in the assessment and valuation processes, and thus to be used by managers and policy makers, it is necessary to create a solid juridical, legal and institutional framework, in local and national terms, and in some cases, even in international ones. This framework should present a detailed legislative description of those criteria, methods and techniques, as well as specific institutional bodies which must be able to ensure their supervision, control and effective application.

Furthermore, in terms of the contents that must be valuated, it is crucial to establish interdisciplinary cooperation between natural scientists and social scientists in order to identify the key elements in conducting an ecosystem services valuation more completely and in a socially acceptable manner[28], as well as between these scientists and the local indigenous community. In that way, the relation between scientific knowledge and traditional knowledge will be able to provide more comprehensive information about the conditions and characteristics of the ecosystems and their services, and about the sociocultural context that surrounds it.

In the specific case of the valuation of ITK, the information about the sociocultural context should include:

1. An analysis of the demographic, economic and legal contexts of the local indigenous people and community, including both religious and moral norms, the rights and traditional forms of conflict resolution, and the rights and entitlements which are specifically guaranteed in the national, regional and international Law;
2. An analysis of the historical and social local context, in order to investigate historical situations of colonization, migration, invasion and conflicts with squatters, land invaders, loggers and miners, etc., and the social, political and economic effects on local indigenous people and community;
3. The ITK of local indigenous people and community;
4. The indigenous narratives about their beliefs, stories and religion;
5. The complex forms of relationships and the level of dependence of the local indigenous people and the community in the ecosystem in which they live;

---

27 The addition of an approach more integrated and adaptable to the specific needs and characteristics of local groups in some sub-global assessments of MA has shown results with greater credibility and legitimacy, such as the assessment processes occurred in Peru and Costa Rica. In those places, the conceptual structures of MA were adapted to local cosmologies in order to "allow for more dynamic interplays between variables, to capture fine-grained patterns and processes in complex systems, and to leave room for a more spiritual worldview". For further details, *cf. MA* (2005a), *supra*, note 11, p. 84-87.

28 *UK NEA*, *supra*, note 13, p. 15.

6. The local indigenous expectations and aspirations about the projects and/or ventures implemented, or under implementation, in areas that may directly or indirectly affect them;
7. The demands of the local indigenous community relating to future generations.

That information is key to understanding the local conditions, because each indigenous people or community has its own and different cultural, social, economic and historical characteristics. Moreover, it must guide not only the valuation processes, allowing values to be analysed in their own context, but also, and mainly, the planning, management and decision-making, the environmental conservation policies, the economic, land and social policies, the spatial planning, amongst others.

In practice, by and large, the identification of these and other information about the ecological and cultural conditions of a particular ecosystem, and of its services, is presumed by researchers, managers and officials as though they were self-evident, with no participation of stakeholders in this process.[29]

For an adequate and legitimate valuation process, it is decisive that a thorough understanding of the potential damage to the ecosystem is arrived at and that the people who are directly or indirectly likely to be affected can vocalize why the incorporation of participatory and deliberative approaches in all of its stages is necessary, through a procedure that should be open and transparent enough to enable dialogue, collaboration and participation of the various stakeholders (institutions of environmental representation, government authorities, public bodies, international organizations, businesses, NGO, civil society, communities, research institutions, universities, etc.), albeit with a particular emphasis on the active participation of the indigenous peoples.

4. THE ACTIVE PARTICIPATION OF INDIGENOUS PEOPLES IN PLANNING, MANAGEMENT AND DECISION-MAKING PROCESSES AS A MEANS OF IMPROVING THE EFFECTIVENESS OF THE ENVIRONMENTAL LAW

Apart from the importance of the participation of indigenous peoples to ensure that the ecosystem services valuation is a legitimately and effectively performed process, this participation is also extended to environmental planning, management and decision-making processes, as well as to environmental policies, actions and protection programs which are an important strategy to ensure the greater legitimacy of decisions arising therefrom and, consequently, to improve the effectiveness of Environmental Law.

29 *K. M. A Chan* et al, *supra*, note 19, p. 745.

Thus, these processes will benefit from indigenous knowledge, data, opinions and expertise, in addition to incorporating a human and cultural perception to the already existing and efficient scientific and analytical methods, which will also be a way to help overcome the gaps that currently bring about scientific uncertainties and weakness to the environmental governance, weaknesses which are greatly responsible for undermining the effectiveness of Environmental Law.

Moreover, as the perceptions and behaviours of individuals or even of entire societies are influenced by factors such as ethics, values and cultural norms, the ITK can be used to change the behaviour of nonindigenous societies both in terms of the way people relate to nature and in terms of their consumption choices, which will give rise to positive consequences for the conservation of ecosystems and consequently to a better effectiveness of the Environmental Law.

The requirement of free prior consultation, informed consent (FPIC)[30], and the participation of indigenous peoples at all levels of planning, management and decision-making processes that may affect them in ways not felt by others in society[31], is a fundamental human right derived from the fundamental right of indigenous peoples to self-determination[32] and from its related principles of democracy and popular sovereignty, as well as being "a corollary of a myriad of universally accepted human rights, including the right to cultural integrity, the right to equality and the right to property."[33]

The FPIC is not, however, something new. It has been a common practice in indigenous customary law with regards to the community decision-making processes[34], even though it has only found support in international regulatory

30 The elements of "free", "prior" and "informed" are the terms and conditions required to constitute a valid and effective agreement with the indigenous peoples. They are defined as follows: "The element of "free" implies no coercion, intimidation or manipulation; "prior" implies that consent is obtained in advance of the activity associated with the decision being made, and includes the time necessary to allow indigenous peoples to undertake their own decision-making processes; "informed" implies that indigenous peoples have been provided all information relating to the activity and that that information is objective, accurate and presented in a manner and form understandable to indigenous peoples;" (*UN EMRIP (2011). Expert Mechanism Advice* No. 2 (*2011*): Indigenous *Peoples* and the *Right* to Participate in Decision-Making, A/HRC/18/42, Annex, § 25.).

31 *J. Anaya* (2009). *Report of the Special Rapporteur on the situation of human rights and fundamental freedoms of indigenous people.* Promotion and Protection of All Human Rights, Civil, Political, Economic, Social and Cultural Rights, Including The Right to Development, Human Rights Council, 22th session, Agenda item 3, A/HRC/12/34, 15 July 2009, § 43, p. 15.

32 About the design of the CLIP as a right stemming from the right to self-determination, see: *UN EMRIP, supra*, note 31, § 18; *IAITPTF & IPF* (2011). *Handbook on Free, Prior and Informed Consent*: For Practical Use by Indigenous Peoples' Communities, MISEREOR, Chiang Mai, Thailand, p. 9 e 11; and *J. Anaya* (2009), *supra*, note 32, § 41, p. 14-15.

33 *J. Anaya* (2009), *supra*, note 32, § 41, p. 14-15.

34 *IAITPTF & IPF, supra*, note 33, p. 10 e 18.

requirements[35] and in domestic law only recently.[36] However, this entire legal framework, featured at the national and international levels, has already shown itself to be insufficient to ensuring the effective participation of indigenous peoples[37], especially when there are significant economic interests at stake, which raises the question about the limits and effects of FPIC, that is whether it is merely limited to the consultation itself or if it also includes the veto power.[38]

In order to demonstrate the consultation procedure's formal requirement to achieve FPIC's insufficiency, some emblematic cases can be cited for States who

---

35 Some international regulatory requirements on consultation, FPIC and participation of indigenous peoples:
Articles 6, 15(2), 16(2), 17(2), 22(3), 27(3), 28(1) (consultation); 6(2), 16(2) (FPIC); 2(1), 6(1b), 7(1)(2), 15, 22(1)(2), 23(1), 27(2), 29 (participation) of the ILO Convention N°. 169 (1989);
Articles 15(2), 17(2), 19, 30(2), 32(2), 36(2), 38 (consultation); 10, 11(2), 19, 28, 29(2), 32(2) (FPIC); e 5, 18, 23, 27, 41 (participation) of the UNDRIP (2007);
Articles 8 (j) (participation) of the CBD (1992)
General Recommendation XXIII on the Rights of Indigenous Peoples of the Committee on the Elimination of Racial Discrimination (CERD), and the following Specific Recommendations, among others: CERD/C/CAN/CO/18; CERD/C/NZL/CO/17; CERD/C/IDN/CO/3; CERD/C/COD/CO/15; CERD/C/ECU/CO/19; CERD/C/USA/CO/6; CERD/C/NAM/CO/12; CERD/C/SWE/CO/18;
General Comment n. 23 on the Rights of Minorities (Article 27 of the International Covenant on Civil and Political Rights) of the Human Rights Committee, and the following Specific Recommendations, among others: CCPR/C/NIC/CO/3; CCPR/C/BWA/CO/1; CCPR/C/CRI/CO/5; CCPR/C/CHL/CO/5;
Other decisions and comments from various international and regional organizations such as the United Nations organizations, the Inter-American Commission and the Inter-American Court of on Human Rights, the World Commission on Dam, the European Union, the Association of South-East Asia Nations; the UN specialized agencies and programs; the financing institutions such as the World Bank and development banks such as the Asian Development Bank, the Inter-American Development Bank; donor agencies and donor countries; international NGOs and indigenous peoples' organizations.

36 Some domestic law on consultation, FPIC and the participation of indigenous peoples: Brazilian Biodiversity Law (Act. N° 13.123/2015) – Brazil; The Indigenous Peoples Rights Act (Republic Act No. 8371/ 1997)- Philippines; Law on Biological Diversity (2000) and Organic Law of The Indigenous Peoples and Communities (2005) – Venezuela; Law of the Right to Prior Consultation to Indigenous or Native Peoples, recognized in the Convention 169 of the International Labour Organization (ILO) (Law N°. 29785/2011) – Peru; among others.

37 The *Former UN Special Rapporteur* on the Rights of *Indigenous Peoples*, Sir James Anaya, has stated that frequently, and in a wide variety of situations, the legal requirement of the duty to consult has not been enough to ensure compliance by States, governments and other stakeholders, which has led to conflictive situations with indigenous peoples. (J. Anaya (2009), *supra*, note 32, § 36, p. 12).

38 For further discussion on the limits and effects of FPIC, see: *J. Anaya* (2009), *supra*, note 32, § 2, 14, 2, 23, 28, and 34; ICHR (2007). *Case of the Saramaka People v. Suriname*. Judgment of November 28, 2007. Series C N. 172, § 134, p. 40; *J. Grutzner & E. Salim* (2003). *The World Bank Group and Extractive Industries*: Extractive Industries Review. World Bank Group, Washington, p. 50; *CHR (2005). Legal Commentary on the Concept of Free, Prior and Informed Consent*: Standard-Setting., Sub-Commission on the Promotion and Protection of Human Rights, Working Group on Indigenous Populations, 23rd session, Item 5 (b) of the provisional agenda, E/CN.4/Sub.2/AC.4/2005/WP.1, July 14, 2005, p. 12-13; *IAITPTF & IPF*, *supra*, note 33, p. 15, 20, 27.

have failed to fulfil their duty of consultation, which have generated direct effects on the physical and cultural survival of the indigenous peoples; for example: the construction of the Belo Monte Dam in the Brazilian Amazon without the consent of the affected indigenous peoples and ignoring the measures imposed by the Inter-American Commission on Human Rights[39] and the recommendations made by the *United Nations Special Rapporteur* on the Rights of *Indigenous Peoples* at the time[40], the Marlin mine, a mining project authorized by the Guatemalan government in the Maya people's territory located in rural San Marcos, without the consent of the Mayans[41], the granting of concessions and licenses by the Surinamese government for foreign companies for conducting logging and mining operations in the ancestral territory of the Saramaka indigenous people[42] and for conducting mining operations, besides the establishment and continuity of three natural reserves, in the ancestral territories of the Kaliña e Lokono Indigenous Peoples of the Lower-Marowijne[43], without their consultation or consent; the authorization, granted to Monsanto by the Mexican federal government, to plant genetically modified soybeans within the ancestral territories of the Pac-Chén and the Cancabchén indigenous communities located in the Yucatan Peninsula, without due consultation with the Maya indigenous people that live there[44],

---

39 *Inter-American Commission on Human Rights (IACHR)* (2011). *Precautionary Measure n. 382/10*, Indigenous communities of the Xingu River Basin, Brazil; and *Brazil, MRE* (2011). Nota n. 142: Solicitação da Comissão Interamericana de Direitos Humanos da OEA de 5 de abril de 2011. Brasília, DF.

40 *J. Anaya* (2010). *Report by the Special Rapporteur on the Situation of Human Rights and Fundamental Freedoms of Indigenous Peoples.* Addendum: Cases Examined by the Special Rapporteur (June 2009 – July 2010), Human Rights Council, 15th session, Agenda item 3, A/HRC/15/37/Add.1, 15 Sept. 2010.

41 *A. M. Fulmer; A. S. Godoy & P. Neff* (2008). Indigenous Rights, Resistance, and the Law: Lessons from a Guatemalan Mine. *Latin American Politics and Society*, University of Miami, v. 50, n. 4, p. 91-121.

42 ICHR (2007), *supra*, note 33; *(IACHR)* (2006) *Report on Admissibility and Merits N. 9/06*. Case 12.338, The Twelve Saramaka Clans (LOS), Suriname, March 2, 2006; *FPP & ASA (2007). Free, Prior and Informed Consent: Two Cases from Suriname*. FPIC Working Papers, Forest Peoples Programme, Moreton-in-Marsh; T. Ward (2011). The Right to Free, Prior, and Informed Consent: Indigenous Peoples' Participation Rights within International Law. *Northwestern Journal of International Human Rights*, v. 10, n, 2, p. 54-84.

43 ICHR (2015). *Case of the Kaliña and Lokono Peoples v. Suriname*, Merits, Reparations and Costs, November 25, 2015, Series C Nº. 309; *FPP & ASA, supra*, note 43; *V. Weitzner* (2008). Shifting Grounds: Indigenous Peoples and Mining in West Suriname. The Association of Indigenous Village Leaders in Suriname, The North-South Institute & The Inter-American Development Bank; Association of Indigenous Village Leaders in Suriname (VIDS) (2008). Decision-Making in the Lokono Communities of West Suriname. The Inter-American Development Bank; *V. Weitzner* (2011). Inclinando la Balanza del Poder – Logrando que el Consentimiento Libre, Previo e Informado Funcione: Lecciones y orientaciones políticas obtenidas en 10 años de investigación acción sobre actividades extractivas con pueblos indígenas y afro descendientes en las Américas. The North-South Institute, Ontario.

44 *Amicus Curiae (2015). Comparative and International Standards on the Right to Free, Prior and Informed Consent*: English Summary. Supreme Court of Justice of Mexico, Second Chamber, September 2015.

the concession, granted to third parties by the Belizean government, to carry out logging and oil exploration within the ancestral territory of the Mopan and Ke'kchi Maya People of the Toledo District of Southern Belize, without proper consultation and related FPIC[45]; the authorization, granted to a private oil company by the Ecuadorian government, to operate within the ancestral territory of the Kichwa People of Sarayaku, without their consultation or consent[46], the forcible removal of Endorois people from their ancestral lands located in the Rift Valley Province in Kenya, without proper prior consultation and consent, as well as without the adequate and effective compensation[47], among others.

Despite the failures and gaps shown by the current FPIC framework, it remains seen, by indigenous movement and by indigenous peoples alike, as an important mechanism for the recognition of indigenous people's rights as a whole. This is why it is important to improve its methods and procedures so that it can meet the aspirations and needs of indigenous peoples and can become an effective and legitimate mechanism for the realization of their right to self-determination.

For this reason, in addition to the formal requirements of FPIC, already established by international and domestic law (which are in most cases defined by open and loose rules that do not identify specifically how the consultation should take place, who should be consulted and what effects it should present), further measures and procedures should be taken to ensure the active and effective participation of indigenous peoples "in all levels of decision-making, including in external decision-making, if the indigenous peoples concerned so choose and in the forms of their choosing, including, where appropriate, in co-governance arrangements."[48]

First of all, the suitability and validity of the FPIC process depends on the recognition and understanding of the different indigenous worldviews which can influence the way indigenous peoples understand the project or policy concerned, as well as their relationships with other stakeholders. Each indigenous people group has its own forms of political, social, economic and spiritual organization, which are added to their historical experiences resulting from situations of colonization, forced displacement, migration, invasion, conflicts with squatters, land invaders, loggers and miners, amongst others. It is likely that the needs and priorities of indigenous peoples may conflict with the demands and concerns of other stakeholders as a result of the complexity and specificity of indigenous worldviews, which requires that ways be found to balance the ethical, spiritual and aesthetic considerations of indigenous peoples, which are essentially non-

45 *IACHR* (2004). *Maya Indigenous Communities of the Toledo District vs. Belize*, Report N°. 40/04, Case 12.053, October 12, 2004; *T. Ward*, *supra*, note 43.

46 *ICHR* (2012). *Case of the Kichwa Indigenous People of Sarayaku v. Ecuador*, Merits and reparations, June 27, 2012, Serie C N°. 245; *T. Ward*, *supra*, note 43.

47 ACHPR (2010). *Centre for Minority Rights Development (Kenya) and Minority Rights Group International on behalf of Endorois Welfare Council v. Kenya*, 276/2003, February 4, 2010.

48 *UN EMRIP*, *supra*, note 31, § 29.

monetarisable with those market perspectives of the other stakeholders, which are essentially based on utility and profit.[49]

Therefore, although it is not possible to draw up a single FPIC framework applicable to the most diverse indigenous realities, some measures and procedures should be minimally observed.[50] The first is the transmission of all of the relevant information concerning the project or policy under discussion, properly translated into the native language of indigenous communities and peoples concerned to ensure that the proposals and commitments are fully understood and freely agreed. Specific training and empowerment programs must also be offered in the native language of each indigenous people group or community involved and according to their own ways of learning and transmission of knowledge, which will require that their configuration and monitoring be undertaken with the assistance of anthropologists and indigenous teachers with intercultural bilingual *education.*

After receiving the appropriate information and training, indigenous peoples must have their own spaces and opportunities for deliberation and decision-making, which will take place within the indigenous territory to avoid tensions and constraints with unnecessary travel, and shall also respect the indigenous time in order to avoid pressures arising from the imposition of restricted and inflexible deadlines. Those spaces and moments should be open and transparent enough to enable effective dialogue, collaboration and participation and to ensure respect for local rules and governance structures, including their collective decision-making practices[51], so that they can express their concerns and needs in relation to the project or policy in question properly and freely.

Obtaining FPIC is, therefore, a real opportunity to enable indigenous peoples concerned to carefully consider the proposal submitted by expressing and discussing different points of view until it is possible to reach a collective decision, free from any influence or external pressure. Moreover, that the FPIC is part of a process where the decision does not mean the end of debates and deliberations,

---

49 *UK NEA, supra*, note 13, p. 14.

50 Several indigenous communities and peoples around the world are working on establishing their own protocols of consultation to make possible obtain their FPIC in accordance with the complexity and specificity of their cosmovisions. The following protocols can be cited as examples:
Conselho das Aldeias Wajãpi (Apina), Associação dos Povos Indígenas (Apiwata)& Associação Wajãpi Terra, Ambiente e Cultura (Awatac) (2014). Wajãpi kõ omõsãtamy wayvu oposikoa romõ ma'ẽ: Protocolo de Consulta e Consentimento Wajãpi. RCA, Iepé, Macapá – AP.
Federación por la Autodeterminación de los Pueblos Indígenas (FAPI) (2013). *Propuesta de protocolo para un Proceso de Consulta y Consentimiento con los Pueblos Indígenas del Paraguay.* PNUD, Paraguay.
First Peoples Worldwide (2012). Indigenous Peoples Guidebook on Free, Prior, Informed Consent and Corporation Standards. First Peoples Worldwide, International Indian Treaty Council (IITC) and Trillium Asset Management; among others.

51 *UN EMRIP, supra*, note 31, § 30. On the collective nature of the FPIC, see also *IAITPTF & IPF, supra*, note 33, p. 13.

but instead can and should continue existing as long as the effects of the project or the policy persist, must be taken into account; as the IAITPTF and IPF have stated: "FPIC is not a one step process wherein once a decision is reached, the process ceases. For indigenous peoples the end result of the FPIC process is an empowered community – the people are capacitated to arrive at decisions, implement such and when necessary amend the decisions."[52]

The difficulties and challenges that indigenous participation may present to managers and policy makers notwithstanding, the knowledge and information provided by indigenous peoples and communities will allow a better understanding of the links between biodiversity and human well-being and, consequently, will ensure the adoption of more effective and efficient responses, ensuring, thereby, legal certainty for the final decisions and their better understanding and acceptance by the populations affected.

5. CONCLUSION

The ecosystem services theory has been used as a means of improving the planning, management and decision-making processes through an integrated management strategy that promotes the conservation of the most diverse ecosystems and the sustainable use of their natural resources, and at the same time, recognizes that humans, with their cultural diversity, are an integral component of ecosystems.

In this context, recognizing the ITK as a kind of cultural ecosystem service might help indigenous peoples give visibility to their disproportionate vulnerability in relation to losses and changes in biodiversity and thereby might serve as a weapon in the fight against constant threats to ecosystems on which they depend for their physical and cultural survival.

The ITK is nonmaterial benefits arising from the intrinsic relationship between indigenous peoples and nature. Apart from providing livelihood, cultural identity, beliefs, spirituality, knowledge, ethical values and a certain way of life for indigenous peoples, these benefits also give relevant contributions to human well-being at large, especially in the improvement of medicine, pharmaceutical and cosmetic industries, agriculture, fisheries, hunting and management of plants and forests. Its importance and value for present and future generations is therefore incalculable.

On the other hand, it will be necessary to overcome some failures and gaps regarding the economic valuation of ecosystem services in order to make it possible to use the ecosystem services theory for an adequate and effective protection of that ITK. To this end, we propose here a new conceptual and methodological framework for the ecosystem services valuation, with a particular emphasis on the cultural ecosystem services valuation, which includes ITK.

---

52 *IAITPTF & IPF*, *supra*, note 33, p. 14.

Our framework embodies a multi-method and multi-criteria approach, participatory and deliberative techniques and methodologies arising from anthropology, sociology and ethics, in addition to quantitative and qualitative methods analysis, flexible and adaptive management and participation structures.

For that to become a reality in the practice of the ecosystem services' research and valuations, this framework should be supported by a solid legal, judicial and institutional framework, both nationally and internationally, which presents a thorough legislative description of its criteria, methods and techniques, and also a specific institutional body that ensures their supervision, control and effective execution. Once operational, our framework will be able to include the material and nonmaterial ecosystem values and benefits, as well as the local knowledge and interests in the planning, management and decision-making processes, which will make them more effective and legitimate and will bring positive consequences regarding their acceptance and adoption by the local and general public.

In turn, extending the possibility of active participation among indigenous peoples and movements in all stages of planning, management and decision-making, and in the policies, actions and environmental protection programs, would result in the overcoming of the gaps that bring scientific uncertainties and the weakness of the current environmental governance, which are greatly responsible for the decrease in the effectiveness of Environmental Law.

Despite the difficulties that may arise from the implementation of the criteria and methods proposed, our framework aims to provide a more effective, legitimate, democratic and socially acceptable realization of planning, management and decision-making processes in the environmental field by providing decision-makers with a better understanding of the local specificities and conditions and the cultural diversity and complexity of indigenous peoples, and by, at the same time, empowering indigenous peoples, communities and movements to effectively communicate their concerns and aspirations.

As a result, the active participation of indigenous peoples as part of the current environmental and global governance structure will give rise to better governance practices, in addition to keeping the dream alive that it is possible for humans to maintain a unified and integrated way of living and to get along with nature, thereby raising awareness around the world for the need for preservation of the environment and sustainability.

CHAPTER 8

PROMOTING ELECTRICITY FROM RENEWABLE ENERGY SOURCES IN FRANCE

Is French Law Appropriate for Achieving the Objectives?

Marie LAMOUREUX
Professor, Aix-Marseille University, CERIC/UMR 7318

ABSTRACT

Like many of her neighbours in Europe, France has set ambitious targets for the development of renewable energies and, especially, for the development of electricity generation from renewable sources. Before the EU imposed a target of a 23% share of energy from renewable sources in final energy consumption in 2020, France imposed this objective herself, and the recent "Energy Transition Act" has increased those objectives. Nevertheless, as a matter of fact, France is in quite a specific position, given the actual share of nuclear power in France's electric mix.

However, beyond the important political debates on the respective places of nuclear and renewable energies in the French electric mix, this raises the question of the juridical tools that are to be used to promote renewables in good economic conditions, as French law expressly requires. If specific tools have been created, the question of their ability to reach their goals remains. We have to admit that, for now, the development of renewable electricity in France suffers from several legal barriers, such as excessive complexity and instability. Furthermore, French law has to deal with European rules, especially regarding State aids, and will need to reconsider the ways to support the promotion of renewables.

INTRODUCTION

The promotion of renewable energies has become a centrepiece of French energy policy, as well as of the European Energy Policy. The development of renewables, in the electricity sector particularly, is now considered to be an essential means to achieve the general objectives of French and European Energy policies. Indeed, promoting electricity from renewable energy sources contributes to the security of supply, energy independence and to the fight against climate change. Thus, it is not surprising that both French and European energy policies will insist on the necessity to develop electricity from renewable sources massively over the next few years. But the question that remains is whether or not this objective can be met. Considering that law is an essential factor in this process, this chapter addresses the question of the ability of energy law to drive behavioural changes in order to reach that goal. Indeed, the promotion of renewable energies not only requires the elimination of technological and economic barriers; it also implies fighting against legal ones. Therefore, the objective will be to determine whether or not French law can be described as effective in reaching the ambitious target of the promotion of renewable sources in the electricity sector.

As a starting point, some elements of context might serve useful here. In France, one cannot talk about renewable energies in the electricity sector without talking about atomic energy. Indeed, considering electricity, France is mainly known as a nuclear country. France made the choice during the 1970s, in the aftermath of the first oil crisis, to develop the nuclear industry massively, in order to become self-sufficient and to offer citizens low-cost electricity. The result is that, at the present time, nuclear power still represents almost 78%[1] of French power production.

This number speaks for itself and shows how essential the nuclear industry is in the French background considering the development of renewables: renewables have to face the powerful nuclear industry and the fact that the entire nuclear system is in the hands of one operator – EDF –. He is therefore in a position to offer nuclear electricity at a very good price and benefits from a dominant position in the markets.[2] This is, maybe more than elsewhere in Europe, challenging the competitiveness of renewables. Even if the most recent studies show that the cost of the nuclear industry has been quite widely underestimated in France[3], French nuclear power is still considered to be one of the least expensive electricity

1 See the last report on the French energy balance (July 2015): www.developpement-durable.gouv.fr/IMG/pdf/Ref_-_Bilan_energetique_de_la_France_2014.pdf.

2 See, recently, P. Sablière, Production nucléaire d'électricité et monopole, *AJDA* 2015, p. 2076.

3 See, especially, the report from the "Cour des comptes" on the costs of the nuclear sector: "*Les coûts de la filière électro-nucléaire*", rapp. public thématique, January 2012 (www.ccomptes.fr/Publications/Publications/Les-couts-de-la-filiere-electro-nucleaire), and its update "*Le coût de production de l'électricité nucléaire, actualisation 2014*", May 2014 (www.ccomptes.fr/Actualites/Archives/Le-cout-de-production-de-l-electricite-nucleaire).

sources in Europe, and remains, in France at least, an open option to providing low-carbon electricity.

We have to pay attention to the very specific position of France in Europe in this regard. Since the Fukushima accident, some European Member States consider that the risks related to nuclear energy are no longer acceptable. Therefore, some public policies on nuclear energy have changed, while others continue to see nuclear energy as an open option, considering that it remains an affordable source of low-carbon electricity generation. National choices in Europe, concerning nuclear power, differ considerably from state to state, and, given the actual share of nuclear power in electricity generation in France (almost 80%), the French case is quite difficult to compare with other European countries (even if, obviously, since the accident of Fukushima, the necessity to further improve nuclear safety in France, as elsewhere, has become more important than ever).

Moreover, one could say that as France is already self-sufficient, thanks to her nuclear industry, there is no need to develop renewables in the electricity sector for the sake of energy independence. Furthermore, nuclear power being a low greenhouse gas emissions industry, one could add that the fight against climate change is not a convincing argument in favour of renewables in the French context, once again, because of the nuclear industry.

Nevertheless, these arguments, which have been decisive for a long time, are now in decline. To be truthful, though, renewables were never been ignored in France. Actually, one renewable source, hydropower energy, has been used for a very long time to produce electricity and is, at the present time, the second electricity source, comprising about 12% of French power production. It is, by far, the first renewable electricity source and it has been promoted since the beginning of the 20th century.

Today, the objective is to develop all of the other renewable sources that have a good potential in France, such as wind power, solar power or marine energies (energy produced by the waves, by marine currents and tides ...). But for the moment, their share in power production is very low: wind power represents about 3% of French power production, solar power only 1%, and most marine energies are not yet in operation and are still in the demonstration phase.[4] All in all, only 16% of French power production comes from renewables and, as can be seen, this is largely thanks to hydropower energy. The other renewable sources are still relatively marginal in the French electric mix.

But the time has clearly come, not to replace nuclear energy with renewables in France, but to at least diversify the electric mix, and we can say that, for the last ten years, the mentalities and the law have evolved in this regard considerably. For the last decade, the objective to develop renewables became one of the French

4 But they could become one of the most important ones in the future, given the extended French seacosts.

energy policy's priorities. The major steps in this evolution will be traced (1.), before wondering, subsequently, if the French legal framework is appropriate to reaching this goal (2.).

1. FRENCH AND EUROPEAN ENERGY POLICY

1.1. 2005 PROGRAMMING LAW ON ENERGY POLICY

With respect to the evolution of French energy policy, the first text that needs to be mentioned is the programming law on energy policy[5], adopted in 2005, which is the first Parliamentary Act that clearly sets the main goals of French energy policy.

According to this text, these goals are: to ensure security of supply, to maintain a competitive energy price, to protect human health and the environment and to assert a right of access to energy for all people. It also stated that the main actions to be carried out in order to achieve these objectives are the improvement of energy saving and energy efficiency, and support for renewable energies. It established a quantified target of a 10% share of renewable energies in final energy consumption by 2010. We can say, now, that this target has been achieved, but it was not really all that ambitious in the first place.

1.2. 2009-2010 THE GRENELLE ACTS

Two years later, in 2007, the government engaged in a national consultation on sustainable development called the "Grenelle Environment Forum" ("*Grenelle de l'environnement*"). Two Parliamentary acts followed, in order to give legal value to the priority targets that emerged during this consultation, and to create a new model of sustainable development, based on energy efficiency and the development of renewables specifically. The first "Grenelle Act"[6], adopted in 2009, established a quantified target of a 23% share of renewable energies in final energy consumption by 2020, and stated that France would develop "all renewable sources in sustainable economic and ecological conditions".[7]

---

5 *Loi n° 2005-781 du 13 juillet 2005 de programme fixant les orientations de la politique énergétique*. This text has been partly integrated in the "Energy Code" adopted in 2011. Especially, the first Articles of the 2005 Act are now part of the preliminary provisions of the French energy code (art. L. 100-1 et seq.). For a commentary on this text, especially on the objective of promotion of renewable energies, see B. Le Baut-Ferrarese & D. Landbeck, La loi du 13 juillet 2005 sur l'énergie et les énergies renouvelables, *AJDA* 2016, p. 189.

6 *Loi n° 2009-967 du 3 août 2009 de programmation relative à la mise en œuvre du Grenelle de l'environnement*. The "Second Grenelle Act" was adopted one year later: *Loi n° 2010-788 du 12 juillet 2010 portant engagement national pour l'environnement*.

7 L. n° 2009-967, Art. 19: «*l'Etat favorisera le développement de l'ensemble des filières d'énergies renouvelables dans des conditions économiquement et écologiquement soutenables*".

1.3. 2015 ENERGY TRANSITION FOR GREEN GROWTH ACT

The most recent Act of Parliament that needs to be mentioned is the "Energy Transition for Green Growth Act" adopted last summer, on the 17th of August 2015.[8] This is clearly a major text in terms of energy policy, which is aimed to state the principles that will lead France on the pathway towards energy transition.

It can be noted that, curiously, the law on energy transition does not define energy transition, but we can say that it is a strategy for a long-term structural change in the energy system, implying a strong reduction of oil consumption and a more efficient and sustainable economy, based on two pillars, which are, again, energy saving/energy efficiency and the development of renewables.

But it must be observed that this is not only a new manner to say what we already knew. There is a clear shift in perspective between this text and the previous ones, especially on the question of the respective places of nuclear and renewable energies in the French energy mix. Over ten years ago, in 2005, the law stated that France needed to develop renewables, but it insisted, at the same time, on the necessity to protect the nuclear industry, presented as the French "industrial sector of excellence", thanks to which: "France has the advantage of benefiting from one of the least expensive electricity in Europe", an advantage that "has to be strengthened" (art 2). It also declared that the State had to "keep nuclear energy's important place in French electricity production, which participates in the security of supply, energy independence, competitiveness, (and) fight against climate change" (art 4).

In 2015, on the contrary, far from singing the praises of the nuclear industry, the energy transition act provides, for the first time in France, the objective of limiting nuclear production. It sets a target to bring the proportion of nuclear energy in the electricity generation down to 50% by 2025 (we should recall that, at the present time, it is about 78%). In the French context, as previously referred to, this is an historic decision.

Nevertheless, we have to pay attention to the fact that this is not a real limitation, in the sense that the law does not require the immediate closing of any nuclear power plant.[9] But the law introduces a limitation of the installed nuclear capacity, capped at a level (63.2 GW) that represents the current installed capacity.[10] Therefore, the law forbids the creation and operation of any new

---

8 *Loi n° 2015- 992 du 17 août 2015 relative à la transition énergétique pour la croissance verte.* Among all commentaries, see, in particular, Ph. Billet, Transition énergétique et croissance verte: itinéraire et ambitions d'une loi, *Energie, environnement, infrastructures* oct. 2015, dossier 6; P. Sablière, Le pilotage de la production d'électricité dans la loi de transition énergétique, *Energie, environnement, infrastructures* oct. 2015, dossier 7; B. Le Baut-Ferrarese, Les energies renouvelables en transition, *Energie, environnement, infrastructures* oct. 2015, dossier 8.

9 It has been one of the most sensitive issues, which, by the way, has created strong disagreements between both Houses of Parliament.

10 *Loi n° 2015- 992 du 17 août 2015 relative à la transition énergétique pour la croissance verte,* art. 187, creating Articles L. 311-5-1 et seq. of the Energy code.

nuclear power plant if an existing one is not closed.[11] Even if some say that this is not enough, it is still the first time in France that such a decision has been taken, which constrains the operator to close nuclear power plants if he wants to open new ones. It is, at least, a clear political signal in favour of the development of alternative energy sources.

Precisely, the Energy Transition Act sets new targets for the development of renewables, which are clearly ambitious: it sets a target to bring the share of renewables to 32% of final gross consumption by 2030, and it is specified that to reach this objective, it will be necessary to bring the share of renewables in electricity production to 40% by 2030[12] (we should remember that it is about 16% at the moment). In other words, an objective which involves doubling the share of renewables in the electricity generation over the next fifteen years.

At the same time, the Act sets an objective of reducing national final energy consumption by 50% by 2050 in relation to the 2012 benchmark, with an intermediate target of 20% by 2030. Of course, no one can tell if such an ambitious goal will be achieved. But, in any case, it can be noted that we have to read the general objective of development of renewables in energy consumption in relation to this objective to reduce energy consumption drastically.

In any event, as can be seen, French energy policy is now clearly and firmly in favour of the massive development of renewables, especially in the electricity sector. France wants to show that she intends to become a major producer of renewable energy. Of course, objectives and good intentions are not sufficient and are just a first step, but it is an important one: the development of renewables needs a clear and strong political commitment legally transposed.

1.4. EUROPEAN CLIMATE AND ENERGY POLICY

It is also important to recall that the development of renewables is not only a French intention and choice; it is also a European objective and, to some extent, an obligation.

Indeed, the promotion of renewable energies has become one of the pillars of the European integrated climate and energy policy, and it is easily understandable why this is. The consumption of fossil fuels has contributed significantly to the increase of greenhouse gas emissions. One could even say that the energy sector,

---

11 The Constitutional Council was asked to rule on the conformity of these provisions with the Constitution. He ruled that there was no violation of any constitutional principle, and that the objective to promote a diversification of the energy mix and to reduce the proportion of nuclear energy in the electricity generation pursued a public interest purpose: Décision n° 2015-718 DC du 13 août 2015, *Loi relative à la transition énergétique pour la croissance verte*.

12 It can be noted that the general objective of development of renewables is stated in relation to energy consumption; but, with regards to the electricity sector, the objective is stated in terms of electricity production.

and the consumption of fossil fuels particularly, produces the lion's share of man-made greenhouse gas emissions. Therefore, promoting low-carbon energy systems is an important challenge for climate change mitigation, and this observation is especially true in the eyes of the European Union. Considering the key role played by energy consumption in the historic increase of greenhouse gas emissions, the European Union has developed an integrated energy and climate change policy and has set ambitious climate and energy targets for 2020[13], targets which were implemented by a "climate and energy package" of binding legislation in 2009. The 2009 directive on the promotion of the use of energy from renewable sources[14] imposes mandatory targets on Member States, in order to reach a general target of a 20% share of energy from renewable sources in overall Union energy consumption by 2020. For France, the mandatory target is 23%.

A few years later, the 2030 climate and energy framework was adopted.[15] A centrepiece of this framework is the target to reduce the EU's greenhouse gas emissions by at least 40% below the 1990 level by 2030. Again, renewable energy is presented as an essential part of this framework, which sets an objective of increasing the share of renewable energy to at least 27% of the EU's energy consumption by 2030. More specifically, in the electricity sector it will be 45%; it should be specified that at the present time 26% of the EU's power is generated from renewables.

For the longer term, the European Commission has elaborated a strategy for 2050. The European Commission published a "roadmap for moving to a competitive low carbon economy in 2050"[16] in 2011, which presents possible actions that could enable the EU to meet a target of a drastic reduction of greenhouse gas emissions by the middle of this century.[17] This roadmap intends to show how different sectors could help to reach this goal and it should be noted that the electricity sector is presented as the first key sector. Power generation should become almost completely carbon-free by the mid-century[18] to achieve the general target of decarbonising the economy, and this requires a significant increase in the use of renewables. On this point, the European roadmap for moving to a low-carbon economy is supplemented by the Energy 2050 roadmap[19],

---

13 See, especially, European Commission, Limiting global climate change to 2 degrees Celsius, The way ahead for 2020 and beyond, COM (2007) 2 final.

14 Dir. n° 2009/28/CE of 23 April 2009 on the promotion of the use of energy from renewable sources and amending and subsequently repealing Directives 2001/77/EC and 2003/30/EC.

15 European Commission, A policy framework for climate and energy in the period from 2020 to 2030, COM (2014) 15 final.

16 Communication from the Commission to the European Parliament, the Council, the European Economic and Social Committee and the Committee of the Regions, "Roadmap for moving to a low-carbon economy in 2050", 8 march 2011, COM (2011) 112 final.

17 – 80 to – 95% by 2050, compared to 1990.

18 – 93 to –99% of greenhouse gas reductions compared to 1990.

19 Communication from the Commission to the European Parliament, the Council, the European Economic and Social Committee and the Committee of the Regions, "Energy Roadmap 2050", 15 December 2011, COM (2011) 885 final.

which explores the specific challenges in the energy sector, by presenting different scenarios. They all imply strong support schemes for renewable energies leading to a very high share of renewables in electricity consumption.

Thus, in the eyes of the European Union, renewable energies in the electricity sector are a key part of the transition to a low-carbon economy, and constitute the first pre-requisite for a sustainable energy system. Furthermore, the development of renewables is now a pillar of the new "Energy Union" strategy, announced last year by the European Commission.[20] Among other things, the European Commission has announced a substantial revision of the directive on renewable energy sources for the period after 2020.

2. THE (IN)EFFECTIVENESS OF THE FRENCH LEGAL FRAMEWORK

But, just after reading the last European report on renewable energy progress one could have some fears, because France is identified as one of the Member States who may miss its obligation under the 2009 directive. Therefore, the European Commission has said that we should "assess whether (our) policies and tools are sufficient and effective"[21] to meet the target. This is, of course, the main question here. The political will to promote renewables has been declared: but is it effective? Is it really possible to reach the target? The question is even more important since, as observed previously, the energy transition act has increased the goal significantly.

We have to pay attention to the fact that the law is an essential factor in this process. Law can create incentives or, on the contrary, slow down the development of renewables if it is not well designed, if it creates excessive burdens or if it is too uncertain, so that it can discourage investors and projects developers. The development of renewables not only requires the elimination of technological and economical barriers; it also involves fighting against legal barriers.

It is impossible to explain in detail all of the legal difficulties that can slow down the realization of renewable projects but, in a few words, we can say that several major legal barriers remain in France, which include complexity, inconsistencies and instability.

---

20 See, especially, the communication from the European Commission "A Framework Strategy for a Resilient Energy Union with a Forward-Looking Climate Change Policy", 22 Feb. 2015, COM (2015) 80 final.

21 Report from the Commission to the European Parliament, the Council, the European Economic and Social Committee and the Committee of the Regions, Renewable energy progress report, 15 June 2015, COM (2015) 293 final.

2.1. COMPLEXITY AND SLOWNESS OF ADMINISTRATIVE PROCEDURES

Of course, French law has created many incentives to support the development of renewables (investment aids, tax exemptions or reductions …). But, generally speaking, the legal framework is too complex and sometimes creates excessive burdens on the shoulders of projects' holders. It is largely caused by a lack of coordination between the different legislations involved in the implementation of renewable projects, such as energy law, planning law, environmental law, maritime law, etc. These legislations duplicate procedures, involve different authorities in charge of each authorization procedure, creating administrative red-tape, slowness in the project's implementation and, in the worst case, litigation that may drive the project to a fatal end.

This problem has been clearly identified and everyone seems to agree that the simplification of administrative procedures is an important challenge to the deployment of renewable energies. Therefore, a movement towards simplification has recently begun, in order to reduce regulatory constraints and to reduce costs and the time taken by procedures.

For example, two years ago[22], a single permit procedure was created, which is a one-stop-shop system, merging the different authorization procedures required by energy law, environmental law and planning law. This is certainly a good thing, even if it is just an initial step.

More generally, simplifying the regulations governing renewable energy projects is one of the objectives declared in the Energy Transition Act adopted last summer. But, unfortunately, this new legislation emphasizes how the simplification of the law is a tricky subject. This Parliamentary Act claims to simplify procedures regarding renewable energies in order to promote them, and to some extent this is true.[23] But it also creates dozens of new rules and the law provides for the adoption of almost two thousand implementing decrees in the next few months. There are doubts as to whether all of these new rules could possibly simplify the law governing renewable energies.[24]

---

22 In 2014, it was on an experimental basis and in limited areas (*Ordonnance n° 2014-355 du 20 mars 2014 relative à l'expérimentation d'une authorisation unique en matière d'installation classée pour la protection de l'environnement*). The Energy Transition Act extends this measure and provides for its widespread implementation throughout France (*Loi n° 2015- 992 du 17 août 2015 relative à la transition énergétique pour la croissance verte*, art. 145).

23 It is true regarding the single permit, for example, or with regards to the reduction of grid connection time. This delay has been limited to 18 months, with some exceptions. Financial compensation can be granted if this time limit is exceeded (*Loi n° 2015- 992 du 17 août 2015 relative à la transition énergétique pour la croissance verte*, art. 105, creating art. L. 342-3 of the energy code).

24 This is so confusing that a web page has been created to follow the progress of the adoption of the implementing decrees (on the website of the public service for the dissemination of law): www.legifrance.gouv.fr/affichLoiPubliee.do;jsessionid=355A1277A1707A21BCF65A8

2.2. INCONSISTENCIES

Furthermore, another problem is, sometimes, a lack of coherency. For example, the development of onshore wind power regularly faced inconsistencies between the objectives declared and the rules adopted. Thus, the Second Grenelle Act, adopted in 2010[25], declared the desire to promote a new model of sustainable development based especially on the promotion of all renewable sources; but it created new burdens at the same time, by submitting wind turbines to the heaviest authorization procedures required for the facilities classified for environmental protection. At the time, it was said that the law was blowing hot and cold[26], and this led to some contestation.[27]

Likewise, the Energy Transition Act, while declaring a desire to reduce regulatory constraints, creates, once more, new ones on wind farm projects by modifying, for example, the rules on the distance between wind turbines and houses.[28] Given France's population density, implementing this new provision is not an easy task, and it is already questioning the survival of some wind farms projects that had been planned.

But, of course, this emphasizes the difficulty of reconciling the conflicting interests involved in a wind farm project (energy policy, environmental issues such as effects on ecosystems and town planning requirements, etc.), which is one of the most challenging issues for the deployment of onshore wind power. More broadly, we need to keep in mind that a massive development of renewable energies not only involves the deployment of hundreds of new production facilities, but also of grid infrastructures that may have severe environmental impact and that involve major social acceptance issues.[29]

1DA551084.tpdila08v_1?idDocument=JORFDOLE000029310724&type=echeancier&typeLoi=&legislature=14.

25 Cited note 6.

26 See J. Duval, Grenelle 2: Un traitement ambivalent des énergies renouvelables, *Environnement*, oct. 2010, étude p. 11; L. Le Corre, Nouveau durcissement du régime juridique des éoliennes en perspective, *Envir. et dév. durable* 2010, étude 13; J.-C. Rotouillie, Eoliennes terrestres: les enjeux de l'application de la police des ICPE, *BDEI* nov. 2011, p. 45; L. Wolff & Ch. Puel, La soumission des éoliennes terrestres au régime des installations classées: obligations et conséquences, *JCP G* 2011, 1032.

27 One of the arguments regularly invoked is that this kind of measure slows down the deployment of renewable energy facilities and that, consequently, it would be contrary to the sustainable development principle enshrined in the French Charter for the Environment and to the European objective of promotion of renewable sources defined in the 2009 directive on the promotion of renewable energy. But the «Conseil d'Etat» has repeatedly rejected these arguments. See, especially, CE, 16 avril 2012, n° 353577, *Sté Innovent, Environnement* janv. 2013, p. 48, note A. Fourmon; CE, 13 juillet 2012, n° 353565, *Volkswind France & Innovent, Gaz. Pal.* 12-13 sept. 2012, p. 13, note A. Fourmon; CE 26 décembre 2012, n° 357152, *Association France Energie Eolienne, Envir. et développement durable* février 2013, comm. 11, note A. Fourmon.

28 The 500 meters rule is now a minimum, and the exact distance has to be decided on a case-by-case basis by the competent authority: *Loi n° 2015- 992 du 17 août 2015 relative à la transition énergétique pour la croissance verte*, Art. 139 (modifying art. L. 553-1 of the Environmental Code).

29 This is, more broadly, one of the many illustrations of the greatest difficulties that we can have in defining sustainable energy. On the different approaches of energy sustainability, see

2.3. INSTABILITY AND LEGAL UNCERTAINTY

Complexity, slowness and inconsistencies notwithstanding, the most serious legal barrier is instability and legal uncertainty. A good example can be taken from the main tool used in France to support the development of renewables in the electricity sector, which is the feed-in tariff.

The French support scheme. Indeed, renewables in the electricity sector suffer from a lack of competitiveness compared with other methods of electricity generation, especially in the French context where the nuclear industry benefits from relatively low production costs. Therefore, at the present time, public support is still necessary to attracting investments and the French public support scheme rests on the feed-in tariff.[30]

Any producer of renewable electricity is entitled to benefit from the long-term purchase contract of his production. This contract is, most of the time, concluded with EDF, which is under the legal obligation to contract and which has to buy the electricity at a price fixed by regulation. This price is designed to be above the market value of electricity, in order to guarantee a return on investment and a sufficient remuneration to the producer. This is, of course, a powerful incentive to invest in the renewable sector, since it offers a guaranteed access to the grid, a stable and long-term purchase agreement (typically, 15 or 20 years), and a guaranteed price based on the cost of renewable energy generation, one above the market price. Therefore, it offers a secure and stable market for investors and project developers.

It also creates some difficulties and even pernicious effects. The best example is that of the solar sector. In the beginning, the feed-in tariff was very attractive in the photovoltaic sector. It was even so attractive that hundreds of purchase contracts were concluded and, quickly, the French government noticed that the objective of development of the photovoltaic sector would be achieved faster than expected. But it was not only good news, because it appeared that the feed-in tariff was also going to cost much more than expected. It should be noted that the final cost of this system is borne by final consumers, who have to pay the public contribution to the electricity service ("*contribution au service public de l'électricité*").

Thus, the success of the feed-in tariff started to raise concerns about a drastic increase of consumers' bills. Therefore, the government decided to put the brakes on public support for the photovoltaic sector and it reduced the feed-in tariff several times in one year in 2010, in order to limit the purchase contract

---

Challenges and approaches in energy transition in the EU, L. Squintani & H.H.B. Vedder with M. Reese and B. Vanhausden (eds), EELF Book Series, vol. 1, 2014, and especially S. Gaines, The energy revolution as sustainable development, p. 7.

30 Art. L. 314-1 et seq. of the Energy Code.

applications. But it was not enough: there were still just as many applicants hoping to benefit from the system. Then, a few months later, the government decided on a more drastic measure, a moratorium suspending the feed-in tariff system in the photovoltaic sector.[31]

It was just a temporary measure, but it has been a dramatic one. There has been a drastic decline of the solar sector in France since this decision, because investors had completely lost confidence. Furthermore, some of the companies who had made their investment plans just before the moratorium have not survived it. More generally, since the moratorium has troubled the expectations of hundreds of companies, it has led to hundreds of legal actions.[32]

Of course, the question of the public cost of the development of renewables is an essential one and, if it is found that one sector is costing too much, it is necessary to make adjustments thereto. But this example also shows how much we have to be careful of legal certainty if we do not want to undermine our chances of reaching the goals of the development of renewables. The investors' confidence needs legal certainty, and if we want an important development of renewables, we need to attract investments now.[33] It does not mean that there can be no evolution in the French support scheme. It only means that changes have to happen in a more predictable and clear manner.

European regulation of State aids for renewable energy. It is all the more important now, since France has to reconsider part of this support scheme, because of the European regulation of State aids for renewable energies. Indeed, another difficulty is that the deployment of renewable energies has to deal with competition rules, and that public support schemes such as feed-in tariffs can be described as State aid, liable to distort competition in the European internal market.

---

31 *Décret n° 2010-1510 du 9 décembre 2010 suspendant l'obligation d'achat de l'électricité produite par certaines installations utilisant l'énergie radiative du soleil.*

32 Most of them are still on-going. Some of them were seeking to hold the State liable for the financial loss suffered, resulting from the moratorium. But the "Conseil d'Etat" ruled that the State did not incur any liability, either on the ground of fault-based liability or on the ground of strict liability, even if there was financial damage: CE, 25 septembre 2015, n° 376431, *Sté Planet Bloo, Energie, environnement, infrastructures*, décembre 2015, comm. 88, note B. Le Baut-Ferrarese, *AJDA* 2016, p. 450, note A. Minet-Leleu; see, also, CE, 16 novembre 2011, n° 344972, *Sté Ciel et Terre*, Lebon T. 746.

33 Considering the photovoltaic sector, French authorities now promote the use of calls for tender, in order to promote the deployment of large-scale photovoltaic installations. It is now considered as the best way for public authorities to redirect investments towards the most efficient and productive locations. This is why the Energy Transition Act has reduced the delays and complexities associated with the call for tenders process, see Articles L. 311-10 et seq. of the Energy Code, as amended by the Energy Transition Act, and Articles R. 311-12 et seq, as amended by the implementing decree n° 2016-170 du 18 février 2016 relatif à la procédure d'appel d'offres pour les installations de production d'électricité.

Until now, the European Commission has declared this kind of state aid to be compatible with the common market, considering that public support was essential to reaching the European target of promotion of renewables.[34] For example, the 2009 directive on the promotion of renewable energies stated that "public support is necessary to reach the Community's objectives with regards to the expansion of electricity produced from renewable energy sources, in particular for as long as electricity prices in the internal market do not reflect the full environmental and social costs and benefits of energy sources used".[35]

But it will be less common in the future, given that the European Commission has announced that the state aids will have to regress as the competitiveness of renewables progresses. Obviously, in the eyes of the European Union, the energy transition must be a cost-effective one.

We have to recall that, even if the European Union has a strongly integrated energy and climate policy today, the first goal of the European energy policy remains an effective operation of the internal energy market. This is how the European Union – and the European Community before it – started to deal with energy issues a few decades ago, and it is still a centrepiece of the European energy policy.[36]

Therefore, it has become necessary to take the fact that the costs of some renewable technologies are going down into account, and that large disparities exist in maturity between the different renewable energy production sectors, so that public support can be redirected where it is still most useful.

This is why the new European guidelines on State aid for environmental protection and energy, adopted in 2014 (covering the 2014-2020 period), intend to avoid excessive support for mature sectors that can create unnecessary market

---

34 Nevertheless, in France, there has been great concern in recent years, because the French regulations on the feed-in tariffs had not been notified to the European Commission. It has particularly troubled the onshore wind power sector for a few years and the "Conseil d'Etat", after seeking a preliminary ruling from the Court of Justice on the question of whether the French support scheme constituted State aid (CJEU, 19 dec. 2013, case C-262/12, *Association Vent de Colère! Fédération nationale and others:* the Court held that the French mechanism for offsetting the additional costs arising from the obligation to purchase the electricity generated by wind turbines felt within the concept of an intervention by the State through State resources), has cancelled the ministerial orders on the feed-in tariff in the onshore wind-power sector: CE, 28 mai 2014, n° 324852, *Association Vent de colère! Fédération nationale et autres*. The same problem is now growing in the photovoltaic sector, see CA Versailles, 8 dec. 2015, n° 14/02549, ERDF c/ SAS Ombrière Le Bosc, seeking a preliminary ruling from the European Court of Justice.

35 Directive 2009/28/EC, 23 April 2009, cited note 14, point 27.

36 For example, Article 194 (1) TFEU has been drafted in this way. It states that the Union policy on energy shall aim to:
"(a) ensure the functioning of the energy market;
(b) ensure security of the energy supply in the Union;
(c) promote energy efficiency and energy saving and the development of new and renewable forms of energy; and
(d) promote the interconnection of energy networks".

distortions and the growth of consumer bills. Therefore, they promote a gradual move to market-based support for renewable energy. In particular, the guidelines foresee the gradual replacement of feed-in tariffs with feed-in premiums.

France has already taken these guidelines into account, on the occasion of the Energy Transition Act, which creates a new support scheme for mature renewable energies, called additional compensation ("*complément de rémunération*")[37], which is a form of a feed-in premium. The producer will sell the electricity directly on the market, but they will benefit from a premium, that is to say an additional remuneration. Thus, this system reduces the market price risk for the producer. As for the feed-in tariff currently used, this mechanism will rest on a long-term contract, concluded with EDF, who will pay the additional remuneration to the producer. This new support scheme is intended to support the deployment of renewable energies in a way that contributes to the increased integration of renewables in the electricity market and, therefore, to something more compatible with the European internal market principles.

For sure, these changes in the public support scheme will create new challenges, and we have to hope that we will avoid the pitfalls of the past and limit the difficulties created by regulations, which are too unstable. The legal risk must be kept to a reasonable degree, as it is a decisive factor that affects investment decisions.

3. CONCLUSION

More generally, it is far from certain that France will meet the target of development of renewables, especially when we see that the law increases the objectives, while we have to decrease public support. But, despite these difficulties, we have to keep in mind that renewable electricity is a fast-growing sector that shows a very high potential for development, which will certainly increase tomorrow and in the days to come, when some technologies that are not yet functioning will be in operation. Energy is a sector in which technological innovations are moving very fast, so it is not impossible to think that what seems very difficult to achieve today could become realistic in the short-term perspective.

And, after all, even if the target is not achieved, this does not mean that French energy policy, in favour of renewables, is completely ineffective. Of course, effectiveness can be defined, in this context, as the ability to reach a certain goal, but this goal is just a number; it is not an end in itself. What really

[37] See *Loi n° 2015- 992 du 17 août 2015 relative à la transition énergétique pour la croissance verte*, art. 104, creating a new section in the Energy Code (art. L. 314-18 et seq.); A. Fourmon, L'évolution des mécanismes de soutien applicables aux énergies renouvelables pour la transition énergétique: premiers commentaires sur la notion de complément de rémunération, *Energie, environnement, infrastructures* août 2015, étude 15.

matters is to develop renewables in good conditions, considering all parameters (environmental, economical and so on …). This is the real issue and this is how renewable energies could contribute, in a long-lasting way, to the effectiveness of larger objectives, such as sustainable development and the fight against climate change.

CHAPTER 9

CHANGING PATTERNS OF INTERNATIONAL ENVIRONMENTAL LAW-MAKING: ADDRESSING NORMATIVE INEFFECTIVENESS

Owen McINTYRE
Senior Lecturer and Director of Research at the School of Law, University College Cork, Ireland

ABSTRACT

However we characterise normative "effectiveness", international environmental law must be adaptable and capable of evolving to address new challenges and pursue ever-higher standards of environmental protection. Conventional regimes tend to be based on framework agreements, which institutionalise cooperation by establishing institutional machinery capable of elaborating more detailed environmental norms and standards. Older conventional instruments may also be understood in the light of current environmental standards and practices due to the "evolutionary interpretation" envisaged under the Vienna Convention. The almost universal participation of States in key global environmental treaties, as well as the pervasive influence of environmental norms on non-environmental treaty provisions, means that this "systemic integration" can promote more coherent and effective conventional regimes for environmental protection. In addition, a relatively relaxed approach is taken to recognition of the closely related customary rules, upon which environmental treaty rules tend to be based, due largely to the powerful law-making effect of a wealth of declarative instruments which rationalise the general principles of law relevant to environmental protection.

Quite apart from the traditionally recognised sources of international law, international environmental law relies heavily on atypical normative forms including, in particular, non-binding soft law instruments, which promote voluntary compliance, facilitate bilateral and multilateral environmental negotiations and provide a basis for the development of more specific binding norms. The rich infrastructure of intergovernmental-specialised agencies and programmes also plays a key role in providing the technical expertise required to achieve scientific consensus. International environmental law also tends to be procedurally sophisticated, requiring an open participative approach, especially where the environmental values concerned overlap with human rights requirements, thus ensuring that it can respond effectively to evolving societal expectations.

Finally, this field of international law is increasingly characterised by multi-level governance as well as by new forms of rules, standards and procedures emerging from non-traditional actors involved in the law-making process, suggesting a fluidity in the formation and evolution of international environmental rules, something which enhances their technical currency, broad legitimacy and applicability and, thus inevitably, their effectiveness.

1. INTRODUCTION

As a new body of rules which has emerged very rapidly in recent decades, the "effectiveness" of international environmental law has long been a matter of concern, causing commentators to focus on various aspects of normative design and implementation.[1] Chambers notably focuses on the robustness of environmental treaty regimes and notes that many have 'built-in ... scientific mechanisms or effectiveness review systems', as well as 'additional built-in systems that allow treaty renegotiation [to] take on deeper commitments'.[2] Commentators also stress the complex interlinkages between international environmental law and other fields, such as international human rights law and international trade law, worrying that traditionally, '[f]ailure to see these linkages has also undermined the effectiveness of international law'.[3] Leary and Pisupati express concern that 'the effectiveness of international environmental law ... will also be

---

1 See, for example, D. Bodansky, *The Art and Craft of International Environmental Law* (Harvard University Press, Cambridge, 2010), Chapter 12, 'Effectiveness'; E. Louka, *International Environmental Law: Fairness, Effectiveness and World Order* (Cambridge University Press, Cambridge, 2006); E. L. Miles *et al*, Environmental Regime Effectiveness: Confronting Theory with Evidence (MIT Press, Cambridge, 2002); J. Vollenweider, 'The Effectiveness of International Environmental Agreements', (2012) 13 *International Environmental Agreements: Politics, Law and Economics* 343-367; A Byrne, 'The 1979 Convention on Long-Range Transboundary Air Pollution: Assessing its Effectiveness as a Multilateral Environmental Regime after 35 Years', (2015) 4 *Transnational Environmental Law* 37-67.

2 W. B. Chambers, *Interlinkages and the Effectiveness of Multilateral Environmental Agreements* (UNU Press, Tokyo, 2008), at 128-129. See further, D. Leary and B. Pisupati, *The Future of International Environmental Law* (UNU Press, Tokyo, 2010), at 7-8.

3 Leary and Pisupati, *ibid.*, at 8. See further, E. Brown Weiss, 'New Directions in International Environmental Law', (United Nations Congress on Public International Law, New York, 1995), reproduced in D. Craig, N. Robinson and K. L. Koh (eds.), *Capacity Building for Environmental Law in the Asian and Pacific Region* (Asian Development Bank, Manila, 2002) at 13.

partly dependent on us breaking out of the pernicious influence of the pervasive concept of state sovereignty in international law', and warn that rigid adherence to traditional understandings of the sources and processes of the formation of law in this field 'is to deny the reality that a range of non-state actors now shape world affairs and responses to the major global environmental challenges of our times'.[4] Thus, thinkers concerned with the problem of effectiveness appear to anticipate shifting patterns in international environmental law-making.

International law, relating to the protection of the natural environment, is not a clearly defined, distinct or systematically constructed corpus of international rules. Instead, it arises from the application of general rules and principles of "classical" international law and comprises a somewhat *ad hoc* collection of, *inter alia*, formal international instruments, both binding and non-binding, established and evolving State practice, various transnational governance frameworks, fora and institutions, and the decisions of various international courts and tribunals in inter-State disputes concerning the natural environment. Thus, the scope of international environmental law-making is both wide and uncertain, with unclear boundaries which overlap with those defining law-making for the utilization of natural resources, human rights, international trade, investor protection, and other related fields.

However, while the sources of international environmental law are the same as those for all other fields of international law formally, the development and adoption of international environmental rules involves a number of unique challenges for the international legal system, which militate against 'taking too narrow a view of the traditional sources of international law'.[5] Any examination of the now-extensive and wide-ranging corpus of international environmental rules requires a discussion of the means by which such rules have emerged and of the forces that have shaped the law-making processes involved. The particular challenges presented by international environmental law-making include the often-urgent need to develop inclusive and comprehensive regimes in areas where few if any controls existed in the past. This need has led the international community to employ more flexible, yet often more complex, instruments than in other fields, such as framework agreements, which only specify general objectives and principles, but also create specialist institutional mechanisms to facilitate the elaboration of more detailed rules. At the same time, the use of consensus negotiating procedures and so-called 'package deal' diplomacy in the agreement of global framework agreements have been vital to securing almost universal participation in key global law-making treaties[6], such as the 1985 Vienna

4 *Ibid.*, at 9-10. See further, E. Brown Weiss, 'International Law in a Kaleidoscopic World', (2011) 1/1 *Asian Journal of International Law* 21-32.

5 P. Birnie, A. Boyle and C. Redgwell, *International Law and the Environment* (3rd ed) (Oxford University Press, Oxford, 2009), at 14.

6 See Birnie, Boyle and Redgwell, *ibid.*, at 13. See also S. Maljean-Dubois 'The Making of International Law Challenging Environmental Protection', in Y. Kerbrat and S. Maljean-

Convention for the Protection of the Ozone Layer[7] and the 1992 Rio Conventions on Climate Change[8] and Biodiversity.[9]

Similarly, the need to develop novel, yet inclusive, frameworks of coherent environmental rules and principles has required considerable reliance on so-called 'soft-law', where States (or other actors) advance rules and principles through the adoption of various kinds of non-binding recommendations, declarations, codes of conduct, guidelines and codifications. Such instruments function to permit otherwise hesitant States to engage in the early iterations of many international environmental 'legislative' regimes, without risking any unanticipated and unintended loss of sovereign discretion, while incrementally building confidence in the type of cooperative arrangements proposed. Of course, while broad adherence to such soft-law codes generate the consistent State practice and evidence of *opinio juris* necessary for identifying emerging customary rules, generally accepted soft-law standards will also often become formalised in global or regional treaty arrangements. Such interactions between the classical and non-classical sources of international law give rise to quite a particular culture of law-making in this field, which is dynamic, yet ultimately convergent around a number of widely accepted general principles.

Another means of ensuring inclusive international environmental law-making, whilst retaining the capacity of regimes adopted to evolve normatively, has been that of formulating and including broad environmental principles which, though widely accepted by States, particularly in the non-binding declaratory instruments adopted by global and regional conferences, tend to be somewhat vague and ill-defined in terms of their normative content and significance. References to the precautionary principle, the polluter pays principle, common but differentiated responsibility and intergenerational equity are ubiquitous in international environmental agreements and declarations. The role of these principles cannot be overstated as they,

'play a part in the foundations of institutional and normative frameworks developed in the field of the environment and they guide the interpretation of commitments. States can foster legitimate expectations by relying on these principles, even though, very often, their legal status cannot be clearly identified.'[10]

Each of these principles is designed to reconcile conflicting values and approaches originating in a number of different technical systems, prompting one leading commentator to describe them as 'open-textured norms' with an 'inter-normative nature'.[11] For example, the principle of precaution is intended to

---

Bubois (eds.), *The Transformation of International Environmental Law* (2011, A. Pedone & Hart, Paris and Oxford), 25-54, at 36.

7 (1987) 26 *ILM* 1529.

8 UN Framework Convention on Climate Change, (1992) 31 *ILM* 851.

9 Convention on Biological Diversity, (1992) 31 *ILM* 818.

10 L. Boisson de Chazournes, 'Features and Trends in International Environmental Law', in Kerbrat and Maljean-Bubois (eds.), *supra*, n. 6, at 9-20, at 11.

11 *Ibid.*

accommodate the difficult interaction between uncertain environmental science and the flexible normative standards inherent to international environmental law. Indeed, since the universal adoption of the Rio Declaration in 1992, the overarching objective of sustainable development has been employed by the international community[12] to guide the development of international environmental law in a manner that is balanced with the economic and social needs of States, and to ensure the integration of considerations of environmental protection into a range of related fields of international law-making.[13]

In identifying patterns of modern international environmental law-making, it is necessary to examine the sources of international rules in this field in order to understand the particular manner in which such sources, both traditional and non-traditional, are employed by the international community. Though any examination of "law-making" necessarily entails a great deal more than a mere survey of "sources" of law, including, for example, an investigation of the myriad institutional, cultural and geopolitical factors which impact upon the development and application of international rules, a discussion of such sources provides a logical structure within which observations may be made upon the singular features of international environmental law-making. Therefore, this chapter commences with a discussion of international environmental law-making by means of the classical sources of international law, before proceeding to a discussion of features of law-making in this field which challenge the narrow boundaries of the traditional sources of law, enumerated under Article 38 of the ICJ Statute.

2. ENVIRONMENTAL LAW-MAKING THROUGH CLASSICAL SOURCES

Article 38(1) of the 1945 Statute of the International Court of Justice[14] remains 'the only generally accepted statement of the sources of international law to be applied

12 To date, approximately 300 international treaties include reference to sustainable development, see V. Barral, 'Sustainable Development in International Law: Nature and Operation of an Evolutive Legal Norm', (2012) 23 *European Journal of International Law* 377, at 384. See further, K. Bosselman, *The Principle of Sustainability: Transforming Law and Governance* (Ashgate, Aldershot, 2008); U. Beyerlin, 'Sustainable Development' in R. Wulfrum, (ed.), *The Max Planck Encyclopedia of International Law* (2015), at http://opil.ouplaw.com/home/EPIL; N. Schrijver, *The Evolution of Sustainable Development in International Law: Inception, Meaning and Status* (Brill, Leiden, 2008).

13 For a concise account of the differing views of key commentators on the normative status and quality of the concept of sustainable development, see U. Beyerlin, 'Different Types of Norms in International Environmental Law: Policies, Principles and Rules', in D. Bodansky, J. Brunnée and E. Hey, *The Oxford Handbook of International Environmental Law* (O.U.P., Oxford, 2007) 425, at 443 *et seq.*

14 Available at http://treaties.un.org/doc/Publication/CTC/uncharter.pdf.

by the ICJ', though '[i]t is open to question whether it represents an exhaustive listing' as regards the sources of international environmental law.[15] Despite the extraordinary proliferation of international bodies, both inter-governmental and non-governmental, and legislative, judicial and technical, which function to elaborate environmental rules and standards, and the expansion of international environmental rules to encompass rights and duties for individuals and other non-State actors, Article 38(1) lists only international conventions, international custom and general principles of law as the primary sources of binding international law and, 'as subsidiary means for the determination of rules of law', judicial decisions and the work of the most highly qualified publicists. However, the recent frenetic pace of this extensive corpus of rules development, and their resulting fluidity, may give rise to some confusion as to the source or provenance of any putative rule or principle. As the Permanent Court of Arbitration has noted, '[t]here is considerable debate as to what, within the field of environmental law, constitutes "rules" or "principles"; what is "soft law"; and which environmental treaty law or principles have contributed to the development of customary international law'.[16]

2.1. INTERNATIONAL CONVENTIONS

Given that international environmental law is a relatively new field, often involving the development and implementation of highly complex technical regimes, it stands to reason that conventions, and multilateral law-making conventions in particular, should provide the most important source of rules and principles in this area.[17] It is estimated that in excess of 500 multilateral environmental conventions have been agreed upon to date[18], at the global or regional levels, though an even greater number of bilateral, trilateral or otherwise "localized" treaties exist, which serve to facilitate environmental cooperation amongst neighbouring States.[19] Many of these treaties, and in particular those which are widely ratified, capable of global application and intended to create an enduring regulatory regime, may be considered '"law-making treaties" in the sense that they have been concluded for the purposes of laying down general rules

15 Birnie, Boyle and Redgwell, *supra*, n. 5, at 15.

16 *Belgium / Netherlands (Iron Rhine Arbitration)*, PCA (2005), at para. 58. Available at: www.pca-cpa.org/showpage.asp?pag_id=1155.

17 For a detailed treatment of the process of international environmental law-making by means of conventions, see T. Gehring, 'Treaty-Making and Treaty Evolution', in Bodansky, Brunnée and Hey, *supra*, n. 13, at 467-497.

18 See Maljean-Dubois, *supra*, n. 9, at 41.

19 See, for example, the extensive list of environmental agreements recorded in B. Rűster and B. Simma (eds.), *International Protection of the Environment* (1975-1993), cited in P. Sands and J. Peel, *Principles of International Environmental Law*, 3rd ed., (Cambridge University Press, Cambridge, 2012), at 98.

of conduct among a large number of states'.[20] An obvious example is provided by the 1992 Convention on Biological Diversity[21], as supplemented by the 2000 Cartagena Biosafety Protocol[22] and the 2010 Nagoya Protocol on Access and Benefit-Sharing.[23] Of course, many more treaties create obligations relating to environmental protection, though they are not intended to address environmental matters primarily. Prominent examples include regional trade agreements and the globally applicable 1947 General Agreement on Tariffs and Trade (GATT), under which environmental concerns may provide an exception to the general prohibition on non-tariff barriers to trade[24] and the 1982 UN Convention on the Law of the Sea (UNCLOS).[25]

For various reasons, including the urgency of securing initial international agreement, the technical complexity of the rules required and simple diplomatic expediency, many multilateral environmental conventions may be described as "framework" conventions, which merely provide a broad outline of the key principles, substantive objectives and institutional mechanisms of the intended regulatory regime, leaving the detailed rules to be developed subsequently. Under the auspices of the relevant "framework" convention, the States parties proceed to conclude more specific agreements or protocols, or adopt detailed technical guidance, often facilitated or assisted by specialist institutional mechanisms established under the convention. A range of such "framework" approaches has been employed. While the 1985 Vienna Convention on the Protection of the Ozone Layer[26] required the 1987 Montreal Protocol[27] to give it practical effect and the 1992 Framework Convention on Climate Change[28] similarly relied on the 1997 Kyoto Protocol[29], the 1979 Bonn Convention on Migratory Species of Wild Animals (CMS)[30] requires the conclusion of specific agreements between range States.[31] Alternatively, framework conventions may take the form of

---

20 Sands and Peel, *ibid.*, at 96-97. On law-making treaties generally, see C. Brőlmann, 'Law-making Treaties: Form and Function in International Law', (2005) 74 *Nordic Journal of International Law* 383.

21 *Supra*, n. 9.

22 39 *ILM* (2000) 1027.

23 Available at: www.cbd.int/abs/doc/protocol/nagoya-protocol-en.pdf.

24 55 *UNTS* 194. GATT, Article XX(b) and (g).

25 21 *ILM* 1261. Though UNCLOS is primarily concerned with such matters as maritime territorial delimitation and rights of maritime navigation, it also addresses the conservation and management of the living resources of the high seas (Arts. 116-120) and protection of the marine environment (Art. 145).

26 *Supra*, n. 7.

27 26 *ILM* (1987) 1550.

28 *Supra*, n. 8.

29 37 *ILM* (1998) 22.

30 19 *ILM* (1980) 15.

31 To date, seven associated binding agreements including, for example, the 1995 Agreement on the Conservation of African-Eurasian Waterbirds (AEWA), which entered into force on 14 August 2002, as well as 18 Memoranda of Understanding, have been adopted under the auspices of CMS.

"umbrella" agreements, linked to additional treaties on specific issues. Examples include the 1982 UN Convention on the Law of the Sea (UNCLOS)[32], parts of which are given effect through implementation agreements such as the 1995 Fish Stocks Agreement[33], and the 1976 Barcelona Convention for the Protection of the Mediterranean[34], in relation to which detailed commitments are set down in seven further Protocols.[35] Thus, though there has been a marked slowdown in the conclusion of multilateral, law-making environmental treaties since the high-point of the 1990s[36], 'this has been matched by increased activity within existing treaty regimes to consolidate and expand rules to cover new issues or to implement new mechanisms, such as non-compliance procedures or liability provisions'.[37]

Maljean-Dubois lists a number of advantages associated with this framework approach to explain why such conventions are 'the most operative type of interstate cooperation':

'because they allow international cooperation to be based on a specific foundation ...; because they allow the institutionalization of cooperation, the development of collective means of inciting compliance and reacting to non-compliance; and finally because they allow the initial regime to evolve through treaty modification, adoption of protocols or, more simply, secondary law.'[38]

Sands and Peel point out that many framework agreements employ a 'three-tiered approach (framework agreement, protocol, annex/appendices) [which] introduced flexibility by allowing legal amendments or other changes in

32 *Supra*, n. 25.
33 34 *ILM* (1995) 1542.
34 15 *ILM* (1976) 290.
35 1976 Protocol for the Prevention of Pollution of the Mediterranean Sea by Dumping from Ships and Aircraft (amended 1995); 1976 Protocol concerning Co-operation in Preventing Pollution from Ships and, in Cases of Emergency, Combating Pollution of the Mediterranean Sea; 1980 Protocol for the Protection of the Mediterranean Sea Against Pollution from Land-Based Sources (amended 1996); 1982 Protocol concerning Specially Protected Areas and Biological Diversity in the Mediterranean (amended 1995); 1994 Protocol for the Protection of the Mediterranean Sea Against Pollution Resulting from Exploration and Exploitation of the Continental Shelf and the Seabed and its Subsoil; 1996 Protocol on the Prevention of Pollution of the Mediterranean Sea by Transboundary Movements of Hazardous Wastes and their Disposal; and 2008 Protocol on Integrated Coastal Zone Management in the Mediterranean.
36 On the phenomenon of "treaty congestion", whereby the sheer number of environmental instruments might hamper effective implementation, see D. K. Anton, '"Treaty Congestion" in Contemporary International Environmental Law', in S. Alam, M. J. H. Bhuiyan, T. M. R. Chowdhury and E. J. Techera (eds.), *Routledge Handbook of International Environmental Law* (Routledge, Abingdon, 2013) 651-666.
37 Sands and Peel, *supra*, n. 19, at 97. Consider, for example, the UNECE 1992 Helsinki Convention on the Protection and Use of Transboundary Watercourses and International Lakes, 31 *ILM* (1992) 1312, which has recently established an Implementation Committee to support implementation and application of and compliance with the Convention, while the Convention has been amended to allow accession by non-members of UNECE from the end of 2013. See further www.unece.org/env/water/text/text.html.
38 *Supra*, n. 9, at 43.

accordance with political, scientific or economic developments'.[39] Birnie, Boyle and Redgwell stress the advantages of arrangements 'to separate such technical standards from the basic provisions of the treaty in order to allow for ease of amendment in the light of technical or scientific experience'[40], and describe the role of 'ecostandards', provided in the 'resolutions, recommendations, and decisions of other international organizations, and by the conferences of parties to treaties' as that of 'amplifying the terms of environmental treaties'.[41] In addition, because they are systematized and recorded in written form, conventional regimes are also the source of the international environmental rules most likely to directly influence the development of domestic environmental law.

The specialist institutional structures, established under the auspices of multilateral framework conventions, play a key role in the ongoing elaboration of the rules of international environmental law.[42] Noting that '[t]he making and evolution of international environmental law are related to the establishment of numerous separately institutionalized multilateral treaty systems', Gehring observes that '[u]pon their establishment, they become machineries for the making of new law and for the development of existing law in their respective areas of competence'.[43] Detailing the significant role played by such institutions in developing the normative content of the regulatory regime established by each agreement and in supervising the States parties' implementation of, and compliance with, that regime, Churchill and Ulfstein describe such bodies as "autonomous", in that they are 'freestanding and distinct both from the states parties to a particular agreement and from existing IGOs' and that 'they have their own law-making powers and compliance mechanisms'.[44]

Of course, environmental conventions will generally share a similar format and characteristics to other international treaties and are subject to the general, and largely customary, rules on treaties set out in the 1969 Vienna Convention on the Law of Treaties.[45] However, as regards the adaptability of environmental conventional instruments, the limited "evolutionary interpretation" envisaged under Article 31(3)(c) of the Vienna Convention, whereby account shall be taken in the interpretation of treaty provisions of any other 'relevant rules of international law applicable in the relations between the parties', allows older instruments to

39 *Supra*, n. 19, at 98.

40 *Supra*, n. 5, at 18.

41 *Ibid.*, at 19.

42 See further, G. Ulfstein, 'Institutional framework for environmental decision-making', in M. Fitzmaurice, D. M. Ong and P. Merkouris (eds.), *Research Handbook on International Environmental Law* (Edward Elgar, Cheltenham, 2010), 26-47, at 29-41.

43 *Supra*, n. 17, at 495. See M. A. Drumble, 'Actors and law-making in international environmental law', in Fitzmaurice, Ong and Merkouris (eds.), *ibid.*, 3-25, at 9-10.

44 R. R. Churchill and G. Ulfstein, 'Autonomous Institutional Arrangements in Multilateral Environmental Agreements: A Little-Noticed Phenomenon in International Law', (2000) 94/4 *American Journal of International Law* 623-659.

45 (1969) 8 *ILM* 689.

be interpreted in the light of current environmental standards and practices.[46] Such an approach has been employed by the WTO Appellate Body in the *Shrimp-Turtle* case in interpreting the scope of "natural resources" under Article XX(g) of the 1947 GATT Agreement in the light of a range of subsequent environmental conventions and soft-law instruments, including the 1982 UN Convention on the Law of the Sea, the 1979 Bonn Convention on Conservation of Migratory Species, the 1992 Convention on Biological Diversity, and Agenda 21.[47] More generally, in the *Gabčíkovo-Nagymaros* case the International Court of Justice (ICJ) accepted the "principle of contemporaneity", whereby it could consider subsequently developed norms and standards in interpreting and applying pre-existing treaty provisions.[48] Thus, the frenetic activity of recent decades in concluding inclusive multilateral environmental agreements, and the comprehensive sectoral coverage of such agreements, permits the progressive environmental evolution of applicable treaty provisions, both environmental and non-environmental, without requiring their formal amendment. In addition, though the texts of environmental conventions have tended to stipulate a relatively low number of ratifications as a requirement for entry into force[49], several key law-making treaties have struggled to enter into force due to their participation requirements[50], and Article 18 of the Vienna Convention provides that signatory States must refrain from acts which would defeat the objects and purposes of the treaty they have signed, unless they have indicated an intention not to become a party.

Indeed, the idiosyncrasies of the type of process that has emerged for the negotiation and conclusion of international environmental conventions reflect the premium that the international community places on encouraging the broadest possible participation by States in international environmental regimes. As noted above, the widespread use of consensus negotiating procedures and so-called 'package deal' diplomacy in concluding global framework agreements, has played a vital role in securing almost universal participation in such key global law-making treaties as the 1985 Vienna Convention on Ozone Depletion and the 1992 Rio Conventions on Climate Change and Biodiversity.[51] As regards the conventional regime created for the stratospheric ozone layer, developing

---

46 See, for example, the *Iron Rhine Arbitration*, *supra*, n. 16, paras. 58-59. See further, D. French, 'Treaty Interpretation and the Incorporation of Extraneous Legal Rules', (2006) 55 *International and Comparative Law Quarterly* 281; C. MacLachlan, 'The Principle of Systemic Integration in Treaty Interpretation and Article 31(3)(c) of the Vienna Convention', (2005) 54 *International and Comparative Law Quarterly* 279.

47 See, *Import Prohibition of Certain Shrimp and Shrimp Products*, WTO Appellate Body (1998) WT/DS58/AB/R, paras. 130-131, at 48-50. See further, Birnie, Boyle and Redgwell, *supra*, n. 5, at 19-22.

48 *Case Concerning the Gabčíkovo-Nagymaros Project* (1997) ICJ Reports 7, at 78, para. 140.

49 Sands and Peel, *supra*, n. 19, at 102, cite the 20 ratifications required for entry into force of the 1985 Vienna Convention and the 1989 Basel Convention.

50 Notably, the 1997 UN Convention on the Law of the Non-navigational Uses of International Watercourses, 36 *ILM* (1997) 700, only achieved the 35 ratifications required in 2014.

51 Birnie, Boyle and Redgwell, *supra*, n. 5, at 13; Maljean-Dubois, *supra*, n. 9, at 36.

countries were encouraged to join through the recognition of their special needs, while the Convention sought to discourage States from delaying accession by fixing the baseline calculation from which reductions were to be made and by ensuring that States would enjoy no trade advantages by remaining outside of the convention.[52] Ultimately, key States, including China and India, demanded linkage between their agreement to participate in the regime and the satisfaction of other concerns, particularly the provision of development assistance for developing States.[53] Noting that '[t]he scale of linkage in the greenhouse gas negotiations will be an order of greater magnitude', Caron presciently concludes that 'the agreement, as a result, may embody compromises on linked issues and thus have the flavour of a package deal'.[54]

The promotion of the broadest possible State participation in conventional environmental regimes recognises the key role of States' treaty practice in the formation of the rules of customary international law. Indeed, Drumbl even suggests that '[w]hen three quarters (or more) of all states become parties to a global environmental treaty, it assumes what can be called quasi-constitutional status', a phrase which he uses 'in the metaphysical sense of a deeply influential norm-creating and value-ordering document'.[55] He points out that the number of such widely ratified conventional instruments is not insignificant.[56]

In addition, many multilateral law-making environmental conventions either do not permit the use of reservations to specific provisions[57] or severely restrict their use.[58] Sands and Peel offer two reasons for this trend towards limiting the permissibility of reservations. Firstly, that 'many environmental treaties are framework agreements providing general structures and guidelines, rather than specific commitments with implications for a particular activity or practice', with respect to which any reservation might seem excessive or premature. Secondly, in the case of a treaty dealing with

52 See D. D. Caron, 'Protection of the Stratospheric Ozone Layer and the Structure of International Environmental Lawmaking', (1991) 14 *Hastings International and Comparative Law Review* 755-780, at 775.

53 *Ibid.* Caron goes on to explain that the London amendments 'provide for technology transfer and establish a fund to aid implementation of the Protocol by facilitating nonozone-depleting paths for growth in developing countries'.

54 *Ibid.*

55 *Supra*, n. 43, at 16.

56 *Ibid.*, where he notes the following examples:
'CBD (190 parties); CITES (171 parties); Basel Convention (170 parties); Vienna Convention for the Protection of the Ozone Layer (191 parties, the Montréal Protocol also has 191 parties and the London Amendment 185 parties); FCCC (191 parties, the Kyoto Protocol has 173 parties); CCD (191 parties); Ramsar Convention (154 parties); UNCLOS (153 parties); MARPOL 73/78 (143 parties to Annex I/II, totaling 97.98 per cent of world shipping tonnage)'.

57 For example, 1985 Vienna Convention, Art. 18; 1987 Montreal Protocol, Art. 18; 1989 Basel Convention, Art. 26(1); 1992 Biodiversity Convention, Art. 37; 1992 Climate Change Convention, Art. 24; 2001 POPs Convention, Art. 27; 2010 Nagoya Protocol, Art. 34. See Sands and Peel, *supra*, n. 19, at 103.

58 For example, 1982 UNCLOS, Art. 309. See Sands and Peel, *ibid.*

> 'particularly sensitive or controversial matters, especially where important economic interests are involved, the negotiated text will often represent a series of delicate compromises which would be undermined by allowing one or more states to opt out of certain provisions. Flexibility is intended to be built into the text itself'.[59]

Of course, signatory or ratifying States may always proceed to enter 'interpretive declarations' explaining their understanding of a particular treaty provision, the precise legal effect of which remains uncertain.[60]

2.2. CUSTOMARY INTERNATIONAL LAW

Where there no environmental convention in force is applicable, where the relevant treaty regime provides incomplete coverage due to the non-participation of certain States or their use of reservations, or where assistance is required in interpreting vague treaty provisions, States may have regard to 'the customary rules [which] were the first to mark out the field'.[61] Customary rules have the advantage of applying to all States generally, except where a State has persistently objected to the rule in question[62], though 'persistent objectors can at best maintain this position only while the status of a new rule is in doubt; they will be bound once the rule is firmly established'.[63] However, as this is a relatively new field of law, with a limited history of State practice, firmly established principles of customary international law are correspondingly few. The formation of custom must, after all, follow the facts and circumstances[64], and so the very existence of several key environmental principles as rules of customary international law remains hotly debated.[65] However, it is clear that a reasonably relaxed approach has been taken to the recognition of customary rules and principles of international environmental law and it is probably more apt to say in the case of such rules than of any other field of international law that 'the old tests of customary law

59 *Ibid.*, at 103-104.

60 *Ibid.*, at 104-105.

61 Maljean-Dubois, *supra*, n. 9, at 41.

62 *North Sea Continental Shelf Cases* (1969) *ICJ Reports* 3, *Anglo-Norwegian Fisheries Case* (1951) *ICJ Reports* 131.

63 D. Charney, 'The Persistent Objector Rule and the Development of Customary International Law', (1985) 56 *British Yearbook of International Law* 1, cited by Birnie, Boyle and Redgwell, *supra*, n. 5, at 25.

64 G. Abi-Saab, 'Cours general de droit international public', (1987) *Collected Courses of the Hague Academy of International Law*, at 128, cited by Maljean-Dubois, *supra*, n. 9, at 42-43.

65 For a sceptical view of the customary status of the precautionary principle, see, for example, D. Bodansky, 'Customary (And Not So Customary) International Environmental Law', (1995) 3 *Indiana Journal of Global Legal Studies* 105. For a more optimistic view, see, for example, O. McIntyre and T. Mosedale, 'The Precautionary Principle as a Norm of Customary International Law', (1997) 9 *Journal of Environmental Law* 221-241.

are increasingly irrelevant since much new law is not custom in the orthodox sense: "it is recent, it is innovatory, it involves typical policy decisions, and it is the focus of contention".'[66] Birnie, Boyle and Redgwell cite the very powerful law-making effect of instruments such as the 1992 Rio Declaration to illustrate this point. Sands and Peel similarly suggest that the ICJ 'will divine the existence of such [customary] rules by more flexible and pragmatic means'.[67] Ultimately, the existence and normative status of customary rules of international environmental law will be defined by 'the progressive gathering of recurrent treaty provisions, recommendations made by international organizations, resolutions adopted at the end of international conferences, and other texts that can be said to have influenced State Practice'.[68]

One customary rule of international law, however, which is both of central relevance to international environmental law and universally accepted as established custom involves the duty of States to prevent significant transboundary harm.[69] This "duty of prevention" or "no-harm principle", has been linked to several legal maxims and doctrines, prominent in both common law and civil law systems, which might help to explain its broad acceptance.[70] Maljean-Dubois convincingly suggests that if this duty 'manages to assert its customary nature without any problem, it is because it is based on the respect of territorial sovereignty ... [being] ... a fundamental principle for the co-existence and "good neighbor relations" of equal sovereign relations'.[71] Indeed, in the recent *Pulp Mills* case the ICJ recognises this rule of international law as the wellspring of all other rules of customary international environmental law, such as that requiring environmental impact assessment of the transboundary impacts of a proposed industrial facility or activity, which functions to discharge certain of the due

---

66 Birnie, Boyle and Redgwell, *supra*, n. 5, quoting R. Jennings, 'What is International Law and How Do We Tell it When We See It', 37 (1981) *Annuaire Suisse de Droit International* 59, at 67, though these authors also cite Bodansky, *ibid*, for a more skeptical view of the true customary status of many key rules and principles of international environmental law.

67 *Supra*, n. 19, at 114.

68 P. M. Dupuy, 'Overview of the Existing Customary Legal Regime Regarding International Pollution', in D. B. Magraw (ed.), *International Law and Pollution* (University of Pennsylvania Press, Philadelphia, 1991), 61, at 61.

69 See *Trail Smelter Arbitration, 3 RIAA* (1941), at 1965 and (1941) 35 *American Journal of International Law* 684; *Corfu Channel Case,* (1949) *ICJ Reports* 1, at 4 and 22; Principle 21 of the 1972 Stockholm Declaration, 11 *ILM* (1972) 1416; Principle 2 of the 1992 Rio Declaration, 31 *ILM* (1992) 876; *Advisory Opinion on the Legality or Threat of Nuclear Weapons*, (1996) *ICJ Reports* 226, para. 29; *Gabčíkovo-Nagymaros Case*, para. 140, at 77; *Pulp Mills on the River Uruguay (Argentina v. Uruguay)*, para. 101.

70 See S. C. McCaffrey, *The Law of International Watercourses: Non-Navigational Uses* (Oxford University Press, Oxford, 2001), at 349-353, who links the principle to, *inter alia,* the maxim *sic utere tuo ut alienum non laedas* (so use your own as not to harm that of another), the theory of abuse of rights (*abus de droit, Rechtsmissbrauch*), and the theory of good neighbourliness (*droit international de voisinage, Nachbarrecht*).

71 *Supra*, n. 9, at 42.

diligence obligations inherent to the duty of prevention.[72] Maljean-Dubois also suggests that '[w]e could almost consider that the other customary rules [of international environmental law] simply derive from it'.[73] Another commentator even argues that, as a result of the substantive due diligence requirement arising under the duty of prevention to ensure a reasonable level of environmental protection through the implementation of national laws, '[t]he individual is progressively acquiring, at an international level, the right to claim the status of "victim", entitling him to seek compensation, without the intermediary of the State to the jurisdiction of which he belongs'.[74] This blurring of lines traditionally drawn between the personalities of international and national law, and between the realms of each system's application, is increasingly characteristic of modern international environmental law.[75]

Customary rules of international environmental law might be procedural in nature as well as substantive, provided that they are of 'a fundamentally norm-creating character such as could be regarded as forming the basis of a general rule'.[76] In addition to the duty to prevent significant transboundary harm, substantive rules of environmental law likely to qualify as established custom include

'the obligation to cooperate on environmental problems associated with shared natural resources; the obligation to adopt general measures to protect the marine environment from significant damage; and the obligation to take measures to ensure the conservation of, and prevention of harm to, endangered species of flora and fauna.'[77]

In addition, certain customary rules, well-established in related fields of normativity, would be understood as encompassing highly developed environmental values and specific obligations of environmental protection. An obvious example is the obligation to use a shared international watercourse in an "equitable and reasonable" manner, the firmly established cardinal rule of international water resources law.[78] Among the somewhat vaguer "guiding principles" of international environmental law, which might be candidates for customary status, are the polluter pays principle, the precautionary principle and

---

72 See further, O. McIntyre, 'The Proceduralization and Growing Maturity of International Water Law: *Case Concerning Pulp Mills on the River Uruguay (Argentina v. Uruguay)*', (2010) 22/3 *Journal of Environmental Law* 475-497.

73 Maljean-Dubois, *supra*, n. 9, at 42.

74 Boisson de Chazournes, *supra*, n. 10, at 14.

75 Consider, for example, the 1998 UNECE Aarhus Convention on Access to Information, Public Participation in Decision-Making and Access to Justice in Environmental Matters, 38 *ILM* (1999) 517.

76 *North Sea Continental Shelf Case*, *supra*, n. 62, at 37.

77 Sands and Peel, *supra*, n. 19, at 116.

78 On the environmental aspects of this key rule of international water law, see O. McIntyre, *Environmental Protection of International Watercourses under International Law*, (Ashgate, Aldershot, 2007), at 53 *et seq*.

the principle of common but differentiated responsibility.[79] Many procedural rules of international environmental law are unequivocally of a norm-creating character[80] and the closely linked obligations to notify and consult the States likely to be impacted by a proposed project or activity, and to carry out an environmental impact assessment of its potential transboundary effects are now well established as custom.[81]

Given that regional regimes have long played an important role alongside global ones, it is significant for the development of international environmental law that customary rules may be regional in character, reflecting the specific interests, needs and capacities of particular regions. Such flexibility reflects the fact that States in one region may be cautious of the rapid pace of global developments in the field of international environmental law, while others may be frustrated by what they regard as slow progress or unacceptably low standards, and facilitates each in the development of their own normative standards and approaches. Sands and Peel suggest that limitation and prohibition of the importation of hazardous and other wastes might provide an example of an African practice that could crystallize into a rule of regional customary international law.[82]

Of course, 'customary and conventional rules do not work in isolation but, on the contrary, enjoy a close relationship extending as far as fertilization and mutual pollination'.[83] This close relationship of 'mutual interdependence' is illustrated by the fact that conclusion and implementation of a treaty may reflect the existence of a rule of customary law, that a treaty might codify or further develop a rule of customary law and that State practice in treaty-making and in accordance with obligations under treaties can contribute to the ongoing development of customary law.[84] Pierre Marie Dupuy identifies further multi-dimensional linkages between environmental convention and custom, pointing out on the one hand that it is 'precisely *because* international environmental law is based in large part on fragmented treaty law that it also needs a strong unifying basis in customary law', and on the other that

79 Sands and Peel, *supra*, n. 19, at 116. See further, Gehring, *supra*, n. 17, at 439-442.

80 See further, P. Okowa, 'Procedural Obligations in International Environmental Agreements' (1996) 67 *British Yearbook of International Law* 275.

81 *Pulp Mills on the River Uruguay (Argentina v. Uruguay)*, para. 204. On the general linkages between these procedural rules *inter se*, and between these procedural rules and key substantive rules, see O. McIntyre, 'The Contribution of Procedural Rules to the Environmental Protection of Transboundary Rivers', in L. Boisson de Chazournes, C. Leb and M. Tignino (eds.), *Freshwater and International Law: The Multiple Challenges* (Edward Elgar, Cheltenham, 2012), 359-395.

82 Sands and Peel, *supra*, n. 19, at 117. See, for example, the 1991 Bamako Convention on the Ban of the Import into Africa and the Control of Transboundary Movement and Management of Hazardous Wastes within Africa, 30 *ILM* (1991) 775, the normative approach of which contrasts sharply with the almost universally ratified 1989 Basle Convention on the Control of Transboundary Movements of Hazardous Wastes and Their Disposal, 28 *ILM* (1989) 657.

83 Maljean-Dubois, *supra*, n. 9, at 41. See generally, B. B. Jia, 'The Relations between Treaties and Custom', (2010) 9 *Chinese Journal of International Law* 81-109.

84 Sands and Peel, *supra*, n. 19, at 113 and 115.

> 'the recommendations and findings by compliance committees, which are nowadays established under most multilateral environmental agreements, may contribute to the development of customary law, through their non-confrontational monitoring of states' obedience to international environmental law.'[85]

In determining whether a conventional rule may constitute a rule of custom, the ICJ has advised that, '[f]or this purpose it is necessary to examine the status of the principle as it stood when the Convention was drawn up, as it resulted from the effect of the Convention, and in the light of State practice subsequent to the Convention'.[86] The duty of prevention, or "no-harm" rule, which has been recognized as a custom since at least 1941[87] and is regularly incorporated into binding treaties and declarative instruments[88], aptly illustrates this close yet complex relationship. Even a treaty that has not yet entered into force may 'contribute to the development of customary international law, or reflect in clearer terms pre-existing customary international law'.[89] Indeed, it is telling that Sir Robert Jennings should declare in a statement to the 1992 United Nations Convention on Environment and Development in Rio that it is 'a principal task of the ICJ to decide, applying well-established rules and criteria, whether the provisions of multilateral treaties have or have not developed from merely contractual rules into rules of general customary international law'.[90]

2.3. GENERAL PRINCIPLES OF LAW

As regards the reference to 'general principles of law recognized by civilized nations' in Article 38(1) of the ICJ Statute, uncertainty persists as to whether it is intended solely to permit the Court to apply widely employed principles of national law where there might otherwise exist lacunae among the established rules of international law, or also to include the various 'principles' of international

85 P. M. Dupuy, 'Formation of Customary International Law and General Principles', in Bodansky, Brunée and Hey (eds.), *supra*, n. 13, 449, at 464-465 (original emphasis).

86 *North Sea Continental Shelf Cases*, ICJ Reports, para. 60, at 37. See also, *Case Concerning the Military and Paramilitary Activities in and Against Nicaragua (Nicaragua v. United States of America)*, Judgment of 27 June 1986.

87 See *Trail Smelter Arbitration, supra*, n. 69.

88 See Principle 21 of the 1972 Stockholm Declaration and Principle 2 of the 1992 Rio Declaration, *supra*, n. 69. For an example of a multilateral environmental convention incorporating the "no-harm" rule, see Article 7 of the 1997 UN Watercourses Convention, 36 *ILM* (1997) 719.

89 Sands and Peel, *supra*, n. 19, at 103, citing the example of the *Gabčíkovo-Nagymaros* case, where the ICJ referred to the recently adopted, but not yet in force, 1997 UN Watercourses Convention as evidence of the 'modern development of international law', (1997) *ICJ Reports* 7, at 56, para. 85.

90 The text of the statement is reproduced in R. Jennings, 'Need for Environmental Court?' (1992) 22(5/6) *Environmental Policy and Law*, 312, at 313, and in (1992) 1 *Review of* European Community and International Environmental Law, 240.

environmental law commonly included in environmental treaties and declarative instruments, most notably the 1972 Stockholm and 1992 Rio Declarations. The former would include general principles of "natural justice" 'accepted by all nations in foro domestico', which could operate 'to avoid any possibility of a non liquet where there may be gaps in the law'.[91] The doctrines of abuse of rights and good faith are often cited as examples of such "general principles".[92] However, Birnie, Boyle and Redgwell caution that, rather than borrowing mechanically from domestic law, tribunals have only 'invoked elements of legal reasoning and private law analogies', so that 'general principles derived by analogy from domestic law are only marginally useful in an environmental context'.[93] Agreeing that their role has been marginal in the development of international environmental law, Maljean-Dubois suggests that, 'with the purpose of filling the gaps in conventional or customary law, these principles [should] play, a priori, a more important role in new fields such as environmental protection than in more traditional fields'.[94]

The latter would include those guiding principles of environmental law routinely endorsed by States in their conventional and declarative practice, such as the precautionary principle, the polluter-pays principle and the principle of common but differentiated responsibility which, if they are accepted as falling under this source of international law, could exert influence independently of their customary or conventional status. Beyerlin appears to include the guiding principles of international environmental law under this source when he examines

'the various "twilight" norms at the bottom of the normative hierarchy of modern international environmental law, such as "precaution", "polluter pays", "common but differentiated responsibilities", "equitable utilization of shared natural resources", "intergenerational equity", "common concern of mankind", and, last but not least, "sustainable development".'[95]

However, he also casts doubt on their status as rules of law at all, explaining that 'in the grey area between international "hard law" and "soft law", are an ever-growing number of amorphous "concepts" whose nature and normative quality are far from clear'.[96] The ICJ's reliance upon the principle of sustainable development in the Gabčíkovo-Nagymaros case provides 'perhaps the best illustration of the role of internationally endorsed principles in international environmental law'.[97] However, most leading commentators express very real doubts about the autonomy of these principles.[98]

---

91 Birnie, Boyle and Redgwell, *supra*, n. 5, at 26-27.
92 See *Free Zones of Upper Saxony and the District of Gex Case*, Ser. A/B, No. 46 (1932), at 167.
93 *Supra*, n. 5, at 27.
94 *Supra*, n. 9, at 44.
95 *Supra*, n. 13, at 426.
96 *Ibid.*
97 Birnie, Boyle and Redgwell, *supra*, n. 5, at 28.
98 For example, Maljean-Dubois, *supra*, n. 9, at 44.

Among the former category of principles, the concept of "equity", which may be defined in this context as 'considerations of fairness, reasonableness, and policy often necessary for the sensible application of the more settled rules of law'[99], plays a particularly significant role in the establishment, operation and application of the rules of international environmental and natural resources law.[100] As the concept and principles of equity are to be found in many national legal systems, equity can serve as a component of the corpus of norms that constitute international law.[101] That international tribunals may be entitled to apply equitable principles without the express authorisation of the parties to an inter-State dispute was confirmed by Judge Hudson in the River Meuse case, where he stated that '[w]hat are widely known as principles of equity have long been considered to constitute a part of international law, and as such they have often been applied by international tribunals'.[102] The language of equity has long been central to international environmental and natural resources law. Consider, for example, the principles of intra-generational equity[103] and inter-generational equity[104], which have emerged in the context of the law relating to sustainable development and which seek, respectively, to ensure some measure of fairness as between developed and developing States and between present and future generations. Similarly, since 1978 the United Nations Environment Programme (UNEP) has considered equity to be the key requirement in inter-State cooperation 'with a view to controlling, preventing, reducing or eliminating adverse environmental effects which may result from the utilisation of … [shared

99 I. Brownlie, *Principles of Public International Law, 4th Ed.*, (Oxford, O.U.P., 1079), at 26. See also, V. Lowe, 'The Role of Equity in International Law', (1992) 12 *Australian Yearbook of International Law* 54, who states, at 54, that '[a] serviceable definition of equity is: general principles of justice as distinguished from any particular system of jurisprudence or the municipal law of any State', and further notes that 'the pervasive influence of equity on legal rules and principles is at least as strong in international law as in other legal systems'.

100 See further, D. Shelton, 'Equity' in Bodansky, Brunnée and Hey (eds.), *supra*, n. 13, 639-662; O. McIntyre, 'Utilisation of Shared International Freshwaters – The Meaning and Role of "Equity" in International Water Law', (2013) 38/2 *Water International* (forthcoming). See generally, T. M. Franck, *Fairness in International Law and Institutions*, (Clarendon, Oxford, 1995), at 56.

101 Lowe, *supra*, n. 99, at 55.

102 *Diversion of Water from the River Meuse*, PCIJ Series A/B, No. 70, at 76-77.

103 L. Rajamani, *Differential Treatment in International Environmental Law* (OUP, Oxford, 2006); P. Cullet, *Differential Treatment in International Environmental Law*, Ashgate, Aldershot, 2003); P. Cullet, 'Common but differentiated responsibilities', in Fitzmaurice, Ong and Merkouris (eds.), *supra*, n. 42, 161-181; D. B. Magraw, 'Legal Treatment of Developing Countries: Differential, Contextual and Absolute Norms', (1990) 1 *Colorado Journal of International Environmental Law and Policy*, 69.

104 E. Brown Weiss, In Fairness to Future Generations: International Law, Common Patrimony, and Intergenerational Equity, (United Nations University, Tokyo/New York, 1989); C. Redgwell, Intergenerational Trusts and Environmental Protection, (University of Manchester Press, Manchester, 1999); E. Brown Weiss, ' Implementing intergenerational equity', in Fitzmaurice, Ong and Merkouris (eds.), *supra*, n. 42, 100-116.

natural] resources'.[105] Indeed, in 1974 the ICJ sought an 'equitable solution for the allocation of shared fisheries stocks'.[106] International environmental law increasingly relies on equity in declaratory and conventional instruments, with high-profile examples including Principle 3 of the 1992 Rio Declaration, Articles 3(1) and 4(2)(a) of the 1992 Climate Change Convention, and Articles 1 and 15(7) of the 1992 Biodiversity Convention. Of course, the concept of equity is absolutely central to the principle of sustainable development, the overarching objective of modern environmental law universally accepted by States at UNCED in Rio, and this has prompted Sands and Peel to remark that, '[i]n many respects, UNCED was about equity', largely because, '[i]n the absence of detailed rules, equity can provide a conveniently flexible means of leaving the extent of rights and obligations to be decided at a subsequent date'.[107] Thus, such flexible general principles can greatly enhance the effectiveness of the law-making process. This trend continues with Articles 9 and 10 of the International Law Commission's 2001 Draft Articles on the Prevention of Transboundary Harm from Hazardous Activities, requiring States to seek 'acceptable solutions regarding measures to be adopted in order to prevent significant transboundary harm ... based on an equitable balance of interests'.[108]

2.4. JUDICIAL AND ARBITRAL TRIBUNALS

Though they are described as a "subsidiary" source of law under Article 38(1), judicial and arbitral tribunals play 'a particular role in the environmental field both by participating in the legal formulation of principles and rules and by implementing them, and thus contributing to their effectiveness'.[109] Consider, for example, the ICJ's recognition of the binding legal character of the principle of "sustainable development" in *Gabčíkovo-Nagymaros*, which it understood as the 'need to reconcile economic development with protection of the environment'[110], and the Court's finding in *Pulp Mills* that THE application of the principle of sustainable development to large-scale construction projects translates into

---

105 UNEP, Draft Principles on Conduct in the Field of the Environment for Guidance of States in the Conservation and harmonious Utilization of Natural Resources Shared by Two or More States, UNEP Governing Council Decision 6/14, 19 May 1978.

106 *Fisheries Jurisdiction (UK v Iceland)* (1974) ICJ Reports 3; *Fisheries Jurisdiction (UK v Federal Republic of Germany)* (1974) ICJ Reports 174.

107 *Supra*, n. 19, at 213-214.

108 ILC, *Draft Articles on the Prevention of Transboundary Harm from Hazardous Activities*, Report of the International Law Commission on the Work of its Fifty-Third Session, UN Doc. A/56/10, 2001. The Commission goes on to provide an indicative list of factors relevant to achieving such equitable solutions, rather as in the case of conventional articulations of the principle of "equitable and reasonable utilization", the cardinal principle of international water resources law.

109 Boisson de Chazournes, *supra*, n. 10, at 17.

110 *Supra*, n. 48.

'a requirement under general international law to undertake an environmental impact assessment where there is a risk that the proposed industrial activity may have a significant adverse impact in a transboundary context, in particular, on a shared resource.'[111]

Though there is no formal doctrine of precedent in the ICJ or in other international courts or arbitral tribunals, judicial and arbitral decision-makers provide an authoritative determination of the current state of the law, and of its correct practical application to factual situations. Thus, such decisions provide 'a source of identification and interpretation rather than creation of law', but contribute to the development of international law through a process of 'normative accretion'.[112] Through the accumulation of decisions and awards, judicial and arbitral decision-makers can provide the clarity required to help practitioners to navigate the burgeoning and complex corpus of interrelated international environmental rules, many of which are intended to balance the multi-dimensional conflicting interests of the parties in dispute. Indeed, international courts might simply set out and elaborate upon the legal principles applicable in a given dispute, in order that the parties may cooperate in its effective resolution themselves.[113]

International courts and tribunals have been pronouncing on environmental matters since the *Fur Seals* arbitration of 1893[114], and commentators note that States are increasingly likely to submit such disputes to adjudication and arbitration.[115] Sands and Peel point out[116] that inter-State disputes submitted to formal third-party dispute resolution have concerned, *inter alia*, transboundary air pollution[117], the diversion or damming of international rivers[118], the conservation of fisheries resources[119], the protection of the marine environment[120], import restrictions on environmental grounds[121], environmental protection and

111 *Supra*, n. 69, at paras. 14 and 83.

112 Maljean-Dubois, *supra*, n. 9, at 45, quoting G. Abi-Saab, 'Cours général de droit internalional public', (1987) 207 *Collected Courses of the Hague Academy of International Law*, at 129 and 131.

113 See, for example, the Judgment of the ICJ in *Gabčíkovo-Nagymaros*, *supra*, n. 185, and the Order of the International Tribunal of the Law of the Sea (ITLOS) in the *Mox Plant Case (Ireland v. United Kingdom)*, 3 December 2001, available at www.itlos.org/fileadmin/itlos/documents/cases/case_no_10/Order.03.12.01.E.pdf.

114 *Rights of jurisdiction of the United States in the Bering Sea and the preservation of fur seals (United States v. United Kingdom)*, Arbitral Award of 15 August 1893.

115 See, for example, Sands and Peel, *supra*, n. 19, at 137 and Maljean-Dubois, *supra*, n. 9, at 45.

116 *Ibid.*

117 *Trail Smelter Arbitration*, *supra*, n. 69.

118 *Lac Lanoux Arbitration (Spain v. France)* (1957) 24 *ILR* 101, *Gut Dam Arbitration (United States v. Canada)* (1969) 8 *ILM* 118, *Gabčíkovo-Nagymaros Project*, *supra*, n. 69.

119 *Fisheries Jurisdiction Case*, (1974) ICJ Reports 3, *Southern Bluefin Tuna Cases*, ITLOS Order of 27 August 1999.

120 *MOX Plant Case (Ireland v. United Kingdom)*, ITLOS Order of 3 December 2001.

121 *United States – Measures on Yellow-Fin Tuna Imports*, GATT Doc./ DS21/R (1991); *United States – Import Prohibition on Certain Shrimp and Shrimp Products*, (1999) 38 *ILM* 118.

the protection of foreign investors[122], access to environmental information[123], procedural obligations to notify and consult in respect of environmentally harmful activities[124], environmental impact assessment[125], the rehabilitation of lands after mining activities[126], the transboundary effects of pesticide spraying[127], environmental obligations in respect of seabed activities[128], and marine protected areas.[129] It is apparent from the cases listed above that, in addition to decisions in cases which are directly concerned with environmental issues, the decisions of other courts and tribunals are relevant to the development of rules of international environmental law, including the International Tribunal of the Law of the Sea (ITLOS), international investment arbitration tribunals established under the auspices of the International Centre for the Settlement of Investment Disputes (ICSID) or NAFTA /UNCITRAL, regional human rights courts, and the Dispute Settlement Body and Appellate Body of the WTO.

2.5. PUBLICISTS

While the work of the 'most highly qualified publicists', referred to by Article 38(1), will be cited by international courts and tribunals from time to time, and relied upon by practitioners of international law to inform their understanding of the rules and principles that they seek to obey, apply and develop on a daily basis, the impact of such doctrine is 'difficult to quantify'.[130] However, certain codifications, prepared by the International Law Commission (ILC) and by learned associations, such as the Institute of International Law (IIL/IDI) and the International Law Association (ILA) can be extensively relied upon. For example, practically every modern agreement on shared international watercourses has substantially followed or deferentially referred to the ILA's seminal 1966 Helsinki Rules on the Uses of the Waters of International Rivers[131], while the ICJ has on numerous occasions relied heavily on draft articles and related commentaries prepared by the ILC.[132]

---

122 *Metalclad Corporation v. Mexico*, (2001) 40 *ILM* 35.

123 *MOX Plant Case, supra*, n. 120.

124 *Pulp Mills Case, supra*, n. 69.

125 *Gabčíkovo-Nagymaros Case, supra*, n. 69.

126 *Certain Phosphate Lands in Nauru (Nauru v. Australia)*, (1992) *ICJ Reports* 240.

127 *Ariel Herbicide Spraying (Equador v. Columbia)*, pending before the ICJ.

128 Advisory Opinion on *Responsibilities and Obligations of States Sponsoring Persons and Entities with Respect to Activities in the Area* (Seabed Disputes Chamber of ITLOS), case No. 17, 1 February 2011.

129 *Dispute Regarding the Marine protected Area (Mauritius v. United Kingdom)*, see ITLOS press release regarding the appointment of arbitrators in this dispute at www.itlos.org/fileadmin/itlos/documents/press_releases_english/press_164_eng.pdf.

130 Maljean-Dubois, *supra*, n. 9, at 45.

131 ILA, *Report of the Fifty-Second Conference of the International Law Association* (1966).

132 For example, Maljean-Dubois, *supra*, n. 9, notes, at 45, that the Court relied to a significant degree on the work of the Commission in its decision in the *Gabčíkovo-Nagymaros Case*, 'particularly on the notion of the state of necessity'.

3. INNOVATIVE FEATURES OF INTERNATIONAL ENVIRONMENTAL LAW-MAKING

In seeking to explore how the effectiveness of international environmental law is enhanced, it is also useful to focus on some of the more unique characteristics of the processes of law-making in this field. Among such peculiarities is that of the key role played by non-binding "soft-law" instruments in the development of rules of international environmental law.[133] Maljean-Dubois also highlights the complexity of the issues falling within the scope of modern international environmental law pointing out, for example, that the boundaries of the concept of "environment" remain fluid, sometimes including cultural heritage and landscape and encompassing understandings that oscillate between anthropocentric and eco-centric values.[134] Indeed, any definition or understanding of "environment" provided will tend to depend on the purpose of the legal instrument or rule in question, with a regime creating liability for environmental harm likely to be restrictive, but clear, in scope.[135] Further peculiarities include the shifting of the traditional boundaries between international, transnational and municipal law in the field of environmental protection and the resulting involvement of new actors, as well as the increasing integration of environmental norms into other fields of normativity.

3.1. RELIANCE ON "SOFT-LAW"

As many leading commentators have noted, '[i]t is a feature of environmental law that it is characterized by the production by States of numerous forms of non-binding declarations and guidelines and non-binding sets of rules and

---

133 See generally, D. Shelton, 'The Environment and Natural Resources', in D. Shelton (ed), *Commitment and Compliance: The Role of Non-binding Norms in the International Legal System* (OUP, Oxford, 2003), at 121-242.

134 The ICJ demonstrated a quite anthropocentric conception of the "environment" in its Advisory Opinion of 8 July 1996 on the *Legality of the Threat or Use of Nuclear Weapons, ICJ Reports* (1996), where it stated, at 242, para. 29, that

'the Court also recognizes that the environment is not an abstraction but represents the living space, the quality of life and the very health of human beings, including generations unborn'.

The Court quoted this statement in the *Gabčíkovo-Nagymaros* case, *supra*, n. 182, at 3, para. 53.

135 However, Maljean-Dubois provides, *supra*, n. 9, at 29, the example of the quite expansive definition of "environment" provided under the Convention on Civil Liability for Damage resulting from activities dangerous to the environment (Lugano, 21 June 1993), which provides that

'"Environment" includes: natural resources both abiotic and biotic, such as air, water, soil, fauna and flora and the interaction between the same factors; property which forms part of the cultural heritage; and the characteristic aspects of the landscape.'

standards'.[136] Though first employed in the field of international economic law, the role of so-called "soft-law" instruments in the formation of rules of international environmental law cannot be overstated.[137] While casting doubt on the customary status of a range of purported norms of customary international environmental law and characterizing them instead as 'declarative', Bodansky concedes that such norms have an important role to play in terms of voluntary compliance and in terms of bilateral and multilateral negotiations, concluding that

> '[declarative] international environmental norms can play a significant role by setting the terms of the debate, providing evaluative standards, serving as a basis to criticize other states' actions, and establishing a framework of principles within which negotiations may take place to develop more specific norms, usually in treaties.'[138]

Dupuy suggests the key role of soft-law in influencing State practice and, thus, in the generation of custom, stating that such guidelines

> 'have penetrated gradually into contemporary State practice. In certain cases, these guidelines bring an important contribution to the definition of international standards on the basis of which the due diligence to be expected from "well-governed" modern States can be established.'[139]

He also highlights the role of such soft-law norms in the interpretation of binding 'hard-law' norms of international law.[140] Hohmann, on the other hand, regards the primary role of soft-law instruments in the identification of custom to be that of 'the solidifying of indicators for a documentation of the opinio juris' of States.[141] Generally, Hohmann notes that, like 'no other area of international law, [international environmental law] is influenced by such a multitude of guidelines, resolutions and other declarations', the grouping of which documents 'in the category of soft law (in contrast to hard law) does not do justice to the peculiarities of modern ways of making international environmental law'.[142] As Judge Tanaka commented, in his dissenting opinion in the *South West Africa*

---

136 M. A. Fitzmaurice, 'International Environmental Law as a Special Field', (1994) 25 *Netherlands Yearbook of International Law* 181-226, at 199. See further, Shelton, *supra*, n. 133.

137 On the origins of "soft-law", see Fitzmaurice, *ibid.*, at 200-201.

138 *Supra*, n. 65, at 118-119. See further, H. E. Chodosh, 'Neither Treaty Nor Custom: The Emergence of Declarative International Law' (1991) 26 *Texas International Law Journal*, 87; and N. C. H. Dunbar, 'The Myth of Customary International Law' (1983) 8 *Australian Yearbook of International Law* 1.

139 Dupuy, *supra*, n. 68, at 61.

140 *Ibid.*, at 62.

141 H. Hohmann, *Precautionary Legal Duties and Principles of Modern International Environmental Law* (Graham & Trotman, London, 1994), at 336.

142 *Ibid.*, at 335.

Case (Second Phase), in relation to repeated pronouncements in UN resolutions and declarations:

> 'This collective, cumulative and organic process of custom generation can be characterized as the middle way between legislation by convention and the traditional process of custom making and can be seen to have an important role from the viewpoint of development of international law.'[143]

Thus, international environmental law makes expedient use of myriad soft-law instruments to advance the normative boundaries of the field in a manner that would not otherwise be possible.

3.2. TECHNICAL COMPLEXITY AND THE ROLE OF INTERNATIONAL INSTITUTIONS

As international environmental law-making comprises the adoption of technically complex rules capable of impacting significantly upon the economic policies and developmental aspirations of States, a wide range of international institutions have played an essential role in facilitating inter-State agreement. The UN and its various specialized and regional agencies and programmes 'have played a leading role in setting law-making agendas and providing negotiating forums and expertise'.[144] Principle among these agencies are the United Nations Environment Programme, the International Law Commission, the United Nations Economic Commission for Europe, the Food and Agriculture Organisation and the World Health Organisation. Of course, consistent with the objective of sustainable development, many international institutions, which are primarily concerned with fields other than that of environmental protection, can play key roles in the elaboration of environmental rules and standards.[145] For example, institutions charged with the regulation of international trade, the settlement of international investment disputes, or the cooperative management of shared international water resources have the potential, and often a clear mandate, to influence the environmental outcomes of the activities with which they are concerned.

Further, the technical complexity of the issues underlying international environmental law dictates that scientific expertise plays an absolutely central role and requires intense interaction between environmental scientists and environmental lawyers at every stage in its development and application. This 'permanent dialogue between science and law becomes a source of difficulty when there is no agreement between scientists', making the need for sophisticated

143 (1966) *ICJ Rep.* 248, at 292.
144 Birnie, Boyle and Redgwell, *supra*, n. at 13.
145 See further, A. Boyle, 'Relationship between International Environmental Law and Other Branches of International Law', in Bodansky, Brunnée and Hey (eds.), *supra*, n. 13, 125-146.

international institutions to inform the decision-making process very clear.[146] In relation to the international climate regime, Maljean-Dubois points to the significance of the work of the Intergovernmental Panel on Climate Change (IPCC).[147]

The majority of conventional environmental regimes utilize scientific institutions to address technical and scientific questions and thereby assist the regimes' progressive evolution. Largely based on the experience of the IPCC, in April 2012 the international community established a similar institution in the field of biodiversity, the Intergovernmental Platform on Biodiversity and Ecosystem Services (IPBES), which is designed to address the fact that

> 'decision-makers need scientifically credible and independent information that takes into account the complex relationships between biodiversity, ecosystems services and people. They also need effective methods to interpret this scientific information in order to make informed decisions. The scientific community also needs to understand the needs of decision makers better in order to provide them with the relevant information. In essence, the dialogue between the scientific community, governments, and other stakeholders on biodiversity and ecosystem services needs to be strengthened.'[148]

Clearly, such institutional mechanisms constitute the 'focal points of a broad, legally significant communication process'[149], as required for the effective elaboration of a technically complex and scientifically contested field of international normativity.

3.3. MULTI-LEVEL AND MULTI-POLAR GOVERNANCE

International environmental law is also characterized by multi-level governance, where rules may be adopted, and may apply simultaneously, at the bilateral, regional and global levels.[150] Over time, as scientific understanding of the interconnected nature of ecological components and of environmental impacts

146 Maljean-Dubois, *supra*, n. 9, at 29-30.

147 She notes, *ibid.*, at 30, that
'the four IPCC reports (1990, 1995, 2001, 2007) have punctuated the progression of international negotiations … [f]rom the adoption of the Framework Convention on Climate Change (1992) to that of the Kyoto protocol (1997), which complements the Framework Convention, followed by the signature of the Bonn-Marrakesh Agreements (2001) which brought into force the Kyoto Protocol, then that of the 2007 Bali Roadmap'.

148 See www.ipbes.net/about-ipbes.html.

149 T. Gehring, 'International Environmental Regimes: Dynamic sectoral legal systems', (1990) 1 *Yearbook of International Environmental Law* 43, at 44, quoted in Maljean-Dubois, *supra*, n. 155, at 30.

150 See further, J. L. Dunoff, 'Levels of Environmental Governance', in Bodansky, Brunnée and Hey (eds.), *supra*, n. 13, 85-106.

has deepened, the focus of States in environmental law-making has shifted from bilateral arrangements intended to ensure cooperation amongst neighbours to multilateral arrangements intended to protect the regional or, increasingly, global common interest of States in effective environmental protection. Whereas normatively inconsistent regimes at different levels may give rise to confusion, and a lack of shared values at the global level may cause concern over a Western bias, the principle of common but differentiated responsibility can play a key role in reconciling such differences. While regional cooperation remains important, and often more effective, especially as regards discrete localized ecological units, such as regional seas or shared river basins, the shift to global arrangements involves a fundamental change in the underlying objective of international environmental law, so that 'the most convincing characterization is no longer that of neighbourly relations, but of environmental trusteeship ... [and] a concern for community interests at a global level, not merely those of states *inter se*.'[151] Of course, this shift inevitably involves profound change in the practice of international environmental law which 'constitutes a real revolution in terms of technique, procedures and legal concepts'.[152] Indeed, Maljean-Dubois goes so far as to suggest that this tendency in international environmental law leads the way in the "communitarization" of State action on a global scale, going beyond traditional "liberal" international law, with limited functions of regulation and coexistence and based on reciprocal obligations, '"to a multifunctional providential law, regulating the life of States and individuals and considered the ultimate guardian of collective well-being" the implementation of which "does not depend on a corresponding implementation by the other parties"'.[153] According to Maljean-Dubois, 'the special nature of the environment plays a large part in the transition from an international law of coexistence to an international law of cooperation', which 'is grounded not on an obligation not to do something, but on an obligation to do something, or positive obligations, because it comes from the idea of action or common tasks, which cannot be done or done well when done individually.'[154]

Noting the 'prolific nature of international environmental law' and the new, non-traditional roles played by the various rules, standards and procedures which are continually emerging from the numerous actors involved in the law-making process, one leading commentator observes that international environmental law 'incites, accompanies and guides expected behavioural changes; it legitimizes new situations, and contributes to the elaboration of a politically accepted language' and, significantly, that '[a]ll normative means are useful to this end'.[155]

151 Birnie, Boyle and Redgwell, *supra*, n. 5, at 39. See Maljean-Dubois, *ibid*, at 33.
152 Maljean-Dubois, *ibid*.
153 *Ibid*., at 34, quoting from various writings by E. Jouannet.
154 *Ibid*., at 34-35.
155 Boisson de Chazournes, *supra*, n. 10, at 10. See also, S. Maljean-Dubois, *ibid*., who notes, at 27, that international environmental law is '[s]ometimes presented as the most vigorous and innovative field of international law – as a "laboratory" for tomorrow's international law'.

Pointing out that, 'in the field of environmental protection, the law still makes very few prescriptions but mainly accompanies changes in behavior', Boisson de Chazournes cites the example of 'the ISO 26000 norms, the normative effects of which could be important, [but which] cannot find their place in the classical structure of the sources of international law'.[156] Of course, standards adopted by the International Organisation for Standards (ISO) provide a prime example of rules which may be explained by the phenomenon of "global administrative law", employed to address the rapidly changing realities of transnational regulation, which increasingly involves, *inter alia*, various forms of industry self-regulation, hybrid forms of private-private and public-private regulation, network governance by State officials, and governance by inter-governmental organizations with direct or indirect regulatory powers.[157] Proponents of this kind of analysis of many of the modern forms of international environmental rules suggest that these disparate regulatory regimes, some voluntary and some mandatory and operating at various levels (sector-specific, national, regional and global),

> 'together form a variegated "global administrative space" that includes international institutions and transnational networks involving both governmental and non-governmental actors, as well as domestic administrative bodies that operate within international regimes or cause transboundary regulatory effects.'[158]

The same authors provide a broad definition of the "global administrative bodies", which generate global administrative law norms and to which such norms might apply, to include:

> 'intergovernmental institutions, informal inter-governmental networks, national governmental agencies acting pursuant to global norms, hybrid public-private bodies engaged in transnational administration, and purely private bodies performing public roles in transnational administration.'[159]

Kingsbury further explains that the identification of such a "global administrative space" 'marks a departure from those orthodox understandings of international law in which the international is largely inter-governmental, and there is a reasonably sharp separation of the domestic and the international', and that it

156 *Ibid.* The standards set out under ISO 26000 provide guidance on how businesses and organisations can opera in a socially responsible way, assisting them to act in an ethical and transparent manner that contributes to the health and welfare of society. See www.iso.org/iso/home/standards/iso26000.htm.

157 See B. Kingsbury, 'Global Environmental Governance as Administration: Implications for International Law', in Bodansky, Brunnée and Hey (eds.), *supra*, n. 13, 63-84.

158 B. Kingsbury, *et al*, 'Global governance as administration: national and transnational approaches to global administrative law', (2005) 68 (3/4) *Law and Contemporary Problems* 1-13, at 3. See also, C. Harlow, 'Global administrative law: the quest for principles and values', (2006) 17(1) *European Journal of European Law* 187-214.

159 Kingsbury, *et al*, *ibid.*, at 5.

reflects the practice of global governance, whereby 'transnational networks of rule-generators, interpreters and appliers cause such strict barriers to break down'.[160] While emphasizing that 'there is no single unifying rule of recognition covering all of global administrative law', he includes among its sources the traditional sources of public international law, *i.e.* treaties, customary rules of international law and general principles of law, as well as certain principles associated with "publicness" in law, such as 'the [public] entity's adherence to legality, rationality proportionality, rule of law, and some human rights'.[161]

In the specific context of international environmental and natural resources law-making, Blanco and Razzaque note that 'transnational social and economic actors (*e.g.* multinational corporations, non-governmental organisations) have become forceful in the global context and play a crucial role in natural resource management', before concluding that '[w]eak regulation or exclusion from relevant governance institutions of non-state actors needs to be superseded by an inclusive system of participation and responsibility'.[162] In pointing out that the emerging international "law of cooperation", exemplified by international environmental law, 'must principally regulate the conduct of private individuals, conduct that classic international law only impacted indirectly', Maljean-Dubois suggests that

> '[t]his explains the current search for new tools (development of standards, normalization and certification, social responsibility of companies, Global Compact, public private partnerships, type II commitments of the World Summit on Sustainable Development, etc.)'.[163]

Thus, it appears that the legal significance of certain non-traditional sources of international environmental rules and standards, whilst failing to qualify under

---

160 B. Kingsbury, 'The concept of "law" in global administrative law', (2009) 20(1) *European Journal of European Law* 23-57, at 25.

161 *Ibid.*, at 23. Indeed, Kingsbury further identifies, at 34, three broad categories of public global administrative activity to which the rules and principles of GAL might apply, and which in turn generate practices which can give rise to such rules and principles. These include:
The institutional design, and legal constitution, of the global administrative body
The norms and decisions produced by that entity, including norms and decisions that have as their addressees, or otherwise materially affect:
other such public entities
states and agencies of a particular state
individuals and other private actors
Procedural norms for the conduct of those public entities in relation to their rules and decisions, including arrangements for review, transparency, reason-giving, participation requirements, legal accountability and liability.

162 E. Blanco and J. Razzaque, *Globalisation and Natural Resources Law* (Edward Elgar, Cheltenham, 2011), at 3-4. See further, E. Morgera, 'Multinational corporations and international environmental law', in Alam *et al, supra*, n. 36, 189-205; P. J. Spiro, 'Non-Governmental Organizations and Civil Society', in Bodansky, Brunnée and Hey (eds.), *supra*, n. 13, 770-790.

163 *Supra*, n. 9, at 35.

the formal sources of international law enumerated under Article 38(1), can be explained by the phenomenon of "global administrative law", which is in turn made relevant by the structural changes occurring within international law as applied to environmental issues. As noted above, by Boisson de Chazournes, the vigorous co-option of such diverse non-traditional forms of normativity enables international environmental law to engage with actors and to impact fields of activity which would otherwise remain formally out of bounds.[164]

3.4. PARTICIPATION AND PROCEDURAL SOPHISTICATION

Quite apart from the burgeoning corpus of procedural rules contained within international environmental law *per se*, it is quite clear that all instruments of international environmental law would now be interpreted and applied so as to require that States generally facilitate a participative approach, especially in respect of projects or policies that might impact on human rights, by ensuring the adoption of procedures by which interested groups, individuals or communities likely to be affected by such projects or policies can receive and access relevant information, meaningfully participate in decision-making and, if necessary, have access to some appropriate means of legal recourse.[165] For example, in the *Ogoni* case the African Commission on Human Rights gave a broad participative reading to Article 24 of the African Charter on Human and Peoples' Rights, which acknowledges all peoples' right to a generally satisfactory environment, to include specific procedural guarantees concerning the carrying out of environmental and social impact assessment. According to Cullet and Gowlland-Gualtieri

> 'it indicated that compliance with the spirit of Article 24 must include a requirement to undertake and publicize environmental and social impact studies prior to major industrial development, as well as the appropriate monitoring of environmental conditions, the provision of information to communities exposed to hazardous

164 See further, J. d'Aspremont, *Epistemic Forces in International Law: Foundational Doctrines and Techniques of International Legal Argumentation* (Edward Elgar, Cheltenham, 2015), Chapter 3: 'Law-Making', which examines new processes outside of traditional diplomatic channels and involving non-State actors which may be said to qualify as law-making.

165 See generally, P. Cullet and A. Gowlland-Gaultieri, 'Local Communities and Water Investments', in E. Brown Weiss, L. Boisson de Chazournes and N. Bernasconi-Osterwalder, *Fresh Water and International Economic Law* (2005, Oxford University Press) 303. See further, J. Ebbesson, 'Public Participation', in Bodansky, Brunnée and Hey (eds.), *supra*, n. 13, 681-703; J. Razzaque, 'Human rights to a clean environment: procedural rights', in Fitzmaurice, Ong and Merkouris (eds.), *supra*, n. 42, 284-302; J. Razzaque, 'Information, public participation and access to justice in environmental matters', in Alam *et al* (eds.), *supra*, n. 36, 137-154; O. McIntyre, 'The Role of the Public and the Human Right to Water' in M. Tignino and K. Sangbana (eds), *Public Participation and Water Resources Management: Where Do We Stand in International Law?*, (UNESCO, Paris, 2015) 139-146.

> materials and activities, and the provision of meaningful opportunities for individuals to be heard and to participate in the development decisions affecting their communities.'[166]

Similarly, the Inter-American Commission on Human Rights has, in the context of Article 11 of the 1988 Additional Protocol on the right to a healthy environment, repeatedly recommended the adoption of domestic legislation providing for meaningful and effective participatory mechanisms for indigenous peoples in the adoption of political, economic and social decisions that affect their interests.[167] In the *Awas Tingni Mayagna (Sumo) Indigenous Community* case[168], the Inter-American Court of Human Rights recognised, in the context of Article 21 of the American Convention on Human Rights guaranteeing the right to property, related participatory rights for indigenous peoples in the case of activities relating to the exploitation of natural resources.[169] In addition, the European Court of Human Rights has held in the *Guerra* case[170] that Article 8 of the European Convention on Human Rights, which guarantees the right to respect for private and family life, imposes a positive duty of States to impart information with respect to the risks and the measures to be taken in the case of a major environmental accident as 'the right protected is infringed unless the subject can obtain information about the health risks to which she or he is exposed'.[171]

Quite apart from the inference of procedural rights and duties in the environmental sphere into human rights instruments, in recent years multilateral development banks (MDBs) and other development agencies have played a major role in implementing the procedural aspects of sustainable development though the application of their environmental and social safeguard policies.[172] These policies

---

166 *Ibid.*, at 313-314, citing Communication No. 155/96, *The Social and Economic Rights Action Center and the Center for Social and Economic Rights v. Nigeria*, African Commission on Human and Peoples' Rights, 30th Ordinary Session, (13-27 October 2001), at para. 53.

167 See, Chapter X of the Second Report on the Situation of Human Rights in Peru, Inter-American Commission on Human Rights; Chapter IX to the Report on the Situation of Human Rights in Ecuador, Inter-American Commission on Human Rights, OEA/Ser.L/V/II.96, doc. 10 rev. 1 (Recommendations) (24 April 1997); Case 7615 (Brazil), Inter-American Commission on Human Rights, 1984-1985 Annual Report 24, OEA/Ser.L/V/II.66, doc. 10, rev. 1 (1985), the *Yanomami* case. See Cullet and Gowlland-Gaultieri, *supra*, n. 165, at 314-315.

168 *Awas Tingni Mayagna (Sumo) Indigenous Community v. Nicaragua*, Judgment of 31 August 2001, Inter-American Court of Human Rights, (Ser. C), No. 79 (2001).

169 See Cullet and Gowlland-Gaultieri, *supra*, n. 165, at 315-316.

170 *Guerra and Others v. Italy* (1998) 26 *European Human Rights Reports* 357.

171 Cullet and Gowlland-Gaultieri, *supra*, n. 165, at 316.

172 See, for example, See, in particular, G. Handl, *Multilateral Development Banking: Environmental Principles and Concepts Reflecting General International Law and Public Policy* (Kluwer Law International, London, 2001). See also, C. E. Di Leva, 'International Environmental Law, the World Bank, and International Financial Institutions' in D. D. Bradlow and D. B. Hunter (eds.), *International Financial Institutions and International Law* (Kluwer Law International) 343; B. Richardson, *Environmental Regulation through Financial Organisations* (Kluwer Law

routinely employ procedures for environmental and social impact assessment of development proposals and for meaningful and inclusive consultation with persons likely to be affected as well as other stakeholders.[173] Of course, such environmental and social safeguard policies and participative procedures fall squarely within the rubric of the "global administrative law" phenomenon outlined above.[174]

3.5. ENVIRONMENTAL TREATY CONGESTION, FRAGMENTATION AND INTEGRATION

Despite concern over "treaty congestion", which may lead to inefficiencies in implementing environmental agreements[175], and the general "fragmentation" of international law, which poses a risk of inconsistency in the law due to the emergence of specialized and relatively autonomous spheres of legal rules and institutions[176], international environmental norms have tended to be 'pervasive' and have proven capable of finding

> 'many ways of penetrating other bodies of norms, whether by inserting specific norms on environmental protection into other bodies of norms, or through techniques of

International, The Hague, 2002); A. N. Gowland Gualtieri, 'The Environmental Accountability of the World Bank to Non-State Actors' (2001) 72 *British Yearbook of International Law*, 213; P. T. B. Kohona, 'Implementing Global Standards – The Emerging Role of the Non-State Sector' (2004) 34/6 *Environmental Policy and Law*, 260; S. Nanwani, 'Directions in Reshaping Accountability Mechanisms in Multilateral Development Banks and Other Organizations', (2014) 5/2 *Global Policy*, 242-251; D. D. Bradlow and A. Naudé Fourie, 'The Operational Policies of the World Bank and the International Finance Corporation: Creating Law-Making and Law-Governed Institutions', (2014) 10 *International Organizations Law Review* 3-80; O. K. Fauchald, 'Hardening the legal softness of the World Bank through an Inspection Panel?', (2013) 58 *Scandinavian Studies in Law*, 2013, 101-127; A. Naudé Fourie, 'The World Bank Inspection Panel's Normative Potential: A Critical Assessment, and a Restatement', (2012) *Netherlands International Law Review*, 199-234.

173 See, for example, D. D. Bradlow and M.S. Chapman, 'Public Participation and the Private Sector: The Role of Multilateral Development Banks in the Evolution of International Legal Standards', (2011) 4 *Erasmus Law Review* 91-125.

174 B. M. Saper, 'The International Finance Corporation's Compliance Advisor/Ombudsman (CAO): An Examination of Accountability and Effectiveness from a Global Administrative Law Perspective', (2012) 44 *New York University Journal of International Law & Politics*, 1279-1329; O. McIntyre, 'Development Banking ESG Policies and the Normativisation of Good Governance Standards: Development Banks as Agents of Global Administrative Law' in K. Wendt (ed.), *Responsible Investment Banking – Risk Management Frameworks and Soft Law Standards* (Springer International, Switzerland, 2015) 145-157.

175 See Brown Weiss, *supra*, n. 3, at 13. See further, Anton, *supra*, n. 36.

176 See International Law Commission, *Fragmentation of International Law: Difficulties arising from the Diversification and Expansion of International Law*, UN Doc. A/CN.4/L.682 (13 April 2006); M. Koskenniemi, *The Politics of International Law* (Hart Publishing, Oxford, 2011), at 67 and 337; P. Webb, *International Judicial Integration and Fragmentation* (OUP, Oxford, 2013). Regarding fragmentation in international environmental law-making specifically, see Gehring, *supra*, n. 17, at 475-6; Anton, *supra*, n. 36, at 662-663.

> interpretation or, even by resorting to rules defining the relationships between the different bodies of norms.'[177]

Environmental considerations are included among the few exceptions permitted to the free trade rules contained under the General Agreement on Tariffs and Trade (GATT) and redress for breach of environmental norms and standards is routinely sought under international human rights law. Indeed, the WTO Dispute Settlement Procedures[178] and the administrative and judicial enforcement bodies established under regional human rights conventions provide a very important avenue for the enforcement of international environmental standards and the settlement of environmental disputes. For example, the 1997 report on Ecuador of the Inter-American Commission on Human Rights found that the 'considerable risk posed to human life and health by oil exploration activities ... through, *inter alia*, contamination of water supplies'[179] could impact upon the right to life and the duty to protect the physical integrity of the individual under the 1969 American Convention on Human Rights.[180]

In addition, it is increasingly likely that recently established environmental rules may come to be integrated into pre-existing treaty arrangements through techniques of interpretation based on Article 31(3)(c) of the Vienna Convention on the Law of Treaties.[181] Applying this interpretive requirement, the PCA Arbitral Tribunal in the *Iron Rhine* case concluded that 'international environmental law has relevance to the relations between the Parties'[182] and, thus,

> 'applied concepts of customary international environmental law to treaties dating back to the mid-nineteenth century, when principles of environmental protection were rarely if ever considered in international agreements and did not form any part of customary international law.'[183]

Boisson de Chazournes suggests that this approach 'provides an opportunity to take a major step forward, offering a sort of modernization of treaties through an interpretation, which takes contemporary environmental requirements into

---

177 Boisson de Chazournes, *supra*, n. 10, at 14. See further, A. Boyle, *supra*, n. 145.

178 See, for example, *European Communities – Measures affecting Asbestos and Products Containing Asbestos*, Appellate Body Report, 12 March 2001.

179 Inter-American Commission on Human Rights, *Report on the Situation of Human Rights in Ecuador*, OEA/Ser.L/V/II.96, Doc. 10 rev. 1 (24 April 1997).

180 1144 *UNTS* 123; (1969) 9 *ILM* 673; (1971) 65 *AJIL* 679 (22 November 1969).

181 Available at http://untreaty.un.org/ilc/texts/instruments/english/conventions/1_1_1969.pdf
Article 31(3)(c) provides that, in interpreting a treaty,
'There shall be taken into account, together with the context:
(c) any relevant rules of international law applicable in the relations between the parties.'

182 *Iron Rhine Arbitration*, *supra*, n. 16, para. 58.

183 See *Indus Waters Kishenganga Arbitration between Pakistan and India*, Partial Award, 18 February 2013, para. 452.

account'.[184] The International Court of Justice (ICJ) has given qualified support to this position, recognizing that treaty terms are, in some situations, capable of evolving, so as to make allowances for developments in international law.[185] However, the PCA Arbitral Tribunal in the recent *Indus Waters Kishenganga Arbitration* found, unequivocally, that '[i]t is established that principles of international environmental law must be taken into account even when ... interpreting treaties concluded before the development of that body of law'.[186] Thus, the processes involved in the formation of norms of international environmental law appear to be capable of ensuring its convergence into a relatively integrated and coherent body of rules.[187]

4. CONCLUSION

Therefore, the unique nature of the issues that international environmental law seeks to address, the idiosyncratic law-making processes and institutions involved, and the resulting peculiarities of the legal landscape created by this body of rules and principles, all function to enhance its effectiveness considerably. Many of these idiosyncrasies function to secure the conclusion of broadly inclusive multilateral environmental framework agreements, the taking of a liberal approach to the recognition of new customary rules, and the adoption of novel forms of normative or sub-normative measures to guide inter-State cooperation, as well as the behavior of other actors. However, it remains clear that certain characteristics of international environmental law-making, such as increased reliance on technically competent and autonomous institutional structures for the ongoing elaboration of international environmental rules, and increased recognition of non-traditional sources of normativity and of the interests of non-State actors under international environmental regimes, may ultimately result in fundamental alteration of the essential processes of international law-making, with implications for the effectiveness of international law reaching far beyond the field of environmental protection. In the light of these changing patterns of law-making, Kim and Mackey characterize international environmental law as a "complex adaptive system", 'where treaties and institutions self-organize and

184 *Supra*, n. 10, at 16.

185 *Dispute Regarding Navigational and Related Rights (Costa Rica v Nicaragua)*, Judgment of 13 July 2009, para 64. See also *Case Concerning the Gabčíkovo-Nagymaros Project (Hungary/Slovakia)*, Judgment, *ICJ Reports* (1997) 7, at 78, para. 140; *Case Concerning Pulp Mills on the River Uruguay (Argentina v Uruguay)*, Judgment, 20 April 2010, para. 204.

186 *Supra*, n. 183, at para. 452.

187 Regarding this phenomenon of evolutionary normative "convergence" in the field of international water law, see further O. McIntyre, 'Chapter 16 – Water', in E. Morgera and K. Kulovesi (eds.), *Research Handbook on International Law and Natural Resources* (Edward Elgar, Cheltenham, forthcoming 2016).

exhibit emergent properties', and in which 'international environmental law as a whole is adapting to exogenous changes through an institutional process akin to natural selection in biological evolution'.[188]

---

188 R. E. Kim and B. Mackey, 'International Environmental Law as a Complex Adaptive System', (2014) 14 *International Environmental Agreements: Politics, Law and Economics* 5-24, at 5.

CHAPTER 10

THE EFFECTIVENESS OF EU NATURE LEGISLATION: A LONG BATTLE TO SECURE SUPPORTING SECTORAL POLICIES

Sandra JEN
Consultant Environmental Policy and Law, advisor to European Policy Office

1. EFFECTIVENESS OF EU NATURE LEGISLATION FROM CONFLICTING TO SUPPORTING EU POLICIES – THE LONG BATTLE TO SECURE COHERENCE WITH EU NATURE LEGISLATION

The European Union has been involved with the protection of wildlife and natural habitats for over thirty-five years, starting with the signature of the Bonn Convention on the conservation of migratory species of wild animals (23/06/1979) and the Bern Convention on the conservation of European wildlife and natural habitats (19/09/1979). The Directive on the conservation of wild birds (hereafter the Birds Directive)[1] and the Directive on the conservation of natural habitats and of wild fauna and flora (hereafter Habitats Directive)[2] put the necessary legal framework for the coordinated implementation of these conventions in the Member States in place. The Habitats Directive provides for the establishment of the Natura 2000 network, a coherent network of sites selected on the basis of scientific criteria for the protection of species and habitats identified in application of the Habitats Directive or of the Birds Directive.

The question of the effectiveness of the EU's nature legislation came to the forefront of the EU political agenda in 2014 with the launch of a European Commission "Fitness Check" on these two directives. The challenges of

1 European Parliament and Council Directive (EC) No 147/2009 on the conservation of wild birds, OJ 2010 L 20, p. 7-25.

2 Council Directive (EEC) 92/43 on the conservation of natural habitats and of wild fauna and flora, OJ 1992 L 206, p. 7-50.

implementing the Nature Directives and of establishing the Natura 2000 network are no secret, with numerous conflicts being brought all the way up to the European Court of Justice. However, the timing and opportunity of launching a "Fitness Check" on the Nature Directives five years ahead of the EU Headline target of "Halting the loss of biodiversity and the degradation of ecosystem services in the EU by 2020, and restoring them in so far as is feasible while also stepping up the EU contribution to averting global biodiversity loss"[3], and less than five years after the adoption of the new Strategic Plan (2011-2020) of the Convention on Biological Diversity with the 20 Aichi Targets[4], has been questioned by many. With the mission letter from the new President of the European Commission Jean-Claude Juncker calling on the Environment Commissioner Karmenu Vella "to carry out an in-depth evaluation of the Birds and Habitats directives and assess the potential for merging them into a more modern piece of legislation"[5], NGOs have questioned the objectivity of the process. The fate of the Nature Directives seemed to have been decided even before the full procedure of the "Fitness Check" was set in motion. Mobilized under a so-called "Nature Alert" campaign, BirdLife, the European Environmental Bureau, Friends of the Earth and the WWF organized a large coalition and mobilized over 500,000 signatures and contributions across Europe to support the full implementation of these directives rather than their revamping.[6] While the Commission report on the results of the Fitness Check was expected for spring 2016, EU Environment ministers in their December 2015 conclusions on the "Mid-term Review of the EU Biodiversity Strategy to 2020" already reiterated their support to Target 1 of the EU biodiversity strategy[7] and the need to – "fully implement the Birds and Habitats directives", reaffirming that "the Birds and Habitats Directives are essential components of European nature protection and that their effectiveness depends on consistent implementation and adequate financial resources, as well as on the integration of biodiversity into other sectoral policies and [...] that full implementation of the Birds and

3 Environment Council Conclusions, 15 March 2010, Biodiversity: Post-2010 EU and global vision and targets and international ABS regime, point 2. p. 4; http://register.consilium.europa.eu/doc/srv?l=EN&f=ST%207536%202010%20INIT and European Council Conclusions, 25/26 March 2010, EUCO/7/10 REV 1, point 14, p.9. http://data.consilium.europa.eu/doc/document/ST-7-2010-REV-1/en/pdf.

4 Convention on Biological Diversity, 10th Conference of the Parties, 18-29 October 2010, Nagoya, Aichi Prefecture, Japan, Decision X/2, Strategic Plan for Biodiversity 2011-2020.

5 Mission Letter, from Jean-Claude Juncker, President of the European Commission to Karmenu Vella, 1st November 2014, p. 4. http://ec.europa.eu/archives/juncker-commission/docs/vella_en.pdf.

6 WWF European Policy Office, Record Breaking Number of EU Citizens Call to Protect Nature, 24 July 2015, www.wwf.eu/keepnaturealive/?249470/Record-breaking-number-of-EU-citizens-call-to-protect-nature.

7 Communication from the Commission, Our Life Insurance, Our Natural Capital: An EU Biodiversity Strategy To 2020, COM/2011/0244 final; Target 1: By 2020, the assessments of species and habitats protected by EU nature law show better conservation or a secure status for 100% more habitats and 50% more species.

Habitats Directives is key to achieving the targets of the Strategy".[8] Furthermore they underlined "the importance of maintaining the goals and of not lowering the nature protection standards of the Birds and Habitats Directives in order to achieve the 2020 headline target for biodiversity and of maintaining legal certainty for all stakeholders, including businesses and Member States' authorities".[9] Carole Dieshbourg, Luxembourg's Environment Minister and President of the Council declared that: "Ministers listened to all the citizens who raised their voice for ambitious biodiversity policies. [...] biodiversity has many co-benefits for society. The existing Nature Directive works, deliver and should not be re-opened".[10] This position was clearly reiterated with the European Parliament Resolution of 2nd February 2016 on the Mid-Term Review of the EU Biodiversity Strategy.[11] With these unequivocal statements, the debate seems to have been brought to a close for a few years, hopefully at least until the assessment of progress against the 2020 headline target will have to be undertaken.

Nevertheless, the recurrent discussion of the effectiveness of the Nature Directives combined with the specific questions on coherence raised as part of the "Fitness Check" prompt an interest to look back on key aspects of the conflicting interaction between other EU policies and the implementation of these directives. This can be particularly striking when looking at the establishment of Natura 2000 given the territorial dimension of the network stretching over 18% of the EU's land area and almost 6% of its marine territory.[12] Considering the implementation of policies which also have a strong territorial dimension, such as the Regional and Cohesion policy, the Common Agriculture Policy or the Common Fisheries Policy (CFP)[13], the establishment of Natura 2000 can appear in many cases as a race against habitats destruction driven by other EU policies and their implementation at national level. It has been a long battle to secure provisions in EU regulations in order to ensure the minimum of coherence with the Nature Directives and avoid destruction of habitats and species faster than they could be protected. This chapter looks back on some of the critical developments to secure coherence between the Regional and cohesion policy and the implementation of Natura 2000 (I) and the developments in the Common

8 Environment Council Conclusions, 16 December 2015, Conclusions on the "Mid-term Review of the EU Biodiversity Strategy to 2020", point 20 p. 7 www.consilium.europa.eu/en/meetings/env/2015/12/16/.

9 Id, at point 25, p. 8.

10 Carole Dieschbourg, Minister for the Environment of Luxembourg, 16 December 2016; www.consilium.europa.eu/en/meetings/env/2015/12/16/.

11 European Parliament Resolution of 2 February 2016 on the mid-term review of the EU's Biodiversity Strategy (2015/2137(INI)).

12 Natura 2000 in a nutshell: http://ec.europa.eu/environment/nature/natura2000/index_en.htm.

13 European Spatial Development Perspective, Postdam May 1999, Chapter on "Influence of Community Policies on the Territory of the EU", p.13. http://ec.europa.eu/regional_policy/sources/docoffic/official/reports/pdf/a13-19_en.pdf.

Agriculture Policy (II) with a view to illustrate the challenging policy context in which the directives have been implemented in the last decades. The analysis will be restricted to the terrestrial implementation of Natura 2000 and will not consider the implementation of Natura 2000 at sea.[14]

2. THE RACE TO PROTECT FUTURE NATURA 2000 SITES THREATENED BY REGIONAL AND COHESION POLICY PROJECTS

European regional policy was effectively launched in the mid-seventies, with the first European regional fund being established in 1975.[15] It was up-scaled after the entry of Greece, Spain and Portugal to the European Community, the adoption of the Single European Act in 1987 and the new Structural Fund Regulations in 1988. In spite of the provisions of Article 130r (2) of the Single European Act, establishing that "Environmental protection requirement shall be a component of the Community's other policies", and evidence at the time of projects contributing to the deterioration of important natural areas[16], the 1988 Structural Fund Regulations did not include any reference to the protection of the environment. Members States nevertheless were already under the obligation to select and designate Special Protection Areas (SPAs) in application of the Birds Directive and to comply with the provisions of the Bern Convention on the conservation of European wildlife and natural habitats.

2.1. 1993-1999: PROVISIONS ON "COMPATIBILITY AND CHECK"

The strengthening of the environmental integration principle in the Maastricht treaty (1992)[17] provided an important legal basis to help improve the Structural Funds regulations for the period 1993-2000, with provisions on "compatibility and checks'. Article 7 of Regulation 2081/1993 required that "measures financed by the Structural Funds or receiving assistance from the EIB or from another

---

14 For an extensive analysis see H. Schoukens & H. Dotinga, "Natura 2000 and Fisheries, a Question of Competence or Willingness", in *The European Directive in its EU Environmental Law Context*, (C.H. Born, et al., Routledge, 2015), p. 375.

15 Regional Policy, Inforegio, History of the Policy http://ec.europa.eu/regional_policy/en/policy/what/history/.

16 C. Coffey & S. Richartz, *The EU Habitats Directive: Generating Strong Responses*, (IEEP, 2003), p. 16, – www.ecologic.eu/download/projekte/850-899/890/in-depth/eu_habitats_directive.pdf.

17 Article 130 r(2) in Consolidated Version of the Treaty Establishing the European Community: "Environmental protection requirements must be integrated into the definition and implementation of other Community policies.", OJ 1992 C 224/1, p. 52.

existing financial instrument shall be in conformity with the provisions of the Treaties, with the instruments adopted pursuant thereto and with Community policies, including those concerning the rules on competition, the award of public contracts and environmental protection" and Member States had to provide to the European Commission a regional development plan including "an appraisal of the environmental situation of the region concerned and an evaluation of the environmental impact of the strategy and operations referred to above in terms of sustainable development in agreement with the provisions of Community law in force; the arrangements made to associate the competent environmental authorities designated by the Member State in the preparation and implementation of the operations envisaged in the plan and to ensure compliance with Community environmental rules".[18]

However, in many cases these procedures were not implemented effectively. Projects supported by the Funds continued to be controversial, by not always respecting the environmental objectives agreed upon. A recurring conflict arose between the Funds and EU nature conservation legislation, with infrastructure projects contributing to the deterioration of sites suitable for inclusion within the new Natura 2000 network.[19] The development of infrastructure projects was often faster than site identification and the implementation calendar for Natura 2000 kept being delayed. In application of Article 4.1 of the Habitats Directive Member States had to submit their lists of proposed Sites of Community Importance (pSCI) by June 1995 and the adoption of the lists of Sites of Community Importance was due to be completed by June 1998. Assessments by environmental NGOs, such as the 1999 WWF report "Natura 2000 Opportunities and Obstacles", clearly illustrate these situations: "River and wetland engineering works, promoted by EU and national policies, are a major cause of damage to freshwater ecosystems and to terrestrial habitats and species. Flood control, drainage and road works, co-funded by the EU Structural Funds, are causing the drainage of over 300ha of wetlands in the east part of Lake Vistonida, in Greece. This will result in the destruction of several habitat types from Annex I of the Habitats Directive. The works are being carried out adjacent to a proposed SCI and partly inside another. Ironically, the LIFE fund is financing a project for the conservation of the pygmy cormorant (*Phalacro-corax pygmaeus*), which feeds and roosts in the area that will be damaged. In Spain, dam-building projects threaten numerous habitats and species of Community interest. Dams such as Melonares (Seville), Breña II (Córdoba), Irueña (Salamanca) and Andévalo (Huelva) threaten to destroy forest and scrub habitats which, apart from their own value, are used by the Iberian lynx

18 Article 8.4 in Council Regulation (EEC) No 2081/93 amending Regulation (EEC) No 2052/88 on the tasks of the Structural Funds and their effectiveness and on coordination of their activities between themselves and with the operations of the European Investment Bank and the other existing financial instruments, OJ 1993 L 193, Vol 36, p. 11.

19 C. Coffey & S. Richartz. *supra*, note 16.

(Lynx pardina), a priority species on Annexes II and IV of the Habitats Directive and thought to be the most endangered feline on the planet."[20]

Confronted with Member States' delays to notify their lists of SPAs and pSCI, NGOs undertook the task of working with experts to identify sites that qualify under the directives' criteria[21] and to demonstrate the insufficiencies of the lists proposed by Member States. The value of BirdLife's Important Bird Areas inventory, as a 'shadow list' of SPAs, has repeatedly been recognised by the European Court of Justice and the European Commission.[22] These "Shadow Lists" were also useful to actively contributing to the biogeographic seminars in which NGO's experts could argue for the consideration of additional sites on the basis of their complementary scientific inventories.

2.2. 1999 – COMMISSIONERS UNITED FOR COHERENCE AND CONDITIONALITY

NGOs kept pressing the European Commission and the European Parliament to make approval of national programmes for the Structural Funds, including the Rural Development Fund, conditional on effective progress in site selection for Natura 2000.[23] These initiatives were pursued in a context of positive political attention for environmental integration with the development of the Cardiff process.[24] The EC Strategy for integrating the environment into EU policies provided, in particular, for: "the introduction of systematic scrutiny of the environmental impact of projects over ECU 50 million; the integration of the environment as an objective for assistance from the Structural Funds in the framework of proposed new Structural Funds regulations; the appraisal by the Commission of regional development plans as regards environmental protection; the introduction of a partnership involving environmental bodies and non-governmental environmental organisations for the preparation of Cohesion Policy intervention programmes".[25]

---

20 G. Beaufoy, *Natura 2000: Opportunities and Obstacles*, (WWF Austria, 1999) p.17.

21 WWF European Policy Office, *Habitats Directive, WWF European Shadow list*, 15 June 2000, www.wwf.eu/?5364/Habitats-Directive-WWF-European-Shadow-List.

22 BirdLife International, *Designating Special Protection Areas in the European Union*. Presented as part of the BirdLife State of the world's birds website, (2013) www.birdlife.org/datazone/sowb/casestudy/244, and Case C-3/96, Commission v Netherlands [1998] ECR I-3031, para 68-70.

23 *WWF European Policy Office*, *supra*, note 21 at p.3.

24 See Environmental Integration History http://ec.europa.eu/environment/integration/integration_history.htm and Cardiff European Council Presidency Conclusions 15-16 June 1998, in SN 150/1/98 REV 1 (Bulletin of 17.6.1998), points 32 to 36, p.12.

25 See Communication from the Commission to the European Council of 27 May 1998 on a partnership for integration: a strategy for integrating the environment into EU policies (Cardiff, June 1998), Com (1998)0333, p.8; not published in the Official Journal; and European

In this context, the 1999 reform of the Cohesion funds clarified both the obligations of Member States and of the European Commission to ensure not only the integration of the necessary environmental requirements in the preparation of the programmes, but calling for "consistency" in the operation of the funds: "The Commission and the Member States shall ensure that the operations of the Funds are consistent with other Community policies and operations, in particular in the areas of [...] the common agricultural policy, the common fisheries policy, transport, energy and the trans-European networks and the incorporation of the requirements of environmental protection into the definition and implementation of the operations of the Funds".[26] The Guidelines for Structural Fund programmes issued to Member States in September 1999 also stressed that "environmental considerations, and in particular compliance with Community environmental and nature protection legislation, must be incorporated into the definition and implementation of measures supported by the Structural Funds and the Cohesion Fund". The objective was not only to ensure that no structural funds would be allocated to projects, which could be in breach of EU environmental legislation, but also to try channelling an increasing proportion of these funds to projects also associated with the effective implementation of this legislation, such as species inventories and mapping, habitats restoration or information and awareness-raising projects.

On 23 June 1999, Environment Commissioner Ritt Bjerregaard and Commissioner Monika Wulf-Mathies, who was in charge of regional policy, wrote to five Member State governments (France, Germany, the Netherlands, Portugal and Ireland) reminding them of their duties and warning them of possible delays for the approval of programmes and projects if, in particular, notifications of protected sites under Habitats Directive and Wild Birds Directive had not been received. This position, and determination to effectively implement Article 12 of the Structural Fund regulation, was pursued under the subsequent Prodi Commission. Following a written question from MEP Horst Schnellhardt[27], regarding the lawfulness and reasonableness of making the approval of structural funds programmes for Germany conditional on the notification of proposed SCI, Commissioner Barnier stressed the duty of the European Commission to "fulfill its obligations under the EC Treaty (Article 6, ex Article 3c) and Articles 12 and 41 (2) (b) of Council Regulation (EC) No 1260/1999 of 21 June 1999 laying down general provisions on the structural funds" and that "a serious lack of information on protected sites which might jeopardise the Commission's assessment whether

Parliament Resolution on the Commission communication "Partnership for Integration" (COM(98)0333 C4-0410/98), OJ *C 359, 23/11/1998 p. 91.*

26 Article 2.5 of Council Regulation (EC) No 1260/1999 laying down general provisions on the Structural Funds, OJ L 161/1, 26/6/1999.

27 Member of European Parliament Horst Schnellhardt (PPE-DE), written question to the Commission, E 1771/99, 11 October 1999, http://eur-lex.europa.eu/LexUriServ/LexUriServ.do?uri=OJ:C:2000:225E:0018:0019:EN:PDF.

programmes are in conformity with Community law as required by Article 12 of Council Regulation (EC) 1260/1999". On 16 March 2000, the European Parliament adopted a Resolution on "Structural Fund programmes in the Member States and national implementation of EU environmental laws".[28] In this Resolution, the European Parliament "emphasises the potential threat to sensitive sites of the European natural heritage from the direct and indirect environmental impacts of Structural Fund supported projects, which could destroy forever the delicate balance of natural habitats; [...] calls on the Commission to clarify its monitoring role once a plan or programme is approved; [and] to require from Member States a firm commitment that their regional development plans and operational programmes will take full account of the need to protect from any possible negative impact those sites already protected under Natura 2000; [...] calls on the Commission to put in place binding mechanisms which ensure that plans and operational programmes are not changed after Commission approval or first fund allocation, unless the proposed changes are preceded by a full and open reevaluation, the results of which determine if funding is still to be granted". On the same date, the European Commission published a press release about the detailed rules for dealing with the situations of Members States which, on the date of the Commission's approval of programming documents, had not yet provided a list of sites to be protected.[29]

Further to this political mobilization to foster coherence in EU spending, and to improve the effective consideration of environment protection obligations in the assessment of national strategic plans and national operational programmes, the scrutiny of EU funds allocation was effectively improved. Nevertheless, this did not entirely mark the end of attempts by national and regional authorities to use the EU Structural and Cohesion Funds for projects that would undermine the objectives of the EU environmental policies and the effectiveness of the Nature Directives. Examples such as the construction of the Odeluca dam in Portugal show that in some cases, when the payment of the EU funds got suspended because the project was found to be in breach of EU legislation, national authorities simply pursued the works with national or private funds.[30] The prospects of the Spanish national hydrological plan, as adopted by the Spanish Parliament in July 2001, were another example of the level of defiance to the reconciliation of regional

---

28 European Parliament resolution on Structural Fund programmes in the Member States and national implementation of EU environmental laws, 16 March 2000, OJ 29.12.2000, C 377/, p. 333, http://eur-lex.europa.eu/legal-content/EN/TXT/PDF/?uri=CELEX:52000IP0227(01)&from=EN.

29 European Commission press release, Commission spells out linkage between structural measures and Natura 2000 commitments, 16 March 2000, http://europa.eu/rapid/press-release_IP-00-266_en.htm.

30 WWF, *Conflicting EU Funds: Pitting Conservation Against Unsustainable development*, (WWF Global Species Programme, 2006), p. 61.http://awsassets.wwf.es/downloads/eu_conflicting_funds_report.pdf.

development and natural capital preservation.[31] This plan consisted of two main parts: a new water transfer of 1,050 cubic hectometres per year from the Ebro River Basin to another four river basins in the north, south-east and south of the country, and a package of 865 public water works.[32]

2.3. ENLARGEMENT TO NEW MEMBER STATES

Furthermore, during preparations for the accession to the EU of ten new Member States in 2004 and of Bulgaria and Romania in 2007, similar problems were transposed to these countries which encompass large wilderness areas, such as the Carpathian Mountains, the Danube Delta or the Baltic Coast.[33] No transition period was granted to candidate countries for the Natura 2000 network and they were required to designate SPA under the Birds Directive and pSCI under the Habitats Directive at the time of their Accession. However, some plans and projects for large infrastructure developments, to be initiated with EU pre-accession funds, were already representing a potential threat. This concerned the extension of the trans-European transport network (TEN-T) in particular.[34] Regulations on the granting of EU funds in the field of trans-European transport networks have included a general clause on compatibility with environment protection since 1995[35] and improvements have subsequently been made with direct references to the Birds and Habitats directives, to the SEA directive[36] and, finally, also to the Water Framework Directive.[37] However, the implementation of these requirements as not always been fully satisfactory and a number of projects raised serious concerns.[38] NGOs campaigned against several major projects threatening outstanding natural areas such as the Rospuda Valley (Poland) threatened by a

31 WWF, *Seven reasons to oppose the Spanish National Plan*; WWF briefing: SNHP and EU Structural Funds, 29 May 2003 www.wwf.eu/?7247/The-Spanish-National-Hydrological-Plan-and-the-structural-funds-legislation.

32 Barcelona Field Study Center, *WWF Opposition to the Spanish National Hydrological Plan*, June 2002.

33 S. Jen & E. Townsend, *WWF Progress on Preparation for Natura 2000 in Future EU Member States*, (WWF 2003). assets.panda.org/downloads/n2000progressmailing20030122.pdf.

34 BirdLife, CEE-Bankwatch, Friends of the Earth Europe, Transport and Environment, WWF, *Conflict Areas between the TEN-T and Nature Conservation*, Case Studies, 2003. www.transportenvironment.org/sites/te/files/media/conflictareas_0.pdf.

35 See Art. 7 in Council Regulation (EC) No 2236/95 laying down general rules for the granting of Community financial aid in the field of trans-European networks, OJ 1995, L 228, p. 1-7.

36 See Art. 8 in European Parliament and Council Decision (EC) No 884/2004/EC amending Decision No 1692 on Community guidelines for the development of the trans-European transport network, OJ 2004 L167, p.1-38.

37 See Art. 36 in European Parliament and Council Regulation (EU) No 1315/2013 on Union guidelines for the development of the trans-European transport network, OJ 2013, L 348, p. 1-128.

38 See more extensively Transport & Environment www.transportenvironment.org/what-we-do/eu-transport-spending/background.

section of Via Baltica, the motorway linking Warsaw and Helsinki, the Struma motorway going through Kresna Gorge in Bulgaria[39] or TEN-T "corridor VII" along the Danube.[40] The Rospuda Valley case led to the European Commission applying for, and being granted, an injunction (interim measures) by the European Court of Justice to suspend the works given the immediate threat to the Natura 2000 site.[41]

2.4. 2006-2013 FINANCING NATURA 2000 AND BIODIVERSITY MAINSTREAMING

The Cohesion Funds Regulations, adopted in 2006, mark an important development in the explicit contribution of this policy to the implementation of the Nature Directives. With many lists of Sites of Community Importance adopted, financial resources for the management and restoration of sites in Natura 2000 was becoming crucial. Article 8 of the Habitats Directive sets out an obligation of EU co-financing for selected Natura 2000 sites. The costs of upkeep and ecological improvement of the network have been calculated at 5.8 billion euro per year, a modest sum compared to the benefits provided by Natura 2000, estimated at the order of 200 to 300 billion euro per year.[42] For the very first time, the financing of measures for the management of Natura 2000 sites is made clearly possible with the direct reference to "promotion of biodiversity and nature protection, including investments in Natura 2000 sites" under the environmental priorities of the convergence objective of the European and Regional Development Fund.[43]

The 2014-2020 programming period for Cohesion Funds marks a new step for environment mainstreaming. Article 8 of the Common Provision Regulation[44] expands considerably on the reference to sustainable development[45] compared

39 A Neslen, *Bulgarian Motorway Poised to Carve Wildlife Haven*, The Guardian, February, 17, 2016.

40 See WWF, The Danube – a lifeline of just a navigation corridor? (*WWF Danube Carpathian Programme and WWF Austria 2005*) http://wwf.hu/media/file/1180873747_wwf_ten_t_position_paper_2.

41 Case C-193/07, Commission v Poland, ECJ Order April, 18, 2007, OJ 2007 C199/50 p.14.

42 See *European Commission*, Guidance Handbook financing Natura 2000, 2014, p.4.at http://ec.europa.eu/environment/nature/natura2000/financing/index_en.htm.

43 See Art. 4 European Parliament and Council Regulation (EC) No 1080/2006 on the European Regional Development Fund and repealing Regulation (EC) No 1783/1999, OJ 2006 L 210, p. 1-11.

44 European Parliament and Council Regulation (EU) No 1303/2013 laying down common provisions on the European Regional Development Fund, the European Social Fund, the Cohesion Fund, the European Agricultural Fund for Rural Development and the European Maritime and Fisheries Fund and laying down general provisions on the European Regional Development Fund, the European Social Fund, the Cohesion Fund and the European Maritime and Fisheries Fund, OJ 2013 L 347, p. 320-469.

45 For an NGO commentary: WWF, *The Future of Cohesion Policy A view from the WWF European Policy Office*, 2008 http://ec.europa.eu/regional_policy/archive/conferences/4thcohesionforum/doc/contributions/epo.pdf.

to the 2006 Regulation[46] and it includes a direct reference to biodiversity in the list of environmental objectives to be fulfilled together with a clear, shared responsibility between Member States and the European Commission: "The Member States and the Commission shall ensure that environmental protection requirements, resource efficiency, climate change mitigation and adaptation, biodiversity, disaster resilience, and risk prevention and management are promoted in the preparation and implementation of Partnership Agreements and programmes".[47] This explicit reference to the protection of biodiversity, together with the other environmental priorities in the Common Provisions Regulation, is very important to unequivocally promoting the allocation of Cohesion funds to finance the necessary actions towards the 2020 biodiversity goal at the national and regional levels. Initiatives such as "Surf nature – let's improve the use of Regional Funds together" had already been adopted in the previous programming period to enhance regional policies for the promotion and preservation of biodiversity and nature and to improve the opportunities for their funding through the European Regional Development Fund (ERDF).[48]

This overview illustrates the long campaigns to obtain adequate provisions in the different legislations for Cohesion Policy as well as the challenges for their effective implementation. With the Natura 2000 network now becoming a reality, the explicit provisions for its financing, together with the reference to biodiversity in the Common Provisions Regulation, and the experience gained in the implementation of the SEA[49] and EIA directives[50], there can be some grounds to have more confidence in finding concerted solutions to achieving sustainable development[51] in compliance with Article 11 TFUE[52], provided that the Nature

46 See Art.17 in Council Regulation (EC) No 1083/2006 laying down general provisions on the European Regional Development Fund, the European Social Fund and the Cohesion Fund and repealing Regulation (EC) No 1260/1999, OJ L 210, 31.7.2006, p. 25-78.

47 Art. 8 par.2 *supra* note 44.

48 For information on "SURF nature – let's improve the use of Regional Funds together" see www.surf-nature.eu/.

49 Report on the application and effectiveness of the Directive on Strategic Environmental Assessment (Directive 2001/42/EC), COM(2009) 469 final, page 1; the SEA Directive was adopted in 2001 with a deadline for transposition of July 2004 but the Directive was transposed in all Member States only in 2009.

50 European Parliament and Council Directive 2014/52/EU amending Directive 2011/92/EU on the assessment of the effects of certain public and private projects on the environment, OJ 2014, L124/1.

51 For example, see W. Sheate, R. Eales & I. Vaizgelaite, Collingwood Environmental Planning, Appraisals of Sustainability and the New National Policy Statements: Opportunities Missed and Challenges to Come?, Final report to RSPB and WWF, 2010; N. de Sadeleer, *L'évaluation des incidences environnementales des programmes, plans et projets: à la recherché d'une protection juridictionnelle effective*, Revue du Droit de l'Union Européenne, 2/2014, p.231.

52 Article 11 TFUE: "Environmental protection requirements must be integrated into the definition and implementation of the Union policies and activities, in particular with a view to promoting sustainable development", Consolidated version of the Treaty on the Functioning of the European Union O.J. 2008 C 115, p. 53.

Directives or other supportive legislation do not get dismantled in a REFIT process.

The Romanian Transportation Master Plan 2015-2030[53] provides a good example of the latest positive developments towards mainstreaming of biodiversity requirements, good governance and commitments to support the achievements of the Nature Directives while pursuing sustainable development.

Nevertheless, environmental actors have to remain vigilant as some political and administrative decision makers continue to have poor consideration for biodiversity, nature protection and the rules of governance attached to sustainable development. The dramatic case of the Sivens barrage in France is an illustration of this.[54] It also relates to critical aspects of the Common Agriculture Policy.

3. RECONCILING THE COMMON AGRICULTURE POLICY WITH NATURE PROTECTION: STILL A CHALLENGE

The European Common Agriculture Policy (CAP) has its origin in post-war Europe and the early developments of the European Economic Community in the 1950s. Its objectives have formally remained unchanged since their inception in the Treaty of Rome, in spite of the numerous treaty revisions, the strengthening of the environmental integration principle[55] or the qualification of the environmental protection as a "fundamental objective of the European Union".[56]

The CAP objectives, as defined in the treaty, are of a socio-economic nature with an emphasis on agricultural productivity.[57] In 2003, agriculture Commissioner

53 *Environment News Service*, Romania Amends 2015-2030 Transport Plan to Protect Animals, 25 Feb. 2015 http://ens-newswire.com/2015/02/25/romania-amends-2015-2030-transport-plan-to-protect-animals/.

54 N. Forray & P. Rathouis, *Expertise du projet de barrage de Sivens* (Tarn), Conseil Général de l'environnement et du développement durable, October 2014.

55 In 1988, the Court interpreted *Article 130r(2) of the Treaty as reflecting "the principle whereby all Community measures must satisfy the requirements of environmental protection" in* Case C-62/88, Greece v. Council, [1990] ECR I-01527, para. 20, and see J.H. Jan, "Stop the Integration Principle", Fordham International Law Journal 33.3 (2011) p. 1544.

56 *Case 240/83 Procureur de la République v Association de défense des brûleurs d' huiles usagées [1985] ECR 531, para. 8*; Case 302/86 Commission of the European Communities v Kingdom of Denmark [1988] ECR 04607.

57 Article 39 TFUE: "The objectives of the common agricultural policy shall be: (a) to increase agricultural productivity by promoting technical progress and by ensuring the rational development of agricultural production and the optimum utilization of the factors of production in particular labour; (b) thus to ensure a fair standard of living for the agricultural community, in particular by increasing the individual earnings of persons engaged in agriculture; (c) to stabilise markets; (d) to assure the availability of supplies; (e) to ensure that supplies reach consumers at reasonable prices. 2. In working out the common agricultural policy and the special methods for its application, account shall be taken of: (a) the particular nature of agricultural activity, which results from the social structure of agriculture and from

Dr. Franz Fischler qualified the "call for greater production" as being "somewhat anachronistic" and regretted that "the goals of the common agricultural policy in the draft [Constitution submitted by the Convention for Europe] still reflect the deprived post-war economy" ignoring "the major paradigm change in European agriculture away from maximising production and towards sustainability".[58] More recent provisions of the treaty, such as the TFEU's EU energy chapter, refer at least explicitly to the need to preserve and improve the environment.[59] However, the European Court of Justice has given a broader interpretation of the CAP objectives[60], first by qualifying the "protection of consumers or the protection of the health and life of humans and animals" as "requirements relating to the public interest" that the CAP "cannot disregard"[61] and justifying measures adopted to this aim on the sole basis of CAP provisions (Art. 43 EC Treaty now Art. 39 TFEU) then, in the application of the environmental integration principle, the court has explicitly recognized environmental protection as an "objective which also forms part of the CAP".[62] One of the three objectives of the 2013 CAP reform was the sustainable management of natural resources and climate action.[63] However, the 2013 reform of the CAP has not brought the landmark changes expected by many. It is "at its best [presented ...], as a stalemate for the environment"[64], and by other account it is a failure for biodiversity.[65]

structural and natural disparities between the various agricultural regions; (b) the need to effect the appropriate adjustments by degrees; (c) the fact that in the Member States agriculture constitutes a sector closely linked with the economy as a whole." *OJ 2012 C 326 p. 47 – 390.*

58 Dr. Franz Fischeler, Member of the European Commission responsible for Agriculture, Rural Development and Fisheries, CAP Reform and EU Enlargement: The Future of European Agriculture, European Bridge, Leuven, 4 November 2003, http://europa.eu/rapid/press-release_SPEECH-03-515_en.htm.

59 See Art. 194 (1) TFUE: "In the context of the establishment and functioning of the internal market and with regard for the need to preserve and improve the environment, Union policy on energy shall aim, in a spirit of solidarity between Member States, to: (a) ensure the functioning of the energy market; (b) ensure security of energy supply in the Union; (c) promote energy efficiency and energy saving and the development of new and renewable forms of energy; and (d) promote the interconnection of energy networks.", *OJ 2012 C 326 p. 47 – 390.*

60 N. de Sadeleer, C-H. Born, *Droit international et communautaire de la biodiversité*, (Dalloz, 2004), p. 626.

61 Case 68/86 UK v. Council [1988] ECR 06393 para. 12 "Efforts to achieve objectives of the common agricultural policy, in particular under common organizations of the markets, cannot disregard requirements relating to the public interest such as the protection of consumers or the protection of the health and life of humans and animals, requirements which the Community institutions must take into account in exercising their powers.".

62 Case C-428/07, The Queen on the application of Mark Horvath v. Secretary of State for the Environment, Food and Rural Affairs, [2009], ECR *I-06355*, para. 29.

63 European Commission COM (2010) 672 The CAP towards 2020: Meeting the food, natural resources and territorial challenge of the future.

64 I. Doussan & H. Schoukens, "Biodiversity and Agriculture, Greening the CAP beyond the Status Quo?", in *The Habitats Directive in its EU Environmental Law Context*, (C.H. Born, et al.(eds.), Routledge, 2015), p.450.

65 G. Pe'er & al, EU agricultural reform fails on biodiversity, Science magazine, 6 June 2014, p. 1090,92.

As early as 1973, the first Programme of Action of the European Communities on the Environment already stressed the need for the CAP to effectively take into consideration environmental protection both at the stages of the elaboration of the policies and its implementation: "the activities of the Communities in the different sectors in which they operate (agriculture policy, social policy, regional policy, industrial policy, energy policy, etc.) must take account of concern for the protection and improvement of the environment. Furthermore, such concern must be taken into consideration in the elaboration and implementation of these policies."[66] However, the integration of environmental policy with the CAP has been a slow and difficult enterprise[67], crystallizing much resistance from some of the organizations representing farming interests at the European level. In 2009, the results of the first systematic assessment of the conservation status of Europe's most vulnerable habitat types and species protected under the Habitats Directive demonstrated that, in general, all habitat types associated with agriculture are doing significantly worse in terms of conservation status than other types of habitats.[68] Nevertheless, with the CAP financing accounting for about 40% of the overall EU budget, with farmland representing around 40% of the total area included in Natura 2000 and Natura 2000 sites covering over 10% of total agricultural area[69], synergies between the CAP and the implementation of Natura 2000, as well as the backing of farmers themselves, are essential to the effectiveness of the Nature Directives and Natura 2000 in particular.

The successive reforms of the CAP have slowly integrated environmental considerations from 1992 on and have done so more effectively in 1999, with the introduction of the so-called Pillar 2 on rural development policy and the evolution of the status of the agri-environment measures from optional to mandatory for Member States as part of their rural development plans. Different measures have progressively been developed for the "greening of the CAP", some of which are more closely linked with the management of Natura 2000.

3.1. CROSS COMPLIANCE AND THE NATURE DIRECTIVES

The concept of "cross compliance" applied in the US agriculture policy since the 1970s, was introduced on a non-mandatory basis under Article 3 of the Common

---

66 Declaration of the Council of the European Communities on the Programme of Action of the European Communities on the Environment, 22 November 1973, OJ 1973 C 112.

67 See G Beaufoy, *EU Policies for Olive Farming, Unsustainable on all Counts*, WWF & BirdLife, June 2001, www.wwf.org.uk/filelibrary/pdf/oliveoil.pdf, WWF and other NGOs, The Truth Behind the CAP, 2011. https://www.foeeurope.org/sites/default/files/publications/FoEE_13_reasons_for_green_CAP_reform_0611.pdf;.A. Lenshow, *Environmental Policy Integration, Greening Sectoral Policies in Europe*, (Earthscan, 2012) *p.* 102.

68 Commission Staff working paper Impact Assesment Common Agricultural Policy Towards 2020, Annexe 2A Fact Sheet Biodiversity and Agriculture, (SEC (2011/1153 final 2), p.1.

69 Commission Staff working paper Impact Assesment Common Agricultural Policy Towards 2020, Annexe 2 Greening the CAP (SEC (2011/1153) final 2), p.4.

Rules Regulation (1259/1999).[70] National authorities were in charge of taking the "appropriate environmental measures" depending on the circumstances. Non-compliance could result in penalties consisting in a reduction of or a cancellation of the support scheme payments accruing from the support schemes. These provisions were not linked to a specific list of environmental obligations. The margin of appreciation left to the Member States contrasts with the strong call for consistency introduced in the 1999 Structural Funds regulation, both for the European Commission and Member States.[71] The 2003 Mid-Term Review of the CAP turned it into a compulsory measure, linking the receipt of all CAP direct payment by farmers to the respect of a number of basic rules on environment, public and animal health as well as animal welfare.[72] The restriction of the scope of cross compliance to a selection of legal obligation might raise some concerns. It should not be interpreted as setting an option to ignore other provisions and obligations, but rather as a tool for the "reinforcement of compliance with EU legislation".[73] In cases of non-compliance, the farmer would be subject to a reduction or withdrawal of these payments. For environmental protection, cross compliance, applied for selected provisions of the Birds and Habitats Directives from January 1st, 2005 on, the nitrates Directive[74], the Directive on groundwater quality[75] and the Directive on sewage sludge.[76] As from January 2007, the conditionality was extended to the second pillar of the CAP.[77] The exclusion of the Water framework directive from this package was strongly criticized[78] in 2003. After much debate[79], the 2013 reform conceded to its introduction together

---

70 Council Regulation (EC) No 1259/1999 establishing common rules for direct support schemes under the common agricultural policy, OJ 1999 L 160; K. Hart, M. Farmer, D. Baldock "The role of cross compliance in greening EU agricultural policy", in *Economics of Regulation in Agriculture: Compliance with Public and Private Standards*, (F Brouwer, G. Fox, R Jongeneel (eds), CAB International 2012), p.11.

71 *Supra*. note 26.

72 See Art. 3 and Annex III of Council Regulation (EC) No 1782/2003 establishing common rules for direct support schemes under the common agricultural policy and establishing certain support schemes for farmers, OJ 2003 L 270, p. 1-69.

73 D. Baldock "Twisted together, European Agriculture, environment and the Common Agriculture Policy", in *Research Handbook on EU Agriculture Law*, (J. A. McMahon & M. N. Cardwell (eds), Edward Elgar Publishing, 2015), p. 141.

74 Council Directive (EEC) No 91/676/EEC concerning the protection of waters against pollution caused by nitrates from agricultural sources, OJ 1991 L 375p. 1.

75 Council Directive (EEC) 80/68/EEC on the protection of groundwater against pollution caused by certain dangerous substances OJ 1980 L 20, p. 43.

76 Council Directive (EEC) 86/278/EEC on the protection of the environment, and in particular of the soil, when sewage sludge is used in agriculture, OJ 1986 L 181, p. 6.

77 See Art. 51 of Council Regulation (EC) 1698/2005 on support for rural development by the European Agricultural Fund for Rural Development (EAFRD), OJ 2005 L 277, p. 1-40.

78 WWF Press Release, Complete Setback for Sustainable Common Agricultural Policy, January 2003, http://wwf.panda.org/wwf_news/?5422/Complete-set-back-for-sustainable-Common-Agricultural-Policy-WWF.

79 WWF Press Release, The Frankenstein of CAP Reform is Born at Council, June 2012 http://wwf.panda.org/wwf_news/?unewsid=205257.

with the Directive on the Sustainable Use of Pesticides, only once they have been shown to have been properly applied in all Member States and obligations to farmers have been clearly identified.

The scope of cross compliance with the Birds and Habitats directive has been streamlined over the last ten years of CAP reforms, partly to focus on Natura 2000 and individual farmer's obligations, rather than on Member States' ones. While the 2003 regulation[80] provided for compliance with the articles of the Birds Directive dealing with the protection, management and restoration of habitats and biotopes outside of protected areas (Art.3), with SPAs management and protection (Art. 4 (1), (2), (4)), protection of all species of birds in accordance with Article 5, the regulation of hunting in application of Article 7 and 8, and Habitats Directive provisions for the management and protection of Natura 2000 sites (Art.6), the protection of Annex IV plant species in application of Art. 13, the prohibition of indiscriminate means of killing and capture (Art. 15) and the control of the deliberate introduction of non-indigenous species (Art. 22.b), in 2009 the scope of cross compliance[81] with the Habitats Directive is narrowed to Art.6 and Art. 13 (1)(a) and reference is no longer made to Articles 7 and 8 (members states obligations in relation to hunting regulations) of the Birds Directives. With the 2013 reform[82], Article 5 of the Birds directive is no longer covered (this Article concerns the Member States' obligation to take the requisite measures to establish a general system of protection for all species of birds listed in Annex 1 of the Directive).

Complying with the corresponding national legislation provisions at the farm level requires the Member States' competent authorities to detail the measures and goals to be achieved by the farmers. Other measures under the same group of Statutory Requirement Measures (SRM) and under the "Good Agricultural and Environmental Conditions" (GAEC) address important environmental issues such as the ratio of permanent pasture or soil protection.

The cross-compliance system and the other measures, introduced under the CAP over a period of more than fifteen years, illustrate the tight links between agriculture management and the effectiveness of the Nature Directives. The full impact of cross compliance is reported as being "difficult to assess" given the limited investment in the evaluation of the measure at EU level.[83] The 2008 report of the European Court of the Auditor points to the confusion resulting from the combined set of provisions at stake, the lack of indicators, the poor administrative practices and the relatively low level of implementation by Member States. The

80 *Supra* (note 64).

81 Council Regulation (EC) No 73/2009 of 19 January 2009 establishing common rules for direct support schemes for farmers under the common agricultural policy and establishing certain support schemes for farmers Art. 4 and 5 and Annex II, OJ 2009 L 30/16.

82 European Parliament and Council Regulation (EU) No 1306/2013 on the financing, management and monitoring of the common agricultural policy, Annex II, Rule on cross compliance pursuant to Art. 93, OJ 2013 L 347 p. 549-607.

83 Baldock *supra* note 73 at p. 141.

sanctions are reported as being weak with low reduction of payment associated and is, at times, disconnected from the levels or extents of the infringements.[84] In addition to the low level of implementation, and the need for reporting and monitoring, NGO assessments have also pointed to the importance of clearly identifying the nature conservation requirements in the GAEC, in order to avoid the risk that these measures could undermine some of the biodiversity objectives and requirements.[85]

The sites' management plans should provide a suitable framework to define the objectives and measures to be taken at farm level for the measures in relation to Natura 2000. Beyond protected areas, the availability of regional biodiversity action plans, or species action plans, can facilitate the identification and agreement on the most important measures to be pursued. A close cooperation between agencies in charge of agriculture and those in charge of the environment is certainly the key to the success of the scheme.

3.2. NUMEROUS OPTIONS FOR NATURA 2000 FUNDING UNDER THE CAP

Both the European Agricultural Guarantee Fund (EAGF) and the European Agricultural Fund for Rural Development (EAFRD) provide numerous opportunities for Member States to support and to promote the farming systems and agricultural management required for the conservation of Natura 2000 farmland.[86] These include payments to farmers in areas facing natural constraints, payment for young farmers, payments for farmers observing agricultural practices beneficial to the climate and the environment or payments for Natura 2000 measures.[87] These different payment schemes, together with the Common regulation provisions requiring promotion in the preparation and implementation of Partnership agreements and programmes, of environmental protection and biodiversity, among other environmental objectives[88], reflect a large part of the progress achieved in integrating requirements for the funding of Natura 2000 management in farmland.

---

84 *European Court of Auditors*, Is Cross Compliance an Effective Policy? Special Report No 8/2008, for other analysis see also *IEEP*, Cross Compliance in the CAP, conclusion of the Pan-European Project 2002-2005, and *Alliance Environnement*, Evaluation of the Application of Cross Compliance as Foreseen under Regulation 1782/2003, 2007.

85 RSPB, Farmland birds and agri-environment schemes in the New Member States, 2006.

86 More extensively see *European Commission*, Farming for Natura 2000 Guidance on how to support Natura 2000 farming systems to achieve conservation objectives, based on Member States good practice experiences, 2014.

87 Art.30 of European Parliament and Council Regulation (EU) No 1305/2013 on support for rural development by the European Agricultural Fund for Rural Development (EAFRD) and repealing Council Regulation (EC) No 1698/2005 OJ 2013 L 347.

88 *Supra*. note 44.

Agriculture, along with human-induced '*modifications of natural conditions*'[89], are identified as the greatest problems in the decline of the conservation status of all groups of species and habitats protected under the Nature Directive, any shortcomings in the implementation these of "greening" schemes would seriously risk hampering the chances of reaching Targets 1, 2 and 3[90] of the EU Biodiversity strategy. The mid-term evaluation of some of the provisions of the CAP in 2017 could present an opportunity to assess the determination of Member States to make the most of these options to promote sustainable farming[91], and their effectiveness.

4. CONCLUSION

This overview of the EU Cohesion and Common Agriculture Policies' evolution, in relation to the Nature Directives, illustrates the long path towards effective environmental integration. Accounting for the largest part of the EU budget, the PAC and the regional and cohesion policies have had considerable spatial impact on the European territory. The delays in Natura 2000 site selection and implementation of the Nature Directives have allowed decision-makers from all sectors to ignore the requirements for nature protection in Europe for too long. In many cases, the implementation of these policies has been perceived as land use competitions for critical areas, such as estuaries, wetlands, country borders formerly less developed, thereafter becoming trans-European corridors for European transport networks or for semi-arid regions receiving EU funding for irrigated agriculture. This context of poor coordination in policy developments, a lack of strategic land use planning at the European level and competition over land for infrastructure developments, rather than synergies for sustainable development, must be fully taken into consideration in the assessment of the effectiveness of the Nature Directives.

At this stage of the implementation of Natura 2000, with the lists of special areas of conservation finally being adopted, but with sites management being nascent in most places, it would be premature to attempt to assess the network's

89 *European Commission*, The State of Nature in the European Union Report on the status of and trends for habitat types and species covered by the Birds and Habitats Directives for the 2007-2012 period as required under Article 17 of the Habitats Directive and Article 12 of the Birds Directive, COM/2015/0219 final.

90 *Supra*. note 7 EU Biodiversity Strategy; Target 2: By 2020, ecosystems and their services are maintained and enhanced by establishing green infrastructure and restoring at least 15% of degraded ecosystems., Target 3 By 2020, the conservation of species and habitats depending on or affected by agriculture and forestry, and the provision of their ecosystem services show measurable improvements.

91 More extensively see R. Moehler "Is there a need for a mid-term review of the 2013 CAP reform" in *The Political Economy of the 2014-2020 CAP, an imperfect storm (J. Swinnen CEPS (ed) Rowman & Littlefield International, 2015*) p. 532-538.

effectiveness. The 2020 assessment report of the conservation status for habitat types & species of community interest to be done on the basis of Member States report (Article 17 of Habitats Directive) could then be a legitimate opportunity to consider the need to review the directives. This timing will also coincide with the evaluation of the progress towards the EU target of halting biodiversity loss by 2020. For now, the Council conclusions[92] and the European Parliament Resolution[93] on the "Mid-term Assessment of the Biodiversity Strategy" set the agenda and the priorities to boost the implementation of these directives and to consolidate a supportive policy framework towards achieving the European and global 2020 headline target for biodiversity, our life insurance, our natural capital.[94]

92 *Supra* note 8.
93 *Supra* note 11.
94 *Supra* note 7.

2.2. BETTER IMPLEMENTATION

CHAPTER 11

TOWARDS MORE EFFECTIVE PROTECTION OF WATER RESOURCES IN EUROPE BY IMPROVING THE IMPLEMENTATION OF THE WATER FRAMEWORK DIRECTIVE AND THE AARHUS CONVENTION IN THE NETHERLANDS

Ernst Plambeck
PhD Student, Utrecht Centre for Water, Oceans and Sustainability Law, Universiteit Utrecht

Lorenzo Squintani
Assistant Professor European and Economic Law, University of Groningen

H.F.M.W. (Marleen) van Rijswick
Professor of European and Dutch Water Law, head of the Utrecht Centre for Water, Oceans and Sustainability Law, Utrecht University

1. INTRODUCTION

The Netherlands is a country that lives on water and has a long and fascinating history of water management. Yet, water quality in the Netherlands is not good,[1] and a recent prediction made by the Netherlands Environmental Assessment

[1] CBS, PBL, Wageningen UR, *Waterkwaliteit KRW, 2015* (indicator 1438, versie 07, 12 januari 2016). www.compendiumvoordeleefomgeving.nl; www.compendiumvoordeleefomgeving.nl/indicatoren/nl1438-Kwaliteit-oppervlaktewater-KRW.html?i=2-76 (Accessed April 2016). See more extensively F.W. van Gaalen e.a., *Waterkwaliteit nu en in de toekomst. Eindrapportage ex ante evaluatie van de Nederlandse plannen voor de Kaderrichtlijn Water*, Den Haag: PBL 2016.

Agency (Planbureau voor de Leefomgeving),[2] shows that by 2027 between 95% and 60% of Dutch waters will not fulfil the standards established under the Water Framework Directive.[3] Clearly, despite longstanding Dutch experience in water management, the effectiveness of implementation of EU Water law can still be improved upon.

In this chapter, we will provide an initial set of recommendations to improve the effectiveness of European water law by way of a better implementation of the substantive requirements of the Water Framework Directive and the procedural requirements of the Water Framework Directive and the Aarhus Convention in the Dutch legal order. Effective environmental policies, as laid down in EU environmental law, require both substantive and procedural elements.[4] Only if both are implemented well can we speak of effective environmental or water legislation and protection.[5]

Indeed, despite the Ministry having repeated its mantra that Dutch water law is in line with the Water Framework Directive[6] part of the ineffectiveness highlighted above can be attributed to the fact that the Dutch implementation of the Directive diverges from the manner in which the Court of Justice of the European Union (ECJ) interprets the Water Framework Directive.[7] Furthermore, shortcomings could derive from the manner in which the Netherlands implements the Aarhus Convention.[8]

In the so-called *Weser* case,[9] rendered in July 2015, the ECJ clarified that the environmental goals established under Article 4 of the Directive are an obligation binding upon each phase of a decision-making process; hence, at the level of plans

2 W. Ligtvoet and others, *Waterkwaliteit en -veiligheid. Balans van de Leefomgeving 2014 – Deel* 6, Den Haag: Planbureau voor de Leefomgeving 2014. See also http://themasites.pbl.nl/balansvandeleefomgeving/2014/waterkwaliteit (accessed April 2016).

3 Directive 2000/60/EC of 23 October 2000 establishing a framework for Community action in the field of water policy [2000] OJ L327/1.

4 See also E.J.H. Plambeck, 'Paradoxes of the EU Regulatory Framework in Water Management: Developing an Assessment Framework to Put the Governance Approach to the Test', *Journal of Water Law* 2015 (24), p. 275, where he equates input-legitimacy with participation and output-legitimacy, or effectiveness with compliance, while compliance falls apart into substantive norm setting and the use of instruments to pursue compliance.

5 See above, S. Maljean-Dubois, 'Introduction. The effectiveness of environmental law: a key topic', p. 3.

6 *Kamerstukken II*, 2015/16, 31 710, nr. 44.

7 H.F.M.W. van Rijswick, *AB* 2015/262; A.A. Freriks and H.F.M.W. van Rijswick, 'Programmatische aanpak stikstof en programmatische aanpak water: van tweeën een?', *TvAR* 2015/9, p. 399–415; F.M. Fleurke, 'Handhaving van Europees Milieurecht: resultaatsverplichtingen op het terrein van lucht en water', *NtEr* 2015/9, p. 284–291; H.F.M.W. van Rijswick and Ch.W. Backes, 'Ground Breaking Landmark Case on Environmental Quality Standards? The Consequences of the CJEU 'Weser-judgment' (C-461/13) for Water Policy and Law and Quality Standards in EU Environmental Law', *JEEPL* 2015/3–4, p. 363–377.

8 Convention on Access to Information, Public Participation in Decision-making and Access to Justice in Environmental Matters, done at Aarhus, Denmark, 25 July 1998.

9 Case C-461/13, *Bund für Umwelt und Naturschutz Deutschland eV v Bundesrepublik Deutschland*, ECLI:EU:C:2015:433 (*Weser*).

and programmes as well at the level of decisions concerning specific projects.[10] There is, therefore, a direct linkage between the environmental goals of the Directive and the decision to authorise or refuse the development of a specific project that would deteriorate the quality of a specific water body covered by the Directive. Moreover, the *Weser* case clarified what 'deteriorating' means under the Directive. Deterioration occurs as soon as the status of at least one of the quality elements, within the meaning of Annex V to the Directive, falls by one class, even if that fall does not result in a fall in classification of the body of surface water as a whole.[11] In light of the one-out-all-out principle, this assessment takes place for each ecological or chemical quality element taken individually.[12] If an affected ecological or chemical quality element is already in the lowest class, any further worsening will qualify as deterioration.

In section 3, we will show that the linkage between the quality objectives under Article 4 of the Directive and the authorization of specific projects is only an indirect one in the Netherlands, i.e. through the medium of the programme of measures adopted for a specific water body. Moreover, we will explain that the binding character of the quality objectives under Article 4 of the Directive is not as clearly formulated as the Directive requires. Consequently, there is too much room for applying a so-called net-loss approach in the Netherlands.[13]

As effective environmental policies require both adequately implemented substantive and procedural elements, we turn to the second shortcoming in Dutch environmental law. This concerns the manner in which the Netherlands has implemented the Aarhus Convention, which is part of the EU environmental acquis.[14] Both the Water Framework Directive and Dutch water and environmental law can be improved, particularly regarding access to justice. The political shortcomings affecting EU law on this issue,[15] do not justify a breach of the Aarhus rights at the national level.[16] In section 4, we will look at the room available for improving both participation and judicial protection under Dutch

---

10 Van Rijswick and Backes (n 7).

11 *Weser* (n 9), paras 69 and 70.

12 Van Rijswick and Backes (n 7).

13 Dutch academics speak of a 'per balance' approach, e.g. Marlon Boeve and Berthy van den Broek, 'The Programmatic Approach; a Flexible and Complex Tool to Achieve Environmental Quality Standards', 2012 (8) *Utrecht Law Review*, 74–85, 78.

14 Article 216(2) TFEU. Case C-244/09, *Lesoochranárske Zoskupenie VLK*, ECLI:EU:C:2011:125 (Zoskupenie). This is an example of mixed agreement, see. J.M.I.J. Zijlmans, *De doorwerking van natuurbeschermingsverdragen in de Europese en Nederlandse rechtsorde*, Den Haag: Sdu Uitgevers 2011, pp. 46; J.H. Jans and H.H.B. Vedder, *European Environmental Law*, Groningen: Europa Law Publishing 2012, pp. 71–74; and E. Hey and H.F.M.W. van Rijswick, 'Transnational watermanagement', in: O. Jansen & B. Schöndorf-Haubold (eds.), *The European Composite Administration*, Antwerpen: Intersentia 2011, p. 240.

15 For the proposal see COM(2003) 624 final. For the withdrawal see [2014] OJ C153/3.

16 L. Squintani and H.F.M.W. van Rijswick, Improving Legal Certainty and Adaptability under the Programmatic Approach, *Journal of Environmental Law*, 2016/3 pp. 443–470.

water and environmental law by juxtaposing the Aarhus Convention to Dutch water and environmental law.

In light of the findings shown in sections 3 and 4, we will formulate a series of recommendations addressed to the Dutch government and Dutch public authorities responsible for the implementation of the Water Framework Directive on how to improve the implementation of the latter in the Netherlands (Section 5). First, however, section 2 will provide an overview of how water management is structured in the Netherlands.

2. THE STRUCTURE OF WATER MANAGEMENT IN THE NETHERLANDS: AN OVERVIEW

As a decentralised unitary state, there are four kind of administrative bodies responsible for water quality policy in the Netherlands. The Ministry of Infrastructure and the Environment and provinces are generic administrative bodies, the regional water authorities are functional decentralized bodies,[17] and *Rijkswaterstaat* (RWS) is the executive agency responsible for implementing the Ministry of Infrastructure and the Environment's policies and regulations, with six national and seven regional divisions.[18] There is a top-down hierarchical relationship between the state, the provinces and the regional water authorities (see figure 1). Municipalities have a relatively small task in water quality management; they are responsible for waste water collection (but not the treatment thereof) and for granting licenses for discharges of polluted waste water on the sewerage system. Nowadays, almost all these discharges have been regulated by means of general rules that replace the requirement of a license.

Figure 1. Administrative structure of the Netherlands with regard to water quality

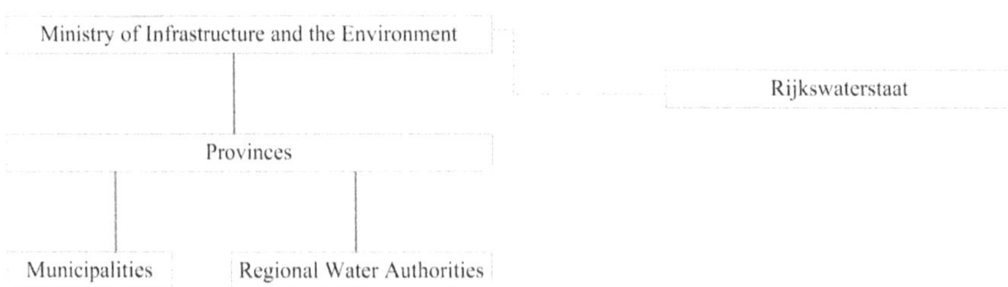

There are twelve provinces, governed by a directly elected Provincial Council (Provinciale Staten) and the Provincial Executive (Gedeputeerde Staten). All

[17] See, on the functional and decentral character of the regional water authorities more extensively, H.F.M.W. van Rijswick and H.J.M. Havekes, *European and Dutch Water Law*, Groningen: Europa Law Publishing, pp. 93–94; pp. 146 ff.

[18] See for more information https://www.rijkswaterstaat.nl/english.

regional water authorities,[19] 22 in total, have a General Council (Algemeen Bestuur) consisting of directly elected members and appointed representatives of several stakeholder groups, and an executive administration (Dagelijks Bestuur).[20]

Figures 2, 3 and 4 show the administrative boundaries within the Netherlands.

Figure 2. Administrative boundaries of the twelve provinces[21]

---

19 See for more information www.dutchwaterauthorities.com.

20 Extensively Van Rijswick and Havekes (n 17), pp. 170 ff.

21 Source: https://simple.wikipedia.org/wiki/Provinces_of_the_Netherlands.

Figure 3. Administrative boundaries of the 22 regional water authorities[22]

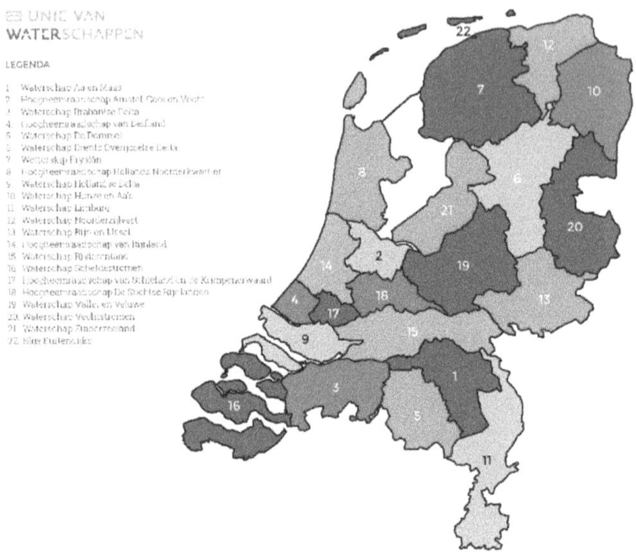

Figure 4. Administrative boundaries of the seven regional divisions of *Rijkswaterstaat*[23]

---

22 Https://nl.wikipedia.org/wiki/Lijst_van_Nederlandse_waterschappen#/media/File:2016-NL-Waterschappen-prov-1250.png.

23 Www.helpdeskwater.nl/publish/pages/36352/rws-regio.png.

With regard to water quality, the main instruments are laid down in the Water Act (*Waterwet*).[24] There are the plans and programmes, laid down in Chapter 4 of the Water Act, and further elaborated upon in Chapter 4 of the Water Decree (*Waterbesluit*). These chapters refer to four kinds of plans: the central government's national water policy plan, regional water policy plans for the sub river basins made by the provinces, the management plans of the Ministry of Infrastructure and the Environment for state waters and the management plans of the regional water authorities for regional waters.[25] These plans and programmes must consist of, among others, the 'river basin management plans' (Art. 13 of the WFD) and 'programmes of measures' (Art. 11 of the WFD). Furthermore, discharges into surface waters are, according to Article 6.2 of the Water Act, prohibited without consent by a permit or by general applicable rules. The general applicable rules are laid down in several Orders of Council, which emanate from central government, or in regional ordinances from the regional water authorities. For specific projects, constructing or modifying a water management structure by or on behalf of a water authority, a decision for the whole project, i.e. a kind of permit with regard to all relevant effects on the water system and its direct environment, is necessary. The *project plan* is laid down in Article 5.4 of the Water Act.

With regard to the judiciary, there is a distinction between civil jurisdiction and administrative jurisdiction in the Netherlands.[26] The Civil Procedures Act (CPA – *Wetboek van Rechtsvordering*) and the General Administrative Law Act (GALA – *Algemene wet bestuursrecht*) contain specific provisions about court competences in civil and administrative cases, as well as on the procedural aspects thereof. With some exceptions, an interested party can contest an appealable decision by a competent authority before the administrative jurisdiction division of a District Court (*rechtbank*). In advance of that, you mainly have to raise objections in a pre-trial proceeding.[27] Appeals against the court's judgment are possible through the Administrative Jurisdiction Division of the Council of State (*Afdeling bestuursrechtspraak van de Raad van State*; ABRvS). If it is not

24 Van Rijswick and Havekes (n 17), pp. 108 ff.

25 *Idem*, pp. 215 ff.

26 See G.T.J.M. Jurgens and F.J. van Ommeren, 'The Public-Private Divide in English and Dutch Law: a Multifunctional and Context-Dependant Divide', *Cambridge Law Journal*, 71(1), March 2012, pp. 172–199, esp. pp. 181 ff. on the distinction between civil and administrative jurisdiction. See for a description of the historical development towards the current court system: R.J.G.H. Seerden and D.W.M. Wenders, 'Administrative Law in the Netherlands', in: R.J.G.H. Seerden (ed.), *Administrative Law of the European Union, its Member States and the United States. A Comparative Analysis*, 3rd edition, Antwerp & Oxford: Intersentia 2012, pp. 131 ff.

27 The main exception is, however, the application of para. 3.4 of the GALA in the preparation of a decision. See more extensively on the substance and requirements of pre-trial proceedings and its relationship with court proceedings, 'Pre-Trial Proceedings in Dutch Administrative Law', in: Ph.M. Langbroek, A. Buijze and M. Remac, *Designing Administrative Pre-Trial Proceedings*, The Hague: Eleven Publishing 2013, pp. 97 ff.

possible to appeal before an administrative judge, appeals can be made to the civil jurisdiction division of a District Court, with the possibility of appeal against its judgment to a Court of Appeal (*gerechtshof*), and for an appeal in cassation to the Supreme Court (*Hoge Raad*).

Some definitions and principles provided in the GALA are particularly important for all administrative procedures in the Netherlands, as well as for decision-making in the field of water quality management, where we focus on in paragraphs 3 and 4. These are listed below.[28]

- An 'administrative authority' is a) an organ of a legal entity which has been established under public law, or b) another person or body which is vested with any public authority (Article 1:1(1) of the GALA);
- an 'order' is a written decision of an administrative authority constituting a public law act (Article 1:3(1) of the GALA);
- an 'administrative decision' is an order which is not of a general nature, including the rejection of an application for such an order (Article 1:3(2) of the GALA), e.g. a water permit; and
- an 'interested party' is a person or legal body whose interests are directly affected by an administrative order (Article 1:2 of the GALA). For example, NGOs can be considered as an interested party, if they look after a specific interest.

3. TOWARDS A BETTER PROGRAMMATIC APPROACH

As indicated in the Introduction, this chapter will focus first on the room available for improving the effectiveness of EU water policy by a sufficient implementation of the Water Framework Directive in the Netherlands. In light of the discussion taking place in the Dutch Parliament on this very issue,[29] we will focus on the main aspects discussed concerning the Dutch implementation of the Directive. First, we will consider the manner in which the quality standards under the Directive have been linked to the authorisation of specific projects (Section 3.1). Second, we will look at the manner in which the Netherlands implements the prohibition of deterioration under Article 4 of the Directive (Section 3.2) and, finally, we will look at the net-loss approach (Section 3.3.).

[28] See further R.J.G.H. Seerden and D.W.M. Wenders, 'Administrative Law in the Netherlands', in: R.J.G.H. Seerden (ed.), *Administrative Law of the European Union, its Member States and the United States. A Comparative Analysis*, 3rd edition, Antwerp & Oxford: Intersentia 2012, pp. 131 ff.

[29] Question of SGP-member Bisschop of 25 September 2015, 2015Z17417; Answered on 12 October 2015, Aanhangsel Handelingen II 2015/16, nr. 273.

3.1. THE LINKAGE BETWEEN QUALITY STANDARDS AND SPECIFIC PROJECTS

The general goal of the Directive is to establish a framework for the protection of inland surface waters, transitional waters, coastal waters and groundwater (Article 1). This general goal is further refined to more specific goals, often placed in a mutual and diffuse relationship.[30] This makes the Directive a complex piece of legislation that is, at times, difficult to grasp – to paraphrase the words of AG Jääskinen.[31] As regards the environmental goals for surface water, Article 4(1)(a) of the Directive establishes that:

(i) Member States shall implement the necessary measures to prevent deterioration of the status of all bodies of surface water, subject to the application of paragraphs 6 and 7 and without prejudice to paragraph 8.
(ii) Member States shall protect, enhance and restore all bodies of surface water, subject to the application of subparagraph (iii) for artificial and heavily modified bodies of water, with the aim of achieving good surface water status at the latest 15 years after the date of entry into force of this Directive, in accordance with the provisions laid down in Annex V, subject to the application of extensions determined in accordance with paragraph 4 and to the application of paragraphs 5, 6 and 7 without prejudice to paragraph 8.
(iii) Member States shall protect and enhance all artificial and heavily modified bodies of water, with the aim of achieving good ecological potential and good surface water chemical status at the latest 15 years from the date of the entry into force of this Directive, in accordance with the provisions laid down in Annex V, subject to the application of extensions determined in accordance with paragraph 4 and to the application of paragraphs 5, 6 and 7 without prejudice to paragraph 8.

These norms do not merely set out the goals of the Directive in a programmatic manner.[32] The Court of Justice did not clarify what it means by a programmatic manner. Squintani and Van Rijswick found that this concept can have different meaning under different EU environmental law directives in 2016.[33] In the broadest of these meanings, EU quality standards are merely long term policy planning objectives, which cannot be used to review the legality of specific decisions, allegedly adopted in breach of such goals. In *Weser*, the Court of Justice made clear that the environmental quality standards, under Article 4 of the Directive, must be respected

30 J.J.H. van Kempen, *Europees waterbeheer: eerlijk zullen we alles delen*, Den Haag: BJu 2012, p. 119–122.
31 Opinion of AG N. Jääskinen of 23 October 2014 in Case C-461/13, *Bund für Umwelt und Naturschutz Deutschland eV v Bundesrepublik Deutschland*, ECLI:EU:C:2014:2324, point 4.
32 *Weser* (n 9), para 43.
33 Squintani and Van Rijswick (n 16).

regardless of the long-term effects of a water plan.[34] They are binding in all phases of the decision making.[35] Furthermore, they must be achieved as regards all water bodies falling under the Water Framework Directive, regardless of whether they have been designated as a protected water body in a national or regional water plan.[36]

In the Netherlands, quality standards for surface water are established in accordance to Chapter 5 of the Environmental Management Act (EMA – *Wet milieubeheer*),[37] as referred to in Article 2.10 of the Water Act.[38] Yet, only the quality standards for the chemical status of water surfaces have been established in accordance with an Order in Council based on Chapter 5 of the EMA (the so-called *Besluit kwaliteitseisen en monitoring water 2009* – Bkmw 2009).[39] No binding provision has implemented the quality standards for the ecological status of surface waters. Some water quality parameters have been established by a group of experts in the so-called '*STOWA-maatlatten*', but this is nothing more than a report with an unclear binding force.[40] It is only a reference framework to be used in the context of monitoring and it is used by Dutch water authorities to motivate their water quality policies. Furthermore, in the Netherlands a distinction is made between designated water bodies as large rivers and lakes and non-designated ones in policies and legislation, although the WFD does not provide for this distinction. With regard to designated water bodies, quality standards, monitoring requirements and general policies all apply. For non-designated water bodies, only the general policies apply.

Another difference between the Water Framework Directive and the Dutch implementation thereof concerns the binding force of the quality standards under the Bkmw 2009. First, it was unclear to what extent it was possible to derogate from the quality standards implementing the Directive for grounds other than those indicated under Article 4 of the Directive. Second, the Dutch government does not consider that quality standards should serve to review the authorization of projects affecting the quality of water bodies covered by the Directive. Of these two differences, only the first one has been deleted. Indeed, as regards the grounds for derogation, the Explanatory Note to the Bkmw 2009 clearly stated that chemical quality standards and ecological standards for certain explicitly designated waters in very good status are binding, and that

34 *Weser* (n 9), para 50.

35 *Weser* (n 9), para. 31.

36 *Weser* (n 9), para 55. See also A.A.H. Smit and others, *Een onmogelijke opgave? Een onderzoek naar de wijze waarop waterschappen invulling geven aan de wateropgaven en de spanningen die zich daarbij voordoen,* Kaderrichtlijn water en Natura 2000, Universiteit Utrecht: Aquaterra Nederland/Leven met water, 2008.

37 *Stb.* 1979, 442, last amended by *Stb.* 2013, 20.

38 *Stb.* 2009, 107, last amended by *Stb.* 2015, 399.

39 *Stb.* 2010, 15, last amended by *Stb.* 2015, 394.

40 D.T. van der Molen and others (eds.), *Referenties en maatlatten voor natuurlijke watertypen voor de Kaderrichtlijn water 2015–2021*, STOWA 2012–31, Utrecht: Stowa 2012. This report is referred to in a Ministerial Decree, the so-called *Regeling monitoring kaderrichtlijn water* (Rmkw), *Stcrt.* 2010, 5615, last amended by *Stb.* 2015, 38398, which, however, does not provide binding force to these parameters as quality standards.

derogations are only possible if they are compatible with those indicated under Article 4 of the Water Framework Directive. However, Article 2.1 of the Bkmw 2009 defined the standards as 'guiding standards' (richtwaarde), from which, in accordance with Article 5.1 of the EMA, it is possible to deviate by means of due motivation.[41] The ambiguity in the formulation of the requirements led to the situation in which several competent authorities considered the quality standards to be not binding.[42] In 2016, with the entry into force of the amended Article 2.1 of the Bkmw 2009, which no longer refers to the term of 'guiding standard', this difference has ceased to exist, although the legal regime is still restricted to chemical quality standards and ecological standards referring to the good status for a small amount of detailed designated water bodies.

As regards the linkage between quality standards and the authorization of specific projects, the Dutch government negates the existence of a direct link.[43, 44] The Dutch Council of State seems to have implicitly accepted this view in 2012.[45] In light of a parliamentary discussion following the *Weser* judgment, the Ministry for Infrastructure and the Environment replied that projects affecting the quality of waters designated under a water plan, 'must be assessed in light of the quality standards', although it is not made clear what these wordings really mean.[46] Indeed, these standards are inserted in the water plans which have less binding force; under Article 6.1a of the Water Decree (*Waterbesluit*) competent authorities must 'take a water plan into account' when granting or refusing a permit. Permits must be refused if the general aims of the Water Act can no longer be achieved and the negative effects cannot be avoided or compensated.[47]

This reasoning fails to take account of the fact that the quality standards in water plans apply only to designated water bodies, which does not cover the

---

41 Additional Explanatory Note to the Bkmw 2009, appendix to *Kamerstukken II* 2009/10, 27 625, nr. 154, p. 6. Cf. J.J.H. van Kempen, *Europees waterbeheer: eerlijk zullen we alles delen*, Den Haag: BJu 2012, p. 131–132, note 93.

42 Ch.W. Backes, A.M. Keesen and H.F.M.W. van Rijswick, *Effectgerichte normen in het omgevingsrecht*, Den Haag: BJu 2012, p. 90–92; H.F.M.W. van Rijswick, 'De betekenis en vormgeving van waterkwaliteitseisen', *M&R* 2007, pp. 395–407; H.E. Woldendorp en M. Thijssen, 'Waterkwaliteitseisen: waterdicht geregeld?', *M&R* 2009, pp. 568–578; H.E. Woldendorp, 'Regulering van de waterkwaliteit: sluitstuk van de implementatie van de Kaderrichtlijn water (I en II)', *BR* 2010, pp. 293–315 and 382–394. Voor de praktijk, zie W.M. Janse and H.F.M.W. van Rijswick, 'De programmatische aanpak in het waterbeheer: een les voor de Omgevingswet?', *M&R* 2012, p. 246.

43 *Kamerstukken II*, 2009–2010, 32 427, nr. 3, p. 3.

44 *Kamerstukken II*, 2015/16, 31 710, nr. 44.

45 ABRvS 8 February 2012 (Waterkrachtcentrale Borgharen), ECLI:NL:RVS:2012:BV3249, paras. 2.21 ff. See also H.J.M. Havekes and H.F.M.W. van Rijswick, *Nederlands waterrecht in Europese context*, Deventer: Kluwer 2014, p. 293.

46 *Kamerstukken II*, 2015/16, 31 710, nr. 44.

47 Article 6.21 in conjunction with Article 2.1 of the Water Act. The management plan for the national waters includes an assessment framework for individual decisions (*Toetsingskader voor individuele besluiten*). The plans of the water managements do not usually include such a framework.

non-designated water bodies that still fall under the Directive.[48] Although water management authorities extend the application of the water quality standards to non-designated water bodies in practice, they lack the legal competence to regulate activities which are not regulated by means of quality standards. This can be problematic in practice. For example, agricultural activities affecting water quality by means of fertilizing activities do not fall under the competence of water management authorities[49] and, hence, the performance of such activities is not subjected to the quality standards. Moreover, an obligation to 'take the quality standards into account' does not carry the same binding force as a requirement 'to act in accordance with' the quality standards. Under Dutch law, when the expression 'take into account' is used in a public law act, derogations are possible.[50] In our case, this would mean that grounds other than those indicated under Article 4 of the Directive could be used to set the quality standards aside and authorise a specific project that would risk the quality of a water body becoming worse. Finally, several human activities do not require a permit to be undertaken, but they simply have to comply with general binding rules.[51] As stated above, there are no general binding rules as regards the ecological quality standards of the Directive. Hence, there is no legal basis to review the legality of the activities undertaken.

3.2. THE MEANING OF THE CONCEPT OF 'NON-DETERIORATION'

As discussed in the previous section, the Directive aims at a good quality status for surface water, unless one of the exceptions under Article 4 apply. The manner to establish this status is provided in the Directive. Indeed, there are two groups of quality elements: the ecological quality and the chemical quality. The ecological element group is further sub-divided in three groups of quality elements: biological elements (water plants and animals), chemical and physicochemical elements (e.g. oxygen and nutrient levels) and hydromorphological elements (water flows and levels; the condition of beds, banks and shores and the continuity of rivers for fish migration), with the latter two sub-categories being supportive of the first one. In

48 It should be added that Best Available Techniques apply as regards the discharge into waters. See, on the arguments against the indirect assessment of quality standards extensively, E.J.H. Plambeck and L. Squintani, 'De bescherming en verbetering van de waterkwaliteit in Nederland, of: hoe vertroebeling niet bijdraagt aan een helder begrip en een juiste implementatie van de KRW', *M en R* 2017/2, pp. 2–14.

49 According to Article 3.84 jo. 3.85 of the Activities Decree (Activiteitenbesluit) there is no room for the competent authority i.e. the water management authority to deviate with 'customised rules' in this case.

50 See also B.A. Beijen (ed.), *Hoofdlijnen milieubestuursrecht*, Den Haag: BJu 2015, p. 83.

51 See A.P.W. Duijkersloot and others, 'Algemeen geregeld, goed geregeld?', *M&R* 2011/167, p. 576–585. The Water Management Authority Rijnland even states that in principle activities are authorised, unless it is proven that they affect water quality, see Water Management Authority Rijnland Toelichting op de Keur Rijnland 2015, p. 1.

turn, each of these sub-groups are composed of specific elements. For example, the biological elements group is composed of a series of elements. These elements are specified for each of the five kinds of water bodies covered by the Directive, i.e. rivers, lakes, transitional waters, coastal waters and artificially and heavily modified surface water bodies. As an example, the biological elements for rivers are: composition and abundance of aquatic flora, the composition and abundance of benthic invertebrate fauna, and composition, abundance and age structure of fish fauna. Each element of the biological elements group can be classified in accordance with one of the following five quality classes: high (H), good (G), moderate (M), poor (P), and bad (B). Chemical and physicochemical elements can only influence status down to 'moderate' and hydromorphological elements down to 'good'. As regards the chemical status, the Water Framework Directive makes use of the quality standards priority substances and/or priority hazardous substances established under the Environmental Quality Standards Directive (Directive 2008/105/EC). Water bodies either comply (good – G – corresponding to gH in a five-stage scale) or not (fail – F – corresponding to an M in a five-stage scale) with this quality standards. The worst of the ecological or chemical elements determines the classification of the quality class for a water body, so-called one-out-all-out principle.[52] Figure 5 provides a visualisation of this system.

Figure 5. The relationship between the qualifications of individual ecological and chemical elements and the qualification of the surface waters status for a whole water body[53]

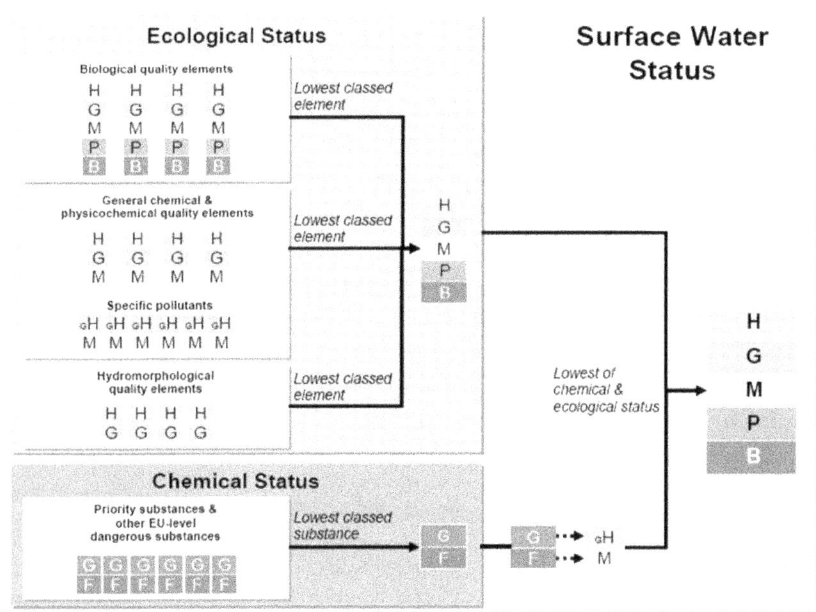

[52] Annex V, points 1.4.2, under i, to the Directive.

[53] Source: www.gov.scot/Publications/2010/03/02155205/4 (accessed Febraury 2017).

The *Weser* judgment makes clear that the prohibition of deterioration under Article 4 of the Directive does not apply at the level of the overall status of surface water quality, i.e. the quality status established at the hand of the worst ecological or chemical group for a water body as a whole. It applies at the level of each sub-element, e.g. an element of the biological quality elements. Therefore, an adverse effect on water quality must be considered as 'deterioration' in the sense of Art. 4 WFD if it deteriorates one quality component to a lower class.

This means that we have to look at the first of the four qualification moments from the perspective of ecological status, i.e. the qualification of a specific element, the qualification of the overall elements sub-group (e.g. biological quality elements), the qualification of the overall ecological status, and the qualification of the overall surface water status.

From the perspective of the chemical status, this means that we have to look at the first of the three qualification moments: the qualification of a specific substance; the qualification of the overall chemical status; and the qualification of the overall surface water status. Deterioration under the Directive occurs when the quality class of any of the elements covered by the ecological or chemical groups is worsened to an extent that it falls to a lower class.[54] When an ecological or chemical element is already at the lowest quality class established for that element, any form of further worsening is a deterioration.

In the Netherlands – but not only in the Netherlands –, there was ample discussion about the meaning of the deterioration ban, and, hence, of its implementation. Some scholars argued that the concept of deterioration applied to the overall quality class, while others argued in favour of an element-by-element approach.[55] Article 16 of the Bkmw 2009 was worded in such a way that it could be read in consistency with the element-by-element approach indicated above. Yet in practice, things were rather different. In the so-called *Nieuwe Meer* judgment, which concerned the ecological elements group, the Dutch Council of State failed to look at each specific element of the ecological elements group.[56] It seems that the Council of State interpreted the Bkmw 2009 as follows: the competent authority could assess the criterion of no deterioration and grant a permission for an activity by only looking at the overall ecological status, hence to the third of the four qualification moments discussed above. As long as the overall status is not deteriorating, the Council of State was of the opinion that a permission can be granted.

---

54 Weser (n 9), paras. 55–70.

55 Y. Uitenboogaart and others (eds.), *Dealing with Complexity and Policy Discretion. A Comparison of the Implementation Process of the European Water Framework Directive in Five Member States*, Den Haag: Sdu uitgevers 2009, pp. 210 ff. for a comparison between different Member States.

56 ABRvS 13 april 2011 (De Nieuwe Meer), ECLI:NL:RVS:2011:BQ1066, r.o. 2.9.7; *M&R* 2011/165 with a commentary by H.F.M.W. van Rijswick; *BR* 2011/138 with a commentary by H.E. Woldendorp.

It is not just the manner in which the Bkmw 2009 has been interpreted that shows a discrepancy between the Directive and its implementation in the Netherlands, regarding the meaning of the non-deterioration concept. The manner in which the quality of water bodies is monitored in the Netherlands also seems problematic from this perspective. Monitoring is of particular importance for determining whether a project will affect the achievement of the quality standards under the Directive.[57] Indeed, despite the silence of the Directive on this point, projections on whether a project will lead to a worsening or deterioration of the water quality of a water body will have to follow the same methodology applied to monitor water quality after that the project has been implemented. This is necessary to ensure that projections are a faithful representation of the changes caused by a specific project to the quality of a water body occurring in practice. The Directive refers to three different kinds of monitoring, i.e. surveillance monitoring, operational monitoring and investigative monitoring.[58] The Court of Justice in *Weser* did not link the concept of non-deterioration to one of these three kinds of monitoring. Yet, given that the operational monitoring aims at assessing any changes in the water status, resulting from the programmes of measures, this seems to be the kind of monitoring that needs to be used to assess whether or not deterioration occurs under the Directive. This means that the monitoring of water quality must happen at the locations and intervals of time indicated for operational monitoring, which differ from those for surveillance monitoring.[59]

In the Netherlands, under the Bkmw 2009, the distinction between surveillance and operational monitoring is not evident. These two kinds of monitoring seem to have been merged.[60] The difference between surveillance and operational monitoring is only made in one of the 'policy' documents referred to in the Ministerial Decree on the establishment of a monitoring programme under the Water Framework Directive (Rmkw),[61] which is based on the Bkmw 2009.[62] This policy document refers to the requirements for the locations and intervals of time prescribed by the Water Framework Directive. Yet, this document only has guiding force, as evincible from its very title, which uses the word *richtlijn* (guideline).[63] There is no legal requirement concerning the responsibility to select a monitoring location. Under the Bkmw 2009, the responsibility for implementing the monitoring programme for surface waters

57 B.A. Beijen, H.F.M.W. van Rijswick and H.T. Anker, The Importance of Monitoring for the Effectiveness of Environmental Directives, A Comparison of Monitoring Obligations in European Environmental Directives. *Utrecht Law Review*, 2014, 10 (2), (pp. 126–135).

58 Article 1.3.1 till 1.3.3 of Annex V to the Directive.

59 Article 1.3.4 of Annex V to the Directive.

60 Explanatory Note to the Bkmw 2009, *Stb.* 2010, 15, p. 72.

61 The Dutch name is '*Richtlijn KRW Monitoring Oppervlaktewater en Protocol Toetsen & Beoordelen*', 2014.

62 *Stcrt.* 2010, 5634, last amended by *Stcrt.* 2015, 38397.

63 Available at www.kaderrichtlijnwater.nl.

rests with the authority that grants the discharge permit under the Water Act.[64] This is problematic for two reasons. First of all, authorities competent for the discharge permit under the Water Act are accustomed to working on the basis of the chemical status. Given that the Directive is based on a mixture of chemical and ecological status, it is unclear how the ecological status is taken into consideration by the authority for the discharge permit. In this respect, we repeat here that the requirements concerning the ecological status are not implemented by means of binding requirements. Hence, although the ecological status is part of the assessment framework for the discharge permit,[65] the specificity of the assessment of the ecological status is unclear. Second of all, the policy document clearly refers to the possibility of *merging* water bodies for the purposes of monitoring. By collecting data at a point at which the water quality of different water bodies merges, it is difficult, if not impossible, to assess the effect that a specific project has on one specific water body, as required under the Directive.

3.3. THE ROOM FOR A NET-LOSS APPROACH[66]

Under a net-loss approach,[67] it is possible to balance the negative effects that one project has on an environmental quality standard with the positive effects that the same project has on a different environmental goal or with the effects that another project or policy measures have on the same environmental goal. While the Water Framework Directive does not explicitedly exclude the possibility of pursuing a net-loss approach, it does severely limit it. Article 4 of the Directive clearly states that deterioration must be prevented, as discussed in section 3.1. According to the Court of Justice in the *Weser* case, this means that:

> *"It follows that, unless a derogation is granted, any deterioration of the status of a body of water must be prevented, irrespective of the longer-term planning provided for by management plans and programmes of measures. The obligation to prevent deterioration of the status of bodies of surface water remains binding at each stage of implementation of Directive 2000/60 and is applicable to every surface water body type and status for which a management plan has or should have been adopted. The Member State concerned is consequently required to refuse authorisation for a project where it is such as to result in deterioration of the status of the body of water concerned or to*

64 Article 14 of the Bkmw 2009.

65 Article 2.1 in conjunction with Article 6.21 of the Water Act.

66 This section provides a summary of what has been written about this topic in Plambeck and Squintani (n 48).

67 Also called 'per balance' approach, Marlon Boeve and Berthy van den Broek, 'The Programmatic Approach; a Flexible and Complex Tool to Achieve Environmental Quality Standards' (2012) 8 *Utrecht Law Review* 74, 78.

> *jeopardise the attainment of good surface water status, unless the view is taken that the project is covered by a derogation under Article 4(7) of the directive.* (para 50)"

The clause '*irrespective of the longer-term planning provided for by management plans and programmes of measures*' used by the Court in this passage makes a linkage between deterioration caused by a project and the effects of a plan or programme of measures. Given the strict interpretation of the concept of non-deterioration, discussed in section 3.2, a net-loss approach between different water bodies and a net-loss approach between different quality elements are excluded.[68]

Still, there seem to be two scenarios for which a net-loss approach is allowed. First of all, the clause '*unless the view is taken that the project is covered by a derogation*' shows that a net-loss approach can be pursued by means of one of the derogation clauses under Article 4 of the Directive. Most relevant for this purpose is the scenario envisaged by Article 4(7) of the Directive, which states:

> "*7. Member States will not be in breach of this Directive when:*
>
> - *failure to achieve good groundwater status, good ecological status or, where relevant, good ecological potential or to prevent deterioration in the status of a body of surface water or groundwater is the result of new modifications to the physical characteristics of a surface water body or alterations to the level of bodies of groundwater, or*
> - *failure to prevent deterioration from high status to good status of a body of surface water is the result of new sustainable human development activities* (...)"

It should be noted that the room for a net-loss approach under this derogation clause is quite limited, given that it only applies to failures due to new modifications to the physical characteristics of a surface water, as in the case of the building of new channels or the strengthening of a dike, or it requires a high status of surface water quality before a new project can be allowed. Moreover, in order to make use of this derogation, Member States must fulfil six cumulative requirements.[69] From these requirements, it appears that Member States must, in particular:

> "*(a) all practicable steps are taken to mitigate the adverse impact on the status of the body of water;* (...)

---

68 This could also be derived from Article 11(5) of the Directive, see also W.M. Janse and H.F.M.W. van Rijswick, 'De programmatische aanpak in het waterbeheer: een les voor de Omgevingswet?', *M&R*, 2012, p. 242–253; H. Sevenster 'Kansarm in Europa?', in: M.N. Boeve and R. Uylenburg (eds.), *Kansen in het omgevingsrecht: opstellen aangeboden aan prof.mr. N.S.J. Koeman*, Groningen: Europa Law Publishing 2010, p. 269.

69 On these requirements see Case C-346/14 European Commission v Republic of Austria ECLI:EU:C:2016:322 (Schwarze Sulm).

(c) the reasons for those modifications or alterations are of overriding public interest and/or the benefits to the environment and to society of achieving the objectives set out in paragraph 1 are outweighed by the benefits of the new modifications or alterations to human health, to the maintenance of human safety or to sustainable development, and
(d) the beneficial objectives served by those modifications or alterations of the water body cannot for reasons of technical feasibility or disproportionate cost be achieved by other means, which are a significantly better environmental option."

These requirements are quite burdensome to meet, especially when they have to be fulfilled by small projects. Hence, in light of the scope of application of this derogation clause, and of the stringency of the conditions for its application, the relevance of this possibility is quite tight.

Secondly, and most relevant, paragraph 50 of the *Weser* judgement suggests that a net-loss approach could be achieved by remaining within the realm of Article 4(1) of the Directive and hence without the need to rely on the derogation clause. Basically, Member States must avoid deterioration from taking place. Primarily, this should occur at project level, i.e. by taking measures aiming at avoiding the negative effects created by the specific project in consideration, given that the Court has explicitly excluded the relevance of the effect of the longer-term planning. This does not mean that the net-loss approach cannot be pursued within the programme of measures itself. Yet, this is, in our opinion, only possible if the programme of measures includes measures aiming at avoiding deterioration coming from the specific project taken into consideration.

Whether the Netherlands implemented the Directive correctly on the issue of the net-loss approach is unclear. The legal framework does not provide sufficient information to establish what kind of net-loss approach is allowed. In the Explanatory Note of the Bkmw 2009, it is indicated that, following the negative advice of the Council of State, a net-loss approach between different water bodies or between different quality elements is not allowed.[70] What is more ambiguous is whether a generic measure in a programme of measures suffices.[71] Moreover, the Dutch implementation mainly links the environmental objectives to the monitoring requirements, instead of implementing them in an independent way. This lack of clarity regarding the monitoring requirements discussed in the section concerning the meaning of the concept of non-deterioration, means that it is difficult to link the status of the water with a specific project. *De facto*, this would allow a net-loss approach.[72] If this is the case, we are of the opinion that the Netherlands does not comply with the Directive.

70 Explanatory Note to the Bkmw 2009, *Stb.* 2010, 15.
71 *Kamerstukken II*, 2015/16, 31 710, nr. 44, p. 9.
72 H.E. Woldendorp, 'Vooruitgang bij 'geen achteruitgang', Het Europese Hof over het vereiste van geen achteruitgang in de Kaderrichtlijn water (zaak C-461/13)', *TOO* 2015/4, p. 479–493.

4. TOWARDS BETTER PARTICIPATION AND JUDICIAL PROTECTION

The shortcomings concerning the implementation of certain substantive standards established by the Directive could be redressed by means of an effective public participation or judicial protection, at least partially. In this section, we will show that, as regards these two procedural aspects, the Netherlands is also still not fully implementing EU law. Substantive shortcomings are piling up on top of procedural shortcomings.

Thanks to the Aarhus Convention, growing amounts of attention are being paid to the participation of the public in the adoption of administrative decisions affecting the environment in the European Union and its Member States. Both the Member States and the European Union are party to this Convention. As the Convention is a mixed agreement, both legal orders are independent from one another and are subjected to the Convention. For the European Union, this means that the provisions of the Convention have a higher rank than EU secondary law.[73] For the Member States, this means that the provisions of the Convention enjoy the same legal force as EU law;[74] hence, they have precedence over conflicting national law provisions.[75] This also occurs as regards those provisions of the Convention that have not yet been implemented by means of EU secondary law.[76] As further discussed below, there are certain provisions of the Convention on public participation (section 4.1) and access to justice (section 4.2) that are relevant in the context of plans and programmes under the Water Framework Directive, which are not yet implemented in EU law.

4.1. PARTICIPATION TO THE DRAFTING OF WATER PLANS AND PROGRAMME OF MEASURES

Participation is one of the three pillars of the Aarhus Convention. Under Article 6 of the Convention, the public has the right to participate in the establishment of decisions on the specific activities mentioned under the Annex to the Convention. Moreover, under Article 7 of the Convention, the public must participate in the decision-making of the plans and programmes that relate to the environment. The participation process shall ensure the following:[77]

73 Article 216(2) TFEU. See also e.g. Case 104/81 Kupferberg, ECLI:EU:C:1982:362; and Case C-344/04, IATA and ELFAA, ECLI:EU:C:2006:10, paras. 35 and 36.
74 Zijlmans (n 14), p. 45.
75 Idem, p. 49.
76 Zoskupenie (n 14).
77 Article 6 (3, 4 and 8) of the Aarhus Convention.

a. The public participation procedures shall include reasonable time-frames for the different phases, allowing sufficient time for informing the public in accordance with paragraph 2 above and for the public to prepare and participate effectively during the environmental decision-making.
b. Each Party shall provide for early public participation, when all options are open and effective public participation can take place.
c. Each Party shall ensure that, in the decision, due account is taken of the outcome of the public participation.

While Article 2 of the Convention defines the 'public' as one or more natural or legal persons and, in accordance with national legislation or practice, their associations, organizations or groups, the concepts of 'plan' and 'programme' are not defined. Still these concepts are formulated in broad terms and seems to cover all plans and programmes made by a public body, regardless of whether they have binding force under national law.[78] If a plan or programme has a regulatory rather than a strategic character and it covers specific activities, it can be qualified as an Article-6 decision, rather than an Article-7 decision.[79]

The requirements of the Aarhus Convention seem to have been correctly implemented in the Water Framework Directive. Article 14 of the Directive has been drafted in advance of the participation of the European Union to the Convention, which finally took place in 2005.[80] Article 14 states:

> "(...) *Member States shall ensure that, for each river basin district, they publish and make available for comments to the public, including users:*
>
> *(a) a timetable and work programme for the production of the plan, including a statement of the consultation measures to be taken, at least three years before the beginning of the period to which the plan refers;*
> *(b) an interim overview of the significant water management issues identified in the river basin, at least two years before the beginning of the period to which the plan refers;*
> *(c) draft copies of the river basin management plan, at least one year before the beginning of the period to which the plan refers.* (...)"

Under this provision, there are three participation moments, which can begin as early as three years before the beginning of the period to which the plan refers. Given that during the preparation of a draft plan competent authorities

78 United Nations Economic Commission for Europe, *The Aarhus Convention: An implementation guide*, second edition 2014, p. 173 stating that plan and programmes have legal value in only some of the legal orders of the Convention parties.

79 L. Squintani and E.J.H. Plambeck, 'Judicial protection against plans and programmes affecting the environment. A backdoor solution to get an answer from Luxembourg', *JEEPL* 2016/3–4, p. 294–324, with further references.

80 Decision 2005/370/EC [2005] OJ L 124/1.

can already make some policy choices, and hence exclude some options, this approach maximizes the chances that participation takes place at a moment at which all options are available. Accordingly, it contributes to the effectiveness of the public participation rights.[81]

In the Netherlands, the duty to ensure public participation in the establishment of water plans has been implemented in two different manners. First of all, draft plans are subjected to the so-called 'public preparatory procedure' (*uniforme openbare voorbereidingsprocedure*), regulated under Division 3.4 of the GALA.[82] This procedure has two shortcomings. First, the participation procedure is required only after the draft plan has been published. Hence, it could be that certain options are already off the table. Paradoxically, the rounds of (structured) informal public participation that public authorities usually undertake, without these being regulated under a legal provision,[83] increase the chances that the official public participation procedure occurs when some options are already off the table.[84] Second, Article 6:13 of the GALA precludes the possibility to start a judicial review procedure if the claimant failed to participate in the uniform public preparatory procedure.[85] This rule shows that the uniform public preparatory procedure is part of the Dutch system for solving conflicts between the public and public authorities. Basically, it equates the uniform public preparatory procedure with an administrative review procedure. Hence, the uniform public preparatory procedure, rather than representing a means of cooperation between the public and competent authorities, it involves or is characterized by conflict or opposition between the public and the competent authorities. It is unclear whether the

---

81 J. Adshead, 'Public participation, the Aarhus Convention and the Water Framework Directive', *Journal of Water Law*, 2006/17, pp. 185 ff.; W. Howarth, 'Aspirations and Realities under the Water Framework Directive: Proceduralisation, Participation and Practicalities', *Journal of Environmental Law* 2009/3, p. 391–417.

82 See Article 4.1(1) of the Water Decree for national plans. Water plans made by the Provinces can be subjected to the same procedure, e.g. Water Regulation of the Province of Zuid-Holland, Water Regulation of the Province of Gelderland, Water Regulation of the Province of Zeeland, Water Regulation of the Province of Noord-Holland, Water Regulation of the Province of Fryslân. See also E.J.H. Plambeck, *Legitimiteit en effectiviteit in het Nederlandse zoetwaterbeleid: het stakeholders' perspectief*, scriptie Universiteit Utrecht, p. 56–58, available at www.uu.nl/ucwosl.

83 See e.g. Code Interbestuurlijke verhoudingen, allowing decentralised auhtorities the possibility to express their opinion. If this possibility is used, interested parties and NGOs are allowed to express their opinions as well.

84 See also B.J. Schueler, 'Wat doen we met de inspraak?', *M&R* 2014/49, p. 239; and A. van den Broek e.a., *Niet buiten de burger rekenen!*, Den Haag: SCP 2016, p. 58–59.

85 The Dutch Council of State has concluded that 6.13 of the GALA is as such in accordance with the Arhus Convention as implemented in the EIA Directive, failing however to appreciate the fundamental difference between a public participation procedure and administrative review procedure, see ABRvS 2 December 2015, ECLI:NL:RVS:2015:3703 paras 21(1–10). See also Ch.W. Backes in his annotation under Case C-137/14, Commission v. Germany, ECLI:EU:C:2015:683: *AB* 2015/447, where he focuses on the case law based on 6:13 GALA restricting an appeal to the arguments a claimant have put forward in the uniform public preparatory procedure is not in line with Directive 2003/35.

adversarial nature of the uniform public preparatory procedure affects the whole, or only part, of the public participation procedure. Neither the Convention nor its implementation under the Directive seems to allow room for equating public participation to administrative review, not even partially. All in all, we are of the opinion that this procedure does not ensure an effective participation, as required under the Directive and the Aarhus Convention.

That alongside the public preparatory procedure, the Netherlands has basically copied Article 14 of the Directive into its Water Decree (Article 4.3 of the Decree) is something that is welcomed. Hence, two extra participation rounds need to be organised. This solves parts of the shortcomings just discussed. Yet, political science studies show that public participation in the Netherlands cannot be considered to have been effective as regards the drafting of the first water plans under the Directive, despite the Commission's positive evaluation on this matter.[86] The main problem seems to be that the public does not have a chance to outweigh the position of those stakeholders, in particular of agriculture and business lobby groups, who take part in the participation rounds at a level which is closer to the decision-maker than the general public.[87] This study confirms a more general trend by which lowly-educated parts of society are not as capable of participating in such a public participation procedure as effectively as highly educated parts of society are, under equal circumstances.[88] This means that in the Netherlands, only certain parts of the public enjoy effective public participation.[89]

4.2. ACCESS TO JUSTICE TO CHALLENGE THE VALIDITY OF WATER PLANS AND PROGRAMME OF MEASURES[90]

In order to ensure the effectiveness of the participation rights, Article 9(2 and 3) of the Aarhus Convention regulates the right to access to justice. Article 9(2) of the Convention applies to Article-6 decisions and, if the parties to the Convention so

86 J. van der Heijden and E. ten Heuvelhof, 'Coping with Mandated Public Participation: The Case of Implementing the EU Water Framework Directive in the Netherlands', *Perspectives on European Politics and Society*, (2013) 14:4, pp. 403–417 and the literature therein referred. This study does not clarify the distinction between formal and informal decision making procedures. The study states that *de jure* the Netherlands comply with the Directive. Yet, this statement is not based on a legal analysis.

87 Ibidem.

88 A. van den Broek and others, *Niet buiten de burger rekenen!*, Den Haag: SCP 2016, pp. 55–61, with further references, in particular, M. Bovens & A. Wille, *Diploma democracy. On the tensions between meritocracy and democracy*, Leiden/Utrecht: Nederlandse Organisatie voor Wetenschappelijk Onderzoek 2009.

89 See further L. Squintani, The Aarhus Paradox: Time to Speak about Equal Opportunities in Environmental Governance, *JEEPL* 2017/1, pp. 3–5.

90 This section offers a summary of what has been written in Squintani and Plambeck (n 79).

decide, to other kinds of acts.[91] Article 9(3) of the Convention applies to Article 7 decisions as established by the Aarhus Convention Compliance Committee (ACCC) in, among others, the *Belgium* and *Armenia* decisions.[92] The position of the ACCC is understandable considering the role that judicial protection has in ensuring the effectiveness of public participation.[93] The Court of Justice also interprets the Aarhus Convention on the basis of a teleological interpretation aiming at ensuring the effectiveness of the Convention.[94] Hence, it can be expected that the Court of Justice will not follow a different interpretation on this issue than the one given by the ACCC. In the field of air quality law, the Court of Justice has already established that parties affected by air quality must be able to challenge the (lack of a) plan, although it did not refer to the Aarhus Convention.[95]

The Water Framework Directive is completely silent on this issue. In light of the Aarhus Convention, and the manner in which the Court of Justice approaches this issue in the context of air quality law, it can be expected that in the field of the Water Framework Directive interested parties should be able to challenge a water plan as well. Still, Member States should set aside their reservations about

---

91 The use of this option will be considered gold-plating, a phenomenon more and more in disuse in the last decade, On this phenomenon, its use in practice, with particular focus on the Netherlands see, e.g. L. Squintani, Gold-plating of European Environmental Law (diss., Groningen) 2013; H.T. Anker and others., Coping with EU environmental legislation: transposition principles and practices, Journal of Environmental Law 2015 (1), p. 17; J.H. Jans, L. Squintani with others, 'Gold Plating' of European Environmental Measures?, jeepl 2009 (4), pp. 417, 418; and L. Squintani, M. Holwerda and K.J. de Graaf, Regulating greenhouse gas emissions from EU ETS installations: What room is left for the member States, in M. Peeters, M. Stallworthy and J. de Cedra de Larragán, *Climate Law in EU Member States*, Cheltenham: Edwin Edgar, 2012, pp. 67–88.

92 United Nations Economic Commission for Europe, *The Aarhus Convention: An implementation guide*, second edition 2014, pp. 173 and 193. See also Aarhus Convention Compliance Committee, Belgium, ACCC/C/2005/11; ECE/ MP.PP/C.1/2006/4/Add.2, 28 July 2006, para. 31; and Armenia, ACCC/C/2004/8; ECE/MP.PP/C.1/2006/2/Add.1, 10 May 2006, r.o. 28–38, in particular paras 35 and 36. See also J. Jendrośka and S. Stec, 'The Aarhus Convention: Towards a New Era in Environmental Democracy', *Environmental Liability Journal* 2006/5, p. 150; and H. Lang, *Public Participation in Environmental Decision-Making in China*, (diss.) Groningen 2014, p. 73. Cf. J. Jendroska, 'Public Participation in Environmental Decision-Making', in M. Pallemaerts (ed), *The Aarhus Convention at Ten*, Groningen: Europa Law Publishing 2011, p. 91–148.

93 United Nations Economic Commission for Europe, *The Aarhus Convention: An implementation guide*, second edition 2014, p. 187. For a recent overview of the literature on this topic, Lang (n 91), Chapter 3 and Jendrośka, (n 59) J. Jendrośka, Public Participation under Article 6 of the Aarhus Convention: Role in Tiered Decision-Making and Scope of Application, in: G. Bándi (ed.), *Environmental Democracy and Law. Public Participation in Europe*, Groningen: Europa Law Pubishing 2014, pp. 113–138, pp. 113–138.

94 E.g. *Zoskupenie* (n 14).

95 Joined cases C-165 to 167/09 Stichting Natuur en Milieu and Others v College van Gedeputeerde Staten van Groningen (C-165/09) and College van Gedeputeerde Staten van Zuid-Holland (C-166/09 and C-167/09), ECLI:EU:C:2011:348, 100 (RWE).

the inclusion of Article 9(3) of the Convention into EU secondary law,[96] and the Directive should be made more explicit on this point.

In the Netherlands, it is not possible to challenge the regulation that sets the environmental quality standards, nor a water plan or water management plan or other policy documents or guidelines before the administrative judge.[97] This is due to the character of environmental standards, laid down in general binding rules and the lack of binding force of plans and policy documents and guidelines which leads to a lack of legal effect or legal consequences.[98] The only way to address these general binding rules, plans and policies before the administrative judge is to have them discussed when challenging an individual decision that can be challenged before the administrative courts. With the adoption of the Bkmw 2009, the Council of State had advised the government to allow administrative review of water plans.[99] The government was ready to take this possibility into account, but this required an act of parliament.[100] No such act has been adopted yet and private law does not seem capable of filling this lacuna. In the Netherlands, generally an action based on tort law with regard to the general binding rules, plans and policies is possible. However, as indicated by the Council of State, such an action is not a desirable alternative with regard to plans.[101] This is understandable considering that an action against a water plan based on tort has little if any chance of success nor would it be clear what remedies should be asked for.[102] The requirement of a causal link between the damage and the unlawful water plan seems a difficult to realized. It is the realization of the project in light of the plan that causes the damage, not the plan itself.[103] In conclusion, Dutch law does not seem to be compatible with the Aarhus Convention on this point.

96 The withdrawal of the Commission's proposal for a (partial) implementation of Article 9(3) Aarhus Convention mentioned at note 13 is emblematic to this extent. See also M. Eliantonio, *Collective Redress in Environmental Matters in the EU: A Role Model or a "Problem Child"?*, *Legal Issues of Economic Integration* 41, no. 3 (2014): 257–274.

97 Article 8:5 i.c.w. Article 1 of Annex 2 to the GALA. See also ABRvS 27 January 2016, ECLI:NL:RVS:2016:152.

98 Havekes and Van Rijswick (n 45), p. 186.

99 Additional Explanatory Note to the Bkmw 2009, appendix to *Kamerstukken II* 2009/10, 27 625, nr. 154, p. 7.

100 Ibidem.

101 Ibidem.

102 L. Di Bella, *De toepassing van de vereisten van causaliteit, relativiteit en toerekening bij de onrechtmatige overheidsdaad*, Leiden: E.M. Meijers Instituut 2014. See also M.G. Faure e.a., Milieuaansprakelijkheid goed geregeld?, The Hague: Boom Juridische Uitgevers 2010. As regards NGOs, see United Nations Economic Commission for Europe, Task Force on Access to Justice, Study on the Possibilities for Non-Governmental Organisations Promoting Environmental Protection to Claim Damages in Relation to the Environment in Four Selected Countries, France, Italy, the Netherlands and Portugal, Unedited informal document, 2015; and M.G. Faure and others, Milieuaansprakelijkheid goed geregeld?, The Hague: BJuU 2010.

103 In other words, it cannot be excluded that the damage would have occurred even if the plan was legal, L. Di Bella, *De toepassing van de vereisten van causaliteit, relativiteit en toerekening bij de onrechtmatige overheidsdaad*, Leiden: E.M. Meijers Instituut 2014, Hoofdstuk 3. See also G.M.

5. CONCLUSIONS

It cannot be contested that Dutch waters do not meet all of the Water Framework Directive's requirements from either a chemical or, mainly, from an ecological perspective. As indicated in the introduction to this chapter, projections do not show a significant improvement that is capable of bringing Dutch waters in line with EU water standards within the agreed upon deadline. In light of the discussion of the Dutch implementation of the Water Framework Directive, examined in sections 2 to 4, it cannot be denied that Dutch water law is responsible for such a finding, at least partially. Put boldly, Dutch water law affects the effectiveness of the Water Framework Directive. Indeed, in section 3 we showed that the Dutch implementation of the Water Framework Directive can be improved as regards several aspects covered by the Directive.

The most important one is the manner in which the quality standards for ecological elements are enclosed within the Dutch legal framework. At the moment of writing this contribution, they are not inserted in a legally binding document, but only in plans which are binding only upon the authorities that have established the plan. The quality standards for the ecological status of waters do not cover all water bodies covered by the directive and cannot be enforced as regards several human activities affecting water quality, such as agriculture. This issue is exacerbated by the fact that in the Netherlands several human activities do not require a permit to be undertaken. Hence, even when such activities fall under the jurisdiction of a competent authority, which has included the ecological quality standards in its water plan, deterioration cannot be prevented.

Another major finding was that, until January 2016, the meaning of the prohibition of non-deterioration was unclear. Although the Minister intended, since the very beginning, to follow an element-by-element approach in applying this prohibition, the way in which the legal rule was framed led to a situation in which public authorities applied this prohibition at the level of overall surface water status.

Finally, monitoring guidelines – there is no binding requirement on all types of monitoring required by the Water Framework Directive – do not ensure that the competent authorities are able to link changes in water quality to specific projects or measures.

In light of the above, no one should be surprised by the quality of Dutch waters being what it is today. The clarity, brought in 2016 as regards the meaning of the non-deterioration prohibition is welcome, but more needs to be done.

The quality standards for ecological elements should be inserted in general binding rules and each authority, charged with scrutinizing human activities affecting the quality of all water bodies in the Netherlands covered by the Directive,

van den Broek and M.K.G. Tjepkema, *De reikwijdte en rechtsgrondslag van nadeelcompensatie in het omgevingsrecht* (preadvies Vereniging voor Bouwrecht), IBR 2015, p. 33–47.

should be obliged to apply these standards in their permitting and enforcement activities. Monitoring requirements should be binding and shaped in such a manner that it is possible to link a variation in the quality of a water body with a specific project. Both amendments concern acts that are adopted by the executive power, i.e. the Bkmw 2009 and the Ministerial Decree on the establishment of a monitoring programme under the Water Framework Directive. Accordingly, there is no need of an Act of Parliament to improve these two aspects of Dutch water law.

Alongside the shortcomings regarding the implementation of the Water Framework Directive, the analysis performed in section 4 highlights shortcomings in the implementation of the Aarhus Convention. Indeed, what is worst about the Dutch implementation of the Directive is that the general public seems to have been kept at a distance in the management of water bodies.

We recognize that public authorities organise informal and formal rounds of public participation, with the latter taking place in line with the Directive. Yet, the manner in which informal rounds of participation take place is unclear. The effects that the informal rounds of participation have on the formal round of participation are also unclear. Given that only the latter serves to implement the Directive and the Aarhus Convention, it is therefore unclear whether Dutch law complies with the Convention. The studies showing that only certain stakeholders can effectively take part in the decision-making process suggests that this is not the case. In general, as far as we could see, there are no mechanisms that allow lowly-educated groups of the public to participate in the decision-making process as effectively as highly-educated groups of the public or formal stakeholder associations can.

Alongside the shortcomings in the system for public participation, we have highlighted the lack of a system for judicial protection as regards regulations (including the quality standards for example), and mainly plans and programmes. Access to justice, to challenge the validity of water plans as such, is indeed impossible via the administrative courts and basically useless via the civil courts. The finding that EU law does not yet implement the Aarhus Convention provisions on access to justice, as regards plans and programmes, at least not explicitly, cannot serve as an excuse for the Netherlands not to assure judicial protection.

Dutch law should be amended on both issues. First, the relationship between the informal participation rounds and the formal participation procedure should be clarified. Legal certainty in the implementation of EU rights, which include the Aarhus rights, dictates the establishment of a legal basis for the informal rounds of participation. Essentially, they have to become formal. Moreover, they must be shaped in such a way that the public, and all the sectors therein, can participate effectively. Here, more attention should be paid to the position of the lowly-educated groups in society. More research on this issue should be financed and performed in order to develop mechanisms that ensure equality between various groups of the public when it comes to effective public participation. Finally, a judicial procedure should be developed to allow for the review of plans and programmes. This can occur by means of an *ad hoc* procedure. Given that the obligation to allow for judicial review of plan and programmes applies as regards all plans and programmes relevant for the environment, which may include land-use and regional development strategies and sectoral planning in transport, tourism, energy, heavy and light industries, water resources, health and sanitation, etc., at all levels of government, this *ad hoc* procedure should be regulated under an environmental act of general application, such as is a done at present by the EMA and will be done by the Environmental and Planning Act in the future. It could also be inserted into the GALA, but must be phrased in such a way to be limited to plan and programmes related to the environment. Under such a procedure, no linkage should be made between the participation in the public participation procedures and access to justice.

CHAPTER 12

ENVIRONMENTAL INSPECTORS AND PUBLIC PROSECUTORS

Is Sharing Information Always Useful?

Carole M. Billiet

Research director Center for Environmental and Energy Law, UGent

Brussels Bar, partner Equal Partners

Sandra Rousseau

Associate Professor, KU Leuven, CEDON

ABSTRACT

In this contribution, we focus on the communication between environmental inspectors and public prosecutors. We model the interaction between both enforcement actors using a sender-receiver model that incorporates the cost factor and the objectives function. The model allows us to identify possibilities by which to optimize the information exchange at this crucial stage of the enforcement chain. We comment on the increasing specialization of public prosecutors in Europe, and in other countries, on the crucial role of effectively written notices of violation and on the issue of strategic information sharing.

"The single biggest problem in communication is
the illusion that it has taken place"
George Bernard Shaw

1. INTRODUCTION

1. Environmental law enforcement is a responsibility shared by a variety of actors. Consequently, many formal and informal interactions between different enforcement actors occur. Police forces, specialized inspectorates, public prosecutors, criminal courts and administrative courts all play a role within countries' environmental administrations. Collaboration between countries is a necessity in the fight against organized crime, cross-border pollution and illegal waste transports.

In this study[1], we focus on the interaction between environmental inspectors and public prosecutors, specifically the communication of information on environmental offences by the inspectors to the prosecution. This interaction is crucial for the enforcement chain and, thus, for environmental policy at large. It triggers the sanctioning process within the criminal sanctioning track. Criminal sanctioning comprises the hard core of law enforcement, next to administrative and civil sanctioning.

The so-called Eco-Crime Directive[2], which had to be implemented by the end of 2010[3], has secured the possibility of criminal sanctioning for the enforcement of serious environmental offences in each EU Member State, whatever its legal tradition in the sanctioning of offences at large and in environmental offences more specifically.[4]

2. We look at the information exchange that occurs when environmental inspectors communicate official records of offences detected while performing

---

1 We closed our source material research on 21 April 2016.

2 Directive 2008/99/EC on the protection of the environment through criminal law (OJ 2008 L 328/28).

3 The deadline for EU Member States to transpose the directive was 26 December 2010 (Art. 8.1 Directive).

4 The twenty-eight Member States display quite some differences in their legal traditions regarding the sanctioning of environmental crimes. Some countries, such as the United Kingdom (UK) and Belgium, used to have sanctioning systems in which the criminal sanctioning track dominated. Many other countries were equipped with sanctioning systems where the administrative track dominated. A recent comparative law overview, for the actual equilibriums in between criminal and administrative sanctioning, can be found on the webpage of the European Commission's DG Justice, in the national reports of Member States on the implementation of the Eco-Crime Directive under the heading "*2. National framework for transposition and implementation of Directive 2008/99/EC*" especially its subdivision "*2.2. Relation between the administrative and sanction systems*". See http://ec.europa.eu/justice/criminal/criminal-law-policy/environmental-protection/index_en.htm, last consulted 21 April 2016. Most of the national reports have been published. For the time being the national reports of the following eight countries are withheld: Bulgaria, Czech Republic, France, Germany, Hungary, Romania, Spain and Sweden. Worth mentioning in appraising the relevance of the criminal sanctioning track is that, today, legal persons can be held criminally liable for environmental crimes in most Member States. The exceptions are Bulgaria, Germany, Greece, Latvia and Sweden. See *G. Vermeulen, W. De Bondt & C. Ryckman*, Liability of legal persons for offences in the EU, 2012, 33-35 and 79-84, as completed by the aforementioned national reports of Denmark, Estonia, Finland, Ireland, Italy, Lithuania, Malta, Poland, Portugal and Slovenia. For Spain, see additionally: www.gccapitalideas.com/2013/01/31/criminal-liability-of-companies-under-spanish-law-what-is-the-real-impact-on-directors-officers-coverage/. This state of affairs matters all the more in view of the fact that several EU Member States have not introduced administrative liability of legal persons for offences. In 2012, these Member States were Austria, France, Hungary, Ireland, Italy, Poland, Slovakia and Slovenia. – *Vermeulen, De Bondt & Ryckman*, *supra*, 35-37.

compliance monitoring duties. In most European countries, and in many other countries besides, the environmental case load of public prosecutors is mainly built up through such official records from inspectorates and police forces with a little more extensive or a highly developed level of specialization in environmental compliance monitoring. A factor contributing to this in EU Member States is the rather recent and growing amount of EU legislation on environmental inspections.[5] In this chapter, we use the term 'environmental inspector', shortened to 'inspector', for each public officer in charge of compliance monitoring, including environmental compliance monitoring, regardless of their specialization level.[6] Whenever an inspector's official record of an environmental offence – a notice of violation – reaches the public prosecutor's office, a file is opened.

Our interest in the communication process lies in the public prosecutor. While inspectors, as well as prosecutors, are obviously elemental in the information exchange, the prosecutor deserves our attention for his pivotal position in the sanctioning system. He has a bridging function between criminals, police forces, specialized inspectorates, criminal courts and possibly also administrative fining authorities. Before reaching the courtroom, and having to convince the court to convict, he decides whom to prosecute, when to settle, when to dismiss the case and, in some legal systems, when to transmit the case to administrative fining

5 This EU-legislation builds on Recommendation 2001/331/EC providing for minimum criteria for environmental inspections in the Member States (OJ 2001 L 118/41). It stimulates the development of specialization in environmental compliance monitoring. Today, legislative provisions imposing minimum standards on environmental inspections carried out by national authorities are stipulated in major pieces of EU environmental legislation such as Directive 2010/75/EU on industrial emissions (integrated pollution prevention and control) (recast) (OJ 2010 L 334/17) (Article 23) and several waste management legislations including Directive 2008/98/EC on waste and repealing certain Directives (OJ 2008 L 312/3) (Articles 34-35), Directive 2006/21/EC on the management of waste from extractive industries and amending Directive 2004/35 (OJ 2006 L 102/15) (Article 17), Directive 2012/19/EU on waste electrical and electronic equipment (WEEE) (OJ 2012 L 197/38) (Article 23) and Regulation (EC) 660/2014 amending Regulation (EC) 1013/2006 on shipments of waste (OJ 2014 L 189/135) (Article 1.3 amending Article 50 of Regulation (EC) 1013/2006). See also the following EU Directives and Regulations: Directive 2012/18/EU on the control of major-accident hazards involving dangerous substances, amending and subsequently repealing Council Directive 96/82/EC (OJ 2012 L 197/1) ('Seveso III'), Article 20; Regulation (EC) 1005/2009 on substances that deplete the ozone layer (OJ 2009 L 286/1), Article 28; Directive 2009/31/EC on the geological storage of carbon dioxide and amending various directives (OJ 2009 L 140/114), Article 15; Directive 2010/63/EU on the protection of animals used for scientific purposes (OJ 2010 L 276/33), Articles 34 and 35; Directive 2009/71/Euratom establishing a Community framework for the nuclear safety of nuclear installations (OJ 2009 L 172/18), Articles 4 and 5, as amended by Directive 2014/87/Euratom (OJ 2014 L 219/42).

6 Thus, for instance, public officers working at specialized environmental inspectorates whose only task consists of environmental inspections, public officers working at customs who monitor waste and wildlife trafficking but also other kinds of crime such as the smuggling of narcotics, and public officers who are part of local police forces in charge of general compliance monitoring, including the occasional waste littering and noise hindrance.

authorities.[7] It is no exaggeration to state, with Rasmusen, Raghav & Ramseyer, that his role "*is one of the most important in criminal justice.*"[8]

We want to get a better understanding of the information exchange happening when a notice of violation, sent by an environmental inspector, reaches a public prosecutor. What exactly is happening in terms of information sharing? Is there any room for the optimization of this crucial communication process? If so, what could it be and why?[9]

3. There is reason to raise these questions.

At first glance, it seems evident that the information sharing between those two actors in the enforcement chain leads to better environmental law enforcement. However, it is important to realize that information sharing between different enforcement actors does not automatically lead to beneficial communication. The cost of information sharing and the objectives pursued by the information senders and receivers, interfere with the communication process. If information sharing is costless, and every party involved shares the same goals, communication is indeed beneficial and everyone will be at least as well off with as without it. However, if information sharing is costly for the sender or for the receiver, this will have a

7 The aforementioned national reports on the implementation of the Eco-Crime Directive give some information on the role of the public prosecutor in the criminal procedure of the EU Member States, most often focussed on the prosecution decision. *Supra* note 4. For more extensive information, detailing the full set of decisions a prosecutor can make and the powers of criminal investigation he has, we refer to comparative legal literature. See for instance *F. Verbruggen & V. Franssen* (eds.), The International Encyclopaedia for Criminal Law, Kluwer Law International, loose-leaf, with recent monographies for a.o. Croatia, Denmark, Finland, Hungary, Italy, Portugal and Spain.

8 *E. Rasmusen, M. Raghav & M. Ramseyer*, Convictions versus Conviction Rates: the Prosecutor's Choice, American Law and Economics Review 2009, (47) p. 48.

9 Our research setting presupposes that the monitoring of environmental compliance, on the one hand, and the prosecution of offences detected, on the other, are tasks performed by distinct public officials, belonging to distinct public entities. Because of the specificity of both tasks, this situation is standard. Exceptions exist, as a rule limited to specific offences. In Norway, for instance, the National Authority for Investigation and Prosecution of Economic and Environmental Crime (ØKOKRIM), set up in 1989, can investigate as well as prosecute environmental crimes. ØKOKRIM, however, specializes in "*the bigger and more complex cases and cases that involve the public interest*", leaving more general compliance monitoring to the local police and environmental agencies – *L. Lavrysen & L. De Geyter*, Summary Report of the Questionnaire – Organization of the courts and tribunals and prosecution policy in the area of environmental crime, EUFJE Annual Conference 2007, p.10, unpublished. See also *H.C. Bugge*, Norway, in *K. Deketelaere* (ed.), The International Encyclopaedia of Environmental Law, Kluwer Law International, loose-leaf, 2004, n° 806. The utility of ØKOKRIM partly stems from the fact that legal persons can be held criminally liable in the country. *Id.*, n° 808.
The fact, however, that environmental inspectors and public prosecutors belong to one same administrative body does not as such imply that the communication issue that we study does not exist. Indeed, the internal organization of this administrative body can confine both tasks to well separated units. Thus, for instance, the Environmental Agency of England and Wales (UK). See the National Report for the U.K., mentioned *supra* note 4, p. 11. Its team of environmental prosecutors, regrouped in the Legal Services unit, does not perform environmental compliance monitoring and inspections.

negative effect on the willingness of some parties to communicate. Moreover, if parties pursue different goals, potential difficulties may arise. Each party has the incentive to only share that type of information that helps in attaining their own objective and, possibly, not the objectives of the other parties.[10]

In this regard, it should be pointed out that the drafting and the reading of notices of violation come at a cost.[11] Depending on the case, this cost factor can be relatively light to very heavy, for the senders, the environmental inspectorates, and the receivers, the public prosecutors. Think, for instance, of a case with a single suspect who admitted he was the one killing a badger last Monday and compare this to a toxic waste fraud case committed bit by bit over months, in several places and involving several perpetrators who are partly denying their involvement. The cost of information sharing is definitely a factor in the communication between environmental inspectors and public prosecutors.

Furthermore, there are theoretical insights and empirical findings on the objectives of public prosecutors that allow us to wonder if their goals and the goals of the environmental inspectors are the same, even if it is doubtless that some overlap in objectives exists.

A decision to prosecute a case automatically implies that resources need to be dedicated to preparing that case and bringing it to trial. Since prosecutors have limited resources, they cannot prosecute every case and need to be selective. Rational prosecutors will use these limited resources only where the benefits they expect exceed the opportunity costs of time and resources. Based on a model that maximizes justice and environmental concerns, Uhlman advises that criminal prosecution of environmental offences "*would be most appropriate when one or more aggravating factors was present: significant environmental harm or public health effects, deceptive or misleading conduct, operating outside the regulatory system, and repetitive violations*".[12] Empirical studies investigating prosecutorial decision-making, support the theoretical proposition of rational selectivity. For the U.S., these studies include those by Forst & Brosi (1977)[13], Myers & Hagan (1979)[14], Glaeser, Kessler & Morrison (2000)[15], Boylan (2005)[16], Rasmusen,

---

10 On the importance of closely related goals, see for instance *V.P. Crawford & J. Sobel*, Strategic Information Transmission, Econometrica 1982, pp. 1431-1451, specifically p. 1450.

11 This cost is not to be confounded with the cost of information generation. With regard to environmental offences, the generation of information can be very costly, for instance when repeated sampling and expensive laboratory testing are needed.

12 *D.M. Uhlmann*, Prosecutorial Discretion and Environmental Crime, Harvard Environmental Law Review 2014, (159) p. 214.

13 *B. Forst & K.B. Brosi*, A Theoretical and Empirical Analysis of the Prosecutor, The Journal of Legal Studies 1977, pp. 177-191.

14 *M.A. Myers & J. Hagan*, Private and Public Trouble: Prosecutors and the Allocation of Court Resources, Social Problems 1979, pp. 439-451.

15 *E.L. Glaeser, D.P. Kessler & A. Morrison*, What Do Prosecutors Maximize? An Analysis of the Federalization of Drug Crimes, American Law and Economics Review 2000, 259-290.

16 *R.T. Boylan*, What Do Prosecutors Maximize? Evidence from the Careers of U.S. Attorneys, American Law and Economics Review 2005, pp. 379-402.

Raghav & Ramseyer (2009)[17] and Uhlman (2014).[18] Outside the U.S., empirical studies regarding prosecutorial decision-making are scarce. Billiet et al. (2010) investigated criminal transaction offers by prosecutors in Flanders, Belgium.[19] Almer and Goeschl (2011) studied the environmental criminal justice system in Germany, including the enforcement decisions made by prosecutors.[20] The different empirical studies confirm the concept of the prosecutor as a rational decision maker, typically balancing expected benefits in the form of successful prosecutions – in terms of convictions and sentences – against the opportunity costs of time and resources. However, they also indicate that the benefits this rational decision-maker expects and incorporates in his decisions, depend on the objectives he pursues. Justice and social concerns notwithstanding, other goals can enter a prosecutor's objective function, personal career-related goals for instance. Public prosecutors are thought to also pursue these objectives, especially in systems with elected prosecutors, such as in the U.S.[21]

4. In the following section, we use a communication model to analyse the potential of information-sharing between environmental inspectors and public prosecutors. We model the communication between those two enforcement actors by using a basic sender-receiver communication model. The modelling incorporates the cost factor and the objective function, allowing us to distinguish four hypotheses where costs and objectives[22] combine in different ways. For each of these, we discuss the decision process of the information sender (the environmental inspector), as well as the decision process of the information receiver (the public prosecutor), looking at outcomes regarding information sharing happening, or not, and regarding the benefits of the information shared (2. Modelling communication between environmental inspectors and public prosecutors). In the third section, we confront the actual environmental enforcement process with the conceptual framework. This allows us to comment on the increasing specialization of public prosecutors in several countries, on the crucial role of effectively written notices of violation and on proof-driven selectivity while recording offences in notices of violation. (3. Relevance for policy development and practice) Finally, we conclude with possibilities by which

---

17 *Rasmusen, Raghav & Ramseyer, supra* note 8, pp. 47-78.

18 *Uhlmann, supra* note 12, 159-216.

19 *C.M. Billiet et al.*, Minnelijke schikkingen voor milieumisdrijven in Vlaanderen, Panopticon 2010, pp. 78-84.

20 *C. Almer & T. Goeschl*, The Political Economy of the Environmental Criminal Justice System: a Production Function Approach, Public Choice 2011, pp. 611-630.

21 *Glaeser, Kessler & Morrison, supra* note 15; *Boylan, supra* note 16. See also *A. van Aaken, L.P. Feld & S. Voigt*, Do Independent Prosecutors Deter Political Corruption? An Empirical Evaluation across Seventy-eight Countries, American Law and Economics Review 2010, pp. 204-244.

22 In this chapter, we use the words 'objectives' and 'utility' as synonyms.

to optimize information-sharing between environmental inspectors and public prosecutors and make suggestions for a wider use of our findings (4. Conclusions)

5. Our focus on the communication issue, underpinning the public prosecutor's decision making adds, to our knowledge, to existing literature. In general, previous theoretical and empirical studies have studied the prosecution decision on its own or as a game between prosecutor and judge. The latter type of studies mostly centre around the process of plea bargaining. Moreover, Almer & Goeschl have adopted a system approach and have included interactions between police, prosecutor and judge in an empirical/political economy model.[23]

2. MODELLING COMMUNICATION BETWEEN ENVIRONMENTAL INSPECTORS AND PUBLIC PROSECUTORS

2.1. MODEL SETUP AND SCENARIOS

6. Whenever environmental inspectors send information on offences to a public prosecutor's office, we have a one-directional information exchange with the inspector on the sender's side and the prosecutor on the receiver's side. This communication set-up is reflected in the model we have chosen to analyse in the communication process: the sender-receiver model.

7. The sender-receiver model, developed shortly after World War II, is the most basic communication model (see Figure 1).[24] As such, it has inspired most other communication models. Its general set-up contains a sender who has an idea or a concept that he wants the receiver to appreciate and, thus, sends a message to communicate it. The message can be distorted by 'noise'. 'Noise' is defined as anything in the communication process that interferes with the intended receiver getting and understanding the message sent.[25] Once the receiver gets the –

---

23 *Almer & Goeschl, supra* note 20.

24 *C.E. Shannon*, A Mathematical Theory of Communication, The Bell System Technical Journal 1948, pp. 379-423 and 623-656; *W. Weaver & C.E. Shannon*, The Mathematical Theory of Communication, University of Illinois Press, 1949.
Speakers or writers are often referred to as 'encoders', and listeners or readers as 'decoders'. When putting ideas or information into words and other signs, you encode them. When you translate the sound waves that hit your ears, or the signs on the screen or paper you are looking at, in ideas and information, you are decoding. *J.A. DeVito*, The Essentials of Human Communication, Pearson Publishing, 8th ed., 2013, p. 5.

25 *Id.*, p. 8. The four main categories of noise are physical noise (e.g. difficult-to-read format types or background noises), physiological noise (e.g. hearing loss or poor eyesight), psychological noise (e.g. feelings of irritation, prejudices or distraction) and semantic noise (e.g. an insurance

possibly distorted – message, he reads it, assesses the (distorted) idea or concept and then takes – or does not take – action.

Figure 1. Sender-receiver model

Within this general set-up, we distinguish four different model scenarios according to two dimensions (see Table 1): the first dimension deals with the costs of sharing information and the second with the differences between the objectives pursued by both parties. Firstly, depending on the cost of encoding, sending and decoding messages, communication can be costless or costly. When communication is costless, the model assumes 'cheap talk'. The classic cheap talk set-up, with an informed sender and an uninformed receiver, was developed by Crawford & Sobel.[26] Secondly, we can distinguish a setting in which sender and receiver have identical objectives and one in which they have different objectives. The model presented by Crawford & Sobel, for instance, showed that communication can be more informative when sender's and receiver's preferences are more similar.

Table 1. Model scenarios

	Information sharing is costless for sender and receiver ('cheap talk')	Information sharing is costly for both sender and receiver
Identical objectives	MODEL 1	MODEL 3
Different objectives	MODEL 2	MODEL 4

2.2. MODELLING THE INFORMATION SHARING FROM ENVIRONMENTAL INSPECTOR TO PUBLIC PROSECUTOR

8. The actual modelling of the information sharing from an environmental inspector, the information sender (S), to a public prosecutor, the information receiver (R), starts here. The modelling will allow us to analyse what happens in the communication process, from inspector to prosecutor, in a structured, complete and transparent way. The model findings will establish the conceptual

salesperson using the jargon of the insurance industry to talk to someone not trained in such topics). *Id.*

26 *Crawford & Sobel, supra* note 10.

touchstone for our further policy analysis. We are especially interested in the combined effects of cost levels and objective functions, even if, at the outset, we can intuitively guess that information sharing will be more beneficial in a setting with costless information and identical goals. Besides testing our intuition for these rather simple settings, the modelling gives us a solid theoretical understanding of, and a complete and clear insight into, the process of information sharing, including the mutual influences of costs and goals.

We will work in five steps. First, we formulate the assumptions underlying our model. This provides transparency, particularly regarding questions such as: 'Can the environmental inspector be dishonest and send false information?' and: 'How might we understand the cost of a unit of information? Is each unit as costly as the others, or does the price go up or down the more information is shared?' (2.2.1). Next, we model the decision of the environmental inspector, the sender (S), to encode/send information (2.2.2). Thereafter, we model the decision of the public prosecutor, the receiver (R), to decode/receive the information (2.2.3). We continue with an analysis of the information sharing that results from both decisions (2.2.4). We conclude with a summary of our findings (2.2.5).

To help readers who are not familiar with the maths, we explain all formulas and graphs with words. This adds significantly to the length of this part, but we think that sharing this relevant information with our reader is worth incurring that drawback. Our recommendation to readers who feel that the modelling remains too hard to approach and digest, is to have a quick glance at the assumptions and to jump over what follows in a straight line to the summary of the findings.

2.2.1. Model assumptions

9. Our model assumptions on the information sharing from environmental inspectors, the information senders (S), to public prosecutors, the information receivers (R), are the following ones.

1) There is no 'noise'; the message sent thus equals the message received.
2) The information that can be shared is based on objective facts and lying is not possible. So, we basically assume honesty: the message contains information that is true.
3) Yet, this true information might only be part of the available information (partial information) or it might be hidden in other irrelevant information (redundant information). Thus, the message contains a certain amount of information y_S. The information content varies from extremely minimal and not so useful, over just right and directly useful, to very elaborate and costly to use.
4) Increasing the information content of the message comes at a unit cost of c_S. Thus, a message with an information content y_S costs $c_S y_S$ to send. Next, the receiver can decode the message at a unit cost c_R per unit of information

content y_S. The receiver decides on an enforcement action a based on the received information, modeled as a linear function of the information:

$$a(y_S) = \delta y_S. \qquad (1)$$

5) Both actors maximize their expected utility, the objectives they pursue. However, their utility functions are not necessarily equal. The utility of the sender depends on the expected benefit B_S from the action a taken by the receiver and on the cost of sending a message:

$$U_S(c_S, a) = B_S(a(y_S)) - c_S y_S \qquad (2)$$

The utility function of the receiver differs from the utility function of the sender: b represents the bias relative to the sender. The bias b can be smaller or larger than one (b < 1 respectively b > 1) and measures the degree to which the sender's and receiver's objectives are aligned. A bias equal to one (b = 1) implies identical utility functions. A bias smaller than one (b < 1) implies that the benefits from the information sharing are smaller for the sender than they are for the receiver, while a bias larger than one (b > 1) implies the reverse. Further, the receiver's utility also depends on the expected net benefit B_R from the enforcement action taken and the cost of decoding the message:

$$U_R(c_R, a, b) = B_R(b, a(y_S)) - c_R y_S. \qquad (3)$$

2.2.2. Decision making process of the sender (environmental inspector)

10. The sender decides to share information or not to share it, and if he shares information, he has to decide how much to share. On the one hand, this decision depends on the costs of sharing information: e.g. sending an email, picking up the phone, writing a short report or writing a long analysis with technical annexes. On the other hand, the decision depends on the expected benefits of sharing information: i.e. how will the information change the behaviour of the receiver? From equation (2) we can derive the optimal amount of information y_S^* to send, i.e. the amount of information that maximizes the utility function of the sender:

$$\frac{\partial B_S}{\partial a}\frac{\partial a}{\partial y_S} - c_S = 0$$

Assuming the marginal benefit of information sent (MB_S)[27] is a linear function equal to $MB_S = \frac{\partial B_S}{\partial a} = \beta_{S0} - \beta_1 a(y_S)$ and using equation (1), we have:

$$y_S^* = 0, \; if \; c_S > \beta_{S0}$$

$$y_S^* = \frac{\beta_{S0} - c_S}{\delta \beta_1}, \; if \; c_S \leq \beta_{S0} \qquad (4)$$

[27] Marginal benefit of information sent: benefit per additional unit of information sent.

So, the sender prefers not to communicate when the costs of sending information are too high $(c_S > \beta_{S0})$. However, when those costs are sufficiently low $(c_S < \beta_{S0})$, the sender will send information. The amount of information shared increases if the cost decreases and if the usefulness of the information increases. This equilibrium is illustrated in Figure 2 for the hypothesis where the costs are sufficiently low ($c_S < \beta_{S0}$). Both the marginal benefit of information sent (MB_S) and the marginal cost of information sent (c_S) are expressed in euros. We can distinguish two scenarios: firstly, when sending information is costless ($c_S = 0$), we find the solution for Model 1 and Model 2, and secondly, when sending information is costly ($c_S > 0$), we find the solution for Model 3 and Model 4.

Figure 2. Decision process of sender

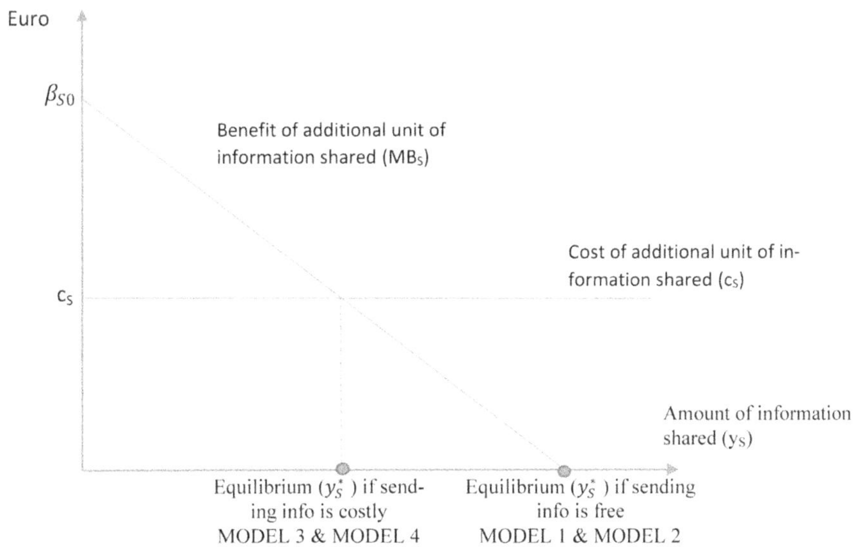

2.2.3. Decision-making process of the receiver (the public prosecutor)

11. The receiver decides to actively process the information he receives or not to do so. This decision depends on the costs of processing information: e.g. reading emails, updating files or verifying and studying information. Moreover, the decision to decode the message and assess its information content also depends on the possible benefits that the receiver associates with the information: i.e. how could the information change his behaviour, and would this change be beneficial for him? These benefits depend on the objectives the receiver pursues.

Given the information y_S^* received from the sender, the utility derived by the receiver from decoding the message equals:

$$U_R(c_R, a, b) = B_R(b, a(y_S^*)) - c_R y_S^*.$$

The receiver will decide to decode the message as long as:

$$B_R\left(b, a\left(y_S^*\right)\right) - c_R y_S^* > B_R(b, a(0)).$$

Otherwise, the message will be ignored.

However, the information received from the sender may not be optimal for the receiver. Therefore, we now derive the amount of information that would be optimal for the receiver and that would maximize his utility. From equation (3) we can derive the optimal amount of information y_R^* from the point of view of the receiver:

$$\frac{\partial B_R}{\partial a}\frac{\partial a}{\partial y_R} - c_R = 0$$

Assuming the marginal benefit of information received (MB_R)[28] is a linear function equal to $MB_R = \frac{\partial B_R}{\partial a} = \beta_{R0} - \beta_1 a(y_R)$ and using equation (1), we have:

$$y_R^* = 0, \text{ if } c_R > \beta_{R0}$$

$$y_R^* = \frac{\beta_{R0} - c_R}{\delta \beta_1}, \text{ if } c_R \leq \beta_{R0} \tag{5}$$

So, the receiver prefers not to communicate when decoding information is too costly $\left(c_R > \beta_{R0}\right)$. However, when costs are sufficiently low $\left(c_R < \beta_{R0}\right)$, the receiver would like to receive information. Again, the preferred amount of information increases if the cost decreases and if the usefulness of the information increases. This derived equilibrium is illustrated in Figure 3 for $c_R \leq \beta_{R0}$. We can distinguish two scenarios. Firstly, when sending information is costly ($c_R > 0$), we find the solution for Model 3 and Model 4. Secondly, when sending information is costless ($c_R = 0$), Figure 3 illustrates the solution for Model 1 and Model 2.

Using the parameter b to represent the extent to which objectives differ between sender and receiver, we assume that the marginal benefit function of the receiver is a linear shift of the marginal benefit function of the sender. This is:

$$MB_R = \beta_{R0} - \beta_1 a(y_R) = b\beta_{S0} - \beta_1 a(y_R)$$

Thus, if b = 1, meaning that sender and receiver have identical utility functions, the two curves coincide and both parties derive the same marginal benefit from an additional unit of enforcement effort made by the receiver. If b<1 (b>1), the marginal benefit from an additional unit of enforcement effort for the receiver is lower (higher) than the marginal benefit for the sender. For simplicity's sake, Figure 3 only models two situations: the situation where b =1 and the situation

28 Marginal benefit of information received: benefit per additional unit of information received.

where b>1. Both the marginal benefit of information received (MB_R) and the marginal cost of information received (c_R) are expressed in euros.

If $c_R \leq \beta_{R0}$, we can rewrite equation (5) as follows:

$$y_R^* = \frac{\beta_{R0} - c_R}{\delta\beta_1} = \frac{b\beta_{S0} - c_S}{\delta\beta_1} + \frac{c_S - c_R}{\delta\beta_1} \qquad (6)$$

Figure 3. Decision process of receiver

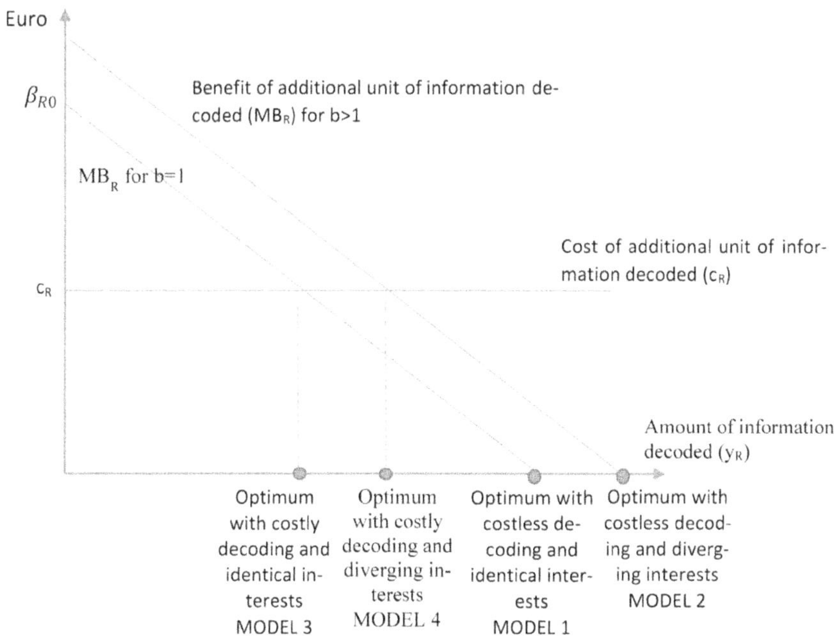

2.2.4. *Model results*

12. We now discuss the implications of equation (6) for the four different conceptual models presented in Table 1.

2.2.4.1. Model 1: costless information sharing and identical objectives

13. In this setting we assume that senders can send information without cost ($c_S = 0$) and receivers can decode messages without cost ($c_R = 0$). Moreover, objectives between the two parties are perfectly aligned and the benefits from information sharing are identical for both sender and receiver (b = 1). Looking at equation (6), the expression now simplifies to

$$y_R^* = y_S^*$$

Thus, the amount of information sent by the sender is optimal for both parties and maximizes both the sender's utility and the receiver's utility. To conclude, sharing information will always happen since it is costless in this model. Moreover, if we define welfare in a utilitarian way (i.e. as a sum of both utility functions), information exchange in this model leads to a welfare optimum.

2.2.4.2. Model 2: costless information sharing and diverging objectives

14. In this setting we still assume that senders can send information without cost ($c_S=0$) and receivers can decode messages without cost ($c_R=0$). However, objectives between the two parties are no longer assumed to be aligned ($b\neq1$) and, thus, the benefits of information sharing differ between sender and receiver. Looking at equation (6), the expression now simplifies to:

$$y_R^* = b y_S^*$$

The amount of information sent by the sender is a factor 1/b different from the optimal amount of information desired by the receiver. Thus, if b > 1, the sender sends a message that will optimize his own objectives, but this message will not optimize the objectives of the receiver since it contains too little information content $\left(y_R^* > y_S^*\right)$. If b < 1, the message will only be partly decoded since the receiver does not need all of the information in the message. Then the action taken by the receiver will optimize his own objectives, but will not lead to an optimum for the sender $\left(y_R^* < y_S^*\right)$.

2.2.4.3. Model 3: costly information sharing and identical objectives

15. In this setting we assume that both sending information and decoding messages is costly ($c_S > 0$ and $c_R > 0$). However, objectives between the two parties are aligned (b=1) and the benefits from enforcement actions are identical for both sender and receiver. Looking at equation (6), the expression simplifies to:

$$y_R^* = y_S^* + \frac{c_S - c_R}{\delta\beta_1}$$

We can distinguish three cases, depending on the relative size of the cost of sending and receiving information:

i) sending and receiving information is equally costly ($c_S = c_R$);
ii) sending information is more costly than receiving it ($c_S > c_R$) and
iii) sending information is less costly than receiving it ($c_S < c_R$).

First, we look at the first case in which sending and receiving information is equally costly ($c_S = c_R$). In this case, if information is shared, the amount of information in the message is optimal for both parties and it maximizes both sender's and receiver's utility. However, information will not always be shared since it is costly to do so. From equations (4) and (5) we know that a sender will only send a message if $c_S \leq \beta_{S0}$ and that a receiver will only decode the message if $c_R \leq \beta_{R0} = \beta_{S0}$. Two possible solutions can be distinguished. If the costs of sharing information are too high ($c_S = c_R > \beta_{S0}$), no message is sent. If the cost of sending is sufficiently low, a message will be sent and it will be decoded. So, in this first case, sharing information will not always happen, but, if it happens, it will be beneficial for both sender and receiver.

In the second case sending information is costlier than receiving it ($c_S > c_R$). No message is sent if the costs of sending information are too high ($c_S > \beta_{S0}$). If the cost of sending is sufficiently low, a message will be sent and it will be decoded since $c_R < c_S$. In this case, sharing information will, once more, not always happen, but if it does happen, it will be beneficial for both sender and receiver.

In the third case, sending information is less costly than receiving it ($c_S < c_R$). We can observe, again, that no message is sent if the costs of sharing information are too high ($c_S > \beta_{S0}$). If the cost of sending is sufficiently low, a message will be sent. However, it will not necessarily be decoded since $c_R > c_S$. Only if $c_R \leq \beta_{S0}$, the message will be decoded and used by the receiver. In this case, useful information will not always be shared and, if a message is sent, it will not always be decoded and used by the receiver.

2.2.4.4. Model 4: costly information sharing and diverging objectives

16. In this setting we assume that both sending information and decoding messages are costly actions ($c_S > 0$ and $c_R > 0$). Moreover, the objectives between the two parties are not aligned and the benefits from enforcement actions differ between sender and receiver ($b \neq 1$). Looking at equation (6), we have:

$$y_R^* = \frac{b\beta_{S0} - c_S}{\delta\beta_1} + \frac{c_S - c_R}{\delta\beta_1}$$

In this case, information will not always be shared and, even if a message is sent, it will not always be decoded, since it is costly for the receiver to do so. From equations (4) and (5) we know that a sender will only send a message if $c_S \leq \beta_{S0}$ and that a receiver will only decode the message if $c_R \leq \beta_{R0} = b\beta_{S0}$. Four possible solutions can now be distinguished (see Table 2). If the costs of sharing information are too high $c_S > max\{\beta_{S0}, b\beta_{S0}\}$, no message is sent. If the cost of sending is sufficiently low, a message will be sent. Next, depending on the relative size of the decoding costs and the bias in its utility function, this message will be decoded ($c_R \leq b\beta_{S0}$) or not ($c_R > b\beta_{S0}$) by the receiver.

If a message is sent, then we can observe two scenarios. Firstly, if $b>1$, the sender sends a message that will optimize his own objectives, but this message will not optimize the objectives of the receiver since it contains too little information content. Secondly, if $b < 1$, the message will only be partly decoded since the receiver does not need all the information in the message. Then the action taken by the receiver will optimize his own objectives, but will not lead to an optimum for the sender.

Table 2. Possible solutions

	$c_R \leq \beta_{R0}$	$c_R > \beta_{R0}$
$c_S \leq \beta_{S0}$	Message is sent and decoded	Message is sent but not decoded
$c_S > \beta_{S0}$	No message is sent	No message is sent

2.2.5. Summary of the model results

17. Using the four different conceptual settings we are able to derive conditions that make sharing information more likely and the conditions that make sharing information more useful (see Table 3). Obviously sending information is more likely, the lower the costs of sending messages are and the more benefits the resulting information sharing brings about. Further, a message is more likely to be decoded, the lower the decoding costs and the higher the benefits associated with the information sharing are for the receiver compared to those for the sender. Finally, the message will include the optimal amount of information when the objectives of both parties are closely aligned (b = 1). If the benefits of the information sharing are more beneficial for the sender than they are for the receiver (b<1), then the receiver can reach his optimum, while the sender cannot. On the other hand, if the benefits of the information sharing are less beneficial for the sender than for the receiver (b>1), the sender can reach his optimum and the receiver cannot.

Table 3. Summary of model results

	Information sharing is costless for sender and receiver ('cheap talk')	**Information sharing is costly both for sender and receiver**
Identical objectives	MODEL 1 Sharing information will always happen and will always be beneficial (nobody will be worse off)	MODEL 3 Sharing information will happen if total benefits exceed total costs (nobody will be worse off; but, sometimes useful information might not be shared because sharing is too costly overall)
Different objectives	MODEL 2 Sharing information will happen if it is beneficial for the sender (sender will never be worse off; impact on receiver is ambiguous; sometimes useful information might not be shared because it does not benefit the sender)	MODEL 4 Sharing information will happen if benefits for sender exceed costs for sender (sender will never be worse off; impact on receiver is ambiguous; sometimes useful information might not be shared because sharing is too costly for the sender)

3. RELEVANCE FOR POLICY DEVELOPMENT AND PRACTICE

18. We can now explore the relevance of the insights provided by the conceptual model for the communication between environmental inspectors and public prosecutors in practice. To this end, we can discuss three different topics: first, the impact of increasing specialization of public prosecutors; second, the informative quality of notices of violations and thirdly, the prioritization of environmental offences in prosecution.

3.1. SPECIALIZATION OF PUBLIC PROSECUTORS: 'ENVIRONMENTAL PROSECUTORS'

19. In Europe, a trend exists towards increasing the specialization of public prosecutors in the field of environmental crime.

We have observed this development in Belgium since 2008. At country level, an evolution towards a structurally formalized specialization of public prosecutors in several highly technical crime areas, including environmental offenses, started in January 2008 on a local scale.[29] It involved the judicial resorts of two courts of first instance; thus, two prosecutors' offices. The initiative spread to the whole of the Province of West-Flanders (November 2010, four judicial resorts), part of the Province of Antwerp (January 2011, two out of the three judicial resorts) and the Province of East-Flanders (December 2011, all three judicial resorts).[30] The essential part of this cooperation effort was that the same prosecutor, or prosecutors of the same prosecutors' office, would deal with all environmental files throughout all of the cooperating judicial resorts. This same prosecutor was also responsible for actually prosecuting the defendant in court and for requesting the appropriate sanctions from the court judge.[31] This move towards specialization was consolidated throughout the country on 1 April 2014 when the judicial reform that reduced the existing twenty-seven Belgian judicial resorts to twelve entered into force. One of the main objectives of the greater scale

---

29 *D. Leestmans*, Gedaan met het exclusief locale denken? Juristenkrant 27 January 2010, 8-9; *W. Haelewyn*, Criminal offence policy with respect to combating environmental offences in Belgium, in: Instituut voor Gerechtelijke Opleiding – Institut de Formation Judiciaire (ed.), Investigation, prosecution and judgment of environmental offences. European seminar for members of the judiciary specialized in combating environmental offences (conference proceedings), Durbuy (Belgium) 24-27 May 2011, 63-67; *J. De Clercq*, Parketsamenwerkingsverbanden inzake milieu en stedenbouw, presented at Vlaamse Vereniging voor Omgevingsrecht, Debating Evening 6 June 2013.

30 *De Clercq, id.*

31 *Leestmans, id.; Haelewyn, id.; De Clercq, id.*

of the resorts is precisely to allow for specialization in crime areas that need it, such as environmental crime.[32]

The tendency towards specialization, giving rise to the emergence of 'environmental prosecutors', appears to be developing throughout Europe. This is illustrated by the creation, in 2012, of the European Network of Prosecutors for the Environment (ENPE)[33] and by ENPE's recent successful bid on an EU LIFE program (2015-2020) supporting its statutory goals.[34]

20. When comparing the situation with structurally formalized specialization to the situation without structurally formalized specialization, it is clear that specialization gives a systematic chance to develop useful expertise as well as to refine prosecution policy objectives. Both evolutions can lead to less costly communication and to more closely aligned objectives between environmental inspectors and public prosecution offices. Nobody needs to be convinced of the complexity of environmental legislation. Specialization obviously helps to overcome the cost of complexity and, thus, helps to bring down the costs of decoding the information contained in the notice of violation. Moreover, the narrowing of the goals of the public prosecutors' policy from a prosecution policy including a wide range of crimes to a prosecution policy encompassing only environmental crime, is another important aspect. Insofar as specialization exists (positive perspective)[35], it implies that communication and the associated enforcement actions are more likely to fulfil the objectives of the environmental inspectors as well as the prosecutors, rather than the objectives of only one of these parties. Communication will then be more efficient. More efficient communication will logically lead to a more efficient prosecution policy. Insofar as specialization does not exist yet (normative perspective), it is a situation to

---

32 Act from December 1st 2013 "tot hervorming van de gerechtelijke arrondissementen en tot wijziging van het Gerechtelijk Wetboek met het oog op een grotere mobiliteit van de leden van de rechterlijke orde" [to reform the judicial resorts and to modify the Judicial Code so as to allow an increased mobility to members of the judicial order] (Belgian Official Journal, 10 December 2013).

33 See www.environmentalprosecutors.eu/.

34 Project reference: LIFE14 GIE/UK/0043. The project, stretching from July 2015 to July 2020, did obtain a funding of 1.072.400 euro (EU-contribution: 643.439 euro). Its objectives are to: (1) develop ENPE to a sustainable network of European environmental prosecutors, (2) improve the collection and dissemination of data on environmental crime and its prosecution, and (3) to bring together environmental prosecutors to share knowledge and expertise, cooperate and share intelligence, and improve capacity in prosecuting environmental crime. Its partners include the European Union Forum of Judges for the Environment (EUFE) (www.eufje.org), the National Environmental Crimes Unit at the Swedish Prosecution Authority and the Office for Serious Fraud and Environmental Crime of the Dutch National Public Prosecutor's Office. See http://ec.europa.eu/environment/life/project/Projects/index.cfm?fuseaction=search.dspPage&n_proj_id=5353&docType=pdf.

35 See, for instance, the specialized prosecutors working at the Environmental Agency of England and Wales (UK), mentioned *supra* note 9.

pursue, a goal to support in view of achieving a more efficient and effective sanctioning of environmental offenses.

3.2. INFORMATIVE QUALITY OF NOTICES OF VIOLATION

21. Our communication model highlights the importance of the informative quality of notices of violation in the interface between environmental inspectors and public prosecutors.

Irrespective of the type of environmental inspector – from a highly specialized environmental inspector to a police officer in charge of general compliance monitoring – notices of violation are the main tool to open a case at the public prosecutor's office. In Belgium, for instance, empirical data show that 95% to 99% of all environmental cases at the prosecutors' offices are opened following the receipt of a notice of violation. Cases provided by other sources, such as through complaints of private parties directly addressed to the prosecutor's office, form an utterly small fraction of the case intake.[36] Environmental compliance monitoring by public officers dominates compliance monitoring because of factors such as the necessity of manpower and other costly means to develop and uphold the monitoring, the technicality of many environmental compliance issues and the legal authority required to visit industrial and other premises. We may reasonably assume that, for same reasons, the situation is roughly similar throughout Europe and in many other countries. In EU Member States, the rather recent and expanding EU legislation on environmental inspections[37] is an additional factor supporting it.

Drafting a notice of violation concerning one or more environmental offences is always costly[38], even if some notices are costlier than others. The cost stems from the effort the environmental inspector invests in 'encoding' the facts of the offence: administrative data, such as data detailing the identity of suspects and the environmental permits of the factory involved; the facts providing the evidence; information relating to eventual antecedents; background data helping to understand and size up the evidence (cartographic material, business records, ...); data useful for assessing the illegal benefits generated by the offence; ... An additional part of the effort can consist in the encoding of a first analysis of all data considered as a whole. The more complex the case, in terms of facts and perpetrators, the costlier the encoding. At the receiver's end, the costs

---

36 *T. Van der Beken & A. Balcaen*, Strafrechtelijke sanctionering van milieurecht: stroomschema van PV tot vonnis (working paper), UGent – IRCP, www.environmental-lawforce.ugent.be – Lawforce Working paper 2007/2; *Vlaamse Hoge Raad voor de Milieuhandhaving*, Milieuhandhavingsrapport 2013. 5 jaar Milieuhandhavingsdecreet (2009-2013), 2014, 143-145.

37 *Supra*, nr. 2, note 5.

38 In terms of our model: $c_S > 0$. See *supra*, nrs. 10 and 15-17.

of decoding the information will more or less follow this same rule of thumb. The cost of notices of violation brings the communication from environmental inspectors to prosecutors' offices in the realm of our conceptual analysis, more specifically in the realm of the models which assume that information sharing is costly for both sender and receiver (Model 3 and Model 4).

Considering the crucial role of notices of violation in the enforcement chain, and in the encoding and decoding costs they bring along, the technical dismissal rate by prosecutor's offices deserves attention. A technical dismissal happens when the notice of violation lacks usefulness in view of the evidence needed, which is evidence regarding the offence as well as the offender. In Belgium, the rate of technical dismissals for environmental offences was 25% in the years 1993-2002.[39] The hope would be that this rate was due to the then-recent acquaintance[40] with environmental law enforcement. This idea does not find support in recent data. The dismissal rate decreased only slightly in the years 2009-2013, to some 20–22% of all cases.[41] An important waste of law enforcement efforts is involved in this communication failure. Each technical dismissal stands for encoding/ sending costs amounting to nothing. It also stands for some decoding/reception costs coming to nothing.

It is important to know more about this fraction of failed communication. Thus, for instance, we know for Belgium that an important fraction of technical dismissals is explained by the lack of proper evidence on the identity of the perpetrator of the offences.[42] But it is unclear to what extent this lack of evidence is due to factors that can be solved, such as a shift in information generation efforts from inspectors to prosecutors, whether it signals flaws in encoding skills, such as an improper understanding of the level of evidence required, or is due to wholly different difficulties, such as ill-drafted laws, which give next to no chance to find a culprit. An example of this kind of legal provision could be a provision forbidding to place poison-baits to control predator populations in the countryside. What is the chance of identifying the person placing such a bait somewhere in Flanders fields, the Irish grasslands, a Spanish Sierra or in a German forest?

22. Our model highlights the importance of costs in communication. Lessening the costs stimulates efficient communication. Considering all of the above, a well-thought out investment in lessening the costs involved with notices of violation

---

39 Information given in the answer to a parliamentary question raised in the Belgian Senate: Vr. en Antw. Senaat, 2003-04, Vr. nr. 3-243, 5 september 2003 (H. VANDENBERGHE).

40 E.g. *M. Faure*, Preadvies Milieustrafrecht, 1990, 163 pp.

41 Flanders: *Vlaamse Hoge Raad voor de Milieuhandhaving, supra* note 36, pp. 156-159. Belgium (statistics for 2009-2011): *Federale Overheidsdienst Volksgezondheid, Veiligheid van de voedselketen en Leefmilieu*, Tweede federaal milieurapport. Deel 2: de andere aspecten van het federale milieubeleid, 2015, p. 145.

42 Belgium (statistics for 2009-2011): *Federale Overheidsdienst Volksgezondheid, Veiligheid van de voedselketen en Leefmilieu*, Tweede federaal milieurapport. Deel 2: de andere aspecten van het federale milieubeleid, 2015, p. 145.

will stimulate efficient environmental prosecution. In policy terms, this stresses the importance of an ongoing investment in the conceptualization of well-made and usable notices of violation (*'Notices of violation for Dummies'*) and in the training of environmental inspectors in drafting such well-made and usable notices of violation. We also find that a better knowledge and understanding of technical dismissals would matter.

3.3. PRIORITIZATION OF ENVIRONMENTAL OFFENCES IN PROSECUTION

23. The last point we would like to make, draws from an empirical observation. This observation is the following one.

In Flanders (Belgium), we built a dataset gathering all verdicts of environmental case law at seven courts of first instance and in the Court of Appeal of Ghent, from 2003 to 2007, as well as precursory decisions by the public prosecutors of three of the seven prosecutors' offices involved, covering the year 2005.[43] The criminal sanctioning policy observed, regarding environmental offences, was dominated by three articles of law. Over 62% of the transaction settlements concluded by public prosecutors[44] and 55% of the accusations in the cases brought to court[45] deal with infringements of (1) the prohibition to discard waste (Article 12 Waste Decree), (2) the environmental permit obligation (Article 4, § 1, Environmental Permit Decree) (EPD) and (3) the obligation to comply with the environmental permit exploitation conditions (Article 22, § 1, EPD). Considering the vast amount of environmental legislation, filling literally thousands of pages in the European[46] and Belgian official journals, this finding is puzzling.

The focus of the enforcement efforts on the environmental permitting legislation, can be explained however. Just as in the rest of the EU, this legislation is a centrepiece of environmental legislation in Belgium. What is intriguing, however, is the relative importance of offences against the environmental permit obligation (Article 4, § 1 EPD) compared to offences against the obligation to respect permit conditions (Article 22, § 1, EPD) in the case load; the public prosecutor concluded by a transaction settlement and in the case load he brought to court. It can be observed that infringements of Article 22, § 1, EPD, offences

43 *C.M. Billiet et al.*, Milieurechtshandhaving: een databestand voor onderzoek naar de penale en bestuurlijke sanctioneringspraktijk, Tijdschrift voor Milieurecht 2009, pp. 128-150; *Billiet et al., supra* note 19, p. 80.

44 *Billiet et al., supra* note 19, p. 83.

45 *Billiet et al., supra* note 42 p. 140. See also *C.M. Billiet, T. Blondiau & S. Rousseau*, Punishing Environmental Crimes: an Empirical Study from Lower Courts to the Court of Appeal, Regulation & Governance 2014, (472) 478.

46 EU official journal: think of the extensive body of EU regulations in the field of waste management, toxic substances and wildlife traffic, which directly apply in the EU Member States.

which, as a rule, imply actual pollution and/or hindrance and, thus, are really harming the environment and/or public health, are dealt with by a transaction settlement twice as often (18.3%) than infringements of Article 4, § 1 EPD (7%), an offence that does not necessarily imply actual pollution and/or hindrance. In the case load brought to court, this proportion is reversed, with a less outspoken, yet neat, preponderance of Article 4, § 1 EPD accusations: 16.3% as opposed to 13.2%. One possible reason for this observed prosecution policy is that communication on offences against emission standards is less straightforward and, thus, more costly to decode than information on the other type of offenses.[47] This would induce prosecutors to opt more easily for a transaction offer as a means of closing a case, since this is a choice where the issue of proof only appears in a limited way and does not require detailed debate and discussion in court.

24. Starting with this observation, and the questions it raises, it could be argued that the communication, through notices of violation, should not only take care of lowering the cost at the sender's side but also at the prosecutor's end. More specifically, the environmental inspectors could systematically, and strategically, pay attention to the reporting of offences that not only matter in terms of protection of the environment and/or public health, but are also, on the more, documented using information that is relatively easy to decode. Such offences are, in our understanding, mainly of two categories. The first category includes authorization obligations of all kinds, as they are often pivotal in the operation of, limited or extended, sets of conditions that protect humans and the environment from harm. Having or not having the authorization required by law, makes a rather simple case to prove, decode, also in the prosecutor-judge relationship. A second category includes paperwork obligations, specifically in environmental domains for which the control of activities essentially happens through paperwork, such as waste, hazardous substances, manure, etc. Remember Al Capone, who was brought to court and put in jail for tax offenses[48]: paperwork offenses. Here again, the communication issue, including proof, is quite straightforward.

4. CONCLUSIONS

25. The simple communication model developed in this chapter highlights two characteristics of communication. Alongside the cost of communication, which is a commonly noticed issue, the model also stresses a rather less often detected characteristic; namely, the issue of the similarity or difference in objectives of communication partners. We clearly show that the communication between

---

47 This explanation finds support in *Forst & Brosi*, *supra* note 13, who find that prosecutors are "*more sensitive to strength of evidence than to crime seriousness*" – *id.*, p.190.

48 Https://en.wikipedia.org/wiki/Al_Capone.

environmental inspectors and public prosecutor is distorted by the fact that communication is costly and also because of differences in the actual objective functions. While at first glance both parties aim to maximize deterrence and to minimize environmental harm, upon closer examination some differences can be identified. More specifically, the opportunity costs of prosecution are not directly relevant to the decisions made by the inspectors, while they are clearly relevant to the prosecutor. Thus, improvements in the communication strategy are possible from a joint perspective.

We have identified three possibilities to improve communication in this crucial stage of the enforcement chain.

1) The specialization of public prosecutors is beneficial to communication. Considering a case with a given complexity, specialization lowers decoding costs. It also aligns the prosecutor's objectives more closely with the environmental inspector's objectives.
2) The effective encoding of information on environmental offences in notices of violation needs ongoing attention, at a conceptual level (*'Notices of violation for dummies'*) and at the implementation level (training of inspectors drafting notices of violation)
3) Inspectors should be attuned to the constraints the prosecutor faces while allocating scarce office resources. Strategic encoding of offences detected, combining environmental concerns with attention to offences that are cheap to decode at the prosecutor's end, ultimately at the judge's side, will pay off in terms of intake into the prosecution and successful convictions in court.

The phenomenon of technical dismissals needs to be better known and understood. What is going wrong and why? It might be that technical dismissals for some types of environmental crime signal a necessity to adapt legislation, by introducing provisions that, while being effective in terms of policy goals, raise the chance to identity an offender from a near to inexistent chance to a reasonable one, for instance. This is a topic worthy of further research.

26. The environmental inspectors' – public prosecutors – interface is a crucial one in the enforcement chain. It is decisive for the intake of a case into the criminal judicial system. However, all of the other interfaces in the enforcement chain matter too. The insights drawn from the communication model we have developed can be applied to other links in the enforcement chain such as, for instance, the interface prosecutors – judges.

27. Last, but not least, an extension of our analysis to environmental networks seems possible. Environmental networks exist in many shapes: formal, informal, with a homogenous membership and with a heterogeneous membership, local and supranational, regional and international. Enforcement networks with supranational homogenous membership are, for instance, IMPEL (European Network for the Implementation and Enforcement of Environmental Law)[49] and the aforementioned ENPE and EUFJE.[50] The INECE (International Network for Environmental Compliance and Enforcement)[51] offers an example of a worldwide formal network with a heterogeneous membership. Informal local networks exist everywhere, between environmental inspectors and public prosecutors having niches for meeting when coping with their duties for instance. Whatever its size and shape, a network thrives through information sharing. Information sharing belongs to the core business of all networks

The communication model proposed here helps to gain insight into the vulnerabilities that networks, formal and informal, face when coping with an information sharing process that is costly for both sender and receiver. For networks with heterogeneous members, such as INECE, the analysis emphasizes the importance of cheap or even costless communication in order to get communication going.

49 Www.impel.eu/.
50 *Supra*, nr. 19.
51 Http://inece.org/.

CHAPTER 13

ENVIRONMENTAL DAMAGE CAUSED BY OIL EXPLOITATION IN BRAZIL

The "Conduct Adjustment Agreement" (TAC) as a Means to Circumvent Civil Liability Ineffectiveness

Carina Costa de Oliveira
PhD in International Law Paris II Panthéon-Assas
Professor at the University of Brasília – UnB

Liziane Paixão Silva Oliveira
PhD in International Law, Aix-Marseille III
Professeur at the University of Tiradentes -UNIT
Coordinator of the Master in Law at the University of Tiradentes -UNIT

Priscila Pereira de Andrade
PhD in International Law Paris I Panthéon-Sorbonne
Associate Professor at Brasília University Center – UniCEUB
Postdoctoral researcher PNPD-CAPES

ABSTRACT

Even though some Brazilian and foreign companies have been sued for environmental damage, due to oil spills which occurred under Brazilian jurisdiction, the system based on civil liability does not provide proper reparation for environmental damage. In this context, extrajudicial instruments, such as the Conduct Adjustment Agreement (TAC), can contribute to improving the prevention and reparation of environmental damage. This chapter will focus on the analysis of its contribution to circumventing civil liability ineffectiveness by taking the increasing importance in the use of TACs on environmental matters into account.

Keywords: Civil liability, extrajudicial instruments, "Conduct Adjustment Agreement", environmental damage, oil spill

1. INTRODUCTION

The exploitation of oil in Brazil has already caused serious environmental damage in States such as Rio de Janeiro, São Paulo, Paraná, Espírito Santo and Bahia. A great part of this damage is caused by oil spills related to the activities that occur on the offshore platforms. In these cases, civil liability has not sufficiently contributed to the prevention and to the reparation of environmental damage. Other public and private instruments should be used in order to achieve greater effectiveness in environmental protection. Extrajudicial instruments, such as the Conduct Adjustment Agreement (in Portuguese *Termo de Ajustamento de Conduta* – TAC), widely used in Brazilian Law, can help to improve environmental protection. Therefore, it is important to briefly highlight the context of oil exploitation in Brazil, the limits of the Brazilian environmental liability system to repair damage caused by oil spills and the role Conduct Adjustment Agreements may play in this scenario.

Oil exploitation is a central economic activity in Brazil, which started in the 1930s and represents, along with the gas sector, 13% of the Brazilian Gross Domestic Product (GDP).[1] Actually, there are around 135 oil platforms fixed, floating and functioning in Brazilian maritime space.[2] Furthermore, there are at least 52 ships transport oil or derivatives.[3] In order to prevent environmental and social damage, the oil sector has to comply with Brazilian security norms.[4] Simultaneously, it is expected that Brazilian State control be done efficiently, in a manner based on norms and on a precautionary approach.

However, since 1960, many oil spills have been reported in Brazil.[5] The large oil spill that occurred in January 2000 in the Guanabara Bay, due to a leaking pipeline operated by the Brazilian company *Petrobras*, is a well-known example.[6]

1 Portal Brasil, Setor de petróleo e gás chega a 13% do PIB brasileiro, 2014, available at: <www.brasil.gov.br/economia-e-emprego/2014/06/setor-de-petroleo-e-gas-chega-a-13-do-pib-brasileiro>.

2 Available at: <www.petrobras.com/pt/quem-somos/>.

3 Available at: <www.transpetro.com.br/pt_br/areas-de-negocios/transporte-maritimo.html>.

4 Some examples of Brazilian security norms are Federal Law n. 6.938/1981; Resolution of CONAMA n. 237/1997; Portaria n. 423/2011; Portaria MMA & MME n. 198/2012. For more information on these specific norms see: *J. S. Carvalho Filho*, Manual de Direito Administrativo, 26 ed., 2013, p. 35.

5 According to the International Tanker Owners Pollution Federation Limited (ITOPF), the first oil spill recorded on the Brazilian coast was due to the tanker *Sinclair Petrolore*. On this topic see: <www.itopf.com/>.

6 *M. Taam*, The Guanabara Bay Oil Spill Incident – "The Brazilian Exxon Valdez" An Institutional Perspective, US EPA Archive Document, available at: <https://archive.epa.gov/emergencies/content/fss/web/pdf/taampaper.pdf>.

In 2004, the Chilean chemical tanker *Vicuña* explosion in the Paranaguá Port contaminated many areas of high environmental sensitivity.[7] In 2011, the *Chevron* case occurred, discharging more than 50,000 litres of crude oil into the Campos Basin situated in the state of Rio de Janeiro. In 2014, the National Agency of Petroleum, Natural Gas and Biofuels (ANP) reported a significant increase in the number of communications concerning oil spill accidents.[8] More recently, at the beginning of 2015, a major oil accident occurred on an offshore production facility called *FPSO Cidade de São Mateus* belonging to the BW Offshore group.[9] In this last case, not only was there an environmental impact, but also nine people were killed.[10] These oil spills also illustrate how environmental, social and economical consequences may be difficult to repair. Activities such as tourism, commerce, sports and fishing are directly disrupted.

Many of the cases mentioned above contribute to the analysis of how environmental liability and reparation is taking place and if it is effective. As we will demonstrate in this chapter, even if some Brazilian and foreign companies have been sued for environmental damages that occurred in the area under Brazilian jurisdiction[11], the system based on civil liability does not provide proper reparation for environmental damage. In this context, extrajudicial instruments, such as the TAC, can contribute to improving environmental damage prevention and reparation.

The TAC was originally established by the 1985 Brazilian Public Civil Action Act[12] and reaffirmed by norms that deal with collective and diffuse rights such as norms on environment protection[13], children's rights[14]and consumer rights.[15] It is a preventive and, at the same time, it is a punitive agreement which can be negotiated before or after the damage occurs. When its terms are not complied with, then the payment of fines may be imposed.[16] The overall objective of the TAC is to enforce compliance among physical persons and legal entities in order

7 International Tanker Owners Pollution Federation (ITOPF), Oil spills in Brazil: case histories, available at: <www.itopf.com/knowledge-resources/countries-regions/countries/brazil/>.

8 *ANP*, Relatório anual de segurança operacional das atividades de exploração e produção de petróleo e gás natural, 2014, p.57.

9 For more information see: <www.bwoffshore.com/news1/in-memoriam/>.

10 For more information see: <http://economia.estadao.com.br/noticias/geral,em-cinco-anos-50-acidentes-fatais-ocorreram-na-petrobras,1633061>.

11 For instance: See: *Tribunal Regional Federal da 2ª Região* Judgment: Case n. 2005.51.02.006331-0, Decision of December 18, 2013; *Tribunal Regional Federal da 2ª Região* Judgment: Case n. 2005.51.01.003821-4, Decision of November 25, 2014. *Tribunal Regional Federal da* 3ª Região Judgment: Case n. 10607 SP 0010607-88.2011.4.03.6104, Decision of November 06, 2014; *Tribunal Regional Federal da 2ª Região* Judgment: Case n. 2009.50.01.0011512-6, Decision of April, 14 2015.

12 Brazil, Federal Law n. 7.347/1985.

13 Brazil, Federal Law n. 9.605/1998, Article 74-A which provides for environmental crimes.

14 Brazil, Law n. 8069/90, Article 211.

15 Brazil, Federal Law n. 7437/1985, Article 113.

16 *E. Milaré*, Manual de Direito Administrativo, 9th ed, Editora Revista dos Tribunais, 2014, p.1401.

to adopt measures that effectively prevent and/or repair the damage. For instance, this can be done by requiring conduct adjustments on the illegal or harmful action caused or not yet caused to the environment, by asking for specific measures such as the return to the *status quo* before the accident.[17] Environmental issues related to construction inadequacies, deforestation, biodiversity and landfill are the subjects of many TACs.[18] This use of TACs can be connected to some of this instrument's characteristics, such as celerity.[19]

Taking the importance in the use of TACs on environmental matters into account, this chapter will focus on the analysis of the effectiveness of the TACs negotiated between public entities, such as Public Prosecutors, environmental executive bodies (IBAMA) and oil exploitation companies.[20] The objective is to analyse these TACs in order to identify the clauses, the actors, the advantages and disadvantages of using this method for the reparation of environmental damage related to oil spills.

We will show that there are many gaps that must be analysed carefully. For instance, depending on the obligations provided in these agreements, the company can be more or less engaged in compliance, once compared to judicial enforcement. One of the positive aspects of using the TAC instrument to treat environmental damage is that it can achieve an agreement faster and more efficiently. Furthermore, it can contribute to a participatory approach perspective, due to the possibility of all actors involved in the damage being able to participate.

Research was made concerning these methods in Brazil.[21] However, it was not easy to find and obtain all of the TACs concerning oil spills. Few of them are published on the internet.[22] In some cases it was necessary to use the procedure created by the Access to Information Law to ask for these methods or to visit and personally and interview the public entities responsible for negotiating them.

The three TACs analysed herein were signed by the end of 2014. The first TAC analysed was celebrated between the Rio de Janeiro Public Prosecution Office

17 *R. Jelinek,* Execução de compromisso de ajustamento de conduta, Editora Forense Universitária, 2009; *F.R.V.akaoui*, Compromisso de Ajustamento de Conduta Ambiental, 4th ed, Editora Revista dos Tribunais, 2012.

18 *G. Rodrigues*, Ação civil pública e termo de ajustamento de conduta: teoria e prática, Editora Forense Universitária,2006, pp. 260-298. See:< www.mpf.mp.br/atuacao-tematica/ccr4>.

19 *E. Milaré, supra*, nota 20.

20 It is possible to highlight the following TACs: the TAC between Chevron and Public Prosecutors from Rio de Janeiro in 2013 concerning the 2011 and 2012 oil spill; the TAC negotiated between Petrobras and environmental administrative entities from Rio and the TAC celebrated between the company Coastal BMCAL-4 Ltda and Public Prosecutors from the State of Bahia.

21 *S. Campelli (coord.)*, Compromisso de Ajustamento Ambiental: análise e sugestões para aprimoramento, 2009. See also: *R.N. Viéga; R.G. Pinto & L.F.N. Garzon,* Negociação e acordo ambiental: o termo de Ajustamento de Conduta (TAC) como forma de tratamento de conflitos ambientais, Fundação Heinrich Böll Brasil, 2014.

22 For example the TAC celebrated between Chevron (and others) and the Rio de Janeiro Public Prosecutors Office in 2013 is available on the internet at <www.prrj.mpf.mp.br/frontpage/noticias/mpf-assina-tac-com-chevron-nessa-sexta-feira>.

(MPF-RJ) and Chevron in 2013. The second agreement was negotiated between the Rio de Janeiro State Environment Secretariat (SEA-RJ), the Rio de Janeiro State Environment Institute (INEA-RJ) and Petrobras in 2011. The third TAC was reached between the Bahia Public Prosecution Office (MPF-BA) and the Coastal BM CAL 4 Ltda in 2003. Indeed, other Conduct Adjustment Agreements containing interesting clauses, actors and effects will also be presented as further examples throughout this chapter. Therefore, before analysing how this instrument can contribute to the reparation of environmental damage, caused by the oil spills in Brazil (2), it is first necessary to present in the first place the ineffectiveness of the Brazilian civil liability system to ensure the reparation of pure ecological damage caused by oil spills (1).

2. THE BRAZILIAN CIVIL LIABILITY SYSTEM FOR THE REPARATION OF ENVIRONMENTAL DAMAGE CAUSED BY OIL SPILLS

Many oil spills in Brazil are the object of civil actions. These actions are sometimes limited in guaranteeing the reparation *in natura* of the damage and in granting the adequate monetary reparation. In order to understand these limits, it is necessary to present some general aspects of the Brazilian liability system (1.1) before analysing the limits[23] of this system for the reparation of environmental damage caused by oil spills (1.2).

2.1. GENERAL ASPECTS OF THE BRAZILIAN LIABILITY SYSTEM

The reparation of environmental damages is provided for by Article 225 paragraph 3 of the Brazilian Constitution, and Article 4, item VII of the National Environment Policy.[24] The liability for environmental damage in Brazil is

---

23 Some limits of criminal or civil liability of foreign vessels, concerning the problem of the convenience flag, can be pointed out, but they will not be object of this chapter. Other concerns related to the "orphaned spots" regarding administrative issues will not be subject of this chapter either. These issues will not be analyzed in this chapter because the TAC is not always useful as a complementary instrument in these cases. The limits that will be pointed out concern specifically the reparation in natura and the monetary reparation. For more details on these other limitations see: *M. D. Varella*, A necessidade de repensar os mecanismos de responsabilidade ambiental em caso de riscos de vazamento de petróleo na Zona Econômica Exclusiva do Brasil, RDI 2012(2), pp. 241-251; *I. Lopes*, O direito internacional privado e a responsabilidade civil extracontratual por danos ambientais causados por transportes marítimos à luz do direito brasileiro, RDI 2015 (1), pp.217-241.

24 Brazil, Federal Law n. 6.938, 31August 1981.

objective[25], which means that the fault of the author will not be taken into account when analysing the damage. All persons, physical and legal, have an obligation concerning environmental protection due to the environment's legal nature as a public good.[26] The law n. 7.347 of 1985, which provides for the Public Civil Action Act – the Brazilian class action -, states, in Article 1, the possibility for a person to be held liable for a material, a moral[27] or pure environmental damage. This action can be used in the case of collective[28], individual or diffuse[29] rights violation, depending on the person that had his rights violated individually or collectively. The individuals also have the possibility of using other instruments in order to seek reparation for the environmental damages caused. Therefore, the explanation of who is competent to use this action, what can be required and the positive and negative aspects concerning this system becomes indispensable.

The Public Civil Action Act[30] can be used in the context of the protection of the environment, consumers, historical and artistic assets, amongst others. The competence to use this instrument is limited only for some public and private subjects, such as the Public Prosecution Office (*Ministério Público*)[31], federal entities, private associations created at least one year before the action[32] with the formal competence to protect collective rights related to the areas indicated above. However, this collective action does not exclude the possibility for the victims to exercise their right to ask for reparation individually concerning moral or material personal damage related to the environmental damage.

By this action, a legal or a private person can be held liable for environmental damage with the statement of specific obligations related to doing or not to doing

---

25 Article 14, § 1° of the Federal Law n. 6.938/1981, see also: *J.R.M. Leite & P.A. Ayala*, Dano ambiental: do individual ao coletivo extrapatrimonial. Teoria e prática, 4th ed, 2011.

26 The Brazilian Federal Constitution qualifies the environment as a public good "*bem de uso comum do povo*". It means that this good cannot be appropriated by anyone. Indeed, it states that the management of the environment is an obligation of the public entities and its conservation and preservation is also an obligation of everybody.

27 Superior Court of Justice (STJ) Judgment: Case Special Appeal (Resp) n.791653/RS, Decision of February 6, 2007.

28 It means that these people are not, but can, be determinate due to their integration in a specific group. They are connected by the same legal relation. The damage is not indivisible. See: Article 81, single paragraph, item II of the Law n. 8078, September 11, 1990; *J.R.M. Leite & P.A.Ayala*, *supra*, note 30, p. 249; *E. Milaré*, *supra*, note 20, p. 167.

29 A definition of these rights can be found in: Art. 81, single paragraph, item I of the Consumer Code (Law n. 8.078 of 1990). "Diffuse rights, (...) have an indivisible nature and have as holders undetermined people connected by a factual situation".

30 *J.R.M. Leite & P.A.Ayala*, *supra*, note 30, p.239-263; E. Milaré, supre, note 20, pp. 1460-1534.

31 Article 127 of the Brazilian Constitution states that the Public Prosecutors Office (*Ministério Público*) is a "permanent institution, essential to the jurisdictional function of the State, and it is its duty to defend the juridical order, the democratic regime and the inalienable social and individual interests". Article 129, item III, states the competence of the prosecutors to use the public civil action.

32 Brazil, Federal Law n. 7.347, 1985, Article 5. See also: *C.A.P.Fiorillo*, Curso de direito ambiental brasileiro, 14th ed, 2013, pp. 696-699.

something, to repairing or/and paying for the damage.[33] The law provides for the coexistence between the material, moral and ecological damage.[34] Indeed, the amount due because of environmental damages must be transferred to a public fund, created in 1994 by Federal Decree n. 1.306. This fund is called "*Fundo de Defesa de Direitos Difusos*". It is a fund controlled by the Federal State, Federation Entities of States or Municipalities. The amount received due to material or moral condemnation must be mandatorily used for the reparation of environmental damage. However, the deposit will be made only if there is pure environmental damage. In case of personal damage, which is the most common one, the environmental damage is integrated in the personal damage, which means that pure environmental damage is seldom recognized; consequently, when it does happen, no damage is reverted to the Fund. Despite the existence of the environmental liability system in Brazil, the latter suffers from some limits regarding the reparation of environmental damage caused by oil spills.

2.2. LIMITS IN PROVIDING FOR REPARATION OF ENVIRONMENTAL DAMAGE CONCERNING OIL SPILLS

Cases concerning discharges of oil from shipping, offshore extraction and transport in pipelines have taken place in Brazil. Even if some Brazilian and foreign companies have been sued for environmental damages that occurred by oil spills, and have been found liable[35], the system based on civil liability does not provide reparation *in natura* of the damages and does not respond to the monetary reparation promptly. Some positive aspects of civil liability still need to be highlighted as to, even while this chapter's objective is to demonstrate these limits.

Recent decisions have considered that the criteria to hold a company liable for an oil spill can be connected to the potentiality of the activity concerned to

---

33 Article 3 of the Law n. 7.347/1985. Superior Court of Justice (STJ) Judgment, Special Appeal n. 1.114.893/MG, Decision of February 28, 2012.

34 For the coexistence between the material, the moral and the environmental reparation see: Superior Court of Justice (STJ) Judgment: Case Special Appeal (Resp) n.1.328.753-MG, Decision of May, 28 2013; Superior Court of Justice (STJ) Judgment: Case Special Appeal (Resp) n. 896.863-DF, Decision of May 19, 2011; Superior Court of Justice (STJ) Judgment: Case Special Appeal (Resp) n. 1.180.078, Decision of December 02, 2010.

35 For instance: See: *Tribunal Regional Federal da 2ª Região* Judgment: Case n. 2005.51.02.006331-0, Decision of December 18, 2013; *Tribunal Regional Federal da 2ª Região* Judgment: Case n. 2005.51.01.003821-4, Decision of November 25, 2014. *Tribunal Regional Federal da* 3ª Região Judgment: Case n. 10607 SP 0010607-88.2011.4.03.6104, Decision of November 06, 2014; *Tribunal Regional Federal da 2ª Região* Judgment: Case n. 2009.50.01.0011512-6, Decision of April, 14 2015. For an example of a case where the companies have not been found liable see: *Tribunal Regional Federal da 2ª Região* Judgment: Case Interlocutory appeal n. 2012.02.01.004075-2, Decision of November 27, 2012.

cause environmental damage.[36] Even if there is no clear evidence of the damage, the probability of its occurrence can be used as an argument to prove the environmental damage.[37] Indeed, the argument of force majeure has not been accepted to avoid the liability of the company.[38]

2.2.1. Limits of the reparation in natura

The decisions concerning civil liability in Brazil are not able to properly deal with the reparation *in natura* of the damage. If the public prosecutors are not able to obtain a provisional measure in order to ask for the reparation *in natura*, the procedures last for at least 3 years because of the plurality of appeals that are made before the end of the process. For instance, in the Chevron case, the provisional measure demanded in 2012 was rejected; this has avoided the possibility of compensation *in natura*.[39]

The reparation *in natura* means that the damage will have to be repaired by mitigation or by elimination of the consequences of the damage caused directly to the environment (on the fauna, flora ...). It means undertaking a direct action in nature. The obligation to compensate means producing a similar good to the one that has been destroyed by searching for an ecological equivalent compensation.

Regarding oil spills in Brazil, most of the cases take a long time to be judged. Because of this, many of the decisions provide only monetary compensation for the damage. For instance, an oil spill of four thousand litres that occurred in the *Baía de Vitória*, in the State of Espírito Santo in 2003 was only judged in 2009 when the two companies responsible for the accident were sued by the Public Prosecutors. The ruling of the Court of Appeal (*TRF 2a. Região*)[40] was delivered only in 2015. The reason for the oil spill was related to the heaviness of a ship that sank after collecting too much oil from other ships. Even if the local administrative environmental entity (*Instituto Estadual de Meio Ambiente e Recursos Hídricos (IEMA)*), the responsible entity from the Marine (The *Capitania dos Portos)*, and the company responsible for the port (Vale/SA), tried to contain this oil discharge, around four thousand litres of oil were spilled in the maritime space under Brazilian jurisdiction. An administrative fine was imposed on the companies.

---

36 *Tribunal Regional Federal da 2ª Região* Judgment: Case n. 2005.51.02.006331-0, Decision of December 18, 2013. *Tribunal Regional Federal da 2ª Região* Judgment: Case n. 2009.50.01.0011512-6, Decision of April, 14 2015.

37 *Tribunal Regional Federal da 2ª Região* Judgment: Case n. 2005.51.01.003821-4, Decision of November 25, 2014. *Tribunal Regional Federal da* 3ª Região Judgment: Case n. 10607 SP 0010607-88.2011.4.03.6104, Decision of November 06, 2014.

38 *Tribunal Regional Federal da 2ª Região* Judgment: Case n. 2009.50.01.0011512-6, Decision of April, 14 2015.

39 *Tribunal Regional Federal da 2ª Região* Judgment: Case Interlocutory appeal n. 2012.02.01.004075-2, Decision of November 27, 2012.

40 *Tribunal Regional Federal da 2ª Região* Judgment: Case n. 2009.50.01.0011512-6, Decision of April, 14 2015.

This fine was challenged by the companies before the first instance tribunal. This appeal was refused by this tribunal and also by the Court of Appeals. Indeed, the lower court awarded compensation of 25 thousand *reais* (around 6 thousand dollars) for each company which had to be deposited in the Fund (*Fundo de Defesa dos Direitos Difusos*). The companies tried to argue that the cause of the accident was an event of force majeure, that the spill was insignificant and did not cause environmental damage. Nonetheless, these arguments were not accepted by the Courts in regards to the obligation of the reparation of any damage, even if it may be considered insignificant, which was not the case.[41] Moreover, even if the event was caused by a force majeure, the companies which were potentially connected to the damage would have to repair it. Other similar cases can be pointed out as examples of the same facts and legal reasoning.[42]

In this context, if a provisional measure required in the Public Civil Action proceedings is not deferred, it is almost impossible to achieve reparation *in natura* of the damage. For instance, in the Chevron case, which was one of the biggest oil spills in the Brazilian maritime space, the provisional measure that was postulated in 2012 was rejected. The arguments that prevailed were connected to the need for more evidence in order to hold the companies liable for the damage. Undoubtedly, the plaintiff was not able to prove that other spills would happen if the activity was suspended. The decision to reject the provisional measures averted the possibility of compensation *in natura* of the damage.[43] In addition to these limits, there are other limits concerning the monetary reparation of the environmental damage through civil liability.

2.2.2. Limits of the monetary reparation

With respect to the monetary reparation, some concerns can be pointed out. In Brazil, the material, the moral and the ecological reparation of the damage can coexist. However, there is no provision for the measurement of environmental damage. There is no consolidated methodology to define precisely the quantum of the obligation to indemnity in the case of environmental damage. The lack of parameters for valuation can hinder the monetary reparation of the damage. Given this legal gap, each Court interprets differently using disparate parameters to value the amount of reparation. For instance, criminal parameters linked to the Environmental Crimes Act have already been used as a parameter for civil liability.[44] For cases related to oil spills, some parameters can be identified.

---

41 Article 3, item III, "e" of the Federal Law n. 6.938/81.

42 *Tribunal Regional Federal da* 3ª Região Judgment: Case n. 10607 SP 0010607-88.2011.4.03.6104, Decision of November 06, 2014.

43 *Tribunal Regional Federal da 2ª Região* Judgment: Case Interlocutory appeal n. 2012.02.01.004075-2, Decision of November 27, 2012.

44 Superior Court of Justice (STJ) Judgment: Case Special Appeal (Resp) n. 1.164.630/MG, Decision of November 18, 2010.

For example, in some cases that occurred in the State of São Paulo, the Court of Appeal of the Third Region used parameters designed by the CETESB – *Companhia de Tecnologia de Saneamento Ambiental.*[45] One case was related to an oil spill in Guarujá/SP which resulted in a condemnation by the first instance court in R$ 89,518.60 (around 20,000 dollars). This amount was based on the quantity of biodiesel dumped and the amount of money which was used to repair the damage. However, the Court of Appeal re-evaluated the amount of the damage to US$ 251,188.64 based on the CETESB parameter. Therefore, it can be said that CETESB is the State entity competent to provide for administrative environmental criteria for the reparation of damage caused by oil spills.[46] In other words, the CETESB parameters have been used in some cases judged by this Appeal Court. Nevertheless, as long as there are five different Federal Appeal Courts in Brazil, depending on the court, these CETESB criteria will not be adopted.

With regards to the ineffectiveness of the Environmental Reparation Fund, created by the law n° 7347 of 1985[47], some limits can be pointed out. The amount that must be deposited in the Fund is the value stated by the judge. That said, the condemnation does not generally indicate the amount that must be directed to the fund. Usually, the decisions take only the material or the moral reparation that must be directed to the victims into account.[48] It means that, in most cases, there is no evaluation of the environmental damage independently of the material or the moral damage. Usually, when personal, material and ecological damages are requested, the environmental one is assimilated to the first ones.

Another aspect that can be pointed out concerning the Fund is that each amount received for the reparation of the environment is added to the total amount of the Fund. This means that the destination of the amount received cannot be determined ahead of time. Therefore, even if this amount will be used for the reparation of environmental damage, it is not possible to ensure that it will be used specifically for the reparation of damage related to oil spills. Hence, these limitations explain why it is necessary to search for complementary instruments in order to ensure environmental damage reparation in the context of oil spills.

---

45 *Tribunal Regional Federal da* 3ª Região Judgment: Case n. 10607 SP 0010607-88.2011.4.03.6104, Decision of November 06, 2014. See also: *Tribunal Regional Federal da 2ª Região* Judgment: Case n. 2009.50.01.0011512-6, Decision of April, 14 2015.

46 *CETESB*, Proposta de critério para valoração monetária de danos causados por derrames de petróleo ou de seus derivados no ambiente marinho, available at <http://4ccr.pgr.mpf.mp.br/atuacao/encontros-e-eventos/cursos/curso-de-valoracao-do-dano-ambiental/CETESB_Valoracao_Ambiental.pdf>.

47 Brazil, Federal Law n. 7347/85, Article 13.

48 Superior Court of Justice (STJ) Judgment: Case Special Appeal (Resp) n.1.328.753-MG, Decision of May, 28 2013. Superior Court of Justice (STJ) Judgment: Case Special Appeal (Resp) n. 896.863-DF, Decision of May 19, 2011. Superior Court of Justice (STJ) Judgment: Case Special Appeal (Resp) n. 1.180.078, Decision of December 02, 2010.

The "Conduct Adjustment Agreement", presented in the following section of this chapter, seems to bring quite interesting alternatives.

3. CONTRIBUTIONS OF THE "CONDUCT ADJUSTMENT AGREEMENT" TO THE REPARATION OF ENVIRONMENTAL DAMAGE CAUSED BY OIL SPILLS

The limits highlighted in the first part of this chapter can be mitigated by using the Conduct Adjustment Agreement (TAC). In order to understand the TAC's specific contributions to environmental damage reparation in the oil spill context, it is important to present this instrument's definition, legal nature, legitimacy, main requirements and consequences. Therefore, we will show in the first part of this topic how TACs are negotiated, who the parties in the agreement are and which common provisions are generally included. Afterwards, the specific characteristics of TACs adopted in the oil spill cases will be presented.

3.1. REFLECTIONS ON THE TAC'S MAIN FEATURES

In general, the TAC is a voluntary agreement celebrated to correct environmental and social damage.[49] In some cases it is actually envisioned as being more advantageous for the polluter to celebrate a TAC than to respond to a public civil action.[50] The celebration of the Conduct Adjustment Agreement consists of some indispensable formal aspects, such as: the written form, legal bases, complete identification of the parties, clear definition of the clauses that set the obligations, deadline and, finally, the parties' signature. The TAC negotiation begins with a clear and objective proposal from the public agency, which also observes the interests of the defendants.[51] The TAC should contain the qualification of the parties, the general obligations, the pecuniary obligation, set a deadline for compliance and penalty provisions, such as fines, if necessary. In other words, according to the case, the TAC may establish obligations to do or not to do (affirmative or restrictive covenants), which may be combined with monetary obligations to compensate. Its main purpose, in addition to adapting the conduct of the wrongdoers, is to promptly and efficiently solve the damages caused to the environment and society by avoiding bureaucratic and lengthy judicial proceedings. This explains why the TAC generally provides deadline clauses for

---

49 Article 42 of the Federal Decree n. 99.274, adopted on June 6 1990.

50 *L. Schimit*, Analise critica do termo de ajustamento de conduta no direito ambiental brasileiro, 2002, pp. 89-91.

51 *S. Campelli*, *supra* note 26, p. 70.

the accomplishment of the obligation. According to Article 5 § 6 of Law 7347/85, if the obligations are not met within the prescribed period, the wrongdoer (defendant) will probably be subject to a monetary penalty.

The parties that engage in the TAC are called the "promisee" (*compromitente*) and the "promissor" (*compromissário*). On the one hand, the petitioners who may have legitimacy to negotiate a TAC, and therefore act as a "promisee", are public entities such as the Union, States, Municipalities, Federal District, the Public Prosecutor's Office and Environment protection agencies, such as the Brazilian Institute of Environment and Renewable Natural Resources (IBAMA). Thus, no civil society organization or private foundation has the legal capacity to propose the making of a TAC.[52] On the other hand, the "promissor" has legitimacy as defendant.[53] Furthermore, the subject treated in the TAC should be part of the public agencies' vocation.[54] In the TACs involving oil spills, it is possible to note the high level of participation of both the Federal and State Public Prosecutor's Office as "promisee", that is as the party that proposes the negotiation of the agreement. However, the Superior Court of Justice has already clarified that even if the participation of the Public Prosecutor's Office is desirable, it is not obligatory and its absence does not nullify the Conduct Adjustment Agreement.[55]

The TAC may be negotiated prior to the opening of the civil inquiry or the public civil action, as well as during the course of the investigation and the execution phase. When negotiated before the conclusion of the public civil action, the TAC will have an extrajudicial enforcement nature; however, if it is signed during the execution phase it will be considered to be a judicial enforcement mechanism.[56] For example, in the Chevron case, which will be further analysed in this chapter, the TAC was signed after the petition of the public civil action in order to accelerate the reparation of the damage and also to assure less expensive reparation for the defendants.[57]

Having presented the general and formal aspects of the Conduct Adjustment Agreement, its complementary role in the reparation of environmental damage will be highlighted next by showing how it contributes to specify obligations to repair *in natura* (2.2) and monetary obligations (2.3). Furthermore, preventive obligations also stipulated by some TACs will be presented to show how they can

52 H.N. MAZZILLI, A defesa dos interesses difusos em juízo: meio ambiente, consumidor, patrimônio cultural, patrimônio público e outros interesses, 23ed, 2015, pp. 48-58.

53 *A.L.A. Nery*, Compromisso de Ajustamento de Conduta: teoria e análise de casos práticos, 2010, p. 169.

54 *Id.* at p. 191.

55 Superior Court of Justice (STJ) Judgment: Case n. 114.470, Decision of September 21, 1996. See also *H. Dalla*, The Undertaking Of Adjustment Of Conduct In Brazilian Collective Procedural Law, p.91.

56 *J.C. Santos*, Ação civil pública: comentários por artigo, 1995, p. 225.

57 TAC Chevron (and others) available in Portuguese at <www.prrj.mpf.mp.br/frontpage/noticias/mpf-assina-tac-com-chevron-nessa-sexta-feira>.

contribute, even if indirectly, to the reparation of environmental damages that occur due to oil discharges.

3.2. THE TAC'S CONTRIBUTION TO THE DEFINITION OF THE OBLIGATION TO REPAIR IN NATURA

The TAC procedure helps circumvent some limitations related to judicial proceedings that may postpone the ideal reparation of environmental damage. Put succinctly, the wrongdoers responsible for an act or omission that resulted in oil pollution may commit themselves to repairing the environmental damage or might take action in order to avoid and prevent future damage. The TAC contributes to the definition and precision of the obligations to repair *in natura*. In other words, concrete obligations to rehabilitate, mitigate the consequences and to remove or limit the impact directly caused on the natural environment may be stipulated.[58]

All necessary measures for the effective protection of the public interest, which needs to appear in the TAC, should relate to the same requests that would have been made in a public civil action. It is understood that the public agency acting as petitioner may only make the TAC's terms flexible regarding concerns about the timing, the means and the place for the fulfilment of the obligations. No flexibility related to the obligations *per se* may occur.[59] Therefore, it is the public agencies' duty to include in the Conduct Adjustment Agreement all the obligations *in natura* they deem important for the environmental damage reparation.[60]

Among the obligations *in natura* established, the TAC REDUC[61], reached between the Rio de Janeiro State Environment Secretariat (SEA-RJ), the Rio de Janeiro State Environment Institute (INEA-RJ) and the Brazilian company Petrobras (*Refinaria Duque de Caxias – REDUC*) specifically recommends the implementation of a treatment station on the river Irajá, the implementation of a project to drain rainwater surrounding the REDUC and the adoption of a recycling waste disposal program.

The TAC involving the Bahia Public Prosecution Office (MPF-BA) and the Coastal BM- CAL-4 Ltda (TAC COASTAL) intended to ensure the consistency of the oil and natural gas research and exploration activities undertaken by

---

58 *B. Steinmetz*, Préjudice écologique et réparation des atteintes à l'environnement – Plaidoyer pour une catégorie nouvelle de préjudice, Revue Européenne de Droit de l'Environnement – décembre 2008, p. 407.

59 *S. Campelli*, *supra*, note 26, p. 23.

60 *R. Jelinek*, *supra*, note 19.

61 TAC Reduc, text available in Portuguese at <http://fappbg.blogspot.com.br/2013/11/termo-de-ajustamento-de-conduta-tac-da.html>.

the company with the environment.[62] This agreement lists several objectives, potential partners and establishes future actions to be undertaken to avoid future environmental damage. It determines that the promissor (the COASTAL Company) should finance the zoning of the area of permanent preservation affected by the activity, among other points. This TAC fixes the need to comply with a Strategic Environmental Assessment obligation.[63]

In addition, monetary obligations are also fixed in many TACs in order to finance the implementation of the *in natura* obligations and to compensate for environmental damage due to oil spills. Penalties such as fines also exemplify monetary obligations; however, these only apply when the company does not comply with its commitments.

3.3. THE TAC'S CONTRIBUTION TO THE DEFINITION OF THE MONETARY OBLIGATION TO REPAIR

The definition and precision of the monetary obligation to repair requires the analysis of many aspects. For instance, it is necessary to consider the extent and severity of the environmental damage, the loss of natural resources, the level of pollution of watercourses and the damage suffered by the local economy.[64] The monetary obligation should bring gains to the environment and inhibit the future occurrence of similar behaviours that lead to environmental accidents. A comparative analysis of the agreed upon monetary obligations permits the assumption that the defendant's economic condition influences in the sum fixed as compensatory values. The "TAC REDUC" case involving Petrobras has the highest monetary obligation value, followed by the "TAC Chevron" and finally by the "TAC COASTAL".

In the "TAC REDUC", Petrobras committed itself to providing up to fifty million *reais* in order to comply with all of the obligations *in natura* that were fixed. In addition to this amount, the value of one billion, eighty-nine million and two hundred thousand *reais* should serve adequacy actions.

In the "TAC Chevron" case, the monetary obligation value for the implementation of the compensatory measures was set at R$ 95,160,000 (ninety-five million, one hundred sixty thousand reais). The given value, according to the provisions of the Agreement, would be aimed at biodiversity conservation on the coast, the sustainable use of fisheries resources and environmental

62 TAC Coastal, Clause 1, available in Portuguese at <www.prba.mpf.mp.br/paraocidadao/pecas-juridicas/termos-de-ajustamento-de-conduta/tac_hidrocarboneto.pdf>.

63 TAC Coastal, Clause I.1.2, available in Portuguese at <www.prba.mpf.mp.br/paraocidadao/pecas-juridicas/termos-de-ajustamento-de-conduta/tac_hidrocarboneto.pdf>.

64 *D. M. B. A Costa*, Valoração econômica como ferramenta para compensação de derramamentos de petróleo, 2012.

education.[65] It is interesting to note that in order to facilitate the implementation of the monetary obligations in this TAC, the Brazilian Institute of Environment and Renewable Natural Resources (IBAMA) and the Brazilian National Agency of Petroleum, Natural Gas and Biofuels (ANP) suggested a financial schedule to facilitate the fulfilment of all the obligations set to repair the damage.[66] Semi-annual monitoring reports audited by an independent company should be sent to the latter-mentioned agencies.[67]

In this particular "TAC Chevron" case, some of the *in natura* obligations were not complied with and two fines were imposed by the IBAMA. The first fine, imposed on November 21, 2011, was due to a continuous discharge of oil even after the TAC was made. The fine was set at the amount of fifty million *reais*. The second fine, worth ten million, was imposed on December 23, 2011 for non-compliance with the Individual Emergency Plan.[68] The National Petroleum Agency (ANP) also imposed a fine of three thousand, six hundred and fifty million *reais*. Among the three TACs analysed in this chapter, the monetary obligation clause inserted in "TAC Chevron" is the most precise, in what concerns the fulfilment of the action plan and the penalties for non-compliance.

Finally, in the "TAC Coastal", the environmental monetary obligation set related to the funding of the Environmental Citizenship Project that was established as an *in natura* obligation. The project should receive the investment of R$ 300,000.00 (three hundred thousand *reais*).[69] Moreover, this TAC established a daily fine for non-compliance at the amount of R$ 50,000.00 (fifty thousand *reais*), to be reverted to the National Environmental Fund.[70]

Even if many TACs bring interesting solutions for the adoption of *in natura* and monetary obligations, it is noteworthy that the majority of the obligations inserted in TACs are of a preventive nature. In what concerns specifically the need to repair environmental damage due to oil spills, these obligations to prevent clearly do not function as well as the *in natura* and monetary obligations; however, their indirect contribution should not be ignored. Therefore, the content of some preventive obligations found in the three TACs analysed are worthy of consideration.

---

65 TAC Chevron, Clause 2.2.2, available in Portuguese at <www.prrj.mpf.mp.br/frontpage/noticias/mpf-assina-tac-com-chevron-nessa-sexta-feira>.

66 TAC Chevron, Clause 2.2.3 e 2.2.4, available in Portuguese at <www.prrj.mpf.mp.br/frontpage/noticias/mpf-assina-tac-com-chevron-nessa-sexta-feira>.

67 TAC Chevron, Clause 2.2.7, available in Portuguese at <www.prrj.mpf.mp.br/frontpage/noticias/mpf-assina-tac-com-chevron-nessa-sexta-feira>.

68 *IBAMA*, Nota Informativa n.01/12 – CGPEG/DILIC/IBAMA. Vazamento no Campo de Frade, na Bacia de Campos – Propostas de Monção do CONAMA. p. 2.

69 TAC Coastal, Clause 4, available in Portuguese at <www.prba.mpf.mp.br/paraocidadao/pecas-juridicas/termos-de-ajustamento-de-conduta/tac_hidrocarboneto.pdf>.

70 TAC Coastal, Clause 5, available in Portuguese at <www.prba.mpf.mp.br/paraocidadao/pecas-juridicas/termos-de-ajustamento-de-conduta/tac_hidrocarboneto.pdf>.

3.4. THE TAC'S DEFINITION OF PREVENTIVE OBLIGATIONS THAT INDIRECTLY CONTRIBUTE TO REPAIR

In the TACs analysed, it is possible to identify interesting solutions for environmental degradation resulting from oil spills that actually come from preventive obligations, such as those related to educational projects, management board training and the inclusion of specialized environmental agencies as drivers and controllers of the actions to be developed.

In the "TAC REDUC" agreement, reached between the Rio de Janeiro State Environment Secretariat (SEA-RJ), the Rio de Janeiro State Environment Institute (INEA-RJ) and the Brazilian company Petrobras (*Refinaria Duque de Caxias – REDUC*), the Parties noted the need to implement necessary measures to comply with the operating licenses granted to the refinery. It was defined that the projects, the investment and the implementation schedule should be approved by the Rio de Janeiro State Environment Institute (INEA-RJ) prior to its execution.[71] Among the fixed obligations within this "TAC REDUC", the Petrobras Company accepted to submit semi-annual reports so that the INEA-RJ could monitor the implementation of the Action Plan, the development of which it had contributed to previously.[72]

The TAC COASTAL explicitly stipulates the obligation to develop environmental plans and programs such as an Environmental Emergency Plan and create a funding program for the Environmental Citizenship Project organized by the *Instituto de Defesa, Estudo e Integração Ambiental* – IDEIA).[73] Another obligation negotiated in this TAC consisted in carrying out at least one public hearing into each of the municipalities affected by the oil and gas research and exploration activities.[74] This sort of obligation could actually be classified as preventive and *in natura* since the public hearing may contribute to specify the damages that occurred and need to be repaired directly with the participation of the local communities affected. The TAC COASTAL exemplifies, therefore, how the parties involved may be interested in anticipating and adopting measures to protect and avoid future environmental damage in the affected area.

In the "TAC Chevron"[75] celebrated with the Rio de Janeiro Public Prosecution Office (MPF-RJ) in 2013, the obligations adopted emphasize the company's commitment to the adoption of all "measures of prevention and precaution to

---

71 TAC REDUC, Clause 1.3, available in Portuguese at <http://fappbg.blogspot.com.br/2013/11/termo-de-ajustamento-de-conduta-tac-da.html>.

72 TAC REDUC, Clause 3.1.2, available in Portuguese at <http://fappbg.blogspot.com.br/2013/11/termo-de-ajustamento-de-conduta-tac-da.html>.

73 TAC Coastal Bmcal-4 Ltda, 2003, Clausula II.

74 TAC Coastal Clause III.2, available in Portuguese at <www.prba.mpf.mp.br/paraocidadao/pecas-juridicas/termos-de-ajustamento-de-conduta/tac_hidrocarboneto.pdf>.

75 TAC Chevron (and others) available at <www.prrj.mpf.mp.br/frontpage/noticias/mpf-assina-tac-com-chevron-nessa-sexta-feira>.

avoid environmental incidents and to improve the system of response in case such incidents occur".[76] The agreement also provides more specific obligations, such as the need to install an integrated system that would work continuously for 24 hours a day to detect and monitor oil at sea on the platform and on at least on two vessels.[77]

4. CONCLUSION

Certainly, initiatives such as the adoption of Conduct Adjustment Agreement can develop to achieve important gains if the *in natura*, monetary and preventive obligations *illustrated* and described *herein* are complied with and are enforced. The TAC is flexible enough to guarantee specific prevention and reparation of the environmental damage. Two main contributions have been highlighted in this chapter, but others can be pointed out as well. Despite the identification of these contributions, some of the TACs' general limits should also be kept in mind when analysing if this instrument is an adequate means to circumvent civil liability ineffectiveness. Therefore, one of the central conclusions of this chapter is that a complementary approach between the civil liability system and the TAC procedure should be envisaged in order to strengthen the reparation of environmental damage.

The complementariness of these instruments permits, for example, the adoption of preventive measures that otherwise would not have been adopted if only the liability system was considered. The TAC can be used as an instrument to avoid future damage since the judgements in the liability system do not provide for preventive measures. For instance, in the three TAC cases concerning oil spills analysed in this chapter, it has been possible to identify interesting preventive measures such as educational projects, management board training and the inclusion of specialized environmental agencies as drivers and controllers of the actions to be developed in order to avoid future damage.

Concerning TAC's contribution to the reparation *in natura*, the return to the *status quo ante* environment is possible because of the monetary obligations that are stipulated. The amounts fixed for compensation and fines contribute to ensuring that companies will comply with the obligations indicated in the TAC. Even if, in the end, these monetary obligations are not complied with, it will still always be possible for the victims to resort to the liability system to seek a judicial decision for reparation. This confirms the possibility of complementariness between the TAC and the liability system.

---

[76] TAC Chevron, Clause 2.1, available in Portuguese at <www.prrj.mpf.mp.br/frontpage/noticias/mpf-assina-tac-com-chevron-nessa-sexta-feira>.

[77] TAC Chevron, Clause 2.1.5.

For the participatory approach, some of the positive aspects related to the use of TACs is that their celebration may take the views of different actors into account, something which may contribute to the definition of the environmental aspects that really require an *in natura* reparation. This is done through the inclusion of *in natura* obligation clauses. In some cases, the participation of Universities and Nongovernmental Organizations can contribute to the designing of these clauses. The Strategic Environmental Assessment required to guide the exploration and production of oil and gas in the south of Bahia, and which had to be complied with under the TAC Coastal, was funded by the Coastal company for example, but was devised and executed by a group of environmental management scientists affiliated with the Postgraduate Program in Engineering – COPPE of the Federal University of Rio de Janeiro. Furthermore, this encouraging broad participation, as seen in the TAC Coastal, was also extended to the explicit recognition of the local communities' autonomy to monitor and combat any increase in the devastation of the environment.

On the other hand, as mentioned previously in this conclusion, TACs also have important limitations. If the clauses are not clearly indicated, or if the obligations agreed upon are not specifically related to oil spills, then the TAC's effectiveness has to be questioned. *Paradoxically,* in these cases, the liability system may therefore become the complementary instrument to the insufficiencies of the TAC. Accordingly, if the obligations and the enforcement measures, such as fines, are not presented accurately, the effectiveness of the Conduct Adjustment Agreement may be challenged. Consequently, depending on the case, the TAC can contribute to the reparation of environmental damage and can serve as a complementary and alternative method to civil liability.

CHAPTER 14

CAN MULTILATERAL DEVELOPMENT BANKS BE MORE ENVIRONMENTALLY EFFECTIVE?

Perspectives from the Practice of International Accountability Mechanisms

Vanessa RICHARD

*CNRS Researcher, Aix Marseille Univ, Univ Toulon, CNRS, DICE, CERIC, Aix-en-Provence, France**

The adverse environmental impacts of projects supported by Multilateral Development Banks (MDBs), such as the World Bank or its regional counterparts, have been denounced for decades. The domains in which MDBs operate logically bear environmental and social risk which can be significant: development of transportation, of agribusiness, of energy sources, of extractive industries etc. This includes projects to develop highways, airports, dams and reservoirs, irrigation systems, wind farms, coal power plants, mining, to reorganize land management, to reform the legal framework related to land tenures or else forest concessions etc. Such projects may entail changing land use patterns and natural habitats, or else cause disruptions affecting the water cycle, biodiversity, soil, forests … Not to mention the human impacts: 'involuntary' (in the language of MDBs) and sometimes unwanted resettlement, destruction of cultural or spiritual heritage, loss of livelihoods, forced evictions etc.[1] The poor environmental record of the

---

* *Principal Investigator of the International Grievance Mechanisms and International Law & Governance (IGMs) project, www.igms-project.org. The research leading to these results has received funding from the European Research Council under the European Union's Seventh Framework Programme (FP/2007-2013) / ERC Grant Agreement no. 312514.*

1 The International Consortium of Investigative Journalism (ICIJ), who originated the 'LuxLeaks' and 'Panama Papers' scandals, have conducted a series of investigations on the human consequences of some projects the World Bank supports, untitled "Evicted and Abandoned. The World Bank's Broken Promise to the Poor", which are quite telling on how ugly things can sometimes turn: see www.icij.org/project/world-bank. All the URLs referenced in this contribution were last visited 27 August 2016.

World Bank Group[2] is richly documented, including by the World Bank itself, thanks to the reports of the Operations Evaluation Department, later transformed into the Independent Evaluation Group (IEG).[3] For example, the 2001 OED Review of the Bank's Performance on the Environment notes that:

> "To be sure, these achievements fell short of the expectations of many of its stakeholders. The momentum of the early 1990s dissipated in the face of constraints faced in the operating environment. Internally, environmental sustainability was not adequately integrated into the Bank's core objectives and country assistance strategies. Intellectually, the linkages between macroeconomic policy, poverty alleviation, and environmental sustainability were not explicitly forged. In sum, the institution's environmental efforts have not been consistent nor have they been held to uniform quality standards. Yet, staff have carried out many worthwhile activities related to the environment (...) This OED report finds that the Bank has made progress on the environment, and notes that its commitments were not accompanied by precise goals and performance monitoring."[4]

In 2008, the IEG finds that:

> "When requested, the Bank Group has been generally able to help countries set environmental priorities (although this is ultimately the responsibility of the countries themselves) and private sector clients to identify and address potential direct environmental impacts. However, it has been far less able to integrate these efforts centrally into country programs, incorporate them as requirements for sustainable growth and poverty reduction, and provide lending to help countries address environmental priorities – often because of lukewarm interest in such support from the countries themselves."[5]

---

2 The World Bank Group consists of five organisations: the International Bank for Reconstruction and Development (IBRD) which lends to governments, the International Development Association (IDA) which provides interest-free loans (credits) and grants to governments of the poorest countries, the International Finance Corporation (IFC) which supports private investment ion development, the Multilateral Investment Guarantee Agency (MIGA) which promotes foreign direct investment by offering political risk insurance (guarantees) to investors and lenders, and the International Centre for Settlement of Investment Disputes (ICSID) which provides international facilities for conciliation and arbitration of investment disputes.

3 The IEG "is charged with evaluating the activities of the International Bank for Reconstruction and Development (IBRD) and International Development Association (the World Bank), the work of International Finance Corporation (IFC) in private sector development, and Multilateral Investment Guarantee Agency's (MIGA) guarantee projects and services. The Director-General of IEG reports directly to the World Bank Group's Board of Directors. The goals of evaluation are to provide an objective assessment of the results of the Bank Group's work and to identify and disseminate lessons learned from experience": see http://ieg.worldbankgroup.org/about-us.

4 OED Review of the Bank's Performance on the Environment, 5 July 2001, http://ieg.worldbankgroup.org/Data/reports/oed_environment_review.pdf.

5 IEG, "Supporting Environmental Sustainability: An Evaluation of World Bank Group Experience, 1990-2007", Fast Track Brief, 6 August 2008, http://ieg.worldbankgroup.org/Data/reports/env_ftb.pdf, p. 3.

More recently, the IEG report on projects on forest resources states that:

> "World Bank policy advice and projects that have supported the reform of industrial timber concession regimes have usually neglected or underestimated the nontimber values and uses of the forests with respect to the livelihoods of forest-dependent people, their traditional claims, sociocultural values, and overall sense of security. Evidence is also lacking that concessioned natural forests are being managed sustainably."[6]

One can also think of the findings of the World Commission on Dams – jointly established by the World Bank Group and the World Conservation Union (IUCN) – on the magnitude of the adverse environmental impacts of large dams[7], or the findings of the Extractive Industries Review commissioned by the World Bank Group.[8] Volumes on the adverse environmental impacts of the activities that the World Bank Group finances, or otherwise supports, have been written by non-governmental organizations (NGOs) and advocates of environmental protection and the respect of social and environmental rights, some being very well-informed and acute.[9] Though regional MDBs, such as the African Development Bank Group (AfDB), the Asian Development Bank (ADB), the Interamerican Development Bank (IDB) and others, have not generated as abundant a literature on this topic as the World Bank has, their operations entail the same potential impacts to a large extent, with differences due to their own contexts.[10]

In contrast with this less-than-satisfying environmental track-record, it is remarkable that MDBs, and first among them the World Bank, have adopted environmental standards which, in some areas, are more detailed than the prescriptions of international environmental law and, what is more, may apply

6 IEG, "Managing Forest Resources for Sustainable Development. An Evaluation of World Bank Group Experience", 5 February 2013, https://ieg.worldbankgroup.org/Data/reports/forest_eval2.pdf, p. XV.

7 World Commission on Dams, *Dams and Development. A New Framework for Decision-making*, London/Sterling: Earthscan (2000), *inter alia* available at www.unep.org/dams/WCD/report/WCD_DAMS%20report.pdf.

8 The Extractive Industries Review resulted in 6 reports and a series of additional documents, including Management responses. All documents are available at www.ifc.org/wps/wcm/connect/Industry_EXT_Content/IFC_External_Corporate_Site/Industries/Oil,+Gas+and+Mining/Development_Impact/Development_Impact_Extractive_Industries_Review/.

9 For an expert analysis of both project-level and systemic failures of the World Bank as regard the environment, see for instance Bruce Rich, *Foreclosing the Future. The World Bank and the Politics of Environmental Destruction*, Washington/Covelo/London: Island Press (2013).

10 For example, so far the AfDB has relatively modestly participated in big infrastructure projects, and often joined the pool of donors after that the projects' design had been decided by the largest donor agencies; thus, its responsibility in the adverse impacts remained limited. With the adoption in late 2015 of the new NEPAD-IPPF (New Partnership for Africa's Development Infrastructure Project Preparation Facility) Strategic Business Plan, this is probably going to change: see AfDB, "Donors welcome improved performance of NEPAD-IPPF in project preparation", 17 December 2015, www.afdb.org/en/news-and-events/article/donors-welcome-improved-performance-of-nepad-ippf-in-project-preparation-15236/.

to the private sector. One shining example is the requirement that borrowers, either sovereign or private, conduct an environmental assessment (EA). The first environmental safeguards adopted by the World Bank date back to 1987. In 1989, the United States (US) Congress voted the so-called 'Pelosi amendment', which:

> "requires US Executive Directors at the World Bank and all the regional multilateral development banks (MDBs) to abstain or vote against any proposed action with significant environmental effects if it has not received an appropriate environmental assessment, or if the assessment has not been available to the Executive Directors and the public for 120 days before a vote (...) Environmental assessment and information access procedures have been adopted and put into practice by all the major MDBs, due in large part, most observers agree, to the Pelosi Amendment."[11]

EAs were formalized with the adoption of Operational Directive 4.00 (OD 4.00) in 1989.[12] The combination of lobbying within and from the US Congress, NGOs' pressure and the organisation of the Rio United Nations Conference on Environment and Development in 1992 provided the necessary thrust to the adoption of further environmental standards.[13] As regards EAs in development projects, the World Bank has a natural role as a standard-setter for international development finance agencies, and it's A to C environmental categorization of projects[14], as well as the requirement (at least in theory, as we will see) to complete and disclose the EA prior to the project being approved, have become standard practice in development financing. In 2010, the International Court of

---

11 Jonathan Sanford, Susan R. Fletcher, "Multilateral Development Banks' Environmental Assessment and Information Policies: Impact of the Pelosi Amendment", Congressional Research Service Report for Congress, 12 February 1998, http://congressionalresearch.com/98-180/document.php?study=MULTILATERAL+DEVELOPMENT+BANKS+ENVIRONMENTAL+ASSESSMENT+AND+INFORMATION+POLICIES+IMPACT+OF+THE+PELOSI+AMENDMENT; see also *inter alia* Ian A. Bowles, Cyril F. Kormos, "Environmental Reform at the World Bank: The Role of the U.S. Congress", 35 *Va. J. Int'l L.* (1995), p. 795.

12 See World Bank Environment Department, "Environmental Assessment Sourcebook. Volume I – Policies, Procedures and Cross-Sectoral Issues", World Bank Technical Paper Number 139 (1991).

13 Susan Park, "Norm Diffusion within International Organizations: A Case Study of the World Bank", 8 *J. Int'l Rel. Dev.* (2005), pp. 128-132.

14 "Category A: A proposed project is classified as Category A if it is likely to have significant adverse environmental impacts that are sensitive, diverse, or unprecedented"; "Category B: A proposed project is classified as Category B if its potential adverse environmental impacts on human populations or environmentally important areas--including wetlands, forests, grasslands, and other natural habitats--are less adverse than those of Category A projects"; "Category C: A proposed project is classified as Category C if it is likely to have minimal or no adverse environmental impacts. Beyond screening, no further EA action is required for a Category C project"; "Category FI: A proposed project is classified as Category FI if it involves investment of Bank funds through a financial intermediary, in subprojects that may result in adverse environmental impacts.": OP 4.01, Environmental Assessment, para. 8. Depending on the categorization of the project, the type and extent of the EA will be different and more or less stringent.

Justice (ICJ) recognized the customary nature of the obligation "to undertake an environmental impact assessment where there is a risk that the proposed industrial activity may have a significant adverse impact in a transboundary context, in particular, on a shared resource."[15] The ICJ inferred such obligation from a "practice, which in recent years has gained so much acceptance among States", but also from "due diligence, and the duty of vigilance and prevention which it implies."[16] The ICJ, however, considered that general international law does not specify:

> "the scope and content of an [environmental impact assessment]". [Consequently,] "it is for each State to determine in its domestic legislation or in the authorization process for the project, the specific content (...) required in each case, having regard to the nature and magnitude of the proposed development and its likely adverse impact on the environment as well as to the need to exercise due diligence in conducting such an assessment."[17]

Conversely, OP and BP 4.01 on Environmental Assessment[18] list a series of steps that the Bank's staff working on projects (the Management) must take. Like-standards of other MDBs have very similar provisions.[19] The first step consists in scoping and screening the proposed project, that is to say that Management must evaluate the type of project (which sector/activities), its scale and proposed location, whether it is *prima facie* sensitive or likely to generate significant social and/or environmental impacts. This leads to categorizing the project, which in turn conditions the type and extent of the Bank's requirements as regards the EA, which is carried out by the borrower.[20] If the latter is considered to have inadequate capacity to carry out the EA, then the project must "include components to strengthen that capacity."[21] Category A projects require a full EA, Category B projects require a narrower EA. Category A and B projects require that the borrower consults, as early as is possible, project-affected groups and local stakeholders and takes their views into account. In order to allow for

---

15 ICJ, *Pulp Mills on the River Uruguay (Argentina v. Uruguay)*, Judgment, *ICJ Reports 2010*, para. 204.

16 *Ibidem*.

17 *Ibid.*, para. 205.

18 Which replaced in 1999 OD 4.00 (1989) and then OD 4.01 (1991). The World Bank's Operational Manual is available at https://policies.worldbank.org/sites/PPF3/Pages/Manuals/Operational%20Manual.aspx.

19 William V. Kennedy, "EIA and Multilateral Financial Institutions", Presentation at the OECD Conference on FDI and the Environment, The Hague, 28-29 January 1999, www.oecd.org/investment/investmentfordevelopment/2076277.pdf. For an overview of the EA process that may apply to any entity, see T.C. Dougherty, A.W. Hall, HR Wallingford, "Environmental Impact Assessment of Irrigation and Drainage Projects", FAO Irrigation and Drainage Paper 53 (1995), Chapter 3, www.fao.org/docrep/V8350E/v8350e06.htm#chapter%203:%20eia%20process.

20 OP 4.01, para. 8.

21 *Ibid.*, para. 13.

meaningful consultations, the "borrower provides relevant material in a timely manner prior to consultation and in a form and language that are understandable and accessible to the groups being consulted."[22] The EA:

> "evaluates a project's potential environmental risks and impacts in its area of influence; examines project alternatives; identifies ways of improving project selection, siting, planning, design, and implementation by preventing, minimizing, mitigating, or compensating for adverse environmental impacts and enhancing positive impacts; and includes the process of mitigating and managing adverse environmental impacts throughout project implementation. (…) [It] takes into account the natural environment (air, water, and land); human health and safety; social aspects (involuntary resettlement, indigenous peoples, and physical cultural resources); and transboundary and global environmental aspects. EA considers natural and social aspects in an integrated way. It also takes into account the variations in project and country conditions; the findings of country environmental studies; national environmental action plans; the country's overall policy framework, national legislation, and institutional capabilities related to the environment and social aspects; and obligations of the country, pertaining to project activities, under relevant international environmental treaties and agreements. The Bank does not finance project activities that would contravene such country obligations, as identified during the EA. EA is initiated as early as possible in project processing and is integrated closely with the economic, financial, institutional, social, and technical analyses of a proposed project."[23]

The Management of the Bank then reviews the EA provided by the borrower, checks whether it is consistent with its EA policy, whether additional information, consultations or studies are needed. Officially transmitted EAs are disclosed by the Bank to the public.[24] After approval by the Board, the borrower must report, during the implementation of the project, about its compliance with the EA and, if relevant, with the Environmental Management Plan.[25]

In most MDBs, the EA requirements are not differentiated between sovereign borrowers and private clients.[26] However, the World Bank Group and, this

---

22 *Ibid.*, para. 15.

23 *Ibid.*, paras 2 and 3.

24 *Ibid.*, para. 18.

25 OP 4.01, Annex A – Definitions, para. 3: "Environmental management plan (EMP): An instrument that details (a) the measures to be taken during the implementation and operation of a project to eliminate or offset adverse environmental impacts, or to reduce them to acceptable levels; and (b) the actions needed to implement these measures. The EMP is an integral part of Category A EAs (irrespective of other instruments used). EAs for Category B projects may also result in an EMP."

26 See Asian Development Bank, "Safeguard Policy Statement", *in* OM Section F1/BP (2013), www.adb.org/sites/default/files/institutional-document/31483/om-f1-20131001.pdf; African Development Bank, "Operational safeguard 1 – Environmental and social assessment", *in* Integrated Safeguards System. Policy Statement and Operational Safeguards (2013), www.afdb.org/fileadmin/uploads/afdb/Documents/Policy-Documents/December_2013_-_AfDB%E2%80%99S_Integrated_Safeguards_System__-_Policy_Statement_and_Operational_Safeguards.pdf; European Investment

is quite recent, the Interamerican Development Bank Group have different standards for public and private operations. The 2012 Sustainability Framework, which applies to IFC and MIGA, is divided into two complementary parts. One is the Policy on Environmental and Social Sustainability[27], which describes IFC's commitments, the other is a set of 8 Performance Standards (PS) which describes the borrower's duties.[28] Though core EA obligations are in essence the same as they are for sovereign projects – to which the World Bank OPs apply – the language of PSs is more tailored to the language of the corporate world. Hence, PS1 does not refer to "environmental assessment" but to "Environmental and Social Management System" (ESMS), defined as "a dynamic and continuous process initiated and supported by management, and involves engagement between the client, its workers, local communities directly affected by the project (the Affected Communities) and, where appropriate, other stakeholders."[29] The purpose and content of ESMSs are not significantly different than those of EAs.[30] Likewise, within the IDB Group since 1st January 2016, the IDB has focused on sovereign-guaranteed projects, while private projects are entrusted to a consolidated Interamerican Investment Corporation (ICC). The IDB applies the 2006 Inter-American Development Bank, Environment and Safeguards

---

Bank, "The EIB Statement of Environmental and Social Principles and Standards" (2009), www.eib.org/attachments/strategies/eib_statement_esps_en.pdf; European Bank for Reconstruction and Development, Environmental and Social Policy (2014), www.ebrd.com/news/publications/policies/environmental-and-social-policy-esp.html …

27 International Finance Corporation's Policy on Environmental and Social Sustainability (2012), www.ifc.org/wps/wcm/connect/7540778049a792dcb87efaa8c6a8312a/SP_English_2012.pdf?MOD=AJPERES.

28 Performance Standard 1 on Assessment and Management of Environmental and Social Risks and Impacts; Performance Standard 2 on Labor and Working Conditions; Performance Standard 3 on Resource Efficiency and Pollution Prevention; Performance Standard 4 on Community Health, Safety, and Security; Performance Standard 5 on Land Acquisition and Involuntary Resettlement; Performance Standard 6 on Biodiversity Conservation and Sustainable Management of Living Natural Resources; Performance Standard 7 on Indigenous Peoples and; Performance Standard 8 on Cultural Heritage: Performance Standards on Environmental and Social Sustainability (2012), www.ifc.org/performancestandards.

29 PS1, para. 1.

30 *Ibid.*, para. 5: "The client, in coordination with other responsible government agencies and third parties as appropriate, will conduct a process of environmental and social assessment, and establish and maintain an ESMS appropriate to the nature and scale of the project and commensurate with the level of its environmental and social risks and impacts. The ESMS will incorporate the following elements: (i) policy; (ii) identification of risks and impacts; (iii) management programs; (iv) organizational capacity and competency; (v) emergency preparedness and response; (vi) stakeholder engagement; and (vii) monitoring and review." Interestingly, contrary to the 'public' arm of the World Bank which has steadily refused to mention human rights considerations in its strategies and standards, the IFC's PS 1 states that "Business should respect human rights, which means to avoid infringing on the human rights of others and address adverse human rights impacts business may cause or contribute to. Each of the Performance Standards has elements related to human rights dimensions that a project may face in the course of its operations. Due diligence against these Performance Standards will enable the client to address many relevant human rights issues in its project": *ibid.*, para. 3.

Compliance Policy[31] and the ICC applies the 2013 IIC Environmental and Social Sustainability Policy.[32] Under the latter, the ICC requires "Environmental and social appraisals." Interestingly, the ICC Environmental and Social Policy introduces a good measure of EES syncretism since it provides that:

> "The IIC assesses potential environmental and social risks and impacts of all proposed investments for compliance with host country laws and regulations and this Sustainability Policy and associated standards and guidelines prior to final approval thereof. These standards (see section VI, paragraph 1) include the IDB Environment and Safeguards Compliance Policy, other IDB safeguard policies and sector guidelines, the Performance Standards (PS) on Environmental and Social Sustainability of the International Finance Corporation (IFC), and the World Bank Group/IFC Environmental Health and Safety (EHS) Guidelines (including both General EHS guidelines and Industry Sector EHS Guidelines). Any subsequent revisions to those standards, policies and guidelines will likewise be incorporated into this Sustainability Policy, unless otherwise provided for by the IIC's Board of Executive Directors."[33]

The standards set by MDBs therefore create specific environmental obligations both directed to the Bank staff and the borrower/client. But do they 'work'? There are many ways to understand effectiveness. As far as the relationship between law and the environment is concerned, this might mean: Are environmental protection rules applied? Are the environmental issues at stake solved / taken into account adequately thanks to the rule? Is the content of the rule appropriate to achieving its environmental purpose? Is the purpose of the environmental rule achieved (irrespective of whether it has concretely solved the environmental problem at hand)? Over the last twenty years, an impressive corpus of literature on the effectiveness of international environmental law has been produced and it considers all of these aspects and even that of the quantification of effectiveness.[34] The present contribution endeavours to contribute to this corpus by exploring a specific angle: that of compliance with the environmental standards of the MDBs, seen through the lens of the cases reviewed by the MDBs' own accountability mechanisms, cases which are brought by the people directly affected by the adverse environmental impacts of projects that MDBs support.

More precisely, what can we learn about compliance, by the staff of MDBs, with the environmental standards adopted by and for the banks, from the cases

---

31 At http://idbdocs.iadb.org/wsdocs/getdocument.aspx?docnum=665902.

32 At www.iic.org/sites/default/files/pdf/iicdocs-346480-v13-sustainability_policy-2_26_13.pdf.

33 Para. 2.

34 Carsten Helm, Detlef Sprinz, "Measuring the Effectiveness of International Environmental Regimes", 45 *Journal of Conflict Resolution* 5 (2000), pp. 630-652; Detlef Sprinz, "The Quantitative Analysis of International Environmental Policy", *in* Detlef Sprinz, Yael Wolinsky-Nahmias (eds.), *Cases, Numbers, Models: International Relations Research Methods*, Ann Arbor: The University of Michigan Press (2004).

borne of projects which somehow went wrong? Such an approach has some obvious biases. Among those, the first is, precisely, that it focuses on projects in which something appeared to have gone wrong enough to justify at least a *prima facie* compliance assessment. This leaves aside all of the projects that did not trigger any compliance issue or any serious allegation of environmental and/or social harm. The purpose of this chapter is, however, not to assess the overall compliance of MDBs with their environmental standards but to shed light on the weak spots in MDB's interventions, these areas in which MDBs could learn and hopefully do better. A second bias is that no one knows how many serious compliance issues related to environmental and social harm have never given rise to the submission of a complaint to the accountability mechanism of the concerned MDB, for lack of knowledge that such mechanism existed, fear of reprisals etc. Nevertheless, most of the MDBs' accountability mechanisms – which are referred to as the International Accountability Mechanisms (IAMs) – now have a significant experience in reviewing the compliance of Management with their bank's standards, and I believe the sample is sufficient to distinguish the general dynamics of non-compliance with environmental standards.

The first part of this contribution introduces the scope and purpose of the control of the IAMs over Management, given that it is a kind of compliance review which is quite specific and distinct from judicial review, and compliance control is based on standards the nature and purpose of which are also very specific. The second part describes the findings of the MDBs' accountability mechanisms, as regards the loopholes and pitfalls related to compliance with environmental standards in the design, implementation and monitoring of the contentious projects and, in the light of these findings, puts forward explanations as to why some problems keep arising again and again.

The research presented here is based on a four-year research program funded by the European Research Council, the International Grievance Mechanisms and International Law & Governance (IGMs) project.[35] The starting point of the project is that although international law was primarily intended only as the legal framework of inter-state relations, made by and for States, it is increasingly called upon to regulate a number of transnational activities, not necessarily performed by States. At the same time, for lack of direct legal connection between the various actors involved in transnational activities, the people affected by these activities often have no appropriate remedy at their disposal to ask some transnational actors to account for their impacts directly. In other words, decisions taken at the international/transnational level (or lack of) can have consequences that are disregarded by the system.[36] The IGMs project intends to explore what can be seen

35 ERC Grant No. 312514 (December 2012-November 2016), www.igms-project.org.

36 On the "problem of disregard in global regulatory governance," that is to say the fact that "the present structures and practices of global regulatory governance often generate unjustified disregard of and consequent harm to the interests and concerns of weaker groups and targeted

as regulation and justiciability 'gaps' in international law and decision-making through an in-depth study of certain international mechanisms that seem to fill some of these gaps. The project focuses on international grievance mechanisms that are not tribunals, but permanent international mechanisms created by non-binding international instruments that nevertheless allow the people affected or potentially affected to ask directly some entities – either public or not – to account for the impacts of their activities when no or hardly any international responsibility/liability mechanism can be triggered. The grievance mechanisms studied include the Inspection Panel[37] (hereinafter IPN in the footnotes, the IAM of the World Bank's IBRD and IDA, created in 1993), the Compliance Advisor Ombudsman[38] (CAO, the IAM of IFC and MIGA, created in 1999), the *Mecanismo Independiente de Consulta e Investigación*[39] (MICI, the IAM of IDB and ICC, first created under the form of an Independent Inspection Mechanism in 1994), the Accountability Mechanism[40] (AM, the IAM of the ADB, first created under the form of an Independent Function in 1995), the Project Complaint Mechanism[41] (PCM, the IAM of EBRD, first created under the form of an Independent Recourse Mechanism in 2003), and the Independent Review Mechanism (IRM) entrusted to a Compliance Review and Mediation Unit[42] (CRMU, the IAM of AfDB, created in 2004). Unfortunately, the IAM of the EIB could not be included in the in-depth study since, until recently (late 2014 or early 2015), no proper registry of the cases was made available to the public and its Complaints Mechanism is the only IAM

individuals", see Richard B. Stewart, "Remedying Disregard in Global Regulatory Governance: Accountability, Participation, and Responsiveness", 108 *Am. J. Intl. L.* (2014), p. 211.

37 Inspection Panel Operating Procedures (with Annex 2 added in February 2016), April 2014, http://ewebapps.worldbank.org/apps/ip/PanelMandateDocuments/2014%20Updated%20Operating%20Procedures.pdf.

38 CAO Operational Guidelines, 2013, www.cao-ombudsman.org/howwework/documents/CAOOperationalGuidelines2013_ENGLISH.pdf.

39 The effective commencement of the ICC's operations on 1st January 2016 has resulted in increased complexity as regards the MICI rules or procedure. The MICI IDB Policy of 17 December 2014 replaced the 2010 MICI Policy. Because of the take-off of the ICC, the Board adopted a second MICI Policy on 15 December 2015, that applies to the ICC's operations (hereinafter the MICI ICC Policy), and amended the 2014 MICI IDB Policy. Thus, the MICI is bound by two sets of rules of procedures, depending on whether the case is related to a project supported by the ICC or the IDB. A preamble was added in the MICI IDB Policy to organize how the cases related to private projects that were managed by IDB should be handled. See Policy of the Independent Consultation and Investigation Mechanism, 17 December 2014 (as amended 15 December 2015), www.iadb.org/document.cfm?id=40153237, and Policy of the Independent Consultation and Investigation Mechanism of the ICC, 15 December 2015, www.iadb.org/document.cfm?id=40151002.

40 Accountability Mechanism Policy, 24 May 2012, OM Section L1/BP, http://compliance.adb.org/dir0035p.nsf/attachments/operations-manual-bank-policy-2012.pdf/$FILE/operations-manual-bank-policy-2012.pdf.

41 Project Complaint Mechanism Rules of Procedure, May 2014, www.ebrd.com/downloads/integrity/pcmrules.pdf.

42 Independent Review Mechanism Operating Rules and Procedures, January 2015, www.afdb.org/fileadmin/uploads/afdb/Documents/Compliance-Review/IRM_Operating_Rules_and_Procedures-january_2015-_En.pdf.

that does not automatically disclose its documents, but instead puts them online only if the parties have agreed to it.[43]

In the framework of this research, the team has performed some sixty semi-directed, qualitative confidential interviews with complainants, persons who work or used to work for the above-mentioned IAMs, and persons who have participated in their creation or revision. In addition, the project's team has created a database of the cases[44], mostly interested in the cases that have led either to a full compliance review – sometimes called 'audit' or else 'investigation' depending on the language of each IAM – or at least to a compliance review assessment, which some IAMs conduct to check whether there are *prima facie* serious grounds for believing that the case deserves a compliance review. On 1st September 2015, this database contained 157 cases.[45] Following a methodology described in the second part of this contribution, the lessons to be learned regarding compliance with environmental standards are largely based on the content of this database.

1. THE PURPOSE AND SCOPE OF IAMs' CONTROL OF THE IMPLEMENTATION OF ENVIRONMENTAL STANDARDS

The International Accountability Mechanisms of MDBs are peculiar creatures. Complainants turn to IAMs as a last resort mechanism, because of a lack of effective remedies – whether amicable or judicial – at the project, local and national levels.[46] IAMs are expected by those affected to be a forum in which they can voice their concerns, and to do something, ranging from stopping the project to alleviating the adverse impacts; it is expected by advocacy organisations to play both the role of a(n independent) white knight and that of a watchdog (with teeth) and; more often than not, it is seen by Management as the "big bad wolf."[47] They

---

43 EIB Complaints Mechanism – Operating Procedures, 28 August 2013, www.eib.org/attachments/strategies/complaints_mechanism_operating_procedures_en.pdf.

44 Available at http://igms-project.org/EN/database/indexbase.html.

45 All the documents related to the IAMs' cases mentioned here are available on the corresponding IAM's website. AM-CRP: http://compliance.adb.org/; CAO: www.cao-ombudsman.org/; IPN: http://ewebapps.worldbank.org/apps/ip/Pages/Home.aspx; IRM/CRMU: www.afdb.org/en/topics-and-sectors/topics/independent-review-mechanism-irm/; MICI: www.iadb.org/en/mici/; PCM: www.ebrd.com/work-with-us/project-finance/project-complaint-mechanism.html.

46 In all the cases about which the IGMs project's team has interviewed complainants, this point has been clearly mentioned.

47 As plainly put by Alistair Clark, Managing Director, Environment and Sustainability Department of the EBRD, during the Open Symposium on the Practice of Independent Accountability Mechanisms (IAMs), organised by the Project Complaint Mechanism of the EBRD, EBRD Headquarters, London, 17 September 2014. See also Jean Aden, "Summary of Targeted Discussions with Bank Management" (2011), http://ewebapps.worldbank.org/apps/ip/Documents/SummaryTargettedDiscussionBankManagement.pdf.

assess compliance with environmental and social standards the content and scope of which is designed by MDBs themselves. In addition, IAMs are independent from their institution in varying degrees and their mandates are not identical, depending on the MDB concerned.

1.1. THE SPECIFIC ROLES OF IAMs

MDBs are international organisations. As such, they are covered by jurisdictional immunities and are very, very difficult to bring before a tribunal, even in cases where their activities ended up with obvious violations of local or international law, even as regards human rights law.[48] Quite recently, an international NGO, EarthRights International, has supported the lawsuit of three fishermen against the IFC before the federal court in Washington DC. The complaint concerns the financing by the IFC of the Tata Mundra Coal Power Plant in India.[49] The complainants point out that although the IFC's own accountability mechanism, the Compliance Advisor Ombudsman (CAO), has found that part of the project does not comply with IFC's environmental and social safeguards[50], the IFC is not taking appropriate action to remedy the harm done to the local population. In March 2016, the judge decided that the IFC had not waived its immunity and, therefore, could not be liable, and dismissed the case without oral argument.[51] The plaintiffs are preparing an appeal.[52] The "untouchability" of MDBs is in stark contrast with the magnitude of the potential impacts of their activities on the

48 See *inter alia* August Reinisch, Ulf A. Weber, "In the Shadow of *Waite and Kennedy*. The Jurisdictional Immunity of International Organizations, the Individual's Right of Access to the Courts and Administrative Tribunals as Alternative Means of Dispute Settlement", 1 *Int'l Org. L. Rev.* (2004), pp. 59-110; Niels Blokker, "International Organizations: The Untouchables?", *in* Niels Blokker, Nico Schrijver (eds.), *Immunity of International Organizations*, Leiden/Boston: Brill/Martinus Nijhoff (2015), pp. 1-17.

49 IFC, Tata Ultra Mega, Project number 25797, approved 8 April 2008, http://ifcextapps.ifc.org/ifcext/spiwebsite1.nsf/78e3b305216fcdba85257a8b0075079d/eab8e042d643a6ec852576ba000e2b15?opendocument.

50 CAO, *India / Tata Ultra Mega-01/Mundra and Anjar*, CAO Audit Report, 22 August 2013. A complaint about the same project has also been filed with the Asian Development Bank's Accountability Mechanism (AM), since ADB also finances part of it. The AM Compliance Review Panel (AM-CRP) has likewise found that the ADB had breached some of its environmental and social standards. See AM-CRP, *India: Mundra Ultra Mega Power Project*, Request 2013/1, CRP Final Report, 7 April 2015 (date of issuance).

51 United States District Court for the District of Columbia, *Budha Ismail Jam, et al. v. International Finance Corporation*, Civil Action No. 15-612 (JDB), Memorandum Opinion, 24 March 2016, www.earthrights.org/sites/default/files/documents/jam_v_ifc_-_order_granting_mtd.pdf.

52 EarthRights International, www.earthrights.org/legal/tata-mundra-coal-power-plant. See also Claire Provost, Matt Kennard, "World Bank Lending Arm Sees off Lawsuit by Indian Fishermen", *The Guardian*, 30 March 2016, www.theguardian.com/global-development/2016/mar/30/world-bank-lending-arm-ifc-sees-off-lawsuit-by-indian-fishermen-power-plant.

ground and their power to influence the course of things. It makes accountability mechanisms all the more precious.

IAMs are not tribunals and they do not look into the legal responsibility of MDBs. They are also distinct from the General Counsel, which is entrusted with the mandate of giving legal advice to the bank. One of the core features of IAMs is that accountability is not polarized on the violation of a norm but on harm, whether it has already occurred or might occur. The logic of the IAMs' accountability process is thus not rights-based but rather wrongs-based. For this reason, except for the Inspection Panel for the public projects (and public-private partnerships) supported by the World Bank Group[53], all other IAMs articulate a problem-solving procedure with a compliance control procedure.

Generally speaking, their role is threefold:

- To assess, upon request of the people affected – or likely to be affected – by the bank's activities, the compliance of the Management of the bank with its own internal rules, that is to say, with its policies and procedures inter alia related to the disclosure of information, environmental and social assessment, indigenous people rights ... If the Management is found not to be compliant, it does not result in the legal implication of the bank but it is expected to adopt corrective measures;
- To offer redress for negative environmental and social impacts, based on a problem-solving approach tailored to the needs of the requesters, using techniques such as fact-finding, mediation, consultation, negotiation ... Except for the IRM and the MICI[54], the latest being the less accessible of all IAMs, access to problem-solving (sometimes called dispute resolution or consultation phase) is not conditioned by the fact that claimants allege a breach of the bank's standards and;
- To provide the bank with lessons learned from the cases, including recommendations related to changes in MDBs' policies and procedures that

53 The 2014 review of the Inspection Panel's Operating Procedures has introduced a highly controversial 'pilot approach to support early solutions' that aims at facilitating dialogue between Management and the complainants before registering the complaint. Though it is not supposed to prevent complainants to access the compliance control procedure if this dialogue fails, the first attempt resulted in some of the complainant seeing the compliance control path barred. See Inspection Panel, 2014 Updated Operating Procedures, *op. cit.*; IPN, *Nigeria: Lagos Metropolitan Development and Governance Project* (Pilot – Not Registered), Case 91, Complaint received 30 September 2013; Amnesty International, "World Bank: Investigate Inspection Panel's Pilot Approach to Early Solutions and Its Application in Badia East, Lagos, Nigeria", 2 September 2014, www.amnesty.org/download/Documents/4000/afr440202014en.pdf.

54 MICI IDB Policy and MICI ICC Policy, para. 24; IRM Operating Rules and Procedures 2014, paras. 1 and 6. Note that in the case of the IRM, the combination of paras. 7c) and 41 reveals that though formally the Operating Rules and Procedures require that the requesters "allege that an actual or threatened material adverse effect on the affected persons' rights or interests arises directly from an act or omission of a member institution of the Bank Group as a result of the failure by the said institution to follow any of its own operational policies and procedures" (para. 1), the question of breach is not considered during problem-solving exercises.

would be needed to prevent future noncompliance situations. In this respect, the CAO used to be the only IAM whose mandate expressly includes direct "advice to the President and IFC/MIGA on broader environmental and social issues related to policies, standards, guidelines, procedures, resources, and systems established to improve the performance of IFC/MIGA projects."[55] The recent revision of the AfDB's IRM has given the CRMU the possibility to propose advisory services.[56] As for the other IAMs, this 'lessons learned' function is part of their compliance review and/or problem-solving roles.[57]

1.2. ON THE BINDING CHARACTER OF THE ENVIRONMENTAL AND SOCIAL STANDARDS OF MDBs

Part of the IAMs' mandate (or almost all of it, in the case of the Inspection Panel) is thus to look into the Management's compliance with the institution's ESSs. From a technical, international law point of view, these ESSs are, according to the terminology of the Draft Articles on the Responsibility of International Organizations (DARIOs), "rules of the organization."[58] Their legal nature is debated and there is no consensus on whether they are part of international law or can only bind the organisation's staff.[59]

Even from the viewpoint of the staff, it is actually not so easy to tell the extent to which the ESSs are binding. In any case, this binding character is usually considered by MDBs' Managements to result from practical considerations, rather than from any *legally binding* character. It first depends on the language of the ESSs: the vaguer it is, the more Management has leeway in interpreting them. Second, the designation of the different kinds of standards indicates that some are considered to be more binding than others: Management seems to be expected to follow policies and procedures, while guidance notes, good practices and so on are only indicative.[60] The first cases submitted to IAMs have given an opportunity

55 CAO Operational Guidelines, para. 5.1.1.

56 IRM Operating Rules and Procedures, para. 71.

57 PCM Rules of Procedure, para. 44 a); MICI IDB Policy and MICI ICC Policy, para. 61; CAO Operational Guidelines, para. 1.2; Accountability Mechanism Policy, paras. 128 vii), 128 viii), 131 xiii).

58 International Law Commission, "Draft articles on the responsibility of international organizations, with commentaries", *Yearbook of the International Law Commission*, Part Two (2011), Article 2b): "'rules of the organization' means, in particular, the constituent instruments, decisions, resolutions and other acts of the international organization adopted in accordance with those instruments, and established practice of the organization."

59 See the debates presented *in* Giorgio Gaja, Special Rapporteur, International Law Commission, "Third Report on Responsibility of International Organizations", 13 May 2005, UN Doc. A/CN.4/553, paras. 18-19.

60 See Daniel D. Bradlow, Andria Naudé Fourie, "The Operational Policies of the World Bank and the International Finance Corporation Creating Law-Making and Law-Governed Institutions?", 10 *Int'l. Org. L. Rev.* (2013), pp. 18-20.

to clarify the 'bindingness' of MDBs' standards. The first Inspection Panel case, related to the *Arun III Proposed Hydroelectric Project* in Nepal, had given rise to a skirmish on the Managements' leeway in interpreting the applicable standards.[61] The Inspection Panel's position in this regard was made clear in the *Western Poverty Reduction Project* case, also called the "Qinghai project":

> "During the course of examining some 20 projects over the past five years, the Panel has encountered certain differences in views among staff on just how the Bank's operational policies and procedures should be applied. (...) For example, a number of staff members felt that the Bank's Operational Directives and other policies were simply idealized policy statements, and should be seen largely as a set of goals to be striven after. Others of equal or more senior rank disagreed with this view. They felt that this interpretation could render the policies virtually meaningless and certainly incapable of being employed as benchmarks against which to measure compliance. (...) In discussions about compliance, staff often pointed out that the policies allow for flexibility of interpretation. The decisions made on the specific matters were thus covered and in compliance. It was simply a matter of "judgement at Management's sole discretion." (...) Other staff argued, however, that the policies are clear enough to distinguish areas that are binding from areas where some reasonable flexibility in interpretation is called for. Read in their entirety, the Panel feels that the directives cannot possibly be taken to authorize a level of "interpretation" and "flexibility" that would permit those who must follow these directives to simply override the portions of the directives that are clearly binding. (...) Faced with these widely divergent views among the staff, the Panel was forced to revisit its views on and experience with Bank policies and compliance. In the end, it returned to the approach reflected in its earlier reports. There is indeed room for some flexibility and interpretation but, as provided in the Resolution that established the Panel, the Operational Directives (and updated OPs, BPs, GPs, etc.) are the primary source of Bank policy for purposes of assessing compliance."[62]

Likewise, the second case before the Inspection Function of the ADB, which was then turned into the Accountability Mechanism, led the IAM of the ADB to vigorously affirm the limits of the leeway Management has in interpreting applicable standards:

> "Management said that ADB's "internal laws" were "not written as rule-based statutes but as operational principles that Staff should apply" and that Management is called upon to make "evaluations and decisions about what is possible and 'doable' while adhering to the integrity and spirit of ADB's internal laws." Management refers to its qualifications and capacity to make professional judgments. (...) Since the issue of professional judgment is referred to at great length and not inconsiderable reliance

---

61 IPN, *Nepal: Arun III Proposed Hydroelectric Project and Restructuring of IDA Credit*, Case 1, Management Response, 22 November 1994, p. 5.

62 IPN, *China: Western Poverty Reduction Project*, Case 16, Investigation Report, 28 April 2000, paras. 9-15.

is placed on professional judgment as a reason for non-compliance with the Bank's operational policies and procedures, the Panel feels obliged to explain at some length why it shares the General Counsel's view that the "internal laws" of the Bank are mandatory. (...) Good governance requires that the affairs of any organization should be conducted in an orderly and reasonably predictable way. This is usually ensured by a hierarchy of norms, including good practices, guidelines, instructions and policy-based operational procedures. Clues to identifying the importance of a norm and the expected level of compliance are ordinarily found in the manner of its formulation and expression and its source. (...) As far as ADB is concerned, it seems to the Panel that the greatest importance is attached to compliance with its procedures anchored in Bank policy and formally declared and prescribed by the Bank's apex governing body – the Board. Their paramount importance and the nature of the compliance expected is reflected in their description as internal "laws" of the Bank. Merely adhering to their "integrity and spirit" is less than what is expected of those from whom obedience is expected. (...) Unless in the circumstances and to the extent prescribed by the Board expressly permitting departures and deviations, compliance is mandatory. There is no choice. It is not a matter for professional judgment as to whether there may or may not be compliance. The need for compliance is not based on any assumption of the qualifications or qualities of any person. It is based on a perceived need of the Board with regard to the conduct it has prescribed."[63]

It must be noted that it results from the different ESSs of MDBs that Management is bound by three overarching obligations: due diligence, supervision and do no harm.

Due diligence refers to the fact that when scoping and screening, the bank staff must act by taking all of the relevant data about the borrower/client and the proposed project into account. For example, Management is expected to make sure that the borrower/client has the capacity to implement requirements.[64] The EBRD PCM stressed for its part that:

"the requirements imposed upon EBRD under the Environmental Policy 2003 primarily amount to 'due diligence' obligations, comprising obligations as to conduct rather than as to result, and so the occurrence of actual harm of the type which the relevant obligation is designed to prevent will not be determinative of non-compliance on the part of the Bank. (...) Therefore, the fact that the Bank exercised appropriate due diligence and discharged its obligations under the Environmental Policy would generally amount to compliance, even in the event that harm nevertheless occurs."[65]

Supervision refers to the duty to make sure that the borrower/client complies with the applicable ESSs and to take the necessary steps in case of non-compliance

63 Inspection Function's *ad hoc* Inspection Panel, *Pakistan: Chashma Right Bank Irrigation Project Stage III*, Final Report, 10 June 2004, paras. 68-72.

64 See for example CAO, *Democratic Republic of Congo / Anvil Mining Congo, SARL-01/World Bank President Request*, Audit Report, November 2005, para. 3.3.4.

65 PCM, *D1 Motorway Phase I (Slovakia)*, Case 2010/01, Compliance Review Report, 11 May 2011, para. 59.

during the full lifecycle of the project. Thus, non-compliance may result from the fact that "key E&S issues identified by IFC in project supervision were not translated into corrective action plans"[66] or:

> "that IFC is not in a position to demonstrate either that its client's monitoring is commensurate to risk (as required by PS1) or that its supervision allows it to meet the stated purposes of supervision as set out in the ESRPs: namely, the development and retention of information needed to assess the status of E&S compliance"[67],

or else that:

> "[d]uring implementation, ADB did not act on early information from its own supervision missions on systemic problems with the functioning of the grievance redress process, and in particular the lack of capacity on the part of the government entities managing this process. Notwithstanding later efforts by ADB to address this issue, the omissions during the early stages of implementation resulted in noncompliance."[68]

Depending on the circumstances of each case, Management's compliance with the supervision obligation may consist of the fact "that Management responded repeatedly and firmly and brought to the attention of the Borrower instances of non-compliance with social safeguards obligations."[69]

Finally, the obligation to 'do no harm' directly stems from the MDBs' standards and, arguably, from the very mission of these *development* banks. For example, the IFC's Policy on Environmental and Social Sustainability states that "Central to IFC's development mission are its efforts to carry out investment and advisory activities with the intent to "do no harm" to people and the environment."[70] The ADB's Safeguard Policy Statement provides that "The goal of the Safeguard Policy Statement (SPS) is to promote the sustainability of project outcomes by protecting the environment and people from potential adverse impacts of projects."[71] The AfDB's Integrated Safeguards Policy Statement indicates that the bank "recognises that human well-being in Africa depends on the quality of the environment and the sustainable use of natural resources. This is why it strives to ensure that Bank operations have no unintended adverse direct or indirect environmental or social impact on communities" ...[72]

---

66 CAO, *Peru / Quellaveco-01/Moquegua*, Investigation Report, 29 August 2014, p. 3.

67 CAO, *India / Tata Ultra Mega-01/Mundra and Anjar*, *op. cit.*, p. 5.

68 AM-CRP, *Greater Mekong Subregion: Rehabilitation of the Railway in Cambodia Project*, Request 2012/2, CRP Final Report, 7 February 2014, para. 136.

69 IPN, *Kenya: Natural Resource Management Project*, Case 84, Investigation Report, 22 May 2014, para. 16.

70 *Op. cit.*, para. 9.

71 *Op. cit.*, para. 1.

72 Integrated Safeguard System, *op. cit.*, p. 15.

What of international law? International organisations are subjects of international law but they hardly subject to it. In sum, international organisations are bound by the terms of their constitutive agreement and by the treaties to which they adhere. As far as I know from my research, no MDB has ever itself adhered to an international environmental, labour or human rights treaty. Being subjects of international law, they may also in theory be subjected to customary international law and to the general principles of international law.[73] The elusive nature of the latter is obvious, but the difficulty of identifying any customary rule which would specifically apply to international organisations is also remarkable.[74] Moreover, both customary international law and the general principles of international law sorely need a judge to decide upon their existence, contours and their applicability to an international organisation.

There is, however, one notable exception to the above statement, namely, that of the European Investment Bank (EIB). The EIB is a body of the European Union (EU). As such, it is required to comply with all of the legal requirements to which the EU has committed, including international environmental treaties. For this reason, failures to comply with some international environmental treaty-based obligations may lead the EIB to face complaints, as a body of a party to these treaties. And it did happen at the international level, before the Compliance Committee[75] of the Aarhus Convention.[76]

The EBRD's Management is, for its part, indirectly but undoubtedly bound by EU environmental law. Though EBRD is not a body of the EU (the EU and EIB are among the 65 shareholders of the bank), its Environmental and Social Policy provides that:

---

73 ICJ, *Interpretation of the Agreement of 25 March 1951 between the WHO and Egypt*, Advisory Opinion, 20 December 1980, *ICJ Reports 1980*, para. 37: "International organizations are subjects of international law and, as such, are bound by any obligations incumbent upon them under general rules of international law, under their constitutions or under international agreements to which they are parties."

74 Daniel D. Bradlow, "International Law and the Operations of International Financial Institutions", ", *in* Daniel D. Bradlow, David B. Hunter eds., *International Financial Institutions and International Law*, Austin/Boston/Chicago/New York/The Netherlands: Kluwer Law International (2010), pp. 1-30; Ole Kristian Fauchald, "Hardening the Legal Softness of the World Bank through an Inspection Panel?", PluriCourts Research Paper No. 13-08 (2013), http://ssrn.com/abstract=2361099, para. 2.4.

75 See Compliance Committee, "Findings with regard to communication ACCC/C/2007/21 concerning compliance by the European Community", 3 April 2009, UN Doc. ECE/MP.PP/C.1/2009/2/Add.1, www.unece.org/env/pp/compliance/Compliancecommittee/21TableEC.html. Communication ACCC/C/2007/21 had been submitted by the Albanian NGO Civic Alliance for the Protection of the Bay of Vlora "regarding compliance by the European Community with its obligations under the Convention in relation to the actions of the European Investment Bank with respect to access to information and public participation in the decision-making on the financing and construction of a thermal power plant in Vlora (Albania)." The EIB was found compliant.

76 Convention on Access to Information, Public Participation in Decision-making and Access to Justice in Environmental Matters, Aarhus, 25 June 1998, 2161 *UNTS* 447; 38 *ILM* 517 (1999).

> "The EBRD, as a signatory to the European Principles for the Environment, is committed to promoting the adoption of EU environmental principles, practices and substantive standards by EBRD-financed projects, where these can be applied at the project level, regardless of their geographical location. When host country regulations differ from EU substantive environmental standards, projects will be expected to meet whichever is more stringent."[77]

Consequently, although formally the EBRD's Management is bound by the Environmental and Social Policy and not by EU law or the international treaties to which the EU adheres, they must apply this policy consistently with the EU environmental law. In addition, in the previous version of the Environmental and Social Policy (2008), the Performance Requirements (PRs) contained direct references to compliance with international treaties and EU law.[78] This has, in many cases, led the PCM to analyse the content of EU law – for example as regards the Carbon Capture and Storage Directive (Directive 2009/31/EC)[79] or the Habitats Directive (Directive 92/43/EEC)[80] – in order to assess whether Management was or was not compliant.

Apart from the special situation of the EIB and the EBRD, it must be noted that the fact that MDBs do not adhere to environmental treaties does not mean that MDBs standards ignore the state of international law, quite the contrary.[81] There are direct references to international instruments, as texts having inspired the drafting of the standards. Thus, the 2009 IDB Environment and Safeguards Compliance Policy "is grounded in the principles of sustainable development as set out in the Declaration of Rio 92, Agenda 21, and most recently reinforced in the World Summit on Sustainable Development in Johannesburg,"[82] the Preamble

---

77 *Op. cit.*, para. 7. Footnote 6 specifies that: "Substantive environmental standards of the European Union are contained in EU secondary legislation, for example, regulations, directives and decisions. Procedural norms directed at member states and EU institutions and the jurisprudence of the European Court of Justice and the Court of First Instance which applies to member states, EU institutions and EU legal and natural persons, is excluded from this definition".

78 Thus, the 2008 version of Performance Requirement 6, on Biodiversity Conservation and Sustainable Management of Living Natural Resources, for example provided that "the Bank is guided by and supports the implementation of applicable international law and conventions and relevant EU Directives": EBRD Environmental and Social Policy (2008), PR6, www.ebrd.com/downloads/research/policies/2008policy.pdf, para. 2.

79 PCM, *Šoštanj Thermal Power Plant (Slovenia)*, Case 2012/03, Compliance Review Report, 23 September 2013.

80 PCM, *Paravani HPP (Georgia)*, Case 2012/01, Compliance Review Report, 1 January 2014; PCM, *Ombla HPP (Croatia)*, Case 2011/06, Compliance Review Report, 1 January 2014; PCM, *Boskov Most Hydro Power (FYR Macedonia)*, Case 2011/05, Compliance Review Report, 1 January 2014; PCM, *D1 Motorway Phase I (Slovakia)*, Case 2010/01, Compliance Review Report, 11 May 2011.

81 See in particular Charles E. Di Leva, "International Environmental Law, the World Bank, and International Financial Institutions", *in* Daniel Bradlow, David B. Hunter (eds.), *op. cit.*, pp. 343-385.

82 *Op. cit.*, para. 2.3.

of the 2013 AfDB Integrated Safeguards System states that "[t]he AfDB (...) views economic and social rights as an integral part of human rights, and accordingly affirms that it respects the principles and values of human rights as set out in the UN Charter and the African Charter of Human and Peoples' Rights"[83] and, for example, its Operational safeguard 3–Biodiversity, Renewable Resources and Ecosystem Services affirms that it:

> "reflects the objectives of the Convention on Biological Diversity to conserve biological diversity and promote the sustainable management and use of natural resources. It also aligns with the Ramsar Convention on Wetlands, the Convention on the Conservation of Migratory Species of Wild Animals, the Convention on International Trade in Endangered Species of Wild Flora and Fauna, the World Heritage Convention, the UN Convention to Combat Desertification and the Millennium Ecosystem Assessment. Its recommendations also align with the International Plant Protection Convention."[84]

One can find similar references to international instruments in the policies of all MDBs.

Finally, it is important to recall that ESSs of MDBs are not only directed to Management but also to borrowers/clients. Being internal rules, they are not as such legally binding over them. It is the loan agreement (or guarantee, or shareholder agreement depending on the kind of support) – which is a legally binding document signed between the MDB and the borrower/client – that creates legal obligations for the latter.[85] Loan agreements stipulate, one way or another, that support from MDBs is conditional on the borrowers/clients' respect of the bank's ESSs related to borrowers/clients' behaviour.[86] Yet, the mandate of the IAMs of MDBs only allows them to assess the behaviour of the bank's staff, not of the borrower/client's.

83 *Op. cit.*, Preamble, p. 1.

84 *Ibid.*, OS3, p. 39.

85 John W. Head, "Evolution of the Governing Law for Loan Agreements of the World Bank and Other Multilateral Development Banks", 90 *Am. J. Int'l L.* (1996), pp. 214-234.

86 Except when the bank forgets to include the environmental and social requirements in the agreement ... This happened in the *Quellaveco* case. "CAO recognizes that this investment was initiated at a time when IFC E&S procedures were relatively underdeveloped. (...) Nevertheless, CAO finds that IFC omitted to include necessary E&S requirements in the Shareholders Agreement which formed legal basis for the investment. This resulted in a significant gap in terms of the Company's E&S obligations, particularly given IFC's undertaking to its Board of Directors in March 1993 that the Project would "comply with all applicable World Bank environmental and occupational health and safety guidelines." CAO finds that the absence of E&S requirements in IFC's investment agreement made E&S supervision difficult": CAO, *Peru / Quellaveco-01/Moquegua*, *op. cit.*, p. 3.

1.3. THE SCOPE OF THE IAMs' REMIT

The IAMs remit is limited in a number of reasons, some being common to all IAMs, others depending on their specific rules of procedure and on the unique culture of each MDB and of each IAM.

First, the IAMs' mandates do not include the power to make decisions on the remedial actions that will be implemented by Management in response to the IAM's compliance review report. All IAMs make findings and some – the PCM, the MICI, the CRMU, the CAO – are also mandated to recommend remedial actions. These recommendations are primarily related to the case at hand, but they can also highlight the systemic changes that might prove necessary at the level of the bank, the need to clarify the procedures that the Management applies for example. The compliance reviews of the Inspection Panel and the AM-CRP[87] have 'only' fact-finding purposes; remedial actions are proposed by Management on the basis of the findings.[88] In any case, it is the Board of the MDB, composed of Executive Directors representing the shareholders (countries), or sometimes the President of the MDB[89] who have the power to decide on remedial actions. Depending on the institution, such power to make the final decision can be purely formal, as it is the case as regards the CAO's reports[90], or gives rise to internal debates that may end with the Board amending the recommendations[91] or even rejecting the whole report.[92]

Second, the fact that IAMs are concerned with MDB's accountability only is a common crucial point. IAMs do not investigate the borrower/client. It is inscribed in the rules of procedures of every IAM. In practice, however, the line is very thin between investigating the bank and the borrower. In order to check whether

87 It has lost its power to make recommendations in the latest version (2012) of its policy, but kept its power to monitor the implementation of remedial actions.

88 Inspection Panel Operating Procedures 1994, *in* Inspection Panel, *Annual Report 1996-1997*, Annex 2, http://ewebapps.worldbank.org/apps/IP/IPPublications/inspectionPanelAnnualReport1996-1997.pdf, paras 52 and 54, and Operating Procedures 2014, *op. cit.*, paras 63 and 67; Accountability Mechanism Policy 2012, *op. cit.*, paras. 79 and 83.

89 CAO Operational Guidelines, *op. cit.*, para 4.4.5; IRM Operating Rules and Procedures, *op. cit.*, p. 1: the IRM "reports to the Boards of Directors of the Bank and Fund (collectively the 'Boards') on approved projects or to the President of the Bank Group (the 'President'), on projects under consideration for financing by the Bank Group."

90 CAO Operational Guidelines, *op. cit.*, para 4.4.5: "CAO will forward the Investigation Report and the IFC/MIGA response to the President. The President has no editorial input as to the content of the compliance Investigation Report, but may take the opportunity to discuss the investigation findings with CAO. Once the President is satisfied with the response by IFC/MIGA senior management, the President will provide clearance for the Investigation Report and the response. The President retains discretion over clearance."

91 It has happened for example in the *Greater Mekong Subregion: Rehabilitation of the Railway in Cambodia Project* case: AM-CRP, Request 2012/2, Board's Decision, 31 January 2014.

92 MICI, *Paraguay – Program to Improve Highway Corridors in Paraguay*, Case PR-MICI002-2010, Final Decision of the Board of Executive Directors, 12 July 2013. The reason is mentioned in the next paragraph of this chapter.

Management is compliant, IAMs must assess whether Management has complied with its due diligence and supervision obligations *vis a vis* the borrower/client's implementation of the safeguards. This possibly implies stating that the borrower/client's capacity was insufficient or did not deliver the environmental and social assessments and plans, as required, before the Board approval, which would trigger the due diligence obligation of Management, or else that the measures necessary to complying with the safeguards have not been properly implemented by the borrower/client, which triggers Management's supervision duty. Thus, IAMs have to look into the shortcomings of the borrower/client in order to make findings on the Management's compliance with the ESSs. Unsurprisingly, some borrower/clients, despite being told that their own accountability is not at issue, do not appreciate feeling investigated.[93] In addition, the Executive Director concerned siting in the Board, and other Executive Directors who defend the same interests, sometimes take up the borrower/client's 'cause' to such an extent that the Board ends up preventing the IAM from doing its job. This has resulted in the Board not authorizing a compliance review despite the fact the IAM finds the complaint eligible[94], or agreeing to a compliance review but on conditions[95] or else, in the end, rejecting the compliance review report.[96]

Indeed, and it is a third point, when looking at the IAMs' remits in detail and putting them in the broader context of each bank's culture, depending on the MDB concerned, there are clear differences regarding the leeway they are granted. The MICI is the least advantaged in this respect. Despite having created its IAM as early as 1994, in the wake of the Inspection Panel's establishment, the IDB has always displayed a great mistrust of its IAM.[97] This has resulted in hardly understandable

---

93 See for example AM-CRP, *Sri Lanka Southern Transport Development Project*, Request 2004/1, 5th and Final Monitoring Report, 5 August 2011, paras. 27-33. Another example is China's refusal to authorize an IAM to make a site visit, thus preventing the IAM to perform an important part of its fact-finding mission: AM-CRP, *People's Republic of China: Fuzhou Environmental Improvement Project*, CRP Final Report, 21 October 2010.

94 MICI, *Bolivia - Santa Barbara- Rurrenabaque Northern Corridor Highway Improvement Program*, Case BO-MICI001-2011, Decision of the Board of Executive Directors, 22 December 2014; MICI, *Brazil - Mario Covas Rodoanel Project - Northern Section 1*, Case BR-MICI003-2011, Decision of the Board of Executive Directors, 10 July 2013; MICI, *Brazil - Mario Covas Rodoanel Project - Northern Section 1*, Case BR-MICI005-2011, Decision of the Board of Executive Directors, 10 July 2013; IPN, *Brazil: Itaparica Resettlement and Irrigation Project*, Case 9, Request received 12 March 1997.

95 IPN, *India: NTPC Power Generation Project*, Case 10, Investigation Report, 22 December 1997 (the Board authorized only a desk study and no on-site fact-finding mission); CRMU, *South Africa: Medupi Power Project*, Request 2010/2, Revised Reassessment and Revision of the Terms of Reference for the Compliance Review, July 2011 (the Board refused that the sixth point of the complaint, which claimed that "the poor people will not benefit from the project", be included in the compliance review's terms of reference.).

96 MICI, *Paraguay - Program to Improve Highway Corridors in Paraguay*, Final decision of the Board of Executive Directors, *op. cit.*

97 Walter Leal Filho, Angel René Rios, *Accountability Issues in International Development Projects*, Frankfurt am Main: Peter Lang (2007), especially pp. 49-146. This point has also been emphasized during the confidential interviews.

delays in the Board making decisions on the MICI's assessments or else, as mentioned above, refusal to follow the MICI's recommendation to proceed with an investigation or rejection of the investigation report, based on what, seen from the outside, looks very much like institutionalised nit-picking.[98] All of the MDB's IAMs except one have the power to monitor the implementation of the remedial actions approved by the Board on the basis of the compliance review report; the Inspection Panel was not granted any monitoring power, which can however be allowed by the Board on a case by case basis.[99] Generally speaking, the IAMs are allowed to use only specific types of standards[100] which do not automatically apply to all of the MDBs' activities. For example, the World Bank's ESSs apply to what they call 'investment project financing,' meaning operations related to specific, circumscribed projects (a dam, a road etc.) but not to 'development policy lending', which supports programs of policy and institutional actions and replaces structural adjustment loans and sectoral adjustment loans, or to the trust funds managed by the bank.[101]

Fourth, depending on the culture of the IAM, harm is more or less important in the triggering of a compliance review. Central to the CAO's mandate are the questions of the IFC/MIGA environmental and social performance, whether the project raises "substantial concerns regarding environmental and/or social outcomes, and/or issues of systemic importance to IFC/MIGA."[102] In order to decide to undertake an investigation, the CAO considers whether:

> "There is evidence of potentially significant adverse environmental and/or social outcome(s) now, or in the future; There are indications that a policy or other appraisal criteria may not have been adhered to or properly applied by IFC/MIGA; There is evidence that indicates that IFC's/MIGA's provisions, whether or not complied with, have failed to provide an adequate level of protection."[103]

---

98 See in particular MICI, *Paraguay – Program to Improve Highway Corridors in Paraguay*, Final decision of the Board of Executive Directors, *op. cit.*

99 Lately the Inspection Panel has made a cautious move in the direction of monitoring and has negotiated with Management some procedures which allow tracking the state of implementation of Management Action Plans in response to the Panel's reports. See IPN Operating Procedures, *op. cit.*, Annex 2 "Enhancing Consultation with Requesters and Tracking Action Plans"; World Bank Management, "Overview of Status of Implementation of Management Action Plans Prepared in Response to Inspection Panel Eligibility and Investigation Reports", April 2016, http://ewebapps.worldbank.org/apps/ip/Documents/Tracking%20Management%20Action%20Plan%20-%20April%202016.pdf.

100 For example, the global and sectoral Strategies of the MDBs cannot be used by IAMs. The CRMU however used AfDB's handbooks, draft policies, and strategies to determine whether there was compliance with applicable standards in the Medupi case, without triggering any noticeable reaction from the Board: CRMU, *South Africa: Medupi Power Project*, Request 2010/2, Compliance Review, 19 December 2011. It is unsure that the CRMU will enjoy this leeway again in the future.

101 On the latter situation see IPN, *Haiti: Haiti Mining Dialogue Technical Assistance*, Case 100, Notice of non-registration, 9 February 2015.

102 CAO Operational Guidelines, *op. cit.*, p. 22.

103 *Ibid.*, p. 23.

The CAO's compliance investigation process is thus not aimed at detecting non-compliance with applicable policies strictly speaking. In contrast, the PCM does not require any allegation of harm. Access to problem-solving is open to: "One or more individual(s) located in an Impacted Area, or who has or have an economic interest, including social and cultural interests, in an Impacted Area" and access to compliance review is open to "One or more individual(s) or Organisation(s)."[104] In its compliance review function, the PCM acts much more like an enforcement device than other like-mechanisms. This does not mean that harm is not considered at all[105], but it is only marginally what is at issue during a compliance review.

2. THE MERRY-GO-ROUND OF LOOPHOLES AND PITFALLS IN THE IMPLEMENTATION OF ESSs

What do the compliance review reports of IAMs reveal about the reasons why a project causes environmental harm and/or why environmental considerations were not properly taken into account? The hypothesis is that a study on the types of findings of non-compliance with environmental standards can contribute to identifying systemic issues that can be remedied.

2.1. METHODOLOGY OF THE STUDY

The first stage in the selection of the relevant cases has consisted of identifying the complaints before the 6 IAMs studied, which actually ended up with a final compliance review report. As mentioned previously, as of 1st September the IGMs' database[106] contained 157 cases of the AM-CRP (9 requests for a compliance review, including one case of the AM-CRP's predecessor – the Inspection Function), the CAO (26 compliance investigations completed or ongoing, 1 CAO

104 PCM Rules of Procedure, *op. cit.*, paras 1 and 2.

105 See PCM, *Tbilissi Railway Bypass 1, 2 & 3 (Georgia)*, Cases 2011/01, /02, /03, Joint Compliance Review Report, 23 July 2012, p. 4: "There is no evidence that the Bank's actions in this regard caused harm to the complainants. (…) Consequently, the complainants did not suffer any harm as a result of this instance of Bank non-compliance and it can be regarded as *de minimus*."; see also Independent Recourse Mechanism (which was replaced in 2009 with the PCM), *Vlore Thermal Power Generation Project (Albania)*, Case 2007/01, Compliance Review Report, 9 May 2008, para. 7: "the potential seriousness of any possible consequences of a breach of EBRD procedures will be taken into account in determining whether that breach amounts to a material violation of a Relevant EBRD Policy along with whether, in the event of a finding of non-compliance, the violation is so critical so as to warrant remedial changes to the scope or implementation of the Project or remedial changes to the Bank's practices and procedures so as to avoid recurrence of such or similar violations in the future."

106 Http://igms-project.org/EN/database/indexbase.html.

sectoral audit and 36 cases which stopped at the stage of the compliance review appraisal)[107], the Inspection Panel (38 cases eligible to an investigation, completed or ongoing), the IRM/CRMU (2 completed compliance reviews), the MICI (14 cases eligible to a compliance review completed or ongoing, including 4 cases of the MICI's predecessor – the Independent Investigation Mechanism – and 6 cases non-eligible to a compliance review), and the PCM (25 cases completed or ongoing, including 2 cases of the PCM's predecessor – the Independent Recourse Mechanism). Among those 157 cases, if one removes the ongoing investigations, the complaints which were finally declared non-eligible or assessed as not meriting an investigation, the cases in which the IAM could not complete the review[108] and the cases in which the investigation was not authorised by the Board, 76 complaints[109] which have resulted in the IAM delivering a compliance review report remain.

The second stage consisted in identifying, from among these 76 cases, those which raise issues of compliance with environmental standards. The discriminating marker used here was the fact the requests filed with IAMs included allegations of environmental harm and/or of the violation of an environmental standard, whether the bank's or a national or international environmental text. This information was retrieved from the columns entitled: "Alleged harm/ Invoked policies & procedures by the claimant(s)" in the tables of the database. Very few complaints that ended up with the IAM performing a compliance review do not include any sort of environmental concern: only 3 CAO cases and 4 Inspection Panel cases. Thus, 69 compliance review reports on cases, in which environmental harm and/or the breach of an environmental instrument were alleged, remained.

The third stage consisted in a systematic exploration of the findings of non-compliance in these 69 compliance review reports, primarily based on the "Outcome of the procedure" column of the database's tables, which are abstracts of the main findings of the IAMs; this was complemented, for greater detail, by an analysis of the synopsis of the cases, which were drafted by the project's

107 The CAO's compliance review appraisals aim at determining if *prima facie* the cases are worth investigating under the compliance review function of the CAO.

108 This happened in the Fuzhou case, about a Category A project. The AM-CRP was denied by China the possibility to make a site visit and the CRP considered that in the absence of a site visit, it was unable to complete the compliance review: AM-CRP, *People's Republic of China: Fuzhou Environmental Improvement Project*, *op. cit.* The CRP asked the Board to clarify or modify the policy in this regard. No consensus on the possibility to deny the CRP a site visit was reached during the negotiation of the 2012 version of the Accountability Mechanism Policy. Consequently, paragraph 82 of the 2012 Accountability Mechanism Policy provides: "in the unlikely event that a site visit is declined, a closure of the compliance review process will be highly desirable, especially from the perspective of the complainants. The CRP will complete its work and deliver its final report without a site visit."

109 AM-CRP: 7 cases, CAO: 16 cases, IRM/CRMU: 2 cases, MICI: 7 cases, IPN: 33 cases, PCM: 11 cases.

team to prepare the field interviews.[110] This allowed some main categories of non-compliances found by the IAMs to be drawn out, with an emphasis on the environmental sub-issues: consultation and/or participation (36 cases), process and content of the EA /Assessment of the management of environmental and social risks (35 cases), information (28 cases), resettlement (23 cases), assessment of borrower's/local institutions' capacities (18 cases), indigenous people (17 cases), social assessment (17 cases), monitoring of the project (15 cases), identification of the affected people (15 cases), biodiversity/natural habitats (13 cases), compensation of affected people (13 cases), economic assessment (13 cases), economic and social impacts (12 cases), cumulative impacts (11 cases), loss of livelihoods (11 cases), water quantity or quality (surface and/ or groundwater, 9 cases), poverty reduction (benefits to population, 9 cases), project-level grievance mechanism (9 cases), cooperation of/coordination with borrower/local institutions (9 cases), categorization of the project (8 cases), pollution (7 cases), cultural and/or spiritual issues (6 cases), disaster risk management (6 cases), health (5 cases), international law (5 cases), security (4 cases), forced evictions (3 cases), gender (3 cases), legacy issues (3 cases), tilted balance between economic interests and environmental considerations (3 cases), climate change (2 cases), human rights (2 cases), compliance with local/national law (2 cases), supply chains (2 cases), environmental and social risks associated with financial intermediaries and their sub-clients (1 case proper and 1 CAO sectoral audit), labour rights (1 cases), country system (use of the borrower's legislation instead of the MBD's standards when it is estimated functionally equivalent, 1 case). It is important to bear in mind that all of this does not relate to the number of references made by IAMs to these issues in their compliance reviews reports, but to actual findings of non-compliance on these issues. This also means that findings of compliance on these issues are not included in this indicative tally.

Besides, some of the main categories of issues proposed here are intertwined and the decision to single some of them out (water, climate change and so on) is obviously arbitrary. Imagine that some complainants allege that a project has partly destroyed the natural habitat of some protected species and that this harm could and should have been avoided; the IAM finds that it is indeed the case and determines that one of the roots of the situation is the fact the Management submitted the project to the Board's approval despite the absence, in the EA, of baseline data studies on the biodiversity of the area. Perhaps the Management knew, and neglected to mention that the EA was failing – for instance because they believed the issue of local biodiversity was not really relevant regarding this project and wanted the project cycle to keep going – or they failed to notice the absence of this data, either way it is a breach of the EA standards of MDBs,

[110] Part of these synopses is available at http://igms-project.org/EN/database/indexbase.html.

which provide for the due diligence and supervision obligations. As such, the case would be listed in the 'EA /Assessment of the management of environmental and social risks' category of non-compliance findings. In addition, because the breach resulted in some unjustifiable and avoidable harm to natural habitats and protected species, the case would also be listed in the 'biodiversity/natural habitats' category.[111]

Admittedly, because the present study is based on data which has already been processed – short abstracts for the tables, long abstracts for the synopses of the cases –, there is a risk that some of the findings were not taken into account and, if truth be told, it is highly likely that this did happen. The aim behind the methodology is, however, not to offer some 'hard' statistical data, but to draw out patterns of non-compliance and, backed up by the interviews of the people who work of have worked in IAMs that the project's team has collected, I believe it provides a good insight into the loopholes and pitfalls in the implementation of the MDBs' environmental and social standards by the Management of MDBs.

This opinion is also supported by the fact that the lessons that emerge from the present study are not ground-breaking at all, in a sense – at least from the viewpoint of any person who knows about the profuse literature on the World Bank's serious shortcomings regarding environmental adverse impacts, which was mentioned in the introduction. It is in itself an interesting output: the issues that the present study identifies, which includes five MDBs with different cultures, some operating at the global level, others at the regional level, are in essence the same that one can find in the reports of the IEG of the World Bank, the slides on the lessons drawn from the cases that the Inspection Panel and its then-Chair, Alf Jerve, presented in 2012[112] and, this is an educated guess, in the upcoming Inspection Panel's report on lessons emerging from cases involving environmental and social assessment.[113]

---

111 This fictional example was *inter alia* inspired by the *Boskov Most Hydro Power* case, related to the EBRD's support to the project of the Macedonian government to build a high dam with a reservoir in the Mavrovo National Park: PCM, *Boskov Most Hydro Power (FYR of Macedonia), op. cit.*

112 Alf Jerve, "The Issue of Consultation and Participation in Panel Cases", Presentation at the World Bank Spring Meetings, Civil Society Organisations Forum, 18 April 2012, http://siteresources.worldbank.org/EXTINSPECTIONPANEL/Resources/Anticonstitutionnellement&Participation_session_Apr2012.pdf; Inspection Panel, "Lessons from Panel Cases: Inspection Panel Perspectives", Committee on Development Effectiveness (CODE) Seminar, 22 October 2012, http://siteresources.worldbank.org/EXTINSPECTIONPANEL/Resources/IPNpresentation_CODE__Oct2012.pdf.

113 Inspection Panel, "Panel Joins Other IAMs at Impact Assessment Meeting in Japan", 13 May 2016, http://ewebapps.worldbank.org/apps/ip/Lists/NewsFromThePanel/NewsFromThePanelDisp.aspx?ID=250&source=http://ewebapps.worldbank.org/apps/ip/Pages/News-fom-the-panel.aspx.

2.2. KINDS OF NON-COMPLIANCE: THE USUAL SUSPECTS

Looking at the categories of non-compliance findings that are proposed here, three appear as being particularly frequent: in about half of the 69 compliance reviews studied, the IAM found non-compliances with consultation and/or participation requirements (in 36 cases) – which are very often coupled with non-compliances with the information obligation (in 28 cases) –, and with requirements regarding the environmental assessment process and content (in 35 cases) – which very often are a consequence of a lack of information, consultation or participation of affected people, or have the consequence that affected people are not informed properly, not consulted or are not given an opportunity to participate.

Non-compliances with environmental standards mix case-specific considerations and systemic shortcomings or loopholes. What can be seen as essentially case-specific considerations is mainly related to highly technical standards, such as letting the client use incorrect sampling methods, which resulted in the baseline ambient air quality data being unreliable and in a breach of the Management's due diligence obligation[114], or else letting the client use less stringent standards than those from the World Bank's Pollution, Prevention and Abatement Handbook (PPAH).[115] Other non-compliance findings, which pop up again and again whatever the MDB at issue is, rather seem to reveal systemic problems and may be summarized as follows: too narrow, too late, too confident.

'Too narrow' essentially relates to the scoping and screening phase. In a number of cases, it is the so-called "area of influence" of the project that has been underestimated. Under OP. 4.01 of the World Bank, it is "[t]he area likely to be affected by the project, including all its ancillary aspects, such as power transmission corridors, pipelines, canals, tunnels, relocation and access roads, borrow and disposal areas, and construction camps, as well as unplanned developments induced by the project (e.g., spontaneous settlement, logging, or shifting agriculture along access roads)."[116] Where Management does define the area of influence too narrowly, some potential environmental and social impacts will not be assessed and no management or mitigation plan can be set up[117] – possibly resulting in neglecting some disaster risks such as floods

114 AM-CRP, *Philippines: Visayas Base-Load Power Development Project*, Request 2011/1, CRP Final Report, 11 April 2012.

115 See the similar findings, about the same project financed *inter alia* by the IFC and the ADB, of CAO, *India / Tata Ultra Mega-01/Mundra and Anjar*, *op. cit.*, and of AM-CRP, *India: Mundra Ultra Mega Power Project*, *op. cit.*

116 OP. 4.01, Annex A, para. 6.

117 IPN, *China: Western Poverty Reduction Project*, *op. cit.*; IPN, *India: Mumbai Urban Transport Project (First Request)*, Case 32, Investigation Report, 21 December 2005; IPN, *Uganda: Private Power Generation Project*, Case 44, Investigation Report, 29 August 2008; IPN, *Ghana: Second Urban Environment Sanitation Project*, Case 49, Investigation Report, 13 March 2009; CAO,

risks.[118] Likewise, failure to correctly identify the scope of affected people – mainly by not taking people who do not have an official title over the land where they live, lower castes, or ethnic minorities into account –[119] has resulted in environmental, social and economic impacts that have not taken the design of the project and costly remedial measures into account. 'Too narrow' may also relate to the fact that alternative sites for the project[120], alternative project design[121] or strategy[122] were not or insufficiently taken into account. In non-compliance findings, it also frequently points at the fact that the full range of environmental matters raised by the project was not assessed, resulting in a lack of environmental and social data that impairs the project[123]or the cumulative impacts of the different operations within and surrounding the project were not considered.[124] The scoping and

---

Honduras / Dinant-01/CAO Vice President Request, Audit Report, 20 December 2013; CAO, *India / Tata Ultra Mega-01/Mundra and Anjar, op. cit ...*

118 IPN, *Argentina: Santa Fe Road Infrastructure Project and Provincial Road Infrastructure Project (Third Request)*, Case 51, Investigation Report, 2 July 2009.

119 IPN, *Nepal: Arun III Proposed Hydroelectric Project and Restructuring of IDA Credit*, Case 1, Investigation Report, 21 June 1995; IPN, *China: Western Poverty Reduction Project, op. cit.*; IPN, *Congo, Democratic Republic of: Transitional Support for Economic Recovery Credit (TSERO) and Emergency Economic and Social Reunification Support Project (EESRSP)*, Case 37, Investigation Report, 31 August 2007; AM-CRP, *Mundra Ultra Mega Power Project, op. cit.*; CRMU, *Uganda: Bujagali Hydropower Project and Bujagali Interconnection Project*, Request 2007/1, Compliance Review, 20 June 2008; MICI (IIM), *Brazil – Cana Brava Hydroelectric Power Project*, Investigation Report, 6 February 2006; CAO, *Honduras / Dinant-01/CAO Vice President Request, op. cit. ...*

120 IPN, *Paraguay/Argentina: Reform Project for the Water and Telecommunications Sectors, SEGBA V Power Distribution Project (Yacyretá)*, Case 26, Investigation Report, 24 February 2004; IPN, *Ghana: Second Urban Environment Sanitation Project, op. cit.*; IPN, *Albania: Power Sector Generation and Restructuring Project*, Case 46, Investigation Report, 7 August 2009; IPN, *Nepal: Power Development Project*, Case 87, Investigation Report, 12 February 2015; AM-CRP, *Philippines: Visayas Base-Load Power Development Project, op. cit.*; PCM (IRM), *Vlore Thermal Power Generation Project (Albania), op. cit. ...*

121 CAO, *India / Tata Ultra Mega-01/Mundra and Anjar, op. cit.*; AM-CRP, *Visayas Base-Load Power Development Project, op. cit. ...*

122 CAO, *Peru / Agrokasa-01/Ica*, Audit Report, 22 February 2011; Inspection Function's *ad hoc* Inspection Panel, *Pakistan: Chashma Right Bank Irrigation Project Stage III, op. cit.*

123 IPN, *Paraguay/Argentina: Reform Project for the Water and Telecommunications Sectors, SEGBA V Power Distribution Project (Yacyretá), op. cit.*; CAO, *Honduras / Dinant-01/CAO Vice President Request, op. cit.*; PCM, *Boskov Most Hydro Power (FYR Macedonia), op. cit.*

124 AM-CRP, Mundra Ultra Mega Power Project, *op. cit.*; CRMU, Uganda: Bujagali Hydropower Project and Bujagali Interconnection Project, *op. cit.*; CRMU, South Africa, Medupi Power Project, Compliance Review, *op. cit.*; MICI (IIM) *Mexico -Termoeléctrica del Golfo Project*, Investigation Report, 21 February 2003; MICI, *Panama – Pando-Monte Lirio Hydroelectric Power Project*, Case PN-MICI001-2010, Compliance Review Report, 19 October 2012; CAO, *India / Tata Ultra Mega-01/Mundra and Anjar, op. cit.*; IPN, *Chad: Petroleum Development and Pipeline Project-Management of the Petroleum Economy Project-and Petroleum Sector Management Capacity Building Project*, Case 22, Investigation Report, 17 July 2002; IPN, *Uganda: Third Power Project-Fourth Power Project and proposed Bujagali Hydropower Project*, Case 24, Investigation Report, 23 May 2002; IPN, *Cameroon: Petroleum Development and Pipeline Project and Petroleum Environment Capacity Enhancement Project*, Case 27, Investigation Report, 2 May 2003; IPN, *Uganda: Private Power Generation Project, op. cit.*;

screening phase may also be too narrow in its time dimension, while failing to take the foreseeable long-term impacts into account[125], but also when using outdated studies and information[126] rather than commissioning new studies. A too-narrow scoping and screening phase might end up with the project's categorization being wrongly downgraded[127], which has serious consequences over the type and stringency of the EA requirements.

'Too late' refers to the fact that the environmental and social studies were not conducted at the time when they were needed to adequately design or to implement the project. It often consists in not presenting the project for approval to the Board with all of the necessary data; it may also refer to the fact that, over the course of its implementation, changes in the project, the discovery of omissions in the necessary data or of new information needs would have warranted an update of the studies or additional ones. A late environmental assessment means that information to stakeholders and consultations were not early enough to meaningfully inform the project's design.[128]

Some 'too late' aspects can be closely related to the 'too confident' pitfall. It may occur when the Management knows that they do not have some important environmental data yet but they nevertheless submit the project to the Board's approval, because they are overly confident that they are going to be able to handle problems later if they arise[129], or because they decide that the missing environmental considerations would not have changed a thing in the Board's decision. Such a practice was denounced in vigorous terms by the PCM:

> "As regards the Bank's environmental and social governance more generally, the approach taken in approving the Ombla HPP Project subject to contractual conditions requiring satisfactory completion of an appropriate biodiversity assessment might amount to an excessive delegation of the Board's decision-making powers and

IPN, *Albania: Power Sector Generation and Restructuring Project*, *op. cit.*; IPN, *South Africa: Eskom Investment Support Project*, Case 65, Investigation Report, 21 November 2011.

125 IPN, *Albania: Power Sector Generation and Restructuring Project*, *op. cit.*; CAO, *Peru / Quellaveco-01/Moquegua*, *op. cit.*

126 IPN, *Ghana: Second Urban Environment Sanitation Project*, *op. cit.*; AM-CRP, *Visayas Base-Load Power Development Project*, *op. cit.*; CAO, *Honduras / Ficohsa-01/ CAO Vice President Request*, *op. cit.* …

127 Inspection Function's *ad hoc* Inspection Panel, *Pakistan: Chashma Right Bank Irrigation Project Stage III*, *op. cit.*; AM-CRP, *Kyrgyz Republic: CAREC Transport Corridor I (Bishkek-Torugart Road)*, Request 2011/2, CRP Final Report, 9 August 2012; CAO, *Brazil / Amaggi Expansion-01/IFC Executive Vice President*, Audit Report, May 2005; CAO, *Indonesia / Wilmar Group-01/West Kalimantan*, Audit Report, 19 June 2009; CAO, *Honduras / Dinant-01/CAO Vice President Request*, *op. cit.*; IPN, *China: Western Poverty Reduction Project*, *op. cit.*; IPN, *Pakistan: National Drainage Program Project*, Case 34, Investigation Report, 6 July 2006; IPN, *Cambodia: Forest Concession Management and Control Pilot Project*, Case 36, Investigation Report, 30 March 2006.

128 PCM, *Paravani HPP (Georgia)*, *op. cit.*; CAO, *Peru / Agrokasa-01/Ica*, *op. cit.*, AM-CRP, *Philippines: Visayas Base-Load Power Development Project*, *op. cit.*

129 PCM, *Paravani HPP (Georgia)*, *op. cit.*

responsibilities in the absence of any clear stipulation that the ultimate decision on the disbursement of funds be referred once again to the Board."[130]

'Too confident' also occurs when the Management estimates that the information they have is sufficient and that they do not have to commission additional studies for supplementary loans[131] or known risks.[132] All in all, the findings of non-compliance which point at 'too confident' behaviours are rooted in situations when the Management's "professional judgement" has taken precedence over the substance and spirit of EESs.

The same threefold root can be seen in the findings of non-compliance with information, consultation and/or participation requirements. Without the appropriate information from correctly identified stakeholders, no real consultation/participation can take place. All MDBs require that borrowers/clients consult project-affected people and local NGOs as early as possible for Category A and B projects, which means before the terms of reference of the EA are finalized; "the borrower provides *relevant* material in a *timely* manner *prior* to consultation and in a *form and language* that are understandable and accessible to the groups being consulted."[133] Compliance review reports describe situations in which the information given, if any[134], was too scarce or incomplete to be useful[135], not in the language of affected people[136], and/or delivered in a form that was inappropriate, for example in written form solely even though part of the project-affected people are illiterate.[137] This, of course, significantly impairs the consultation process and does not allow it to help design a sound, well-founded project. Consultation must also be organised in such a way

130 PCM, *Ombla HPP (Croatia), op. cit.* See also CAO, *Peru / Agrokasa-01/Ica, op. cit.*

131 Inspection Function's *ad hoc* Inspection Panel, *Pakistan: Chashma Right Bank Irrigation Project Stage III, op. cit.*

132 MICI, *Panama – Panama Canal Expansion Program*, Case PN-MICI002-2011-31, Compliance Review Report, 4 August 2015.

133 OP. 4.01., para. 15 (emphasis added). All MDBs have similar standards in this regard.

134 See for example AM-CRP, *Sri Lanka Southern Transport Development Project, op. cit.*, para 116: "there is no evidence that the EIA (...) was brought to public attention other than meeting the legal requirements of a notice in the newspaper that the EIA had been approved"; CAO, *Honduras / Dinant-01/CAO Vice President Request, op. cit.*, p. 7: "The rationale for foregoing consultation as explained by IFC was that the project did not pose adverse impacts to local communities, and therefore that consultation was not required. Given the risks described in the E&S Assessment and acknowledged by IFC in applying E&S category B to the project, CAO finds that consultation was required as part of the E&S Assessment process."

135 IPN, *Uganda: Private Power Generation Project, op. cit.*

136 PCM, *Tbilisi Railway Bypass 1, 2 & 3 (Georgia), op. cit.*; PCM, *Paravani HPP (Georgia), op. cit.*; IPN, *Papua New Guinea: Smallholder Agriculture Development Project*, Case 62, Investigation Report, 19 September 2011; CRMU, *South Africa: Medupi Power Project*, Compliance Review, *op. cit.*; IPN, *Ghana: Second Urban Environment Sanitation Project, op. cit.*; AM-CRP, *Philippines: Visayas Base-Load Power Development Project, op. cit.*; AM-CRP, *Kyrgyz Republic: CAREC Transport Corridor I (Bishkek-Torugart Road), op. cit.*

137 AM-CRP, *Greater Mekong Subregion: Rehabilitation of the Railway in Cambodia Project, op. cit.*

that it allows the people involved to effectively convey their concerns.[138] The information/consultation/participation requirements will also be deeply impacted by the bank's failure to correctly identify the project-affected people. Some compliance review reports highlight the fact that vulnerable groups in a given society – ethnic minorities, lowest castes, women, the marginalized, the poorest – are often disregarded during consultation processes[139], sometimes because the Management is 'too confident' that the borrower/client has provided accurate social baseline data.

Here again, timing is crucial. Consultations that take place after the project's design and location are decided[140] do not make sense, since it is the very purpose of early consultations to inform the project design and location on the people's concerns. In addition, "the lack of adequate consultations [might be] a spark for tension and conflict."[141]

2.3. THE DETAILS THE DEVIL IS IN: SYSTEMIC INSTITUTIONS' SHORTCOMINGS

The study of the IAMs' compliance review reports, of existing literature on the functioning of MDBs and the IGMs' project team interviews of 27 people, who have either participated in the creation or revision of IAMs, or who work or have worked in an IAM, reveal some systemic non-incentives and loopholes.

The first type of non-incentive is the work conditions of the staff. There is a strong pressure on the staff to develop the institution's portfolio and to work quickly, which is probably faring worse and worse in a context of competition with commercial banks and the creation of the Asian Infrastructure Investment Bank. Moreover, neither compliance with ESSs nor the sustainable development

---

138 IPN, *Paraguay/Argentina: Reform Project for the Water and Telecommunications Sectors, SEGBA V Power Distribution Project (Yacyretá), op. cit.*; IPN, *Ghana/Nigeria: West African Gas Pipeline Project*, Case 40, Investigation Report, 25 April 2008.

139 IPN, *Nepal: Arun III Proposed Hydroelectric Project and Restructuring of IDA Credit*, Investigation Report, *op. cit.*; IPN, *China: Western Poverty Reduction Project, op. cit.*; IPN, *Colombia: Cartagena Water Supply, Sewerage and Environmental Project*, Case 31, Investigation Report, 24 June 2005; IPN, *Panama: Land Administration Project (First Request)*, Case 53, Investigation Report, 16 September 2010; AM-CRP, *Sri Lanka Southern Transport Development Project, op. cit.*; AM-CRP, *Greater Mekong Subregion: Rehabilitation of the Railway in Cambodia Project, op. cit.*, IPN, *Cambodia: Land Management and Administration Project*, Case 60, Investigation Report, 23 November 2010; CAO, *India / Tata Ultra Mega-01/ Mundra and Anjar, op. cit.*; AM-CRP, *Mundra Ultra Mega Power Project, op. cit.*

140 IPN, *Argentina: Santa Fe Road Infrastructure Project and Provincial Road Infrastructure Project (Third Request), op. cit.*; IPN, *Colombia: Cartagena Water Supply, Sewerage and Environmental Project, op. cit.*; CAO, *India / Tata Ultra Mega-01/Mundra and Anjar, op. cit.*; AM-CRP, *Mundra Ultra Mega Power Project, op. cit.*

141 IPN, *Peru: Lima Urban Transport Project*, Case 61, Investigation Report, 18 January 2011.

effectiveness of projects is taken into account for career advancement.[142] In addition, several interviewees have emphasised that the high turnover of the Management's staff was a hurdle for any lesson to be learned from the cases.

IAMs' non-compliance findings also show that 'the Management' or 'the staff' is not a one-piece body. Competing interests within the staff sometimes result in tilting the balance between considerations of economic stakes and environmental and social stakes towards the first. A striking example can be found in the CAO *Agrokasa* case. The CAO discovered that:

> "CES [IFC Environmental and Social Development Department] review staff were clear in their recommendations regarding the investment. In the face of resistance from the CAG [IFC Agribusiness Department] and commercial pressure to move ahead with funding of an existing client, CES management were complicit in sidelining specialist(s) assigned to the investment who intensified their concern about the sustainability of the situation in Ica and had pointed out inconsistencies in the apparent permitting of water extractions. The concerns of CES specialists relating to the environmental and social impacts of groundwater extraction in the Ica Valley were not reconciled by consecutive layers of IFC management through engagement with the project team. The resulting capitulation on the requirement for an EA in advance of taking the project to the Board exposed IFC to increased risk and was inconsistent with IFC procedural and disclosure requirements. CAG staff assured the CAO that commercial pressure was not applied to seek to ensure inclusion of the commitment within the 2008/09 program. However, the CAO has reviewed documentation showing clear pressure, culminating in a request from CAG to move the requirements in the ESAP [Environmental and Social Action Plan] to a condition of disbursement rather than a condition of commitment. The CAO concludes that CES management did not play an effective role in supporting the professional judgment of CES specialists, in protecting the broader interests of the IFC in applying its standards, and in protecting the interest of weaker parties in the emerging water conflict over scarce water resources in the Ica Valley. This, in combination with mismanaged client communications, produced an incoherent IFC approach, undermining and fragmenting IFC's position."[143]

Another issue revealed by some IAM's non-compliance findings is the absence or an inadequate number of social specialists, such as ethnologists and anthropologists. This has sometimes caused significant mistakes in the scoping of affected people, with the corresponding non-compliances with standards on information, consultation and indigenous peoples.[144]

---

142 See *inter alia* Robert Wade, "Greening the Bank: The Struggle Over the Environment, 1970-1995", *in* Devesh Kapur, John P. Lewis, and Richard Webb (eds.), *The World Bank: Its First Half Century – Volume 2: Perspectives*, Washington DC: Brookings Institution Press (1997), pp. 611-734; Walter Leal Filho, Angel René Rios, *Accountability Issues in International Development Projects*, *op. cit.*; Bruce Rich, *Foreclosing the Future*, *op. cit.*

143 CAO, *Peru / Agrokasa-01/Ica*, *op. cit.*, pp. 30-31.

144 See for example IPN, *Pakistan: National Drainage Program Project*, *op. cit.*; AM-CRP, *Indonesia: Integrated Citarum Water Resources Management Investment Program – Project 1*, Request 2012/1, CRP Final Report, 10 April 2013.

Finally, compliance review reports show that, in some cases, the loophole is in the lack of a clear indication of what is required from the staff. The vaguer the wording of standards is, the more the staff has leeway in interpreting them and the more they risk taking ill-informed decisions. Thus, in a number of cases IAMs made findings such as "IFC's procedures on categorization are loosely defined however, and implicitly rely heavily on professional discretion. As IFC's procedures do not provide for in-depth public disclosure around decisions on categorization, it is not possible for interested or affected parties to make an informed judgment about IFC's decision-making process."[145] Moreover, some "non-compliances are largely rooted in underlying weaknesses in the Policy and due diligence framework,"[146] when ESSs are unsuitable for the operations they are supposed to cover.[147]

Can MDBs do better? Certainly. Are they willing to make the necessary cultural changes? That one is less certain. In reaction to findings of non-compliance, and in a cultural context in which accountability is felt by part of the staff and part of the Executive Directors as a naming and shaming exercise, the reaction of the Management of all MDBs has been to 'panel-proof' the projects. This is how staff and IAMs call the practice that has been developed to minimize the risk to be subjected to a compliance review, by "omitting important but risky elements"[148] in their projects or by finding a way to transfer those risks on the borrower for example.[149] On the one hand, it spurs Management to make a compliance screening of projects, to check whether they are in line with ESSs' requirements. On the other hand, it has sometimes been described as a box-ticking exercise which may have little to do with the environmental and social effectiveness of projects in the field.[150] Although the world's (im)balances and global concerns have considerably changed since the nineties, the statements of early studies on the Inspection Panel and the *de facto* disregard of the sustainable development effectiveness of MDB-supported projects are depressingly familiar.[151] However,

---

145 CAO, *Brazil / Amaggi Expansion-01/IFC Executive Vice President, op. cit.*

146 PCM, *Paravani HPP (Georgia), op. cit.*

147 Regarding the inadequacy of IFC's procedures applied to financial intermediaries, see CAO, *Compliance Audit of IFC's Financial Sector Investments*, 10 October 2012, released 5 February 2013, www.cao-ombudsman.org/newsroom/documents/FIAUDIT.htm.

148 Edith Brown Weiss, "On Being Accountable in a Kaleidoscopic World", 104 *Am. Soc'y Int'l L. Proc.* (2010), p. 488.

149 Richard E. Bissell, "The Arun III Hydroelectric Project, Nepal", *in* Dana Clark, Jonathan Fox, Kay Treakle (eds.), *Demanding Accountability. Civil-Society Claims and the World Bank Inspection Panel*, Lanham/Oxford: Rowman & Littlefield (2003), p. 41.

150 Jonathan Fox, "The World Bank Inspection Panel: Lessons from the First Five Years," 6 *Global Governance* 3, (2000), pp. 279-318.

151 Dana Clark, Jonathan Fox, Kay Treakle (eds.), *Demanding Accountability, op. cit.*; Jonathan Fox, "The World Bank Inspection Panel: Lessons from the First Five Years", *op. cit.*; Jonathan Fox, David Brown (eds.), *The Struggle for Accountability: The World Bank, NGOs and Grassroots Movements*, Cambridge: MIT Press (1998)°; Daniel Bradlow, "International Organizations

the heated debates on the occasion of the drafting of the World Bank's new Environmental and Social Framework[152] show that such standards can now no longer be decided without the public's scrutiny and input.[153]

and Private Complaints: The Case of the World Bank Inspection Panel", *Va. J. Int'l L.* (1994), pp. 553-613; Dana Clark, David Hunter, "Amplifying Citizen Voices for Sustainable Development", *in* Gudmundur Alfredsson, Rolf Ring (eds.), *The Inspection Panel of the World Bank. A Different Complaint Procedure*, La Haye/Londres/Boston: Martinus Nijhoff (2001), pp. 167-189 ...

152 "World Bank Environmental and Social Framework. Setting Environmental and Social Standards for Investment Project Financing", 4 August 2016, http://consultations.worldbank.org/Data/hub/files/consultation-template/review-and-update-world-bank-safeguard-policies/en/materials/the_esf_clean_final_for_public_disclosure_post_board_august_4.pdf. The new Framework will take effect in early 2018.

153 See the documents on the two-year consultations with governments, development experts, and CSOs at http://consultations.worldbank.org/consultation/review-and-update-world-bank-safeguard-policies.

www.ingramcontent.com/pod-product-compliance
Ingram Content Group UK Ltd.
Pitfield, Milton Keynes, MK11 3LW, UK
UKHW051920100926
8556IPUK00021B/1281

9 781780 684673